MYTH AND MYTHOLOGY

IN THE THEATER OF
PEDRO CALDERÓN DE LA BARCA

MYTH AND MYTHOLOGY

IN THE THEATER OF
PEDRO CALDERÓN DE LA BARCA

Thomas Austin O'Connor

TRINITY UNIVERSITY PRESS

HOUSTON PUBLIC LIBRARY

FOR RAE

My bounty is as boundless as the sea,
My love as deep; the more I give to thee,
The more I have, for both are infinite.

Romeo and Juliet, II, 175-77

Trinity University Press gratefully acknowledges the assistance of the *Program for Cultural Cooperation Between Spain's Ministry of Culture and North American Universities* in making this publication possible.

Library of Congress Cataloging-in-Publication Data
O'Connor, Thomas Austin, 1943-
  Myth and mythology in the theater of
Pedro Calderón de la Barca/Thomas Austin O'Connor.

    p. cm.
    Bibliography: p.
    Includes index.
    ISBN 0-939980-21-5
    1. Calderón de la Barca, Pedro, 1600-1681 – Criticism and
interpretation. 2. Myth in literature. 3. Mythology in literature.
I. Title
PQ6317.M84026 1988   88-16057
862' .3 – dc19   CIP

Reproductions of the woodcuts used throughout this book proceed from the following volumes in the author's personal library: Agustín de Salazar y Torres, *Cythara de Apolo*, vol. I (Madrid, 1681), *Sylva natalicia* (Madrid, 1683), and Calderón de la Barca, *Primera parte de comedias* (Madrid, 1726).

Acknowledgments

I owe a debt of gratitude to Don Gonzalo Torrente Ballester, my master and friend, who first suggested that I examine the poetic and dramatic works of Agustín de Salazar y Torres (1642-1675) for my doctoral dissertation at the State University of New York at Albany. Although I had been concentrating on contemporary literature, the discovery of Baroque theater, coupled with his inspirational seminar on Góngora, sidetracked my original plans and ambushed my youthful enthusiasm. While a faculty member at the State University of New York College at Cortland, I received two SUNY/Research Foundation Fellowships and one Grant-in-Aid that allowed me to investigate in 1973 the myth of Cephalus and Procris in the seventeenth-century *comedia* and to research in 1976 mythological plays in Spanish libraries. In 1975 I received an ACLS Fellowship for library research in North America and a semester's leave that inaugurated what I then called "A History of the Mythological Drama in 17th-Century Spain." The following two summers, with assistance from the SUNY/Research Foundation and a College of Liberal Arts Research Stipend from Texas A&M University, I pursued my investigations in Spain. After I had read more than three hundred plays based on Greco-Roman myth, Calderón's achievements clearly stood above what his fellow dramatists had accomplished. Consequently, my original focus narrowed considerably. It was not until 1984 that I was able to dedicate the time and energy needed to begin writing, and, without a sabbatical leave from Kansas State University in the fall of 1986, I would not yet have completed this book. I am sincerely grateful to former Dean William L. Stamey and current Associate Dean William "Jack" Carpenter for their encouragement and support. Ms. Jerry Harding exhibited exemplary skill and aplomb in following my scribblings and typing them in a legible manner, and considerable patience and dedication in learning two computer programs. But without the considerable editing skills of my wife Rae, her understanding of my preoccupation with Calderón and myth, and her saintly patience, nothing worthwhile could have been accomplished. To Lois Boyd, Director of Trinity University Press, goes my appreciation for her encouragement and enthusiasm. Frederick A. de Armas and the other reader provided many helpful suggestions that improved the present work. To all of the above, I am grateful.

Preface

The 1980s have witnessed an explosion in Calderonian criticism in both quantitative and qualitative terms. Much is attributable to the celebration in 1981 of the tercentenary of Calderón's death and publication of the various proceedings. In addition, several monographs and book-length studies have appeared that challenge current critical opinion while at the same time deepening our appreciation of Calderón's dramaturgy. In 1982 Robert ter Horst's *Calderón: The Secular Plays* inaugurated the general revision by offering a sweeping reappraisal of the *comedias*.[1] Significantly, ter Horst approached the secular corpus from the anachronistic vantage point of *La estatua de Prometeo*, because the myth plays "provide the clearest insights into Calderón's art at maturity" (p. 1), a position with which I wholeheartedly agree. Although he employed *Prometeo* as a model of Calderonian dramaturgy, he virtually left unexplored the sixteen remaining myth plays. Moreover, we must ask whether it is legitimate to read all Calderonian drama, the myth plays included, through this one great work. In the same year Ciriaco Morón Arroyo published *Calderón: pensamiento y teatro*,[2] a study based on the history of ideas approach. Although Morón Arroyo had little to say about the myth plays, he categorized them as "autos sacramentales laicos" (p. 20), a claim that close scrutiny cannot support. The third study published in 1982 was David Jonathan Hildner's *Reason and the Passions in the "Comedias" of Calderón*.[3] Though he examined only one myth play, *Prometeo*, his exploration of the tension between reason and passion as "related to the idea and practice of *aristocratic* behavior" (p. 8) provided new perspectives that challenge the traditional Thomistic approach to these issues.

William R. Blue's 1983 study, *The Development of Imagery in Calderón's "Comedias,"*[4] traces how the dramatic poet's "style changes and develops from his earliest works to his last" (p. i). This book contains a quantitative recognition of the importance of the myth plays, for of the eighteen works studied three are myth plays: *El hijo del Sol, Faetón, Eco y Narciso*, and *El monstruo de los jardines*. In 1984 Francisco Ruiz Ramón's *Calderón y la tragedia*[5] demonstrated beyond doubt that Calderón is a major European dramatist and a consummate tragedian. By close scrutiny of two models of the genre, one configured by the conflict liberty/destiny and the other by honor, he provided illuminating commentary on six plays, not one of which is based on Greco-Roman myth. In the same year Anthony J. Cascardi published *The Limits of Illusion: A Critical Study of Calderón*,[6] in which he plumbed the conflict resulting from Calderón's professional need to employ illusion that as a Christian he is morally forced to abjure (p. ix). While Hildner first broached this tension from a philosophical perspective (p. 18), Cascardi fleshed it out in terms of the conflict "between theatrical form and the themes of illusion" (p. ix). Although he discussed three myth plays, *Los tres mayores prodigios, Eco y*

Narciso, and *Prometeo*, his jaundiced view of court theater precluded any significant critical insight. In this regard he followed James Maraniss's early view of the court spectacle as virtuoso pieces of artificiality (p. 130).[7]

In 1986 Frederick A. de Armas demonstrated the pervasiveness of the myth of Astraea in early Spanish literature and its significance in Calderón's theater in *The Return of Astraea: An Astral-Imperial Myth in Calderón*.[8] Of the thirteen *comedias* included, five were myth plays: *El monstruo de los jardines*, *El golfo de las Sirenas*, *El mayor encanto, amor*, *Ni Amor se libra de amor*, and *Los tres mayores prodigios*. In each work a character appears whose name is Astraea, and de Armas reveals her symbolic significance within the above-mentioned tradition. The same year saw the publication of Dian Fox's *Kings in Calderón: A Study in Characterization and Political Theory*.[9] In this monograph not one myth play appears, even though the rule of kings and gods is a significant dimension of those works. At the same time Susana Hernández-Araico's *Ironía y tragedia en Calderón*[10] explored the humoristic ingredient in Calderonian tragedies. Although she examined *Apolo y Climene* and *El monstruo de los jardines*, she limited their importance to a socio-political commentary (pp. 83-4 and 87-98). In this manner she echoed Sebastian Neumeister's concern to understand the myth play within what Gadamer calls its "Okkasionalität."[11] Whereas Neumeister moved from the literal to the allegorical level of interpretation, Hernández addressed only social and political possibilities in the dramatic texts.

The purpose of the present study is to interpret all Calderonian myth plays from the unique vantage point supplied by *mythos* itself, i.e., from the perspective that mythic narrative contains within itself a meaning that survives adaptations over time and across cultures.[12] I have also endeavored to analyze each play within a broad mythological category, a decision which lengthened the study, but also allows readers to examine individual plays within their unique contexts. It will be obvious to the informed reader that I owe a great debt to the critics mentioned above as well as to others who have preceded them.

The organization of this book requires some comment. The Introduction places the myth plays within a literary tradition that made it possible for them to survive the passage of time and the waning of dramatic interest in Hapsburg court theater. Part I is divided into four chapters. The first introduces the reader to the world of myth that unobtrusively ambushes our notions of reality. The second sets out the critical principles informing the study. The third and fourth chapters establish the fundamental tension between the "christianized" world informing many of Calderón's plays and that of degenerate honor, where providence and grace appear bracketed by a dramatic fiat. Part II organizes Calderón's seventeen myth plays according to clearly defined categories that are not meant to be exclusive. Chapter 5 analyzes *Fortunas de Andrómeda y Perseo* and *Eco y Narciso* from the critical perspective of rites of passage. Chapter 6 examines the illusion of power by which males tend to live, focusing on both the gods, Apolo and Cupido of *El laurel de Apolo*, and men, Jasón, Teseo, and Hércules of *Los tres mayores prodigios* and Hércules alone in *Fieras afemina Amor*. Ulises appears in Chapter 7, and while not blatantly demythologized as Hércules and Apolo were in the previous chapter, he nonetheless fails to live up to his traditional reputation in *El mayor encanto, amor* and *El golfo de las Sirenas*. Chapter 8 explores the importance of love, human and sexual, for the realization of one's true humanity. *La fiera, el rayo y la piedra* depicts love's dual potential, live-giving and life-denying, while *Amado y aborrecido* and *Ni Amor se libra de amor* are enthusiastic representations and celebrations of love's transformational potential. *El monstruo de los jardines* dramatizes the ambiguity of Aquiles's rite of passage to full sexuality and the assumption of the onus of Greek honor. *Fineza contra fineza* provides us with a remarkable view of the world of nobility, similar to *Amado y aborrecido*, but yet fuller and more compelling. *Fineza* is the nutshell term that encapsulates the obligations of noble birth and spells out the risks the nobleman must be prepared to take for the sake of others. The examination of myths of suffering and destruction in Chapter 9 is subdivided into two categories. The first addresses the formation and disintegration of the family in *Apolo y Climene* and *El hijo del Sol, Faetón*. The second explores the death of individuals whose metamorphoses might seem to be apotheosic, but on closer scrutiny appear to be truly tragic in spite of the dramaturgic will to "transcend" tragedy. *La púrpura de la rosa* and *Celos, aun del aire, matan* are operatic librettos which retain their literary and dramatic nature. Chapter 10, the myth of human origins, explores the creation myth contained in the ironic narrative of Prometeo. A brief Conclusion summarizes the study's contributions to Calderonian criticism.

With this study I hope to demonstrate that any serious student of Calderón can no longer ignore or selectively choose from amongst his myth plays, a fact many of the critics cited above realize. I shall show that, first, there is a continuity between Calderón's earlier serious dramas and his later myth plays, and, second, that these myth plays reveal what can be truly labeled a Calderonian mythology, the larger connecting whole within which each dramatized myth signifies in plenitude.

Notes

1 Lexington: UP of Kentucky, 1982.
2 Santander: Sociedad Menéndez Pelayo, 1982.
3 Amsterdam/Philadelphia: John Benjamins, 1982.
4 York, South Carolina: Spanish Literature Publications, 1983.
5 Madrid: Alhambra, 1984.
6 Cambridge: Cambridge UP, 1984.
7 *On Calderón* (Columbia: U of Missouri P, 1978).
8 Lexington: UP of Kentucky, 1986.
9 London: Tamesis, 1986.
10 Potomac, MD: Scripta Humanistica, 1986.
11 See *Mythos und repräsentation* (München: Wilhelm Fink, 1978).
12 Marcia L. Welles's *Arachne's Tapestry: The Transformation of Myth in Seventeenth-Century Spain* (San Antonio: Trinity UP, 1986) addresses the parodic reaction to Greco-Roman myth. For an excellent analysis of *Céfalo y Pocris*, a *comedia burlesca* attributed to Calderón, see pp. 103-30.

Contents

MYTH AND MYTHOLOGY

IN THE THEATER OF
PEDRO CALDERÓN DE LA BARCA

Introduction: On Readers, Reading, and the Myth Plays of Don Pedro Calderón de la Barca.

The Privatization of Theatrical Experience

There are two principal ways to approach dramatic texts of the seventeenth century: first, from the perspective of theatrical history, and, second, from that of literary criticism. The latter category may be expanded to include criticism of actual performances given in our lifetime or recorded for posterity, such as now occurs at the Chamizal Festival in El Paso, Texas.[1] In this case, at least, the interests of theater and criticism meld to enrich both enterprises. Although some may insist on restoring the theatrical heritage to Spain's Golden-Age drama, and by so doing to privilege criticism of performance over that of text, we should be aware that this desideratum reflects seventeenth-century concerns over the destiny of its dramatic texts. With the publication of the *Comedias escogidas* and the *Partes* of famous writers such as Calderón, theater and theatrical interests lost control of the destiny and part of the profitability of those works that were originally written for the stage and not for a reading public. When we consider Hapsburg court theater, we realize how limited the theatrical audience was, principally to the ruling classes resident in Madrid and to the Madrilenian populace admitted to special performances of courtly spectacles open to the public. The very popularity and success of the *comedia* and its various manifestations created a demand for printed versions of those theatrical scripts that widened the basically theatrical and communal experience to include a private and literary enjoyment of them. While *comedias* continued to be performed in theaters all over the peninsula, the *privatization* of theatrical experience, its appropriation to individual and intimate readings, was a factor, both cultural and economic, taken into account by Calderón's first editors and publishers. The reading and criticism of dramatic texts as *dramatic literature* produced an interesting tension and antagonism between theatrical interests and those of the reading public.

In 1636 Don Joseph Calderón de la Barca explained his reasons for publishing the *Primera Parte* of his famous brother's works:

LA Causa, Excelentissimo señor, que me ha movido à aver jútado estas doze Comedias de mi hermano, no ha sido tanto el gusto de verlas impressas, como el pesar de aver visto impressas algunas dellas antes de aora por hallarlas todas erradas, mal corregidas, y muchas que no son suyas en su nombre, y otras que lo son en el ageno. . . .[2]

While the latter motive, to publish a more correct and accurate version of the texts and to clarify their authorship, would become a commonplace for all of Calderón's editors, even those of today, the former sounds strangely exculpatory and disingenuous. Whether Joseph Calderón sincerely wished to see Pedro's works in print, we may never know for certain, but we are indeed certain about the societal pressures and economic demand to make those works available to the reading public. Most likely we are facing formulaic expressions that mask the economic interests at the heart of the will to publish. The real question facing the editor was and remains: Why is my edition better than that which has already appeared? Again Joseph Calderón clarifies the issue in the *Segunda Parte*:

no pudiendo estoruar que otros las imprimiesse [sic] erradas y defetuosas, quise, que saliendo de mi poder fuessen, yà que defetuosas, no por lo menos erradas. Restaurarlas solamente pretendi de los errores agenos. . . .[3]

The public's demand for Calderonian texts brought to bear market forces that, in spite of Calderón's hesitancy or refusal to participate in meeting that demand, encouraged others who were willing and able to provide the goods.

Calderón's obduracy in this matter was not merely a question of personal preference, but of national pride, as the Duque de Veraguas's letter demonstrates (Valencia, 18 June 1680):

permitame V.m. empiece riñendole, pues quanto hà granjeado del mundo en aplausos, parece se lo retribuye en desprecios, y por rigida que sea la Filosofia, no hallo yo, que toquen sus desengaños en ingratitudes. . . .
Que cosa es, que siendo V.m. la gloria de nuestra Nacion, lo que con tanta floxedad este timbre, que no se acuerde de la obligacion en que le impone, para no dexar aventurado el lustre, que à todos los Españoles nos resulta en sus obras, en la Contingencia de su desperdicio.[4]

The good Duke then urges Calderón to continue the publication of his *autos*, even offering financial assistance. Fortunately, he also requested a list of the dramatist's *comedias* and *autos*. We may well imagine an aged and disillusioned Calderón who, on facing rapidly approaching mortality, set his priorities according to those religious and theological principles that form the bases of his dramatic output and personal convictions. Worldly glory has lost its allure, and only the *autos sacramentales* relate in a significant way to eternal verities. The publication in 1677 of the *Primera Parte* of the *autos* only encouraged those like the Duque de Veraguas who recognized Calderón's stature as the pre-eminent figure of Spanish letters and culture. His heritage must not be lost to exaggerated religious scruple. Where Calderón neglected or opposed the publication of his secular and profane works, there would be enterprising and entrepreneurial spirits willing and able to meet public demand for them, as the publication of the spurious *Quinta Parte* in that very same year of 1677 demonstrates.[5]

Public demand for Calderón's works underscores how certain texts become the communal "property" of a *reading* public. John M. Ellis has defined literature as "those [texts] that are used by the society in such a way that *the text is not taken as specifically relevant to the immediate context of its origin*."[6] It is clear that Calderonian plays were passing from theatrical script to literary text, and the implications of this cultural rite of passage were significant. Though Calderón may have wished to control the destiny and fate of his dramatic corpus, it was no longer an issue of individual prerogative.

Although I have emphasized the economic and cultural factors that led to the publication of these dramatic scripts, we should not overlook the fact that Calderón's early editors were keenly attuned to the needs of the reading public and were determined to meet them. Joseph Calderón explicitly, though begrudgingly, admits that his edition (*Primera Parte*) of Don Pedro's plays responds to and satisfies the reader:

Con todo esso he querido, que el que las leyere las halle cabales, enmēdadas, y corregidas à su disgusto, pues las he dado a la estampa con animo solo de que ya que han de salir salgan enteras por lo menos, que si ninguno huviera de imprimirlas, yo fuera el primero q̃ dexara olvidarlas.

In Calderón's dedication of the *Tercera Parte* (Madrid, 1664) to Don Antonio Pedro Alvarez Osorio Gómez Dávila y Toledo, he mentions his editor's desire "a sacar estas doze Comedias de sus originales, procurando (segun dize) restaurarlas de los achacados errores que padecen otras en la estampa...." The editor, don Sebastián Ventura de Vergara Salcedo, explains in his "Papel Al Avtor" how he and others:

sienten el que anden diminutas, y llenas de errores de la Imprenta, assi las sueltas, como las que en partes diferentes de libros se han dado estos años a la Prensa; y tambien el que muchas huelen con el nombre de v.m. no lo siendo, y algunas de v.m. con el ageno; motiuo bastante para q̃ fiado en la merced que me haze, resoluiesse recoger estas doze, y darlas a la estampa, por eximirlas del riesgo que las demas han padecido. Bien reconozco, que es interesse mio en todo; pues aunque su modestia de v.m. quiera sentirlo, le [sic] razō la [sic] ha de obligar a mostrarse gustoso, ademas, que las gracias que espero de tantos aficionados, como v.m. tan condignamente tiene, serà sobrado premio del zelo q̃ me rige. Suplico a v.m. que lo tēga por bien, no solo en estas, sino en las demas que ofrezco juntar....

Besides the *de rigueur* comments on the state of current editions available and on the question of authorship, Don Sebastián openly admits his personal interest and financial motive in the publication of Calderón's plays, even in the face of Calderón's objections or opposition. In addition to the public praise to be garnered from the readers (*aficionados*) served, there was a definite economic motive involved in this publication. The *Suma de Priuilegio* was issued to Domingo de Palacio y Villegas, Mercader de Libros, and not to Calderón. We may conjecture whether friendship and regard for Calderón's talents were somehow commingled with the desire for financial gain, especially in light of Don Sebastián's declared intent to publish additional *Partes*. Apparently Calderón *lo tuvo por mal*, and it is most illuminating that the *Cuarta Parte's privilegio* was issued to Calderón himself, just as those of the *Primera* and *Segunda Partes*. Calderón's regaining financial control of his works would prove to be temporary as the publication of the spurious *Quinta Parte* demonstrates. His plays would appear in print only when someone with determina-tion and motivation came upon the scene, and Calderón's pre-empting of the publication rights to his works from Don Sebastián Ventura de Vergara Salcedo ironically paved the way for the ambitious and prompt Vera Tassis, whose first edition, the corrected *Quinta Parte*, would appear in 1682, one year after Calderón's death.

Don Juan de Vera Tassis y Villarroel would prove to be an indefatigable edi-tor and persistent seeker of Caderón's works. In his "Al Lector" of the *Novena Parte* (Madrid, 1691), he notes even after ten year of effort:

PONGO En tus manos, y en el Teatro comun este Noueno Tomo de Comedias del cèle-bre Poeta Español, Don Pedro Calderón de la Barca: ninguna de ellas la leeràs como andava manuscrita, ò impressa; porque solicitando vnas, y otras originales, se ha pro-curado corregir, y ajustar con la mayor legalidad possible esta impression...."7

With the proper bow to editorial conventions, Vera emphasizes that his plac-ing of these plays in the hands of the reader symbolically transmits them to the public domain and to the use the reading public would deem appropriate. Fourteen years earlier Calderón wrote in "Al Lector" of his *Autos sacramen-tales, alegoricos, y historiales* (Madrid, 1677):

Pareceràn tibios algunos trozos, respeto de que el papel no puede dar de si, ni lo sonoro de la musica, ni lo aparatoso de las tramoyas; si ya no es que el que los lea haga en su imaginacion composicion de lugares, considerado lo que seria sin entero juizio de lo que es, que muchas vezes descaece el que escriue de si mismo por conueniencias del Pueblo, ù del tablado."

With reference to the Jesuit meditation practice of imagining the locale of a Biblical event, Calderón, even in his advanced years, attempts to place his *autos* in their theatrical environment. He wants the reader to read *theatrically*. The tension between *papel* and performance is a fundamental issue for the aging dramatist who always insists on the theatrical nature and dimension of his works. In a letter to Francisco de Avellaneda dated 30 July 1675, Calderón comments on the performance of *El templo de Palas*, given on the name day of Mariana de Austria, an event he was forced to miss due to poor health:

embiè (nò sin disculpada embidia de los que la lograron) à suplicar V.m. me hiciesse favor de remitirme el Borrador, para restaurar en parte la perdida del todo: que aûque es verdad, q̃ el papel no puede dar de si lo vivo de la represẽtaciõ, lo adornado de los trages, lo sonoro de la Musica, ni lo aparatoso del teatro; con todo esto, à los que tenemos alguna esperiencia de quanto desmerece fuera de su lugar este (nada dichoso) genero de estudios: nos es mas facil, que a otros suplir con la imaginacion la falta de la vista, y del oido.... Hela leido, vna, y muchas vezes, con admiracion de que en tan corta esfera quepan tantos primores, como vna Fabula no vulgar reducida a representable metro, en tan elegante, y no afectado estilo....[8]

Whereas in 1677 Calderón commented on the proper theatrical environment for an adequate reading of his *autos*, in 1675 he also insisted, from an elitist position, on reading a myth play in its own theatrical milieu. Background experience is absolutely necessary, according to Calderón, to form a disciplined and active imagination sufficient to re-create a particular genre's setting. This man of the theater manifests both the advantages and disadvantages of an exclusively theatrical perspective. Without the *papel, El templo de Palas* would have had a limited destiny, at least as far as we and Calderón are concerned. Because he was able to read its *Borrador*, this text escaped its immediate environment and expressed purpose to assume another destiny made possible by the act of reading.

On Spectators and Readers

It is to be expected that men of the theater will of course emphasize the theatrical connection when they write about dramatic texts. In his *aprobación* of Calderón's *Segunda Parte* (Madrid, 1637), el Maestro Joseph de Valdivielso praises the twelve plays before him in the following terms:

he visto este Libro de doze Comedias, escritas por don Pedro Calderon, y representadas en los mayores Teatros de España, con aplausos repetidos, en numerosos concursos, ...

Valdivielso confirms his theatrical opinion of Calderón's plays, their quality based on where they were performed and how they were received, by reading the texts submitted to him by the Consejo Real. Forty-seven years later Vera Tassis will insist not only on the theatrical provenance of Calderón's plays but also on their literary status as by now classical texts forming part of the canon. In "Al que leyere" of the *Octava Parte* (Madrid, 1684), Vera states that:

muchas de las Comedias que contiene avràs visto en los Teatros representadas, y en los Libros impressas; pero ninguna en vnos, y otros tan cabal, como las que agora salen à la luz publica....

Nothing highlights more clearly the changes that Spain's theatrical texts were undergoing than these two statements from men of the theater, but of different generations. Vera Tassis makes certain that the value of his edition, its completeness, surpasses what anyone may have seen performed or read beforehand. The importance of reading Spain's dramatic texts for their eventual performance becomes a major concern in Vera Tassis's dedication of the *Novena Parte* (Madrid, 1691) to don Iñigo Melchor Fernández Velasco y Tovar, Condestable de Castilla, Camarero Mayor, and Mayordomo Mayor of Carlos II. After the conventional encomium, Vera gets down to business, stating his purpose in dedicating this *Parte* to Don Iñigo:

entre cuyas ingeniosas Comedias hallarà V.Exc. algunas con que seruir à sus Magestades, à causa de no auerse representado en su Real presencia; y todas tan corregidas de los defectos con que hasta aqui han corrido, que, en mi juizio, no las ha de hallar encuentro la mas critica censura. . . .

Valdivielso praises and admires Calderón's theatrical successes, whereas Vera Tassis becomes a proponent of the staging of those plays in the *Novena Parte* that had not been seen by their Majesties. This transition from commentator to propagandist, while much is due to Vera's interest in the success of his editorial enterprise, reveals just how thoroughly the theatrical viability and survivability of Calderonian texts now depend on the literary tradition they have created.

Because Calderón's myth plays were complex productions involving elaborate staging, state-of-the-art machinery, musical accompaniment, and often the cooperation of at least two theatrical troupes, they were not easily transferred to the *corrales* nor were they restaged at court without considerable planning and expense. Although theatrical history tends to concentrate on Madrid, and in regard to the court theater on the Buen Retiro, the Zarzuela, the Casa de Campo, and the Alcázar, we must keep in mind the other great population centers. Valencia, Sevilla, and Barcelona, and those not so great, such as Almagro, were visited regularly by travelling troupes portrayed so vividly by Cervantes in *Don Quijote* (II, 2). Since there is a vast performance tradition for Golden-Age dramatic texts, the following scheme conveys only part of the trail left by the performances of Calderón's myth plays. In each column I list by day, month, and year the performances cited in the corresponding sources:[9]

	Shergold, *History*	Varey & Shergold, *Fuentes*	Valbuena Briones	Reichenbergers
1. *Amado*	18/I/1676	18/I/1676, 26/IX/1686	before 1657	a. 16/X/1656
2. *Apolo*	mentioned	18/I/1686, 16/II/1686 23-28/X/1686 4/III/1696, domingo de Carnestolendas	pub. 4.a Parte 1672	Carnaval 1661
3. *Celos*		12/II/1679, 10/XII/1684	5/XII/1660	5/XII/1660
4. *Eco*	28/X/1689	29/I/1682, 17/I/1692	12/VII/1661	12/VII/1661
5. *Encanto*	St. John's Night 1635	15/VI/1681	St. John's Night 1635	25/VI/1635
6. *Faetón*	Carnaval 1662 22/XII/1679	22/XII/1679	1/III/1661	1/III/1661
7. *La fiera*	V/1652 Valencia, 1690	6/XI/1685	1652	V/1652
8. *Fieras*	I/1670		I/1670	18/I/1670
9. *Fineza*		3/XII/1682, 25/II/1685, 10/X/1685	Viena, 22/XII/ 1671	22/XII/1671
10. *Fortunas*	18/V/1653		18/V/1653	18/V/1653
11. *Golfo*	17/I/1657 Mon. of Carnaval 1657	6/VIII/1684	17/I/1657	17/I/1657
12. *Laurel*	4/III/1658		4/III/1658	4/III/1658
13. *Monstruo*		23/IV/1684	Sevilla, fall of 1667	VII/1661 (Neumeister)
14. *Ni Amor*	3/XII/1679	3/XII/1679, 26/III/1687	19/I/1662	19/I/1662
15. *Prodigios*	St. John's Night 1636	Carnestolendas, 1676, 4/XI/1678, 7/VII/1687, 25/VIII/1687	St. John's Night 1636	23/VI/1636
16. *Prometeo*		22/XII/1685, 1 and 13/I /1686	pub. 5.a Parte 1677	22/XII/1670? or 1672/74
17. *Púrpura*	5/XII/1660, 17/I? 18/I/1680	25/VIII/1679, 18/I/1680	5/XII/1660	17/I/1660

If we examine the Reichenbergers' bibliography for items listed from the seventeenth and eighteenth centuries, we discover a more detailed trail of the literary tradition of those same myth plays. A brief summary follows:

1. *Amado*: 3 *Partes*, 7 *sueltas*
2. *Apolo*: 2 MSS, 2 *Partes*, 4 *sueltas*
3. *Celos*: 1 MS, 3 *Partes*, 5 *sueltas*
4. *Eco*: 1 MS, 2 *Partes*, 4 *sueltas*
5. *Encanto*: 1 MS, 2 *Partes*, 4 *sueltas*
6. *Faetón*: 4 MSS, 2 *Partes*, 3 *sueltas*
7. *La fiera*: 2 MSS, 2 *Partes*, 3 *sueltas*
8. *Fieras*: 3 MSS, 2 *Partes*, 7 *sueltas*
9. *Fineza*: 2 *Partes*, 11 *sueltas*
10. *Fortunas*: 2 MSS, 2 *Partes*, 3 *sueltas*

11. *Golfo*: 2 MSS, 2 *Partes*, 4 *sueltas*
12. *Laurel*: 2 *Partes*, 4 *sueltas*
13. *Monstruo*: 2 MSS, 2 *Partes*, 8 *sueltas*
14. *Ni Amor*: 1 MS, 2 *Partes*, 4 *sueltas*
15. *Prodigios*: 1 MS, 2 *Partes*, 4 *sueltas*
16. *Prometeo*: 2 MSS, 2 *Partes*, 5 *sueltas*
17. *Púrpura*: 2 MSS, 2 *Partes*, 3 *sueltas*

Performance is an ephemeral event that touches only a small portion of the populace. Printed texts are a cultural resource that is renewable. To bring together information scattered throughout the Reichenbergers' bibliography, I list the Calderonian *Partes* that I have personally checked in the Biblioteca Nacional, Madrid, or in the Cruickshank and Varey facsimile edition (London: Gregg, 1973). If this literary tradition is so rich and varied, responding as it does to the public's demand for printed texts of Calderón's plays, we can only imagine the scope of the performance tradition fragmentarily represented above. Calderón, his editors, his spectators, and readers have left us with a rich heritage that we are only now beginning to examine with care and in detail.

I. *Primera Parte*
1. Madrid, 1636 (QCL)
2. " , 1640 (VSL)
3. " , 1640 (VS)[10]
4. " , 1685 - Vera Tassis edition
5. " , '1685' - pseudo V.T.[11]
6. " , 1726[12]

II. *Segunda Parte*
1. Madrid, 1637 (QC)
2. " , 1641 (S)
3. " , '1637' (Q)[13]
4. " , 1686 - Vera Tassis edition
5. " , '1683' - pseudo V.T.[14]
6. " , 1726
7. " , 1757[15]

III. *Tercera Parte*
1. Madrid, 1664 (Excelmo)
2. " , '1664' (Excelentissimo)[16]
3. " , 1687 - Vera Tassis edition
4. " , '1687' - pseudo V.T.
5. " , 1726
6. " , 1757[17]

IV. *Cuarta Parte*
  1. Madrid, 1672
  2. " , 1674
  3. " , 1688 - Vera Tassis edition
  4. " , '1688' - pseudo V.T.
  5. " , 1731

V. *Quinta Parte*
  1. Barcelona, 1677[18]
  2. Madrid, 1677[19]
  3. " , 1682 - Verdadera 5.a Parte, Vera Tassis edition
  4. " , 1694[20]
  5. " , '1694' - pseudo V.T.
  6. " , 1730

VI. *Sexta Parta*
  1. Madrid, 1683 - Vera Tassis edition
  2. " , '1683' - pseudo V.T.
  3. " , 1715

VII. *Séptima Parte*
  1. Madrid, 1683 - Vera Tassis edition
  2. " , '1683' - pseudo V.T.
  3. " , 1715

VIII. *Octava Parte*
  1. Madrid, 1684 - Vera Tassis edition
  2. " , '1684' - pseudo V.T.
  3. " , 1726

IX. *Novena Parte*
  1. Madrid, 1691 - Vera Tassis edition
  2. " , '1691' - pseudo V.T.
  3. " , 1698[21]

The success of a theatrical performance contributed to the demand for a printed version of the script, thus creating a literary tradition. There was even a practice of publishing commemorative texts of courtly performances. Toward the end of the century and throughout the eighteenth we find that the literary text spawns theatrical performance, as Vera Tassis's dedication of the *Novena Parte* indicates. Those of us who have studied *sueltas* periodically come across copies that have been annotated for performance, and I have one in my possession for Calderón's *Las armas de la hermosura*, Num. 38 (Salamanca, Imprenta de la Santa Cruz, n.d.). It contains notations in two distinct hands with clearly different inks. This apparent prompt copy attests to a theatrical tradition in which *Las armas de la hermosura* formed part of the repertoire of some company in the second half of the eighteenth and perhaps early nineteenth centuries. The literary and theatrical traditions form a symbiotic relationship. The staging of *Celos, aun del aire, matan* in San Antonio, Texas on 12 February 1981, accompanied by an edition and translation by Matthew D. Stroud (San Antonio: Trinity UP, 1981), makes clear just how interwoven these traditions have become. Whereas these two audiences only partly overlapped during Calderón's lifetime, in ours the reader and the spectator have become congruous.

On Performance and Publication: The Economic Factor

It will be remembered that of the four early *Partes* Calderón did not hold the *privilegio* to the *Tercera Parte*. In deliciously tongue-in-cheek remarks regarding the publication of his works by Don Sebastián Ventura, Calderón, referring to him as "mi mas apassionado amigo," proceeds to compliment his editor for the wish to publish a corrected volume and, at the same time, underscores the fact that the twelve plays comprising the volume are stolen:

Biẽ deuiera agradecerle la fineza de q̃ ya q̃ ayan de salir hurtadas, agenas, y defectuosas, salgã corregidas, enmendadas, y cabales. Pero con todo esso no puedo en vna parte dexar de conuertir en quexa el agradecimiento, pues remata la primera noticia que me dà de auer hecho esta Impression, con dezirme, que dexa a mi albedrio el elegirlas Dueño, a cuya autoridad salgan, defendidas, y amparadas de la comun censura, a que nacen expuestas todas las publicas acciones voluntarias.

While Calderón's notorious reluctance to publish his plays contributed to the sorry state of the printed versions available to us, that same reluctance made the theft of his works a very remunerative practice. When we read the dedication of the *Cuarta Parte* in light of the events surrounding the publication of the *Tercera Parte*, we realize that little has changed in the intervening eight years. The dramatist, on an errand to provide books for an absent friend, among which are to figure "los libros de Comedias," discovers that:

y no solo hallè en sus impressiones, q̃ ya no eran mias las que lo fueron; pero muchas que no lo fueron, impressas como mias, no contentandose los hurtos de la prensa con añadir sus yerros a los mios, sino con achacarme los agenos, pues sobre estar, como antes dixe (las ya no mias) llenas de erratas, y por el ahorro del papel, aun no cabales (pues donde acaba el pliego, acaba la Iornada, y donde acaba el quaderno acaba la comedia)....

With this reference to the incomplete version of *El laurel de Apolo* printed in the *Tercera Parte*, there are found the conventional complaints concerning editorial sloppiness and the thieving nature of editors and booksellers. Calderón then lists those plays falsely attributed to him either in *suelta* format or in collected volumes. Calderón's *amigo ausente* of the dedication owes much to Cervantes's friend of the *Prólogo* to the first part of *el Quijote*; whereas the latter allows Cervantes to write the troublesome prologue, the former allows Calderón to criticize his editors and to censure those who have robbed him of his works.

Perhaps the most severe criticism by Calderón of the wrongs inflicted on him by editors, printers, and booksellers appears in his response to the Duque de Veraguas's letter, dated in Madrid, on 24 July 1680.

Yo, Señor, estoy tan ofendido de los muchos agravios, que me han hecho Libreros, y Impressores, pues no contentos con sacar (sin voluntad mia) à luz mis mal limados yerros, me achacan los agenos (como si para yerros no bastassen los mios) y aun essos mal trasladados, mal corregidos, defectuosos, y no cabales; tanto, que puedo assegurar à V.E. que aunque por sus Titulos conozco mis Comedias, por su contexto las desconozco, pues algunas, que acaso han llegado à mi noticia, concediendo el q̃ fueron mias, niego el que lo sean, segun desemejadas las hã puesto los hurtados traslados de algunos ladroncillos, que viuẽ de venderlas, porque ay otros, que viuen de comprarlas."

Besides the obvious *el-perro-del-hortelano* syndrome exhibited here by the dramatist, there is a marked reluctance to publish his plays. There is the clearly stated refusal to have his "errors" made public, perhaps due to religious motives. Underlying this expressed reason there is a societal network of economic factors. Thieves rob Calderón of his plays and live off their ill-gotten gains. In addition to the theatrical people who profit from this trade, there are the printers and booksellers "que viuen de comprarlas," for they do the most damage to Calderón by depriving him of what is properly his and circulating his plays in the public domain. The religious motivation behind the 1677 edition of the *autos* is further emphasized in this letter to the Duke. Stating that he intends to proceed with the publication of the *autos*, Calderón sidesteps the economic factors to lay stress on the importance of an error-free edition:

que son lo que solo hè procurado recoger, porque no corrã la desecha fortuna de las Comedias, temeroso de ser materia tan sagrada, que vn yerro, ò de la pluma, ò de la Imprenta, puede poner vn sentido à riesgo de cẽsura. . . .

Since Calderón evidently disliked serving as editor of his own works, at his advanced age only religious scruple would be sufficient motivation for him to collect his *auto* scripts, to correct them, and to publish them as error-free as possible. This concern for the *autos sacramentales* probably reflects a taking-stock attitude on Calderón's part. In the *privilegio* to the *autos* conceded to him it is stated that "deseauades que saliessen de sus originales corregidos, y enmendados. . . ." But in the "Al Lector" we read the words of a man whose hand is being forced by his fame and prior successes: "a que ya que ayan de salir, salgan por lo menos corregidos, y cabales. . . ."

That Calderón was acutely aware of the financial implications of the publication of his works, there is no doubt. In the dedication of the *Cuarta Parte* he writes:

vna Comedia en su primera estimacion, cuesta al Autor cien ducados; y si le sale mala, no vale el papel en que està escrita; y si buena, no ay precio con que pagarla, porque es vn credito abierto en todos los lugares donde llega nueua; y no pudiendo (digo otra vez) ignorar tampoco el ser hurtada, pues no es su dueño el que la vende, sino el apuntador que la traslada, ò el compañero que la estudia, ò el ingenio que la contrahaze? Con todo esso se la compra, con que dada a la estampa, la que ayer valia cien ducados en casa del Autor, vale oy vn real en casa del Librero, cuyo menoscabo lleua tras si el no aueriguable precio de mañana.

Calderón complains here of the disruption of market forces that governed the economic value of his theatrical scripts. The original script that once cost 100 ducados, or 37,500 maravedís, now that it is available in the bookstall, brings a real or 34 maravedís: From 37,500 maravedís to 34, almost 1/1000 of its original value! No wonder the dramatist complains bitterly of being robbed! Curiously enough those who most likely are the thieves are theatrical people, such as the prompter or member of the troup, or some *memorión* who pirates the text from its performance. A good example of this practice may be seen in the edition of *Tan largo me lo fiáis*, attributed to Calderón, but obviously by Tirso, and based most likely on a pirated text composed by a *memorión*.[22] Two distinct worlds are clashing, that of theater and that of the printed word. The theatrical company that brings a new play to town, especially one that has been successful in Madrid, possesses a script of great value, the *crédito abierto* referred to above. Obviously traditional economic forces and theatrical relations between the principal dramatic troupes who perform in Madrid and elsewhere, as well as the accessibility to novel plays by minor companies touring the provinces, are being severely threatened by the publication of these scripts. What motivates these practices is greed, as Calderón makes clear in "Al Lector" of the *Autos*:

pues no contenta la codicia con auer impresso tantos hurtados escritos mios, como andan sin mi permisso adozenados, y tantos como sin ser mios andan impressos con mi nombre....

Indeed Calderón has been victimized by unscrupulous and greedy individuals in the business of satisfying the public's demand for his plays. Referring to the pirated *Quinta Parte* of 1677, he disclaims any responsibility for the ten plays published there and furthermore hyperbolically renounces authorship, stating:

no ser las quatro mias, ni aun ninguna pudiera dezir, segun estàn no cabales, adulteradas, y defectuosas, bien como trasladadas à hurto para vendidas, y compradas, de quien ni pudo comprarlas, ni venderlas.

Stressing the financial damage wreaked on *his* theatrical world and its charitable connection, he claims an annual loss of 26,000 ducados for the hospitals
and other works of mercy. Once we comprehend the scope of the financial
damage inflicted on Calderón and on theater as a public institution, we begin
to commiserate with the dramatist caught between conflicting economic realities whose interests the judicial system seems unable or unwilling to mediate.

It is interesting to note that, when Don Joseph García de la Plaza received
the *suma de privilegio* (19 October 1725) for the nine volumes of the Calderonian *Partes*, it stated that others could not even publish *comedias sueltas*.[23]
The question of who had the legal right to Calderón's works after his death
vexed Gaspar Agustín de Lara, who claimed that it belonged to la Congrega-
ción del Glorioso Apóstol San Pedro, which inherited Calderón's goods by
sworn testament. Attacking the presumptuous Vera Tassis, Lara emphasizes
the economic value of his friend Don Pedro's plays:

siendo todo el vtil que resultare de sus escritos herencia suya, como no està el Privilegio de la verdadera quinta parte (ni de la sexta, y septima, que ha salido despues de su
muerte) de comedias en su Cabeza? Aviendo valido al Impressor (como dizen todos los
Libreros) en menos de vn año, mas de tres mil ducados, sacada la costa de la impression; con que sea transferible la herencia, y que la aya transferido la Congregacion, se
me podrà responder à esta duda (7¶r).

He summarizes his feelings thus:

yo siempre dudarè, como pueda la Congregacion dexar de ser heredera del Privilegio
de los Libros, y que dexe de tener derecho à percibir lo que han valido las impres-
ssiones. . . .

Lara's appearance on the scene with his *Obelisco funebre, pyramide funesto
que construia, a la inmortal memoria de D. Pedro Calderon de la Barca . . .*
(Madrid, 1684), while it celebrates the genius and accomplishments of the
dramatist, does not hesitate to flail Vera Tassis both as editor and usurper of
Don Pedro's patrimony. Besides the legal questions that Lara raises, a more
fundamental issue is at stake: Who truly serves the memory of Don Pedro
Calderón de la Barca, Don Juan de Vera Tassis y Villarroel or Don Gaspar
Agustín de Lara?

Although Vera Tassis may not have had any legal claim to Don Pedro's dramatic works, as Lara points out, he certainly provided a great service both to
Calderón's memory and to his dramatic and literary legacy. Fray Manuel de
Guerra y Ribera, whose lengthy, detailed, and passionate *aprobación* of the
comedia became its most eloquent defense in the face of severe moral repro-

bation, specifically mentions the public service Vera Tassis provides in his editing of Calderón's works:

Debe rendir el agradecimiento publico repetidas gracias à Don Iuan de Vera Tassis y Villarroel, que sacrifica su cuidado à esta comun vsura de los estudiosos; y dexando sus proprios empleos, dignos de tanta luz, como se la dà el grande ingenio de su Autor, se dedica à la amistad con la memoria: y à la vtilidad publica, limpiando estas Come-dias, que auiendo corrido asta aqui mal copiadas, aun no pudieron, siendo de Don Pedro, librarse de yerros. Oy salen tan cabales, que no hecharà menos Don Pedro su mano, quando la mira tan heredada en quien le venera, y imita.

This perceptive friar recognized the importance and contribution of Vera's labors, but I am not certain how well received they would have been by Calderón. What is evident, however, is that Vera's persistence in seeking the most authoritative versions of the plays was indeed a labor of love.[24]

In the *Séptima Parte*, published by Vera in 1683, he stresses in "Al Discreto, Y Prudente Lector" that:

salen oy . . . limpias, cabales, y desagrauiadas de las graues injurias que de la Pluma, y el Molde padecieron.

As editor, Vera is conscious of how the theatrical scripts were corrected, cut, and copied by innumerable people. Each intervention adulterated the text, and only by locating and editing the original could one be sure that the text represented Calderón's genius rather than someone else's adaptation of it. Printed versions presented the same difficulties. In passing, Vera could not fail to mention Fray Manuel's *aprobación* "para que acaben de romper sus dientes los mordazes detractores, que ociosamente han intentado mellar el inmortal Simulacro de su fama." In brief, Vera intends to publish the most correct and authoritative versions of Calderón's plays that his diligence could locate and his skills could produce.[25] It is indeed noteworthy that when he encounters serious difficulty in locating reliable, if not original, texts, Vera postpones his continuation of the *Partes* to re-edit volumes one through four. There is an unmistakable tone of frustration in "Al que leyere," of the *Octava Parte* (Madrid, 1684), one induced perhaps by Lara's virulent attacks on Vera's ability and character. Our editor writes:

Las demàs que en mi poder quedan, estàn en sus traslados tan inciertas, que hasta conseguir otros mas verdaderos, avrè de suspender el proseguir en el Noueno Tomo; passando à repetir en la Prensa los quatro Primeros, que te asseguro, no tienen menos yerros, que los aduertidos en los que tengo publicados; pues aun no bastò el respeto de su Autor viuo, para eximirse del riesgo que suelen padecer à manos de los traslados, y moldes: y como el verdadero amor es preciso que passe mas allà de la muerte, yo que fui quien mas entrañablemente amè à Don Pedro; pues como *Omni tempore diligit, qui amicus est*, es forçoso que à repetidas instancias de la voluntad, quando parece que acabo, empiece de nueuo à exercitar mi obligacion, tomando esta fatiga por aliuio, para que todo ceda en su obsequio, y en honra, y gloria de Dios, que te guarde.

While we all have reservations regarding Vera's methods and skills as an editor, there is no doubt concerning his perseverance, dedication, and commitment to Calderón's memory.

Burned by criticism and frustrated by his inability to locate reliable versions of the *comedias* yet to be published, Vera Tassis requested permission to
reprint the first four volumes: "por hallarse en vuestro poder los originales"
according to "El rey," dated 11 July 1684 and found in the *Primera Parte*
(Madrid, 1685). This same document noted Vera's purpose in so doing:
"deseauades que dichas Obras saliessen cabales, y corregidas de tantos
yerros. . . ." With considerable hyperbole, Vera notes in "Al que leyere" that
"Estas Comedias, que por desfiguradas desconoció su Autor en su Primera
Parte, yà ilustradas en esta nueva luz con que las retocò el desvelo mio. . . ."
What was meant by the word "originales" is spelled out in the *Advertencia* to
the *Segunda Parte* (Madrid, 1686), where he writes:

hallando diminutas las mas, y defectuosas todas, passè à corregirlas por sus originales,
algunos de la mano de su Autor; otros, por adulterados, de agena letra.

We do not know which versions were based on autograph manuscripts and
which were not, nor do we know a great deal about the extent of Vera's "desvelo" in touching up these early texts. The editorial apparatus had not
evolved well enough to meet our concerns and objections. But Vera was conscious that his editorial enterprise was directed at readers who also could
compare his efforts to those of earlier editors. Announcing the imminent publication of the *Tercera Parte*, he states:

que no tiene menores yerros que los notados, pues concurriendo ignorancia, y negli-
gencia en imprimirle, era forçoso fraguarse los mas desproporcionados, y los que en
este advirtirà el desapassionado Lector, son tan leves escrupulos de la prensa, que
podrà corregirlos, sin desvelado estudio.

This criticism of Don Sebastián Ventura de Vergara's editorial efforts
becomes more detailed in the *Prólogo* to the *Tercera Parte* (Madrid, 1687):

lo qual verificarà el que diligente, ò curioso cotejare la del *Laurel de Apolo* que aora
sale, con la que èl permitiò imprimir, que ademàs de concluirla en vn medio verso,
faltandola mas de ducientos, los demàs en los razonamientos estàn desfiguradas.

Vera's edition of the nine *Partes* stands as a great service to readers, many of
whom never witnessed the production of such plays as *El laurel de Apolo*.
Since we do not wish to undervalue his contributions to Calderón's literary
heritage, we should also not overlook the financial incentives and rewards
that spurred on his efforts.

Don Gaspar Augustín de Lara felt deeply moved in *Obelisco funebre* to honor his friend Don Pedro and to criticize the presumptuousness of Vera Tassis. In many ways Lara continues Calderón's *perro-del-hortelano*-like attitudes, which, I hope to have shown, are attributable both to religious and economic factors. Going right to the heart of the matter, he questions Vera's sources, stating:

De forma, que por ninguna parte pueden averse adquirido verdaderas; porque bien saben todos, que Don Pedro jamàs diò ninguna Comedia suya à la Prensa; y que las que se imprimieron fue contra su voluntad; tanto, que aun corregirlas nunca quiso, aun pidiendolo personas de autoridad; lo mas que dezia, que las corrigiessen ellos, ya que se huuiessen de imprimir sin su gusto (8¶)

Lara may indeed be a faithful representative of Calderón's wishes, but we must recognize the shortsightedness of those wishes and their implications for posterity. We should be grateful to Vera Tassis for his broader understanding of Calderón's legacy and place in Spanish culture, while at the same time we respect the position of Lara who believes that he is faithfully carrying out his friend's expressed wishes. The real issue was whether personal preference should dictate such important concerns as Calderón's legacy to Spain and to the literate world.

Lara's criticism is based not so much on the sources of Vera's editions as on the propriety of the methods he used to acquire them and whether or not their publication respected Calderón's wishes. To further undermine Vera's authority and accuracy, he criticizes the editing of Don Agustín de Salazar y Torres's (m. 1675) *Cythara de Apolo* (Madrid, 1681). As Salazar's *mayor amigo* he should have known that the poet and dramatist was born in Almazán, not in Soria. As editor Vera mistakenly included Don Juan de Jáuregui's *Fábula de Orfeo*[26] among Salazar's poems and a *comedia* by Don Juan Cuero de Tapia among his dramatic works.[27] Vera is an indiscriminate editor who has willy-nilly included "otras Poesias de otros muchos Ingenios, que oy viuen." This broadside without specificity smacks more of spite than of respect for truth. The *mayor amigo* label may be a conventional phrase used by Vera to demonstrate his concern and actions that further his friend's fame and legacy to posterity. Nevertheless, serious doubt has been raised about Vera's methods and achievements as an editor.

Lara raises a real challenge to Vera's editorial enterprise by also questioning the accuracy of his results:

y desta forma, todos los que las imprimieron, y corrigieron en vida de Don Pedro, con los errores, y defectos que le obligaron à desconocerlas por suyas, pueden imprimirlas oy, alegando el lugar del primer Tomo, impresso en el Prologo de sus Autos, que alega el que las està imprimiendo aora, diziendo, que las quita los infinitos errores con que andauan impressas, y trasladas, cosa digna de loor grande, si puede ser possible (6¶).

D.W. Cruickshank has observed "that Vera was capable of allowing his editing to extend into the realms of original composition."[28] Obviously Lara was aware of Vera's practices and warned his readers about them. As with Vera's penchant for publishing works not by Salazar among this author's authentic poems and plays, Lara takes issue with Vera's gullibility regarding Calderonian titles, but particularly with his presumption to "correct" what Calderón wrote and found acceptable:

(procedidos de los malos traslados, y pcores impressiones) se originò el desconocerlas por suyas: De que se debe inferir, que todos los errores que se reconocieren, seràn causadas, de quien pretende enmendar aora, los que no tuvieron, quando su Autor las diò la vltima pcrfeccion, que se reconociò en su primer examen: sièdo la mayor gloria para su posteridad, el q̃ siempre se tengã por perfectas, aun à resistencia de las imperfecciones que el tiempo caduco las pudiere introducir, y la ignorancia balbuciente, presumiere enmendar.

Vera's greatest failing was his desire to serve appearances by making corrections not only to obviously faulty passages and errata but also to those slips and inappropriate words and phrases that he believed damaged Calderón's luster. In fact Vera Tassis was substituting his esthetic sensibility and judgment for those of Calderón.

Vera Tassis stated in the *Quinta Parte*, and Lara quotes him directly in his *Obelisco*, that Calderón's "achacosa edad no permitiò pudiese hazer entero juizio dc sus Comedias" (8¶2r). Taking this assertion as a personal affront to Calderón's honor and memory, Lara replies that his friend conserved "tan sano el juizio" up to the moment of death. How could someone as unfamiliar with Calderón's preferenccs, desires, and habits, as Vera demonstrates, become the arbiter of his works? Vera's lack of intimacy with the real Calderón obviously disqualifies him from such a lofty responsibility. Therefore, Lara states, regarding Calderonian titles:

y assi siempre avràn de ser suyos solos aquellos que èl declarò lo eran; los demàs, aunque estàn en su nombre, bien se dexa reconocer que son supucatoo (8¶2r).

It is amazing how many of the questions raised during Calderón's lifetime and which formed the basis of this Vera-Lara controversy continue to plague Calderonistas and Calderonian studies.

Reading as Anachronism

Calderón wanted to have his *autos* and the *comedias de fábula* read imaginatively and theatrically by those capable of re-creating the proper environment in which they were orignally produced. As a man of the stage, he resisted the divorce between the theatrical script and its intended place of performance. But events were such that Calderón's wishes were ignored. Both spectators and readers demanded access to his works, and there were many enterprising individuals ready to meet that demand, regardless of propriety or legality. These two distinct groups form part of a larger audience I call consumers of Calderonian plays, both in performance and in printed editions of his works. They are the driving force behind the events so meticulously chronicled in the preliminary pages to the *Partes*. With their maravedís, reales, and ducados the Spanish consumers of the seventeenth and eighteenth centuries fueled the confrontation between performance and *papel*. On examining some of the historic players in this confrontation, we get a better sense of what was happening behind the scenes, so to speak. Theatrical interests, Calderón himself, and Gaspar de Lara stood squarely behind the performance objectives of Calderón's dramatic scripts; it is evident that in the first two instances, at least, it was in their financial best interest to do so. In support of the reading public, we have the publishing industry, Vera Tassis, and those like him who, for a variety of reasons, wished to publish corrected and complete editions of Calderón's plays. From our vantage point we cannot but be grateful for the persistence of those individuals who sought to satisfy the demands of the reading public, regardless of the legal and moral issues involved.

What would have become of Calderón's plays in general and of the myth plays in particular if our acquaintance with them had to rely exclusively on a performance tradition? The myth plays survived because they continued to be read within the literary tradition long after they had ceased to form part of the performance tradition or repertoire of Spain's theatrical companies. Reading as anachronism is not in this light a criticism, but the very process that guarantees that these texts will survive the ravages of time and the vagaries of cultural evolution. It is in this sense that Calderón's seventeen myth plays are examined in the present study. I attempt to plumb these texts not so much for their allegorical significance within the historic contexts of their first or any subsequent performance, but for their narrative and symbolic significance in our historic time and place. In so doing I fully recognize where I place myself with reference to Calderón's oft-expressed opinions and desires, but at the same time I acknowledge that I may be more faithful to his theatrical scripts as cultural and literary texts than even the dramatist himself.

Notes

1 Each year the National Park Service sponsors a Golden-Age Drama Festival at the Chamizal National Memorial. Companies from the United States, Mexico, and other nations stage live performances of Spain's dramatic heritage.

2 *Primera Parte* (Madrid, 1636), dedicación a don Bernardino Fernández de Velasco y Tobar.

3 *Segunda Parte* (Madrid, 1637), dedicación a don Rodrigo de Mendoza Rojas y Sandoval de la Vega y Luna.

4 Quoted from Gaspar Agustín de Lara, *Obelisco funebre, pyramide funesto que construia, a la inmortal memoria de D. Pedro Calderon de la Barca. . .* (Madrid, 1684), ¶9r- ¶10r.

5 See D. W. Cruickshank, "The textual criticism of Calderón's *comedias*: a survey," in *The Textual Criticism of Calderón's Comedias* (London: Gregg International, 1973), p. 2, where he states: "If public demand for printed editions of his plays is any indication, Calderón's prestige did not reach its highest point until the 1670s, long after he had ceased to write for the public theaters; but the public's demand was no doubt satisfied in part by the great *Comedias escogidas* series, which began in 1652, and which published a number of Calderón's plays." I would add that Calderón's exclusive dedication to court theater cut off the general public's access to his works, thus heightening the importance of the print medium.

6 *The Theory of Literary Criticism: A Logical Analysis* (Berkeley: U of California P, 1974), p. 44. The importance and pertinence of this definition for my purpose will become evident in the analysis that follows.

7 *Legalidad*, according to the *Autoridades*, signifies "Fidelidad, puntualidad, buen trato y observancia de la ley, ù de la propria obligacion."

8 *El templo de Palas* (Nápoles: Gerónimo Fasvlo, 1675).

9 N.D. Shergold, *A History of the Spanish Stage from Medieval Times until the End of the Seventeenth Century* (Oxford: Clarendon P, 1967). N.D. Shergold and J.E. Varey, *Teatros y comedias en Madrid: 1666-1687. Estudio y documentos* (London: Tamesis, 1974) and *Representaciones palaciegas: 1603-1699. Estudio y documentos* (London: Tamesis, 1682). Pedro Calderón de la Barca, *Obras completas: dramas*, ed. A. Valbuena Briones (Madrid: Aguilar, 1969). Kurt and Roswitha Reichenberger, *Bibliographisches Handbuch der Calderón-Forschung*, vol. I and III (Kassel: Thiele & Schwartz, 1979-1981).

10 Printed illegally in 1670. I rely on Cruickshank for most of the details enumerated here.

11 Pirated edition circa 1700.

12 These eighteenth-century editions are reprints of the Vera Tassis editions, except where noted.

13 Based on QC; printed in 1672 or 1673.

14 Obvious error in the date.

15 A collection of *sueltas* in the format of the pseudo-Vera Tassis edition.

16 Printed within ten years of 1664.

17 See note 15.

18 Printed in Madrid.

19 Reprint of #1.

20 Second edition of 1682.

21 Second edition of 1691. I have not found, nor is there listed in any source consulted, an early eighteenth-century reprint or edition of the *Novena Parte*. Jaime Moll has observed that the *Novena Parte* of 1698 was in fact published around 1731. See

"Sobre las ediciones del siglo XVIII de las Partes de comedias de Calderón," in *Calderón* (Madrid: 1983), I, 230-31.

22 See the edition by Xavier A. Fernández (Madrid: Revista "Estudios," 1967).

23 See *Primera Parte* (Madrid, 1726).

24 Fray Manuel's *aprobación* is dated in Madrid, 14 April 1682.

25 Vera's *Partes* appeared in the following chronological order: 5.a-1682; 6.a-1683; 7.a-1683; 8.a-1684; 1.a-1685; 2.a-1686; 3.a-1687; 4.a-1688; 9.a-1691.

26 This poem was first published in Madrid in 1624.

27 Referring to this play Lara writes: "que yo he visto en sus borradores," but he failed to mention which play it was.

28 "Don Juan de Vera Tassis y Villarroel," in *Aureum Saelculum Hispanum*. (Wiesbaden: Franz Steiner, 1983), p. 49.

Part I

I Myth as an "Ambush of Reality"

homo sum; humani nihil a me alienum puto

Introduction to the World of Myth

The world of myth is at one and the same time diaphanous and opaque. We "see" it depending on the degree of our sensitivity to its truth, its inner laws, and its mode of revealing itself. Poets have generally found myth to be a fertile ground of inspiration, and therefore on the whole they are more familiar with its secrets and treasures. Nathaniel Hawthorne, in his *Tanglewood Tales*, states that "the inner life of the legends cannot be come at save by making them entirely one's own property...."[1] Though in principle I agree with his statement, I find its declaration to be too forceful, too aggressive. A shift in emphasis, perhaps, would correct the exaggeration of believing that myth can be grasped and made one's own. We, in fact, are grasped by myth, and it makes us all participants in its communal life. Even though we live in "enlightened" times, our world has been shaped and continues to be formed by modern myths; only today we take our myths to be facts—facts of science or the results of social research. We construct our myths and in turn are imperceptibly shaped by them. But there is a uniqueness to myth, one that Mark Twain's comment about pedestrian truth allows us to glimpse: "Homely truth is unpalatable."[2] The world of Greco-Roman myth, while it may lack the factual elements we appear to thrive on, retains a wholeness and completeness that defies our accumulated facts. Moreover, its truths are not homely, for I have yet to see "truth" as homely as that found in scientific discourse. Why has Greco-Roman myth continued to fascinate, enthrall, and captivate so many readers of tales, be they of the gods and goddesses or of the heroes? The answer may be simple: its truth is not homely truth, and therefore it is most palatable to those of us fascinated by its beauty and unsuspecting charm that lay hold of us before we have realized it.

Before proceeding we should briefly address what is meant by the term "myth." Stanley Edgar Hyman, in his essay on "The Ritual View of Myth and the Mythic," admonishes us to distinguish myth "from all the other things we loosely call by its name: legend, tale, fantasy, mass delusion, popular belief and illusion, and plain lie."[3] He then links myth with rite. But such a narrow view, while appropriate for the anthropologist, would be unduly restrictive for the literary critic. Stith Thompson suggests a practical solution that is in accord with the European literary tradition and is an appropriate introduction to the present study. Myth encompasses those narratives of gods and heroes handed down from the Greco-Roman tradition.[4]

Yet Hyman's caveat is not without merit, especially in light of those connotative meanings for myth listed above. It is precisely the inferential possibilities, such as "mass delusion, popular belief and illusion, and plain lie," that have left many with a jejune, if not hostile, attitude toward myth. By having expanded the acceptations of "myth" we have correspondingly reduced its revelatory power. In this vein Alan M. Olson has written about the need for a "postcritical naïveté" that has "to do with striving for that difficult position that is guided by criticism but still open to wonder in the face of what myth and symbol have to give."[5] Is there a knowable reality independent of language, ideology, and myth? In his critique of Northrop Frye, Gerald Graff has noted that "Myth is supposed to humanize, order, make sense of experience, yet its separation [by Frye] from any objective ground leaves it without the authority to carry out these functions effectively."[6] Though we may have lost our direct access to being and reality, myth, as well as language, is a mediated access, for through it being and reality whisper their secrets to us all. Without language and myth there would be no way to approach the world, and without value and ideology there would be no meaning in it. In summary, myth is not a childish or primitive form of knowledge, but a perennially vibrant and mature one that requires a sincere openness to its revelatory powers as the condition for the communication of knowledge about our being in the world, that world itself, and the interaction and mutual dependence of the one on the other.

The meaning of the word "myth" has shifted, moreover, from one of univocity to equivocity and even to plurivocity (A. M. Olson, p. 3). In this regard myth participates in a general intellectual movement from monosemy to polysemy. In addition to myth, the scope and definition of literature have experienced a similar expansion to include diaries and other such forms of popular culture. The literary canon itself has faced challenges from right and left. And literary criticism, from New Criticism to deconstructionist expressions, has exploded into such a proliferation of manifestations that indeed it appears the core has dropped out of the Western literary tradition, or at least been significantly, though perhaps temporarily, eroded. In this general cultural welter the concept of myth has undergone a similar transformation or expansion of meaning, so much so that its use may easily lead to misunderstandings, especially by those who hold to a particular definition of myth to the exclusion of other possibilities.

Mythos is concerned with the activity of telling by which the hearer comes into the presence of that which is narrated.[7] By its very nature mythic telling is a dynamic activity. The world of myth is, as David Bidney has characterized it, "a dramatic world, a world of conflicting powers, and mythical perception is impregnated with these emotional qualities."[8] Over the centuries poets and dramatists have heard myth's siren song and been invariably changed by their encounter with it. Aeschylus, Sophocles, and Euripides are numbered among its devotees, and the list is endless: Boccaccio, Racine, Calderón, etc. The Western mythic tradition is fundamentally literary, for the Greek tragedians were already elaborating on "old tales" as well as on older literary renditions and compilations of their basically religious myths. By the time the myths reached the seventeenth century, there were two main repositories of them: the great collections by mythographers, such as Pérez de Moya's *Philosophia secreta* and Baltasar de Victoria's *Teatro de los dioses de la gentilidad*[9] and the literary sources found in Greek and Roman literature, especially Ovid's *Metamorphoses*. From our perspective myth has followed a twisting but clearly perceptible path from various "tellings" through literary renditions and scholarly compilations to further elaboration within both the literary and scholarly domains. One needs only to recall Buero Vallejo's *La tejedora de sueños*, Cocteau's films, or Edith Hamilton's popular, but bowdlerized, *Mythology*. K. K. Ruthven has written that "Change – in the form of creative misunderstandings – is what keeps myths alive."[10] While I could quibble over the use of "misunderstandings" where I would prefer to see "recodifications" or "remythologizations," Ruthven has, nonetheless, accurately perceived the process by which myth survives its detractors and intractable critics.

Nowhere is the tendency to mistrust myth more apparent than in the popular use of the term "demythologizing." Our positivist tendencies have led us to prefer reason over insight and fact over imagination. A recent cartoon by Phil Frank illuminates this point.[11] Cupid is seated on the corner of a park bench, with head in hands, in a state of total dejection. At his feet lies a victim, pierced through with one of his shafts. To the left, a police officer is reading Cupid his Miranda rights. A semiological analysis of the scene would tell us much about our "contemporary" view of love, myth, and victimization, as well as our perception of the justice system. But the tendency to look through myth to its underlying ideology is not a modern passion or obsession. Calderón demythologizes Hércules, "the hero above all other heroes," as Richmond Y. Hathorn characterizes him,[12] in *Fieras afemina Amor*. To stop at this phase, or to concentrate exclusively upon this negative aspect of demythologizing in Calderonian theater, is to fail to see the forest for the trees. On considering Calderón's entire mythic output, one is struck by the positive disposition of his plays towards what A. M. Olson has called a "creative remythologizing" (p. 3) of the Greco-Roman mythic tradition. Bultmannian theology has captured the spirit of this creative remythologizing while at the same time retaining the term "demythologizing." According to Bultmann, every effort is made "to locate the claim which the Bible has on us today."[13] The tension underlying this process depends on the need to apply to the present a text that stands in the past. In the last analysis the text is not the object; we become the "object" addressed by it. In both literary and mythic interpretation we need assume a similar attitude that asks what is speaking to us in and through the text. We humbly face the text asking how we are to understand it.[14] Palmer has summarized the nature of "demythologizing" as a paradigm for literary interpretation: "Demythologizing (which is not the dissolving of myth but the realization that we must see what it is in myth that is meaningful) should, in principle, be the task of literary interpretation" (p. 251). Calderón, as dramatist and interpreter of myth, participates in the demythologizing/remythologizing processes in both their negative and positive manifestations, though the latter is dominant. He is truly a *mythológos*, one who grounds his individual existence in myth.[15]

Evidently the interrelationships of literature and myth are many and fruitful, and it is possible to point to two main perspectives or directions. First of all there is the perspective that myth provides on the literary phenomenon, such as the study of the hero figure, for example, the figure of Ulysses.[16] The second perspective involves the distinctly literary study of myth, which Hyman has characterized as a focus on a specific myth and text in contradistinction to an anthropological study that concentrates on a specific culture and rite (p. 144). In my examination of Calderonian myth dramas, the latter, the distinctly literary study of myth, is the perspective employed in the analyses of individual plays, whereas the former, the distinctly mythic study of literature, is the perspective reflected in the overall organization of the book.

Definitions of Myth and Descriptions of the World of Myth

In an excellent survey article on "Literature and Myth," John B. Vickery has divided the prevailing current extraliterary perspectives on myth into four general groups: the anthropological, the psychological, the sociological, and the philosophical.[17] Using this outline as a taxonomy for various definitions of myth will assist us in appreciating both the complexity and diversity as well as similarity of most definitions of myth.

The Anthropological. The most representative example of this approach is Claude Lévi-Strauss's structuralist studies of myth. In the essay titled "The Structural Study of Myth," he has defined myth in such global terms that it could be included in the philosophical and religious category: "On the one hand, a myth always refers to events alleged to have taken place in time: before the world was created, or during its first stages—anyway, long ago. But what gives the myth an operative value is that the specific pattern described is everlasting; it explains the present and the past as well as the future."[18] The explanatory function of myth is the key to its power, for that which explains also confers meaning and purpose on human activity. For this reason Lévi-Strauss envisages myth as a logical model whose purpose is to overcome the contradictions inherent in life (p. 105). Therefore, when he speaks of myth's instrumentality in effecting a mediation between meaningful oppositions such as birth and death, blindness and lucidity, and sexuality and truth, he naturally denominates myth as "a kind of logical tool."[19] This approach lays bare the manipulative nature of myth, for "mythical thought proceeds from the consciousness of certain oppositions and tends towards their progressive mediation" (p. 224). It is a short step from this perspective to R. Barthes's view of myth as a justificatory system of any ideology.

In addition to the Boaz school, the other main anthropological perspective would be the Frazerian influenced Cambridge School. Lord Raglan has defined myth as "a narrative which, with or without its associated rite, is believed to confer life,"[20] and Hyman, in a streamlined version, as "a story sanctioning a rite" (p. 146). Neither school has had significant literary impact of late.

The Psychological. The theories and influences of Jung and Freud are well known to most. In Jungian terms, "Myths are the original revelations of the preconscious psyche, involuntary statements about unconscious psychic happenings. . . ."[21] For Freud myth, such as that of Oedipus, embodies the hidden impulses of the subconscious that frequently lead to neurotic behavior. Though very different in terms of emphasis, both have had profound influence on mythic and literary studies.

The Sociological. Bronislaw Malinowski is the principal exponent of the sociological perspective, and Vickery's own general definition of myth admits a sociological point of view: "The conviction or convictions, explained in various ways by actions of beings superior in kind and degree to humans, that provide a rationale for existing patterns of belief and behavior..." (p. 72). This approach is also conducive to a critique of myth's justificatory movement, such as that found in Barthes's *Mythologies*.

The Philosophical and Religious. Vickery employs the ideas of Roland Barthes and Ernst Cassirer as models of the philosophical perspective, and in truth just about all the approaches share in some way this perspective's search for ultimates. For comparative religion, "A myth is a type of narrative which seeks to express in imaginative form a belief about man, the world or deity which cannot adequately be expressed in simple propositions."[22] The relation of myth to faith is seen more clearly yet in Hans-Georg Gadamer's categorical definition which states that "myth neither requires nor includes any possible verification outside itself."[23] The self-verifying nature of both excludes any critique not proceeding from within the very nature of belief itself and confirms the authority faith commands and myth suggests. Mircea Eliade shares Gadamer's exclusive view: "The myth defines itself by its own mode of being. It can only be grasped, as a myth, in so far as it *reveals* something as having been *fully manifested*, and this manifestation is at the same time *creative* and *exemplary*, since it is the foundation of a structure of reality as well as of a kind of human behavior."[24] He emphasizes the corollary common to faith and myth, personal commitment. The following definitions neglect this active aspect of myth. Stith Thompson's practical approach states that "myth has to do with the gods and their actions, with creation, and with the general nature of the universe and of the earth" (p. 173). For our Western tradition he amends his definition to include the hero tales. Another cosmological definition is proffered by Alan W. Watts "as a complex of stories—some no doubt fact, and some fantasy—which, for various reasons, human beings regard as demonstrations of the inner meaning of the universe and of human life."[25] In all these attempts to define myth there is a common factor that links myth to faith, whether it is of a philosophical or religious nature. The search for explanations is a constant human endeavor, and the search for the ultimate explanation of the world is endemic to our species and characteristic of our diverse cultures.

Perhaps the most popular perspective over the past twenty years has been the structuralist, whose influence has been felt in fields far beyond the anthropological studies of primitive peoples upon which it is based. At the heart of Lévi-Strauss's approach lies the notion of myth as a logical model, or tool, whose purpose is to mediate meaningful oppositions. Paul Ricoeur has critiqued this concept of myth as a logical operator between propositions, and in his view myth "involves propositions which point towards limit situations, towards the origin and the end, towards death, suffering and sexuality." Therefore, mythical thought gravitates around the *aporias*, or insoluble problems, of human existence.[26] While taking advantage of many of the benefits structural analysis confers as a method, this study will incorporate Ricoeur's insight into the direction of mythical thought.

The Literary. Vickery has pointed out that literature and myth share formal characteristics that almost make them appear identical, such as narrative, character, image, and theme (p. 67). Therefore it is not surprising that several definitions and descriptions have stressed elements that would normally be of prime concern to literature. William Righter defines myth as "the embodiment of human aspiration and its appropriate imaginative form."[27] Alan M. Olson, in a more functional vein, writes that "Myth has to do with a telling that seeks to bring the hearer into the *presence* or *region* of that which is told" (p. 3). On considering the history of Western literature, perhaps it would be appropriate to view literature as the medium that carries on many of the ancient functions of myth. What appears to be common to both is their ability to create meaning and inspire belief, and even to move to action.

The term "mythology" may refer to three broad categories or areas: 1) a treatise on myths, such as Pérez de Moya's *Philosophia secreta*; 2) the science of myths, such as Lévi-Strauss's or Roland Barthes's works; and 3) the collection of myths into a system that embodies a people's beliefs. Again, from the perspective taken, there may be slight changes of focus as the term is employed. For Jean Seznec, mythology is nothing more "than a system of ideas in disguise, a 'secret philosophy'" (p. 321). Such a view accords well with his history-of-ideas approach. For C. Kerényi it is the movement of mythologems, or tales, which are capable of transformation though they remain basically the same.[28] And Jacques Waardenburg stresses the interpretative function in the following definition: "A *mythology* expresses mythical contents which are contained in different stories within a larger connecting whole. It represents a degree of rationalization of myth and the symbolic message which it is supposed to contain, and it facilitates the transfer of meaning of myth as long as it has not decayed into merely amusing stories" (p. 59). In this light my study will be mythological in that, in addition to the interpretation of individual myths dramatized by Calderón, every attempt will be made to relate those interpretations to the larger connecting whole that forms Calderonian mythology. Calderón's dramatic activity is fundamentally mythological in its attempt to recover the symbolic messages veiled in *some* Greco-Roman myths. Interpretation implies a form of rationalization, but that very process underlies the dramatic value of those texts. In short, all of us are involved in the creation of meanings, and, though these exist apart from the consciousness that creates them, in the last analysis those very meanings link one consciousness to another.

What Calderón has dramatized so effectively is the nature of faith and love as transforming forces that involve pain and suffering. Faith in a Supreme Being and love of God and one's neighbor may appear dim in a mythological context, but they are the controlling ideas that allow the Christian dramatist to appreciate, interpret, and put on the stage the pagan tales of old as well as enable us to grasp their relevance to our own present.

Although the selection of Vickery's outline of perspectives on myth is somewhat arbitrary, it does cover fairly well contemporary scholarship. Ruthven suggests another schema that substantially duplicates Vickery's; he suggests the study of myth as 1) history and 2) natural history; as encompassing 3) psychological approaches; as 4) moral didactics, 5) language games, and 6) ritual; and as 7) structural analysis. All in all, "myths are malleable" (p. 47). Bidney, assessing the question from the perspective of the history of mythological theory, concludes that the two basic approaches to the interpretation of myth have been the literal and the symbolic (p. 21). Many contemporary thinkers are uncomfortable with the symbolic and hence either wish to undermine its authority or deconstruct its truth claims. Roland Barthes has written that "Semiology has taught us that myth has the task of giving an historical intention, a natural justification, and making contingency appear eternal."[29] Therefore, the basic movement of myth is from history to nature, thereby eliminating all dialectics and creating a deceitful clarity. To view myth solely as a justificatory system of an ideology is to mute its ability to speak and to deny its validity as a form of knowledge. It would be simplistic to summarize myth as the mediation of oppositions contained in stories of the gods and cultural heroes, or as social delusion or social faith, but structuralist and semiological studies lead us in these directions. Structural analysis presupposes that myth "has a meaning as a narrative of origins" (Ricoeur, p. 217). Its movement is from a surface semantics "to a depth semantics, that of the boundary situations which constitute the ultimate 'referent' of the myth . . ." (p. 217). We can perceive the confluence of these two distinct concerns in that both social structures and mythical thought reveal the deep-rooted conflicts, the human predicaments, and existential perplexities (the *aporias* of social existence) that characterize the human situation throughout history and in all cultures (p. 220).

Myth and the Question of Truth

Though the question of truth occupies the interest of some of the foremost contemporary philosophers, such as Gadamer, Habermas, and Ricoeur, I presume not to enter that particular discussion, but to review what several thinkers see as the relationship between myth and truth, a fundamental issue that needs to be addressed. There is some general agreement about what myth does, but disagreement arises when different individuals interpret from distinct perspectives the meaning of what was actually accomplished. Lévi-Strauss points to the fundamental principle that "myths get thought in man unbeknownst to him."[30] What this insight discloses is that we do not create or invent myths as much as we are created and manipulated by them. The relation to contemporary theories of language is obvious. What myths do is to provide through images a foundation view of humankind and the world from which then all else proceeds. Eliade observes "that *the essential human condition precedes the actual human condition*..." (p. 54). Essence is a given and not the result of existential decisions.

A more pragmatic view of the truth of myth emphasizes that it is a function of the interpretation of myth. Bidney concludes, then, that myth symbolizes either a fundamental religious and metaphysical truth or a sociological one with no cosmic reference (p. 16). These two interpretations are mutually exclusive. What 'truth' exists in myth is evidenced by its effectiveness in motivating people to action; myth is, therefore, "beyond truth and falsity" (p. 20).

In the literary domain, the question of truth takes on a clarity that may be obscured in a more general discussion. In *Myth and Literature*, William Righter suggests that the validity of myth employed in a literary work arises from the context in which it is used (p. 32). It follows, then, that meaning flows not from the myth itself, but from the context created for it (p. 80). Myth illuminates the patterns of life and human participation in it, so much so that we are led to confess that, in spite of myth's remoteness and strangeness, it nonetheless captures something essentially human and true. As Righter expressed it, myth confers a "yes,-life's-like-that" feeling (p. 95). In the final analysis, myth, through its creative power, supplies "viable forms of coherence" (p. 107) that are either in tune with our own experience or sufficiently revelatory as to suggest that life should be that way. In sum, a constant of myth is its sense-making function (p. 108). In this vein Marcelino C. Peñuelas is correct when he asserts "que el mito contribuye a crear, o crea en cierta forma, la realidad." Myth is, then, an operative reality in view of its ability to move people to action.[31] But if myth functions within a context of "invented" meaning, and if its coherence depends on a certain conformity with already held views, myth becomes a quasi solipsism that is self-confirming; its revelatory powers have been trimmed down to human proportion.

A contrasting view is provided by Mircea Eliade who sees myth as ontophany. As the plenary manifestation of Being, "ontophany always implies theophany or hierophany" (p. 15). In phenomenological terms, myth reveals "the structure of reality, and the multiple modalities of being in the world." As a disclosure of the sacred, myth compels the religious person "to comply with general values, with the universal" (p. 18). These two perspectives on the question of myth's truth may not be as disharmonious as they appear at first glance. Eliade speaks of myth in its pure state as a communication between being itself and people who participate in it. Righter speaks of myth as basic plot material to be molded into a meaningful context by the author. Both views are adequate from the perspectives taken; both are valid in their contexts. But what is contrary to both myth making and poetic activity, as Alister Cameron has shown in "The Myth and the Maker," is an orthodox spirit.[32] The openness to what is whispered in myth or suggested in a literary creation is the key to the treasures locked within them.

Myth and Time

Mircea Eliade has written eloquently about the primordial event that is the object of myth. *In illo tempore* the foundation of the human condition was laid by mythic ancestors. In spite of a multitude of images depicting the event, "they all mean the same thing: that *the essential human condition precedes the actual human condition*" (p. 54). Through myth one attempts a *regressus ad originem* to relive that event that took place in time or before time and determined the fate of humankind. Oftentimes the primordial event, such as the fall of Adam, results in an ontological mutation of the human condition, which in turn produces a cosmic schism, of which we at present are its victims (p. 60). In stressing myth's explanatory function, Lévi-Strauss describes how myth refers to that primordial event in such a way as to illuminate a pattern that is everlasting: "it explains the present and the past as well as the future" ("The Structural Study of Myth," pp. 84-85). In the Christian tradition there is the primordial event, the fall of Adam and Eve, and the expiatory event, the redemption by Jesus Christ that supersedes in magnitude and meaning the effect of the former. It is this latter event that radically alters our conception of time.

As Eliade demonstrates, mythical behavior, through its *regressus ad originem*, seeks integration into the primordial event that is explanatory of the present. He describes its four characteristics as follows: first, the exemplary pattern; second, its repetition; third, the break with profane duration; and fourth, the integration into primordial time (p. 31). But Christianity radically alters mythical behavior through its reorientation from preoccupation with the past to longing for the future. As myth seeks to break with profane time,

Christianity realizes that time has become hierophantic in the overall plan of salvation and therefore seeks the partial realization of that plan in the present time. Likewise, Christian eschatology longs for the second coming of Christ at which time time itself will come to an end with death, judgment, heaven, and hell and the integration of all into eternity. In the Judeo-Christian tradition the transcendent God has manifested Himself as immanent through his interventions in history. And the deciding intervention was the Incarnation of Jesus Christ, at which time "all history becomes a theophany." According to Eliade, the result of the Incarnation is that "The conceptions of mythical time and of the eternal return are definitely superseded" (p. 153).

In Calderonian myth plays two distinct conceptions of time operate. The first, typically mythical, depicts a cyclical notion of time. Cyclical time underlies Calderonian tragedy, and it is found in tragic myths such as *Eco y Narciso*. The second, typically Christian, depicts a progressive or teleological notion of time. Human history is not degenerative, from the fall to everlasting damnation, but rather a progressive "building up" of the kingdom of God through the realization of God's divine plan for salvation. Such a teleological conception of time is found in *La estatua de Prometeo* and *Fortunas de Andrómeda y Perseo*, where there are divine "interventions" to better a situation or resolve an impasse. This notion of time underlies Calderonian comedy and by and large defines his dramatic world view. Its most salient representation is found in his *autos sacramentales*.

A Taxonomy for the Study of Myth

The following discussion is based upon Jacques Waardenburg's "Symbolic Aspects of Myth"[33] in which he stresses myth's function as witness to reality, making palpable the hidden aspects and dimensions of human experience. As a symbolic construction of reality, myth operates in two complementary manners: first, it may suggest a deeper order underlying the world of appearances. *La devoción de la Cruz* and the *auto sacramental* function in this way as expressions of Christian mythology, and by this expression I intend nothing derogatory. Second, it may function as a breakthrough transcending ordinary reality. *El médico de su honra* and *Fieras afemina Amor* operate in this manner, providing new insights into truth and reality.

Waardenburg cites Eric J. S. Sharpe's definition of myth as "A type of narration which seeks to express in imaginative form a belief about man, the world or deity which cannot adequately be expressed in simple propositions." The former then goes on to distinguish between two basic kinds of myth. First, explicit myth exists in the form of a particular kind of story; second, implicit myth exists "as elements in speech indicating particular and essential assumptions which give meaning to the life of an individual or community and on which people can fall back in situations of a crisis" (p. 52). Calderón dramatizes both the explicit myths of Greco-Roman mythology and the implicit myths of his society. In plays such as *El médico de su honra* and *Fieras afemina Amor* the movement is from implicit to explicit myth, revealing in the process the social "faiths" from which action and belief are projected. Eric Dardel has commented on this second form of myth as "what we never see in ourselves, the secret spring of our vision of the world, of our devotion, of our dearest notions."[34] The distinction between these two forms of myth is crucial in the analyses of individual plays, for the implicit myths of Spanish society are the ideological codes that undergird each myth and provide an adequate framework for its explication. Another fruitful distinction is suggested by Northrop Frye's *Anatomy of Criticism*, where the myths of the Judeo-Christian tradition are viewed as canonical myths, and those of the pagan, Greco-Roman tradition are viewed as apocryphal myths.[35] From the perspective of our study *La devoción de la Cruz* dramatizes the archetypal myth of all Christianity, and Calderonian *autos* are "glosses" on it. Calderón dramatizes explicit myth and creates explicit myth from the implicit codes that form his world.

Lévi-Strauss opines that mythology is static in that it functions within a closed system in contradistinction to history which operates as an open one (*Myth and Meaning*, p. 40). Such a description would at first glance appear to contradict Waardenburg's view of myth as dynamic, a "moving symbolism" (p. 54). By combining these two insights it becomes evident that myth is dynamic, but ultimately it signifies only within the closed system of mythology in which it participates. In this fashion individual myths dramatized in the Calderonian corpus have indeed dynamic properties that are explained in terms of polysemy. But within the closed system of Christian mythology, they more fully express their mythical contents through reference to the larger connecting whole.

From another perspective Calderón, in light of that dynamic quality attributed to myth, is involved in the process of "liberation from tired myths." This phrase describes three separate activities. First, to make an implicit myth into an explicit one, and then develop a coherent mythology within which to function. The coordinates of this coherent mythology are the transforming properties of love and faith, on the one hand, and the deadly effects of degenerate honor and egotism, on the other. Second, the assimilation of an old myth into a new one that has broader claims and more promising possibilities in regard to the interpretation of reality. This process is seen on the level of individual myths as the remythologizing of the Greco-Roman tradition by which ancient tales are made pertinent to contemporary life. And on the level of Calderonian mythology, those tales fit into an all-embracing *Weltanschauung* that is Christian. Third, to allegorize myth, as demonstrated in the mythic *autos sacramentales*. The clearest examples of this allegorizing tendency in the myth plays are *El mayor encanto, amor* and *El golfo de las*

Sirenas.

One of Calderón's greatest insights into the world of myth is the recognition of myth's antithetical properties. Myth can be an opening to reality that is primarily epiphanic, or it can be a "hindrance to access to reality" (p. 58). Waardenburg describes this latter category as follows: "Myths that detract from reality can be used to blind people and keep them under control. These are the *myths of domination*, which imprison people so that they can see and judge reality only in a particular light. Myth here does not open up reality but narrows it down" (p. 58; emphasis added). In this category I would place the Spanish code of honor as practiced in its most exaggerated and extreme form by the husbands of the honor plays. Calderón demythologizes degenerate honor by revealing its fundamental tenets and dramatizing its horrific consequences. *Fieras afemina Amor* demythologizes the maximum expression of masculine power and heroic valor, Hércules. From the foregoing discussion it is clear that there is an ethic of myth by which a good myth and a good use of it produce a positive influence, whereas a bad myth and a bad use of it produce a negative influence.

Characteristically myth lacks conceptual clarity; the truth it conveys is oftentimes felt rather than logically derived. Waardenburg has described this aspect of myth as a "flash of insight into reality which is reflected upon only later" (p. 59). Therefore a hermeneutics of myth is called for to ascertain the truth claims of a particular myth as well as the extent of its truth. Since criticism damages myth, one must be careful in laying bare the mythic aspects not to wound mortally, through excessive demythologizing, the truth contained in these narratives. Calderón demythologizes the Greco-Roman myths by filtering them through his own Christian mythology. In spite of this "filtering" of myth we yet are entrapped by what Waardenburg has denominated the "naïveté of myth" (p. 61). These quaint tales of a remote past retain their symbolic meanings irrespective of their present use, and it is most likely that insight into those symbolic meanings motivated their further study and quickened their applicability to dramatization. Myth's function as an "Ambush of Reality," in William Alfred's description,[36] is directly related to its apparent naïveté, for through those tales insistent reference is made "to problems which few individuals are able to see and face on their own" (Waardenburg, p. 61).

Myth as a Threat to Orthodoxy

In his monumental study *The Survival of the Pagan Gods*, Jean Seznec provides us with the traditional Christian view on pagan mythology as expressed by St. Augustine: "Omnes dii gentium daemonia."[37] Those ancient tales are not innocent narratives, but the handiwork of the devil, and they sanction all manner of ungodly and licentious behavior. In spite of the traditional theories or perspectives on myth summarized in Cicero's *De natura deorum* as 1) the historical, 2) the physical or cosmological, and 3) the moral and philosophical, in addition to 4) the encyclopedic, as Seznec designates it, which combines the former three, myth was suspect at best and dangerously suggestive at worst for the believer. Given the strength and power of the Church in spreading its message, Seznec's historical survey up to the seventeenth century is all the more amazing in its recounting of myth's survivability in the face of hostility and neglect. One factor that contributed to the persistence of pagan myths was the Christian tendency to allegorize them. Especially in the second half of the sixteenth century, allegory was used by learned churchmen as a moral antidote to mythology (p. 269). Calderón was brought up in this tradition, and the flowering of it in his theater is the *auto sacramental*, religious and theological allegories on all manner of plot material, from the Bible to pagan mythology. Though Calderón allegorized myths, he also sought their own unique messages and dramatized them effectively. At times the allegorizing tendency manifests itself outside of the *auto*, such as in *El golfo de las Sirenas*. But it would be a gross oversimplification to regard Calderonian myth plays as mere allegories, especially as an orthodox allegorical treatment of heterodox material. Frye reminds us that myth has a centripetal structure of meaning, even though it can be made to convey a variety of things. As he expressed it: "The allegorization of myth is hampered by the assumption that the explanation 'is' what the myth 'means'" (p. 341). Myth resists allegorization, and only when taken on its own terms does it fully signify as a manifestation of being and reality and not an artificial, albeit artful, code imposed from without.

It is significant that pagan imagery and licentious tales (e.g. the sexual exploits of Jupiter) continued in vogue in spite of the Council of Trent's warnings. Seznec points out that censure was avoided by the use of allegory, which became a sort of expedient for vindicating humanist learning and practices (p. 271). The Jesuits, under whom Calderón received his intellectual training, harmonized and integrated humanistic learning and Christian instruction through subtle allegorization of the pagan past. In Cesare Ripa's *Iconologia*, according to Seznec, "mythology proclaims philosophical truths and moral concepts" (p. 278). There is something in the nature of myth that lends itself to allegorization. C. Kerényi has observed that "the mythologems were in fact *thought up* for the *purpose* of explanation" (*Essays*, p. 3). In this way both drama and myth fall under interpretive strategies that seek to "explain" what they mean.

At this point it would be helpful to contrast the mythic *auto sacramental* with the myth play proper. In Calderón's *autos*, the explanation subdues and dominates the form; their intellectual clarity results from the ideological code (Christian theology) that provides the key to their correct interpretation. Dramatic action is viewed "through" the religious and theological concepts it is designed to flesh out. In the myth plays the action controls and dominates the form; their dramatic effectiveness results from the nature of the conflict itself (its human dimension) that suggests various possible interpretations (poly-semy). The explanation and interpretation of the dramatic narrative "flow" from that action—the material speaks for itself. Whereas allegory satisfies our desire to know and to interpret well the *auto sacramental*, at least in its historic sense, for the myth plays allegory is nothing more than a veneer sat-isfying orthodoxy's demands. Their deeper meanings invite further, and more profitable, probing.

Conclusion

Eliade stresses myth's function as "exemplary models for human behav-ior;" they "reveal the structure of reality, and the multiple modalities of being in the world" (p. 15). Paul Ricoeur explains how the abolition of first order ref-erence (descriptive, constative, didactic discourse) in narratives frees up a second order reference he terms *Dasein*, being-in-the-world. Thus, in spite of literature's tendency "to destroy the world," nonetheless "there is no dis-course so fictional that it does not connect up with reality" (p. 141). From this Heideggerian vantage point, it is clear that both literature and myth (as a form of narrative) share a common ground. Ricoeur emphasizes that narra-tives encourage imaginative variations of the ego. Reality is metamorphosed by both literature and myth, creating in the individual under their influences a "power-to-be." Though we inevitably experience an eventual distanciation from them, this process of distanciation contributes to wonder and specula-tion on our part.[38] Yes, myth functions as an ambush of reality, and Calderón's myth plays are a dual ambush of reality both as myth and as dramatic litera-ture.

Notes

1 *Tanglewood Tales* (New York: J. H. Sears, n.d.), p.6.
2 *The Adventures of Tom Sawyer* (New York: Harper, 1922), p. 181.
3 In *Myth: A Symposium*, ed. Thomas A. Sebeok (Bloomington: Indiana UP, 1955), p. 153, n 10.
4 See "Myth and Folktales," in *Myth: A Symposium*, p. 173.
5 *Myth, Symbol, and Reality*, ed. Alan M. Olson (Notre Dame and London: U of Notre Dame P, 1980), p. 3.
6 *Literature Against Itself: Literary Ideas in Modern Society* (Chicago: U of Chi-cago P, 1979), p. 183.
7 See Alan M. Olson, p. 3.
8 "Myth, Symbolism, and Truth," in *Myth: A Symposium*, p. 11.
9 See Jean Seznec, *The Survival of the Pagan Gods: The Mythological Tradition*

and Its Place in Renaissance Humanism and Art, tr. Barbara F. Sessions, Bollingen Series XXXVIII (New York: Pantheon Books, 1953), pp. 317-18.

10 *Myth* (London: Methuen, 1976), p. 47.

11 I do not recall from which newspaper I clipped this cartoon.

12 *Greek Mythology* (Beirut, Lebanon: The American UP, 1977), p. 323.

13 See Richard E. Palmer, *Hermeneutics: Interpretation Theory in Schleiermacher, Dilthey, Heidegger, and Gadamer* (Evanston: Northwestern UP, 1969), p. 189.

14 See Palmer's analysis, p. 189.

15 See C. Kerényi, *Prometheus: Archetypal Image of Human Experience*, tr. Ralph Manheim (New York: Pantheon Books, 1963), p. 14.

16 My use of the English or Spanish version of a mythological character's name is not arbitrary. When one appears in Spanish, I am referring to a character in the context of a specific Calderonian play; when in English, as the present case exemplifies, the context is broadly mythological.

17 In *Interrelations of Literature*, ed. Jean-Pierre Barricelli and Joseph Gibaldi (New York: MLA, 1982), pp. 67-89.

18 In *Myth: A Symposiuim*, pp. 84-85.

19 Claude Lévi-Strauss, *Structural Anthropology* (Harmondsworth: Penguin, 1968), pp. 210-24.

20 See "Myth and Ritual," in *Myth: A Symposium*, p. 124.

21 C. G. Jung and C. Kerényi, *Essays on a Science of Mythology: The Myth of the Divine Child and the Mysteries of Eleusis*, tr. R. F. C. Hull, Bollingen Series XXII (Princeton: Princeton UP, 1969), p. 73.

22 Eric J. S. Sharpe, *Fifty Key Words: Comparative Religion* (London: Lutterworth P, 1971), p. 43, quoted from Jacques Waardenburg, "Symbolic Aspects of Myth," in *Myth, Symbol, and Reality*, p. 52.

23 "Religious and Poetical Speaking," in *Myth, Symbol, and Reality*, p. 92.

24 *Myths, Dreams and Mysteries: The Encounter between Contemporary Faiths and Archaic Realities*, tr. Philip Mairet (London: Harvill P, 1960), p. 14.

25 *Myth and Ritual in Christianity* (London, 1953), p. 7, quoted in Philip Wheelwright, "The Semantic Approach to Myth," in *Myth: A Symposium*, p. 154.

26 *Hermeneutics and the Human Sciences: Essays on Language, Action and Interpretation*, ed. and tr. John B. Thompson (New York and Paris: Cambridge UP and Editions de la Maison des Sciences de l'Homme, 1981), p. 161.

27 *Myth and Literature* (London: Routledge and Kegan Paul, 1975), p. 3.

28 See *Essays on a Science of Mythology*, p. 3.

29 *Mythologies*, tr. Annette Lavers (New York: Hill and Wang, 1972), p. 142.

30 *Myth and Meaning* (New York: Schocken Books, 1976), p. 3.

31 *Mito, literatura y realidad* (Madrid: Gredos, 1965), p. 78.

32 *The Identity of Oedipus the King: Five Essays on the Oedipus Tyrannus* (New York: New York UP, 1968), p. 6.

33 In *Myth, Symbol, and Reality*, pp. 41-68.

34 "The Mythic," *Diogenes*, 7 (1954), 33-51; quoted in "Myth, Symbolism, and Truth," p. 20.

35 *Anatomy of Criticism* (Princeton: Princeton UP, 1971).

36 See Herbert Mason, "Myth as an Ambush of Reality," *Myth, Symbol, and Reality*, p. 16.

37 *Enarratio in Psalmos*, Psalm 96 (*PL*, XXXVI, 1231-32), verse 5; quoted in Seznec, p. 17 *n* 17.

38 See Ricoeur, pp. 112 and 142.

II Critical Assumptions

Felix, qui potuit rerum cognoscere causas
Vergil, Georgica, *II, 490*

Method, Explanation, and Truth

It is a sign of our times that the author recognizes the necessity of stating the critical principles or assumptions that underlie his or her study before undertaking the same. For this reason I wish to clarify what are my own critical prejudgments so that this study be evaluated in terms of its original conception and the manner of realizing it. I acknowledge that there are other ways of approaching and handling the mythic material under discussion; likewise, I admit that this material is filtered through my own particular experiences and presuppositions. The actual value of the critical endeavor depends on whether the world revealed through explanation is sufficiently convincing as to satisfy the principles of congruence and plenitude.[1]

Method, as opposed to initial intuition and subsequent reflection on it, smacks of "objectivity" in contradistinction to intuition's "subjectivity." But method does not "explain" anything other than what method has set out to "explain;" it focuses our vision so that the matter under scrutiny may be viewed in minute detail; explanation then follows. What is revealed through explanation is not so much a product or result of the method employed as of the vision or intuition that founded and informs the method. No method or its result can put a closure on discourse; and only in an open polemical situation can the results of various methods vie for ratification by readers.

A very difficult question concerns the nature of "truth" in its relation to method and explanation. Richard E. Palmer has convincingly shown that the literary interpreter, with his method, shapes the meaning of the object by viewing it only in a particular light (pp. 22-23). Method thus limits meaning by interpreting in a particular way the task at hand. Palmer further states that "Truth is not reached methodically but dialectically" (p. 165). Since method tends to prestructure the interpreter's field of vision, the dialectical approach is the antithesis of method and the only corrective to its liabilities. Gadamer has demonstrated that method cannot reveal any new truth, but only that implicit in the method itself.[2] The way to incorporate these insights is to recognize the inevitable movement from a problem of method to one of being. The critical task involves not the denial of method's limitations, but their recognition, so as to undertake a more fruitful course: the disclosure of the structures of being inherent in the linguistic structures of the literary work. The basic operation of the dialectic to be employed concerns the experience of belonging to one or several traditions as well as the alienating distanciation resulting from the oppression those very cultural traditions imply.

The Function and Limitation of Literary Criticism

Wayne C. Booth has written clearly and concisely about the powers and limitations of criticism, observing that works of art present us with manifold perspectives. No single critical method or perspective can ever hope to encompass all that is offered to a reader.[3] Years earlier, R. S. Crane observed that "There is...a strict relativity, in criticism, of statements to questions and questions to 'frameworks.'"[4] It is obvious that at the heart of all criticism lies an insight that has been incorporated into a method. Crane's observation on the role of frameworks allows us to understand better the ultimate relativity of our particular questions put to a literary text. At times the frameworks are adequate, and therefore the questions put to a text will be good, and the statements they in turn will permit us to make will be also good and significant. But critical understanding oftentimes outstrips the narrow confines of critical methodologies. Booth reminds us that "The worst enemy of good reading as of good criticism is the application of abstract rules that violate the life of particular works."[5] The tendency in all critical studies is first to force heterogeneous material into a homogeneous mold that then replicates itself, and second to claim an exclusivity of insight that violates the very nature of literary art.

Jürgen Habermas has demonstrated that language itself contains a hidden agenda masking the structures of domination and social power it embodies.[6] So just as a particular critical idiom is limited in scope and function, language itself may be ideological to the extent that its symbolic framework hides the actual social conditions of its use. Hermeneutical practice which recognizes language's ideological distortions becomes, in Habermas's view, critique of the ideology. The goal of the critique of ideology is universal, undistorted communication (McCarthy, p. 263), in which there will be no boundaries or constraints placed on discussion. Criticism at its best shares this vision of the future, admittedly Utopian, in which communication will serve its emancipatory function. Criticism and critique of ideology coincide in their notion of truth as the ability to pursue one's endeavors "free from unnecessary domination in all its forms" (McCarthy, p. 273), and it is precisely in uncontrolled and unconstrained critical inquiry that their horizons merge. The value of such inquiry lies, ultimately, in its ability to convince others of its correctness; the danger is that instead of heightened vision we may be faced with only chaotic phantasmagoria, each method solipsistically proclaiming its "truth." In the dialectic of critical confrontation with opposite points of view, the limits of method (a particular form of criticism) are defined. Therefore, the challenge of criticism is to test the reference of literary discourse, the truth value of its propositions, its claims, in mimetic art, to reach reality in a significant way. In this manner criticism fulfils one of its primary tasks, which is the recovery of function for literary texts of the past or, as Frye expressed it, "the recreation of function in a new context" (p. 345).

Understanding

Logical understanding is prior to interpretation; it is communication, according to Gadamer, in view of the fact that openness to what a text says allows the latter's being to unveil itself.[7] Understanding is not the grasping of a fact nor the finding of a sense in a work, but, as Ricoeur has stated, the unfolding of "the possibility of being indicated by the text" (p. 56). In other words, "To understand is to follow the dynamic of the work, its movement from what it says to that about which it speaks" (p. 177). And when misunderstanding occurs, it is legitimate to postulate a prior understanding that violates a text's inner coherence and dynamic movement. Such prior understandings are "the pre-eminent meta-critical theme" (p. 77). In the final analysis, we as readers understand ourselves in front of the text (p. 143). This description of understanding is not subjectivistic due to the fact that the reader does not project himself into the text but rather exposes himself to the various possibilities of being unfolded by it. This process involves the imaginative variations of the ego, a process that enlarges the self rather than limits it to its prior understandings.[8]

Literary texts possess an autonomy that Ricoeur summarizes as follows: 1) with respect to the intention of the author; 2) with respect to the cultural situation and sociological condition of the production of the text; and 3) with respect to the original addressee (p. 91). The autonomy of the text is based on its semantic autonomy, for it is no longer possible to view it as dependent on its author, etc., once a text becomes the literary patrimony of a culture. The autonomy of the text as a concept oftentimes is taken as a rationalization of radical subjectivity that once again threatens the entire critical enterprise. But the text's autonomy implies in principle its objectivity. Ricoeur summarizes once more what is meant by the objectivity of the text: "1) the fixation of the meaning; 2) its dissociation from the mental intention of the author; 3) the display of non-ostensive references; and 4) the universal range of its addressees" (p. 210). Because a text is objective, we can approach it and understand it even though it does not come from our own historical moment. A literary text supersedes history. And the meaning of a particular text does not lie hidden behind it but rather discloses itself in front of the text. As Ricoeur has expressed it so well, "Texts speak of possible worlds and of possible ways of orientating oneself in these worlds" (p. 177). Literary texts enlarge our horizons of understanding by exposing us to more "worlds" and experiences than we are capable of on our own. In this regard, though literary works are products of distinct authors, proceed from distinct historical periods, and represent many various locales, in the end they all pertain to my historical present once I commence to read them.

In the passage of time there is a benefit for understanding rather than a liability. Gadamer has shown that "temporal distance" allows the fading of certain prejudgments concerning the nature of the subject, while at the same time bringing forth those that lead to true understanding. Palmer states that the passage of time is "hermeneutically fruitful" (p. 185). In the act of reading, a literary text is decontextualized (decodified) from its origin only to be recontextualized (recodified) in new and different situations. The value of older texts for our own present is realized in this process of recontextualization. Ricoeur expresses this particular quality as follows: "The peculiarity of the literary work, and indeed of the work as such, is nevertheless to transcend its own psycho-sociological conditions of production and thereby to open itself to an unlimited series of readings, themselves situated in socio-cultural contexts which are always different" (p. 91). This transcultural quality of literary texts was brought home to me tellingly by a letter I received from an eminent Hispanist. That letter recounts his first reading of Calderón's *Fieras afemina Amor* "in the middle of a rice paddy in Yunan Province in China."[9] The journey over the Hump for that Calderonian text was long, and the site of its recontextualization, at first glance, appears incongruous or bizarre, but on reflection it should not surprise us. It is the purpose of hermeneutics to overcome cultural distance as well as estrangement from meaning by making those texts from the past vitally relevant to the present. They serve both to solace us in troubled times and to unsettle us in our peaceful moments. Time is bridged, and meaning survives the passage.

A major concern for anyone who reads and writes academic criticism is to distinguish between the literary and nonliterary use of texts. In this latter group the principal tendency is to treat literature as historical texts or to approach it from the perspective of literary history. Paul de Man, in "Shelley Disfigured," comments that, in resisting historicism, reading as disfiguration "turns out to be historically more reliable than the products of historical archeology."[10] The tension between the literary and historical use of texts is long and significant for the demarcation of each field. John M. Ellis, following this train of thought, has observed that "The use of texts in such a way that they are not regarded as limited to and functioning within the original circumstances of their origin is defining for literary texts" (p. 135). As Heidegger, Gadamer, Ricoeur, and others have made clear, literature qua literature is only understood from within the present situation of the reader. Projection of one's subjectivity back into the past psycho-social conditions of production is neither possible for the literary critic nor for the historian. All understanding is, in the final analysis, related to our present situation. McCarthy sums up Gadamer's position as follows: "Once we have given up the view that understanding amounts to a self-transposition into the situation of the author or agent (which enables us 'to see things exactly as he saw them') and have accepted the view that understanding beliefs and practices involves making them intelligible in one's own frame of reference, it follows, according to Gadamer, that the interpreter must 'somehow relate the text to his situation if he wants to understand at all'" (p. 179).[11] This view of literature is significant for our appreciation of the value of literary texts, for, as Ellis has opined, it is only in outgrowing the original, and thereby extremely limited, social situation that literary texts realize their potentialities (pp. 136-37).[12]

An ancillary, though still important, question involves our modern notions of aesthetics. Many critics have been brought up in a tradition that conceptualizes art as sense perception. The noted Greek scholar H. D. F. Kitto pithily expressed this view by stating that "The business of criticism is not to help us to *feel*, but to explain how the artist contrives to *make* us feel" (emphasis added).[13] Gadamer critiqued this position of aesthetic consciousness by demonstrating that great works of art open up worlds rather than provide the outline of forms whose contemplation provides sensuous pleasures. Refining Gadamer's insights, Palmer states: "As soon as we stop viewing a work as an object and see it as a world, when we see a world *through* it, then we realize that art is not sense perception but knowledge" (p. 167). Art transmits not some vague sensation, usually called aesthetic pleasure, but rather the revelation of being. We as readers can understand those worlds created in the past because both those worlds and we participate linguistically in the structures of being.

At this point it would be valuable to review Ricoeur's concept of the "hermeneutical circle." The hermeneutical circle is not a circuit between two subjectivities, those of the reader and author, nor is it, under new guise, the re-presentation of the Romantic notion of projection of the reader's subjectivity into the reading itself. Rather it is a movement from the subjectivistic level to the ontological plane by the process of disclosure-appropriation.

a) By *disclosure* Ricoeur means that "The emergence of the sense and the reference of a text in language is the coming to language of a world and not the recognition of another person" (p. 178). For this process of disclosure to operate one must be "lost" to oneself, the ego distanced sufficiently that understanding may take place. There must first obtain the disappropriation of the ego from its own prejudices before appropriation of the proposed world of the text by that same ego may take place.

b) There are several ways of expressing what *appropriation* signifies. First "the reader understands himself in front of the text, in front of the world of the work" (p. 178). In this way readers do not project themselves upon the text but rather find themselves brought into its world and affected by it; they begin to react to it. But as has been stated, this is not a subjectivistic process due to the fact that the reader must "let the work and its world enlarge the horizon of the understanding" (p. 178) that one has of oneself.

Ricoeur's concept of the "hermeneutical circle" avoids the charge of solipsism imputed to many modern critical methodologies. The hermeneutical circle depends on the dialectic in operation between distanciation and appropriation. Distanciation is the disappropriation of the self and its presuppositions in order to appropriate the proposed world offered by the text. As Ricoeur has stated, "distanciation is the condition of understanding" (p. 144), and appropriation implies a moment of dispossession of the narcissistic *ego* (p. 192).[14]

Interpretation

Though understanding is logically prior to interpretation, the two exist in a symbiotic relationship in which the destiny of the one is fulfilled in realizing the destiny of the other. Ricoeur has written that "Textual exegesis and critique of ideology are the two privileged routes along which understanding is developed into interpretation and thus becomes itself" (p. 111). For this reason ideology impinges on interpretation by narrowing the horizons of the interpreter. Ricoeur has stated the key hypothesis of hermeneutical philosophy as the assertion "that interpretation is an open process which no single vision can conclude" (p. 109). He states further that "to interpret is to explicate the type of being-in-the-world unfolded *in front of* the text" (p. 141). Interpretation, like understanding, involves knowledge and not simply sense perception. Therefore, when a critic such as Richard Levin contends that "The task of interpretation, surely, is to lead us back into the play, to enrich and refine the experience it was designed to produce,"[15] we must examine such a critical assumption in light of our prior critique of "aesthetic consciousness," as Gadamer phrased it. Experience taken as sense perception or sensuous pleasure is but the first step in a process that, though classifiable as a refinement of experience, must lead to critical reflection. And though Levin sees "experience" as knowledge, this knowledge, via interpretation, refers in the last analysis not so much to the play as to the "world" seen through the play.[16]

We have been speaking of "texts," and it is time to clarify what is meant by that term. In other situations we frequently employ the synonym "work." "Work" or "text" is constituted by the closed sequence of discourse (Ricoeur, p. 166). We now generally accept that a text or work decontextualizes itself and recontextualizes itself in the act of reading. What this process of reading involves is the interplay of explanation and interpretation leading to understanding. As Ricoeur has pointed out, reading is the dialectic of explanation of the text's structure and interpretation (p. 152).

1) *Explanation* concerns itself with the *sense of a work*, its internal organiza-

tion, the immanent pattern of its discourse. Structural analysis explicates this aspect of a literary text.

2) *Interpretation* concerns itself with the *reference of a work*, the mode of being unfolded in front of the text. Ricoeur has stated that the reference of a work involves the intentional orientation towards a world and the reflexive orientation towards a self. He has further stated: "the task of interpretation, *qua* interpretation, will be precisely to fulfil the reference" (p. 148). And in this movement of the ego towards the reference of the text, it distanciates itself, "divests itself of itself" (p. 191).

In more philosophical terminology, Ricoeur explains sense and reference as follows: "The sense is the ideal object which the proposition intends, and hence is purely immanent in discourse. The reference is the truth value of the proposition, its claim to reach reality" (p. 140).[17]

Interpretation thus explicates the type of *Dasein*, or being-in-the-world, unfolded in front of the text (p. 141). We as readers must interpret a world in which we could live and move and have our being. In this proposed world I also "could project one of my ownmost possibilities" (p. 142), I could "live" imaginatively in that world and "experience" what the characters experience. Thus this proposed world of the text is a possible world for me, and the existence depicted therein is likewise a possible existence for me.[18]

The world of the text is suggestive in its ability to disclose new possibilities of being-in-the-world. Ricoeur has stated: "For us, the world is the totality of references opened up by texts" (p. 177). The power of the text to open a new dimension of reality potentially creates a recourse against any given reality. At this point the critique of ideology may operate because we have now established the possibility of a critique of the real. Ricoeur emphasizes that in poetic discourse the subversive power contained in a critique of the real is most alive (p. 93). Habermas's critique of ideology is a theory of institutions and of phenomena of domination that focuses on the analysis of reifications and alienations (p. 100). Its goal, as Habermas states, is "the unrestricted communication about the goals of life activity and conduct."[19] For this very reason literature has been suspect in those societies we could label closed, including Spain of the seventeenth century. To control this subversive tendency censorship is instituted to protect the ruling interests' power, position, and privilege. Ricoeur has stated that "poetic discourse distances itself from everyday reality, aiming towards being as power-to-be" (p. 91). We are enlarged by our exposure to a fictionalized world—and we concomitantly experience dissatisfaction with the real world in which we live. We begin to understand the limitations of the real world through exposure to new modes of existence that have not previously formed part of that world.

Just as we saw in the interpretation of myths, literary texts are characterized by their plurivocity or, as Ricoeur expresses it, their openness "to several readings and to several constructions" (p. 212). In this regard the author no longer controls the meaning of a text because he cannot direct or dominate the referential movement of his text. Thus it is possible for the world of the text to "explode" the world of its author (p. 91). In the interpretation of meaning we as a critical community move between two poles that Ricoeur denominates dogmatism and scepticism (p. 213). The validation of interpretations is polemical by nature, and it involves a logic of probability—various interpretations vie with one another attempting to demonstrate superiority by proving that one is more probable than another. But interpretation must go beyond the explicit formulations in the text to the underlying presuppositions that motivate its sense while masking its "interests." Palmer states that "every interpretation must do violence to the explicit formulations in the text," for to do otherwise is a form of idolatry and historical naïveté (p. 148). Calderón's myth plays may induce a certain "reverential" attitude due to their remoteness, or perhaps a historical regard for their original function in the glorification of the Hapsburg dynasty, but as dramatic texts they can only be actualized by the resumption of their referential movement toward new modes of being-in-the-world.

Conclusion

In the following pages I will be guided by the hermeneutical principles outlined above and expounded principally by Paul Ricoeur.[20] Every effort will be made to interpret a complete text first, and second to relate those results to broader issues and concerns inherent in Calderonian dramaturgy. In the interpretation of individual texts I have been guided in my analyses by the frameworks the plays themselves suggest to me. I recognize beforehand that there is always the tendency to "implant" one's own ideas, preoccupations, and presuppositions in the material under study. But at the same time it is incumbent on me to echo Gadamer's axiom that all understanding is related to the interpreter's own situation. Therefore, I am not unduly concerned with the problem of anachronism, for this study will not attempt historical reconstruction nor ape historical "fidelity." I shall analyze and discuss the myth plays on their own terms, concentrating on the issues they raise and confronting the dilemmas they present. In the course of these analyses I would hope to cover the nature and role of myth in the "worlds" of the play, the particular myth dramatized in each play, and the Calderonian use of myth in a very broad and general sense.

I have deliberately avoided the use of the term "mythological plays," preferring "myth plays," because the former term implies a generic commonality which may belie the true nature of individual works. A task of criticism is to establish a working taxonomy which contributes to the understanding of the individual work beyond that supplied by its source or plot material. My particular classification follows broad mythic patterns, thereby assuming a certain thematic consistency. At any rate, such a solution to an otherwise thorny problem is but one *cala* into a significant body of dramatic material that has not been appreciated, much less adequately sampled, to date.

Notes

1 See Paul Ricoeur, *Hermeneutics*, pp. 175-76.

2 See Palmer, p. 165.

3 *Critical Understanding: The Powers and Limits of Pluralism* (Chicago: U of Chicago P, 1979), p. 41.

4 *The Language of Criticism and the Structure of Poetry* (Toronto: U of Toronto P, 1953), p. 26. See also Booth, p. 42.

5 *A Rhetoric of Irony* (Chicago: U of Chicago P, 1974), p. 277.

6 See Thomas McCarthy, *The Critical Theory of Jürgen Habermas* (Cambridge: MIT P, 1978), p. 183.

7 See Jack Mendelson, "The Habermas-Gadamer Debate," *New German Critique*, 18 (Fall 1979), 56.

8 See Ricoeur, p. 94. Philip Vellacott, in *Ironic Drama: A Study of Euripides' Method and Meaning* (Cambridge: Cambridge UP, 1975), p. 16, states that "Understanding is not arrival at established facts, but an increasing perception of coherence."

9 From a personal letter to the author written by Professor Raymond R. MacCurdy, dated 16 April 1983.

10 In *Deconstruction and Criticism* (New York: Seabury P, 1979), p. 69.

11 See also Mendelson, p. 56.

12 Frye expressed this same insight: "Through such an analysis we may come to realize that the two essential facts about a work of art, that it is contemporary with its own time and that it is contemporary with ours, are not opposed but complementary facts" (p. 51).

13 *Greek Tragedy: A Literary Study*, 3rd ed. (New York: Barnes & Noble, 1961), p. 249.

14 McCarthy provides a succinct summary of Gadamer's and Habermas's positions which Ricoeur's concept of the hermeneutical circle seeks to reconcile: "Whereas Gadamer speaks of tradition primarily as a source of insights and values that have to be constantly reactualized in ever new situations, Habermas stresses the elements of domination, repression, and distortion, which are also incorporated in our heritage and from which we must continually strive to emancipate ourselves. Whereas Gadamer speaks of 'the dialogue that we are,' Habermas speaks of the dialogue that is not yet but ought to be. Whereas Gadamer is moved by respect for the superiority (*Überlegenheit*) of tradition, Habermas is motivated by the anticipation of a future state of freedom. As others [principally Ricoeur] have pointed out, there is no need to remain at this kind of impasse. Hermeneutic understanding can be pursued critically, with an interest in enlightenment and emancipation. And critique would remain empty without concrete input from our cultural heritage" (p. 192).

15 *New Readings vs. Old Plays: Recent Trends in the Reinterpretation of English Renaissance Drama* (Chicago: U of Chicago P, 1979), p. 55.

16 In another place Levin writes that "the primary meaning of the play is presented to us" (p. 200). Using Ricoeur's terminology, I would call this the "sense" of the work.

17 Eric D. Hirsch, Jr., in *The Aims of Interpretation* (Chicago: U of Chicago P,

1976), states that "meaning" (the verbal meaning of a text) "is the determinate representation of a text for an interpreter" (p. 79), whereas "significance is meaning-as-related-to-something-else" (p. 80).

18 Frye, though employing a different vocabulary, views this question similarly: "Literary meaning may best be described, perhaps, as hypothetical, and a hypothetical or assumed relation to the external world is part of what is usually meant by the word 'imaginative'" (p. 74).

19 Jürgen Habermas, *Toward a Rational Society: Student Protest, Science, and Politics*, tr. Jeremy J. Shapiro (Boston: Beacon P, 1970), p. 120.

20 Hermeneutics is defined by Ricoeur as "the theory of the operations of understanding in their relation to the interpretation of texts" (p. 43).

III The Mythic Aspects of Christianity

> We know that by turning everything to their good God co-operates
> with all those who love him, with all those that he has called according
> to his purpose. They are the ones he chose specially long ago and
> intended to become true images of his Son, so that his Son might be the
> eldest of many brothers. He called those he intended for this; those he
> called he justified, and with those he justified he shared his glory.
>
> Romans 8:28-30[1]

> pues los cielos
> me han señalado con ella [Cruz],
> para públicos efectos
> de alguna causa secreta.
>
> Eusebio, ll. 335-38[2]

> porque no alcanza
> los misterios al efecto
> quien no previene la causa.
>
> Curcio, ll. 678-80

The Christian Message of "La devoción de la Cruz"

La devoción de la Cruz, as a dramatic work, creates a world that is comprehensible primarily in terms of the Christian message, the Good News of salvation. The mythic pattern underlying the play is the *mysterium paschale*
(Paschal Mystery), which reenacts for the individual Christian his or her participation in the rite of dying and rising again with Christ. One's introduction
into Christ's death is but the prelude to a new life that manifests itself in the
Christian community and reaches fulfillment in eternity. The New Testament
asserts that the redemption of humankind has already taken place and that
salvation is at hand. Buried deep in these two concepts are distinct but complementary notions. Redemption stresses that inevitably good will prevail
over evil, whereas salvation emphasizes the result of that prevalence, the
experience of peace, harmony, and love, disclosing the fact that indeed goodness has overcome evil. The movement in *Devoción* is from redemption as
fact, symbolized in the Cross, to salvation as event, symbolized visually at the
play's conclusion as follows: "Vase Julia a lo alto, asida de la Cruz que está en
el sepulcro de Eusebio" (p. 117). Good has triumphed over evil—but not completely.

Eusebio de la Cruz's (l. 243) story is one of several in the plot that emphasizes alienation. All of Curcio's children experience at one time or another some form of estrangement. Eusebio does not know who his parents are, and feelings of rejection characterize his alienation from society. Due to his exaggerated sense of honor, the patrimony of Curcio and masculine society in general, Lisardo is in conflict with and is estranged from his own brother, Eusebio. Julia is victimized by an oppressive father who does violence to her freedom by choosing her vocation in life – she, in turn, is estranged from both family and society. Lastly Curcio, a victim of his own preoccupation with honor, is alienated from family and society in a more complete and thorough manner. In *Devoción* alienation serves to strip away from the individual all ties to family (the basic unit of society) and to community. In a very real sense Eusebio's alienation includes psychological isolation. Though he lives apart from the community, he seeks reintegration through marriage to Julia. The play depicts not how he is integrated into human society, but how he is brought into God's salvific love and the communion of saints.

Eusebio's salvation is not viewed as an individualistically oriented act, for in it Curcio, Lisardo, Julia, and the whole community are caught up in the social dimension of salvation. Bernard Häring has demonstrated that holiness and sin are "essentially social phenomena."[3] Our Western tradition lays much stress on the individual and individual rights and development, so much so that we may lose sight of the broader context of community as it functions in *Devoción*. Through Eusebio we witness a transformation from an awareness of sin to the demonstration of grace's efficaciousness. St. Paul writes that the Christian is like a dead man brought back to life to fight on the side of God. As a new man he lives not under the law, but under grace: "and then sin will no longer dominate your life, since you are living by grace and not by law" (Romans 6:14). This Christian freedom liberates Eusebio, inspires Julia, but dumbfounds Curcio, who remains mired in honor's tenets. The law, as St. Augustine reminds us, contributes only to the awareness of sin – *posse peccare* – whereas grace liberates humankind – *posse non peccare* – to true freedom.[4] Eusebio's story eventually becomes, for the entire community, an epiphany on a grand scale of God's ability to bring to salvation whom He wills. The *admiratio* experienced at the play's conclusion reinforces faith in God and His word and contributes to the building of a stronger and more dedicated community.

Mythic Plays and "La devoción de la Cruz"

Though drama usually examines the *individual condition* in depth, the mythic plays look beyond the individual condition to the *social condition* of all mankind and womankind. It is not that the individual is ignored or allegorized, but that the individual is viewed in function of participating in something with significance beyond its individualized and particularized meaning—our common humanity. Paul Tillich has commented on the relationship of meanings to being human: "Man's being includes his relation to meanings. He is human only by understanding and shaping reality, both his world and himself, according to meanings and values."[5] According to Waardenburg, myth embodies an insight into truth and reality and reveals an underlying order; *Devoción* does so also, but from a Christian perspective. From a mythic vantage point *Devoción* depends on an organizing and explanatory principle of experience that can only be explained satisfactorily by reference to Christian beliefs. To comprehend the worlds created in the myth plays and to share the horizons they espy, it is necessary to analyze their deep structures that are fundamentally Christian. Approaching *Devoción* from the perspective of myth will contribute to our analyses of the myth plays by making explicit the common structures shared by them both. The meanings and values that constitute their commonality ultimately shape a shared vision of what it is to be human and communicate a sense of the significance of that experience. Ontogyny recapitulates philogyny: the history of Eusebio reenacts for the Christian what should be the history of all humankind.

There are two distinct classes of myth in the Calderonian corpus: 1) *explicit myth*—a) traditional Greco-Roman myths, such as the myth of Andromeda and Perseus, and b) Christian myths, such as redemption and divine providence, which underlie the *autos sacramentales*; 2) *implicit myth*—the possible stories based on the particular organizing and explanatory principles of historical experience as lived in the seventeenth century, such as the code of honor, the role and function of the monarchy, and common notions of love and passion. The two classes of explicit and implicit myth may be further refined into a) *apocryphal myth*, based on the Western mythological tradition, and b) *canonical myth*, based on the Judeo-Christian tradition. In *Devoción* the explicit apocryphal tradition intersects with an implicit Christian myth located in the figure of Eusebio, a new Icarus, a new Phaethon[6] who, as a new Adam, rejects his tragic past on realizing with grace's promptings the salvific potentiality of the Paschal Mystery. The mythological allusions to Phaethon and Icarus are stock illustrations of mortals who aspire too high. They typify youthful foolhardiness.[7] Both figures are doubly significant in that Icarus was implicated in the deeds of his father, Daedalus, whereas Phaethon did not know his father. Both sons suffer in some way due to their paternity. Although *Devoción* relies particularly on the myth of the redemption of humankind, it is structured primarily on the archetypical myth of the Judeo-Christian tradition: the revelation of God as a personal and loving presence who manifests Himself in time and history. The subtle contrast of this divine presence with that of Curcio constitutes the dramatic tension of *Devoción*.

Though my choice of *La devoción de la Cruz* and *El médico de su honra* may appear to be an arbitrary scheme for establishing the basic coordinates of

Calderonian theater, the arbitrariness relates to the choice of particular plays and not to the deep structures contained in each. *Devoción* embodies the myth of divine providence as the significant factor in Eusebio's life, and the full flowering of the insight occurs in the *autos sacramentales*. The *autos* are individual episodes from salvation history that make concrete and visual the religious evolution of the Judeo-Christian tradition. *Médico* dramatizes the secular myth of honor as an antivital factor in the lives of its characters, and the mature manifestation of antivital insights takes place in the myth plays. The myth plays are also individual episodes from secular "history" that make clear the universal scope of destructive tendencies inherent in both the world and its inhabitants. Religion and myth are not opposed. As religion contributes to the realization of what it means to be human, myth contributes to our understanding of what conspires to destroy our humanity.

Frye has stated that plays with religious themes and content, and especially the *autos sacramentales*, are in one way myth plays. They emphasize "dramatically the symbol of spiritual and corporeal communion" (p. 282). *Devoción*, in this sense, is a myth play. But its emphasis is dualistic in terms of the contrast, mentioned before, between the play's protagonist (God) and antagonist (Curcio). On the one hand there is the inheritance of the flesh, the wages of sin, and on the other the free gift of divine grace, an unmerited expression of divine mercy and love. Eusebio is Curcio's son—but in the following quotation from St. Augustine, it is obvious that he is also God's son. The sin and guilt of one's parents may be visited upon the children unless and until grace and mercy intervene:

and it is said, with much appearance of probability that infants are involved in the guilt of the sins not only of the first pair, but of their own immediate parents. For the divine judgment, "I shall visit the iniquities of the fathers upon the children," certainly applies to them before they come under the new covenant by regeneration...and further, because there are other sins of the immediate parents, which, though they have not the same effect in producing a change of nature, yet subject the children to guilt unless the divine grace and mercy interpose to rescue them.[8]

This quotation describes well the case of Eusebio, caught in honor's outrages, but also destined to liberation as a son of God.

Providence and the Question of Protagonist

La devoción de la Cruz, like *El gran galeoto*, is a work in which the protagonist does not appear. It presents a slice of chronology that highlights a divine commitment to humankind for all time: God orders all things to their end.[9] This telic presence operates in the lives of all the characters, and only on considering the play as a dramatic whole do we begin to perceive its fundamental importance. The notion of Divine Providence, or divine intervention in the lives of *all* characters, organizes the various episodes so that the overall dramatic pattern becomes clear. Nevertheless, the maxim that grace follows nature is not forgotten. Providence is the central force bringing to salvation all the members of the Curcio family, but its patriarch opposes it at every turn. In the conflict of these two forces the play's structure rests. Whereas providence is the central myth of *Devoción*, in the honor plays its absence is conspicuous and helps define the honor tragedies as a world in which there is no provident presence, or in which provident concern is ineffectual. Therefore, fate is the underlying myth and force in Calderonian tragedy,[10] while providence imbues Calderonian comedy and plays like *Devoción* with their unique and optimistic outcomes. In *Devoción* in particular providence discloses an untiring, relentless God of love, a person who is overflowing with compassion and mercy. Curcio represents at best the concern and efficaciousness of the *natural order*, and at worst force and violence. Human means cannot save Eusebio from the vengeful *villanos* who seek his death, and in all other cases Curcio is ineffectual—in Lisardo's and Julia's cases, for instance. But *the order of grace*, manifested through constant encouragement and gentle promptings, triumphs. As Eusebio gains insight into his sin, he realizes the full extent of his personal depravity and the misery of being cut off from God.[11] We as witnesses to God's great mercy experience how this unmerited mercy, in St. Augustine's words, "shine[s] forth the more brightly in contrast with the unworthiness of its objects" (p. 674).

Devoción is structured by a series of contrasts between actions "determined" by the rigorous application of the code of honor and others influenced by Divine Providence. It could be said that there are two "dramas" at loggerheads: the first, the honor play, actualizes the secular myth of honor, and its general tone is tragic, perhaps more accurately fatalistic;[12] the second, the religious play, actualizes the myth of redemption of humankind as individual salvation, and its general tone reflects the loving presence and powerful influence of God in time and human history. Phrases like the one that speaks about a God who "loves us and has washed away our sins with his blood" (Rev. 1:5), remain abstract for those who have not witnessed nor felt the effects of God's provident concern for them. Therefore, *Devoción* sets out to depict visually, dramatically, and affectively the miraculous mercy of God. Eusebio's "resurrection" from the dead symbolizes the miraculous nature of God's love for all, for Eusebio is brought first and foremost from the death of sin to the life of divine grace. If the lesson of Scripture is to trust and have faith in God's word, then Eusebio's life conveys most dramatically that no matter what the sin, no matter what the offense, Christ's suffering, death, and resurrection were directed at him and intended to initiate him into the efficaciousness of Christ's victory over death.[13] Eusebio will follow Christ, although he may not be fully conscious of that fact. He will also suffer, die, and rise. The play suggests forcefully, therefore, that Eusebio is a recipient of a divine gift that he in no way earned through his own efforts, and that that divine gift is available to everyone. Reading the final scene in this manner integrates it more fully into the meaning of the play as Julia, Eusebio's twin, also experiences God's provident intervention.

Generic Considerations

Devoción, as pointed out previously, manifests both comic and tragic tones. The latter proceeds from the *drama de honor* being played out in the Curcio family, and the former from the *comedia de santos* it is destined to become. These intersecting structures contribute to the generic problematization that characterizes the play. Its movement is from human tragedy to transcendence of that situation by a series of miraculous interventions. The first act depicts a life-death tension that is played out principally on a human plane. The second act moves that tension to a human-divine plane, and the third act reveals the transcendence of the human-divine tension by the definitive intervention of divine mercy. Throughout the play, but especially in the second act, human beings interpret poorly the events in which they participate. Curcio cannot understand, and thus is incapable of interpreting, the significance of the events that took place previously in the mountains at the foot of the Cross. Unfortunately the Rosmira episode (an honor tragedy in miniature) has taught Curcio little and fails to mitigate his present honor-driven desires for vengeance. The pattern of action unfolding in the present is partly repetitive of past events: Rosmira, Julia, Eusebio were all victimized in that prior episode. Julia will be victimized once more, as well as Eusebio. Julia also interprets the events that took place in the convent as a demonstration of God's denial of forgiveness and sets out to avenge God's refusal of mercy as well as Eusebio's rejection of her. But Eusebio, moved by the powerful, yet to him still hidden, meaning of the Cross, has begun to respond to its deeper significance—divine compassion and love. Thus in Act III the basic motives of vengeance and clemency take on a clearer focus.

The tension between Curcio and Divine Providence demonstrates affectively two very distinct domains. First, Curcio attempts to dominate his world through linguistic manipulation. He imposes his will on all, and the chief vehicle of this imposition is verbal and physical force. His case discloses the tendencies of the human mind to create arbitrary patterns and to impose capricious linguistic schemes on one's world. Second, the presence of the Cross symbolizes a profound commitment of God to the world. The workings of providence are subtle, carrying out through love a foreordained plan for humankind. Divine Providence counterbalances human excess, revealing thereby the eternal truth that "God is with us." The first act demonstrates the distance created between Curcio and his children—he cannot *be* with them; he must *dominate* them. And the vehicle of this domination is *human lan-*

guage with its inherent axiological patterns that establish the relative value of each family member: father, son, wife, daughter. The harsh effects of this domination are readily seen in Julia's almost total lack of freedom. On the other hand, there are glimpses of another mode of being as Eusebio relates his strange and miraculous encounters with the Cross. Although the Cross is a visual symbol of divine love for humankind, its meaning is only intellectually manifest to Eusebio, who is incapable of understanding its various interventions on his behalf. Its *presence* is attested to by concrete past actions that are elaborated in great detail. The characteristic of this presence is its loving concern for the individual. Eusebio, Julia, and Lisardo emerge from Curcio's oppressive world to become caught up in the larger and more benevolent designs of providence.

Curcio refuses to read and act upon the signs that make up his world. But his children do. He continues to impose his private readings of events and the world upon himself and others. There are so many "texts" that he misreads: Rosmira's pregnancy, the miraculous births of Julia and Eusebio, Eusebio's death, Julia's deliverance. Curcio's case demonstrates the futility of arbitrary interpretation, for behind the imposed pattern of Curcio's world there stands the divine pattern of love, mercy, justice, and truth. When one fails to interpret the world and events in accord with the larger pattern of divine design, tragedy results. In this way we may profitably view Eusebio and Julia as Curcio's children, setting out to impose meaning on their chaotic worlds, Eusebio through banditry and Julia through rebellion and murder. Curcio's manner of discourse (ll. 2408-11) imaginatively anticipates the worst; his children do likewise. But this repetitious pattern of character and action is definitively broken and tragedy is averted. Curcio exalts language (ll. 665-68) over presence (ll. 1258-65 and 1351-54); but in the end it is the Cross's presence that prevails, exalting its referentiality to the concrete, yet mysterious, workings of God's love in the present time.[14]

Traditionally the determining attitude of tragedy reveals a desire to amplify the perspective on what we call fate, or perhaps necessity (*diké*). We witness the progressive restriction of human freedom that ordinarily leads to catastrophe. On the other hand, the determining attitude of comedy manifests, traditionally, a desire to open a wide perspective on fortuitous chance or on the possibility of happily exercising human freedom in a world habitually hostile and dehumanizing. In comedy, time is the ally of the protagonist, or at least a redemptive force that assures a solution to all problems, while in tragedy time frequently confirms his destruction.[15] In overall tone, the action of *Devoción* is tragic, as that of *Oedipus in Colonus*, but at the same time it does not fail to contain within itself the *loa* to a divine comedy, the Christian life seen from the perspective of eternity. As the play concludes we witness the *partial* integration of the Curcios into divine "society." Frye has written that tragedy fragments the family and places it in opposition to the rest of society;

this indeed occurs. Comedy integrates the family into society (p. 218); but in *Devoción* family ultimately refers to an eternal context. In their triumph over many worldly perils, the comic spirit palpitates. Only Lisardo Curcio père remains aloof from that divine society, prolonging the tragic tone of the play.[16] Comedy exalts freedom, and Eusebio, Julia, and Lisarado have at last exercised theirs well; tragedy narrows freedom, and Curcio, automaton-like, rages against a world he does not understand and in which his responses are totally predictable. Thus the play exposes a failure of providence at the same time as it celebrates victories in the children's cases. The structure manifests throughout the three acts generic problematization, developing thereby the possibilities offered by the confrontation of these two basic attitudes with their respective tones.

Max Scheler has observed that "In every genuine tragedy we see more than just the tragic event." What is discovered, in the last analysis, is "the very makeup of the world."[17] This insight is valuable, for *Devoción* is more than just the "death of love."[18] The tragic hero reaches universality, according to Robert M. Torrence, by transcending his individuality.[19] Eusebio does so, whereas Curcio is incapable of it. For Eusebio and Julia and Lisardo, tragedy is a prelude to comedy,[20] but as said earlier, a divine comedy, for *Devoción* is a religious drama that stresses the communal dimension of salvation. The problem of evil and retribution are subsumed under the more all-encompassing rubric of divine understanding expressed as follows by Augustine: "For He judged it better to bring good out of evil, than not to permit any evil to exist" (p. 673). This is the transcendental view espoused by the play. After our surfeit of "the old solidarity of corruption," in Häring's words (p. 233), characterized by the "self-glorifying, egocentric way of thinking and manner of existence," or *sarx*, we come upon a new world. The human tragedy depicted in *Devoción* is but a prelude to what we should appropriately call the divine comedy that has been occurring all along. Frye says that "The action of comedy moves toward a deliverance from something which, if absurd, is by no means invariably harmless" (p. 178). Only at the conclusion do we fully realize that deliverance was always at hand.

Bruce Wardropper has argued for a view of Calderonian comedy as a prelude to tragedy.[21] In the three cases of the honor dramas, the so-called *comedias de capa y espada* did not end happily with the marriage of those who loved each other. Here "comedy" was frustrated. It was short-circuited. In our notions of comedy and tragedy we normally find two radically different and mutually contradictory attitudes toward life. What in some comedy, the world of fantasy, is permissible becomes in tragedy, the world of reality, the inevitable and fatal result of those very same attitudes. Only in those works that are truncated comedies do we find the tragic potential. In truncated tragedies we likewise find comic potential. Where passion does not become love, death stalks its victims. If the chaos of passion is not channeled by the socializing and humanizing properties of marriage, then tragedy may result. If overriding love "manipulates" human foolishness, then comedy may result. At the root of so many Golden-Age comedies is the desperate plea for love. Marriage must not be barter, but the free exchange of vows to "love" forever. Comedy is not always a prelude to tragedy – it depends on the nature of the final resolution. Where love triumphs, love will endure; where love is defeated, tragedy may, and will, ensue. *Felix quem faciunt aliena pericula cautem.*

The Transforming Qualities of Faith and Love

St. Paul defines faith as follows: "Only faith can guarantee the blessings that we hope for, or prove the existence of the realities that at present remain unseen" (Heb. 11:1). Tillich, in a modern idiom, writes that "Faith is the state of being grasped by the power of being-itself" (p. 172). Continuing along this line of thought, we may say that faith is at the root of courage to be truly oneself; it is the experiential power of affirmation of one's own being by being itself. For St. Paul, it is also an ontic reality that alters radically human nature. It is the source of the mystic's exclusive dedication, the martyr's singleness of purpose, and the saint's personal conviction. Tillich stresses the courage that flows from the state of being grasped by being-itself:

Courage participates in the self-affirmation of being-itself, it participates in the power of being which prevails against nonbeing. He who receives this power in an act of mystical or personal or absolute faith is aware of the source of his courage to be (p. 181).

Eusebio typifies the courage to be just as Enrico of *El condenado por desconfiado* does positively and Paulo, negatively. At the core of Paulo's despair is the lack, or rejection, of faith. But to represent adequately the nature of faith it is necessary to relate it to love, the energizing theological virtue. Augustine, following Paul, writes: "Now what shall I say of love? Without it, faith profits nothing; and in its absence, hope cannot exist. . . .Wherefore there is no love without hope, no hope without love, and neither love nor hope without faith" (p. 661). The theological virtues transform an individual into a more perfect creature, and in Eusebio's transformation faith, hope, and love are joined to form an inseparable whole.

Perhaps the most difficult aspect of *Devoción* is the apparently gratuitous nature of Eusebio's salvation. But such is the Christian message. Gadamer went so far as to say that faith as a gift of grace appears incomprehensible, and that salvation depending solely on the act of faith is really scandalous.[22] Eusebio and Julia sink into outrageous manifestations of evil, so extreme as to become unsympathetic characters. The depth of their sin makes bold the efficaciousness of grace. One of Augustine's greatest intellectual problems was that of evil, and his solution was to define it as the absence of good (p.

662). What still remains a problem is how good comes into being. According to classical Christian doctrine, God creates it and is solely responsible for it. Its absence is due to human willfulness, for the human will is the source of moral evil. If death is the wages of sin, then Christ's destiny was to triumph over sin and death. In describing the mythic Christian pattern of participation in Christ's death, St. Paul provides the key to Eusebio's transformation: "All I want is to know Christ and the power of his resurrection and to share his sufferings by reproducing the pattern of his death" (Phil. 3:10). The strength of will and completeness of Eusebio's conversion come from his participation in Christ's death and resurrection. A loving God rescues him.

Thomas Merton explains what he calls the pattern and prototype of all sin as:

the deliberate and formal will to reject disinterested love for us for the purely arbitrary reason that we simply do not want it. We will to separate ourselves from that love. We reject it entirely and absolutely, and will not acknowledge it, simply because it does not please us to be loved. Perhaps the inner motive is that the fact of being loved disinterestedly reminds us that we all need love from others, and depend upon the charity of others to carry on our own lives. And we refuse love, and reject society, in so far as it seems, in our own perverse imagination, to imply some obscure kind of humiliation.[23]

All the Curcios are prideful individuals who find it difficult to accept love, with the exception of Julia early in the play. Curcio's tragedy is his continuing rejection of it; his children's triumph is their acceptance of it. At the core of the play's action there is a slavery that exhibits three mutually joined characteristics: 1) the lack of knowledge; 2) selfishness; 3) the lack of identity and purpose. In the Biblical notion of freedom we are freed from something (sin) to do something (love). Heinz Kohut has remarked that the indeterminacy of self does not signal freedom, but fragmentation.[24] While choice limits freedom in one sense, in another it tends to enhance it by focusing freedom and giving it direction. Real choice on the part of the Curcio children comes about with external promptings from God, supplying identity and purpose, knowledge, and finally other-centeredness. Merton writes that the life of the soul is not knowledge but love (p. 191). Once the will is turned toward its proper end, love, then the Curcio children find their true selves. Only the courage of their faith combats the heritage of death and sin.[25] And in the salvation of one of them, that of the others is implicated.[26]

For a non-Christian, the plot of *Devoción* may appear to rest on a superstitious belief in the talismanic power of the Cross. It seems to function as a safe conduct allowing a person all manner of reprehensible conduct while alive, only to be saved at death by its miraculous virtues. But such occurrences dot the history of Christianity. In 1251 Mary appeared to St. Simon Stock promising that those who wore the brown Carmelite scapular would be saved from hell and taken to heaven on the first Saturday after death. Such a belief and practice appear as superstitious as Eusebio's personal devotion to the Cross. At face value it is superstition, but it represents a spirituality not common today: the Carmelite scapular served as a reminder to live a full Christian life. Therefore, the belief and practice appear truly superstitious only if their symbolic value is not understood. The Cross as symbol has many meanings, but it primarily represents the Christian faith and belief in redemption. Underlying this more obvious meaning is the forgiving presence of God, graphically represented at the crucifixion by Jesus, hanging on the Cross and expressing his concern for others: "Father, forgive them; they do not know what they are doing" (Luke 23:34). In the first act, just as in the third, Eusebio was saved from physical death (ll. 297-303) due to his devotion. In the second act, incest[27] was averted by the presence of the Cross on Julia's breast; but more importantly it elicits Eusebio's inner confession of faith:

> Señal prodigiosa ha sido,
> y no permitan los cielos
> que, aunque tanto los ofenda,
> pierda a la Cruz el respeto.
> Pues si la hago testigo
> de las culpas que cometo,
> ¿con qué vergüenza después
> llamarla en mi ayuda puedo?
>
> (ll. 1613-20)

Thus in the third act, as Eusebio goes off to confess his many sins ("más que del mar las arenas / y los átomos del sol" [ll. 2497-98]), he indeed may express: "¡Tanto con el cielo puede / de la Cruz la devoción!" (ll. 2499-2500). Afterwards Alberto repeats almost verbatim the same words: "que tanto con Dios alcanza / de la Cruz la devoción" (ll. 2545-46). Christian faith, as typified in Eusebio, provides the courage of self-affirmation in spite of sin and death, the principal manifestations of non-being for the believer. As Tillich points out, this "courage is the knowledge of what to avoid and what to dare" (p. 81). And the Cross, as ultimate sign of Christ's victory over death (or separation from God), encourages Eusebio to confront death itself, for as Tillich has shown clearly "death can be accepted only through a state of confidence in which death has ceased to be the 'wages of sin'" (p. 170).

In the first act Eusebio recounts how he was found as an infant by a shepherd who was perhaps searching for a lost sheep (ll. 231-32), conjuring up the image of the Good Shepherd. But the overriding biblical image that adequately "explains" *Devoción* is that of the forgiving father welcoming home his prodigal son. The intertextuality of the play with the Bible is obvious, and it also depends on many maxims of classical Christian theology. For the rationalist, *Devoción* is a "difficult" play, especially when considered as part of the

Calderonian corpus, where emphasis on rationality has been perceived as a major characteristic. But this play is an example of faith seeking understanding, the hallmark of Augustinian thought on the relation between faith and reason.[28] Seen through the eyes of faith, there is nothing strange about the play. And perhaps understanding, in the fullest sense of the term, is possible only when the play is viewed in the larger context of salvation through faith, or the *sola fide* doctrine of Paul.

Augustine has insisted many times in his anti-Pelagian writings that man cannot by the effort and initiative of his free will reach salvation. One's righteousness is the work of God, the result of grace. God's mercy, in his words, "goes before the unwilling to make him willing; it follows the willing to make his will effectual" (p. 677). Grace is, therefore, an absolutely free gift that preceeds good works and without it these latter acts are impossible.[29] Eusebio is not totally evil; at times he indeed does a charitable deed, such as carrying Lisarado to be confessed, or rejects temptation, such as fleeing from Julia in the convent scene. He responds to grace. So the question of his good acts, as well as that of his salvation, relates to the mysterious workings of grace, described by Augustine as follows: "'He hath mercy' of His great goodness, 'He hardeneth' without any injustice; so that neither can he that is pardoned glory in any merit of his own, nor he that is condemned complain of anything but his own demerit. For it is grace alone that separates the redeemed from the lost, all having been involved in one common perdition through their common origin" (p. 716). It is plain that the Curcio children are brought to salvation by the will of God as it functions throughout the play. The gift of eternal life "is simply grace given for grace" (p. 721). This realization, especially in the case of Eusebio, shocks our human sense of justice. But here also our notions are inadequate in attempting to capture the nature of God and His *justice*. Justice, for Augustine, "is that love which serves only God and thus brings into the order of salvation all else that is entrusted to man."[30] To question Eusebio's salvation is really to marvel at God's love and to admire His unbounded mercy.

The Symbolism of the Cross

Devoción opens with a comic exchange between Menga and Gil over an unruly *burra* that has been trapped in mud. Mud symbolically represents the entrapment of humankind in sin, to be released only by the intervention of Divine Providence. Eusebio de la Cruz (l. 243) is the beneficiary of a secret cause that operates "behind the scene," so to speak. Early in the play he attempts to explain the mysterious relationship between himself and the Cross as follows:

> pues los cielos
> me han señalado con ella [Cruz],

> para públicos efectos
> de alguna causa secreta.
>
> (ll. 335-38)

The secret cause is the love of God whose divine assistance (grace) carries forth the redemptive wishes of the Godhead (the salvation of the Curcio children). God's antagonist is Curcio, whose honor-driven and fear-motivated world would lead to death if it were not for God's solicitude for His own. In his soliloquy on honor Curcio underscores the need to comprehend the motive for action:

> porque no alcanza
> los misterios al efecto
> quien no previene la causa.
>
> (ll. 678-80)

Two causes, two distinct effects. Even in his attempt to seduce Julia, Eusebio attributes his motivation to a "causa más oculta" (l. 1550) that seeks to link him with his twin. At the same time as he is moved toward her, he is prevented from consummating the union, or raping her: "mas no fué la causa mía, / causa más secreta fué" (ll. 1811-12). Eusebio exhibits an ambiguous attitude toward Julia, experienced even as he is about to seduce her:

> Su peregrina beldad,
> de mi torpe amor objeto,
> hace en mí mayor efeto;
> que a un tiempo a mi amor incito,
> con la hermosura apetito,
> con la honestidad respeto.
>
> (ll. 1471-76)[31]

Their destinies are linked through a secret mystery whose symbol is the Cross they both bear on their breasts (ll. 1813-20). At the conclusion, the acotación demonstrates that they are joined in the profound mystery of salvation both as a saving event and communal act: "Vase Julia a lo alto, asida de la Cruz que está en el sepulcro de Eusebio" (p. 117). The Cross that divided them in the convent scene here symbolically joins them in their common destinies.

For the ancient world, the cross represented a life of dishonor, and death upon one was dishonorable. William Faulkner, in his story "The Bear," writes: "apparently they can learn nothing save through suffering, remember nothing save when underlined in blood."[32] In this light the spiritual sings out: "I know it was the blood that saved me," proclaiming the shocking truth of Christianity. The Cross is a rich semiological sign whose dramatic meanings may be summarized as follows. First of all, the Cross symbolizes the suffering, death, and resurrection of Jesus Christ, a pattern of life that will become Eusebio's own as well as that of all Christians. Second, the Cross is also the sign of Christ's victory over death, ("en que [Cross] animoso y fuerte, / muriendo, triunfó Cristo de la muerte" [ll. 1009-101], as found in later editions of the play). When it is remembered that death as a punishment for sin symbolizes estrangement from God, then the Cross surely points toward sonship and daughtership and life with God.[33] Eusebio himself grasps the symbolic meaning of the Cross in the face of that physical death awaiting him at the hands of the *villanos* who pursue him:

> pero mis pasos impida
> la Cruz, porque desta suerte
> ellos me den breve muerte,
> y ella me de eterna vida.

> (ll. 2277-80)

Third, the Cross as symbol of deliverance will also rescue Julia, bringing the twins to eternal life. It is a sign of the Christian's destiny. The Cross protected Rosmira, and because of it Lisardo was able to confess before dying. Alberto, the priest, is the visible witness, a symbol of Christ's priesthood ever present to assist anyone in need. Eusebio directed himself to the Cross as follows:

> pecador soy, tus favores
> pido por *justicia* yo;
> pues Dios en ti padeció
> sólo por los pecadores.

> (ll. 2291-94; emphasis added)

We should not forget here Augustine's definition of justice as "that love which serves only God and thus brings into the order of salvation all else that is entrusted to man." Häring has written that "The Church is a visible sign of the enduring love of Christ in the World" (p. 148), and in this light Alberto responds, symbolizing the Church's role in the remission of sins (see Augustine, p. 696). In the last analysis, the Cross represents a miraculous love for humankind that surpasses our comprehension; equally important, *Devoción* conveys imaginatively some sense of its "fanatical" devotion to *all* humankind. All the miracles attributed to the Cross throughout the three acts are but reminders that the greatest miracle of all is God's love for the individual — it cannot be explained, only accepted.

The Irony of the Denouement

In several Calderonian plays, as the dramatic action comes to what would normally be the close, meaning opens out to multifarious possibilities. *Devoción* and *Médico* in particular bring up the question of the value of women.

Why does Gutierre marry Leonor, and what does this marriage portend for their life together? Why is Julia rescued in such a miraculous manner, and what does this action signify in terms of the entire play? Julia is delivered from the honor-driven rages of Curcio, in contradistinction to Leonor's being *handed over* to Gutierre, a proven psychopath. Julia freely chooses to return to her convent to begin life anew as a bride of Christ (ll. 2575-78). Her freedom now is truly *God-given*, for we recall her outburst in Act I on being told that Curcio had chosen the religious life for her: "la libertad que me dió / el cielo, es la que te niego" (ll. 613-14). Karl Jaspers captures the spirit of the former passage, albeit from a humanistic perspective:

Man is always something more than what he knows of himself. He is not what he is simply once for all, but is a process; he is not merely an extant life, but is, within that life, endowed with possibilities through the freedom he possesses to make of himself what he will by the activities on which he decides.[34]

What Calderón has added to, or Jaspers subtracted from, the description above is the person of faith's recognition that freedom is choosing what God already foreordained. What Julia denied in her heart to Curcio she joyfully surrenders to her loving Father. Therefore *Devoción* presents us with a proposed, or hypothetical, world in which we could participate imaginatively, one in which two mutually exclusive possibilities of being-in-the-world are dramatized. At the conclusion of the play we realize that Curcio represents a this-world-only attitude in which "man" recognizes only an intrinsic purpose to life—to be a man of honor according to worldly criteria and earn worldly fame. In the cases of Julia and Eusebio we encounter another possibility, the attitude that recognizes the mutability of all worldly things and that seeks, for this very reason, a more permanent state in an extrinsic purpose to life through conformity with divine will.

Throughout Act I Julia manifested a feminine attitude, for example, granting pardon to and demonstrating mercy toward Eusebio after the killing of Lisardo. The play's action, especially her father's lack of respect for her as a person, allows her more unruly passions to come to the fore and dominate her life. But God's love and mercy are constant, never changing, and only through divine constancy will the hatred and vengeance of Curcio's masculine world be superseded by a more "feminine" and forgiving presence.

"La devoción de la Cruz" and the *auto sacramental*

In one sense we may classify *Devoción* as a type of *auto sacramental* destined for the *corrales*. In the first place its content and themes are principally religious. In the second it is a Christian mythic play that dramatically emphasizes the symbol of the spiritual and corporeal communion of all humankind (Frye, p. 282). Since *Devoción* breaks the characteristically mythic model of

behavior, for a more adequate comprehension of the play it becomes necessary to distinguish between mythic comportment in general and Christian
comportment in particular. Mircea Eliade defines the four characteristics of
mythic comportment as: 1) the exemplary pattern; 2) its repetition; 3) the
breaking with profane time; and finally 4) the integration into primordial time
(p. 37). With the Incarnation of Jesus Christ and the Redemption of humankind, mythic time has been definitively replaced by a divine present because
God became man in Time. Now all history is a *theophany* (p. 153). Consequently our outlook is focused on a "divinized" present and not on a past that
contains a wholeness in which the concrete historical person may not participate. Eliade adds that "One is devoured by Time, by History, not because one
lives in them, but because one thinks them *real* and, in consequence, one forgets or undervalues eternity" (p. 242). Christianity looks inevitably towards
eternity, towards permanence, just as myth focuses on the past in the attempt
to discover primordial time, to find, in a realm without time, the essentially
permanent condition of humankind. For the Christian, eternity and permanence are not found on annulling time and history, but paradoxically on realizing their sacred nature. Only by living time and history as the means of God's
plan for salvation may the individual be eternally integrated into the reign of
God.

As a dramatic work *Devoción* is convincing, moving, and highly effective.
But as Christian drama it is incomplete because it lacks the full vision and
implication of the Eucharistic connection so necessary in the *auto*. Häring has
written that the sacraments are "acting signs of unity, speaking signs of the
brotherhood in the family of God" (p. 17). This view is implicit in the confession scene with Alberto, but the full and explicit vision of the Church as the
sacrament of love (p. 14) is missing. The Eucharist, according to Häring (p.
16), "should form us ever more intimately into a community of love," for the
sacraments, in their external form, are social saving events in the life of the
community (p. 161). The Eucharist is the ongoing celebration of humankind's
redemption, and through the Eucharist one is brought steadily and more
deeply into the community of love, the essence and model of which is the
Trinity. In short, through the Redemption one returns to God's grace and
favor, and the Eucharist is the sign of redemption and of God's love in the
here and now—through it one grows in love. The New Covenant is one of
love—the love of God—in community, the witness to God's love (p. 16).[35]

Conclusion

Generally speaking literary criticism of *Devoción* begins with an interpretation of its title, translated into English as *The Devotion to the Cross* and into
French as *La dévotion à la Croix*. According to these translations, which are
based on the traditional criticism of the drama, *Devoción* depends fundamen-

tally on a religious fanaticism that sees in the Cross a talisman against eternal condemnation. Eusebio, as the protagonist in the dramatic action, following this critical presupposition, manifests the benefits that result from such a devotion. The work embraces, however, two perspectives on the plot that, on correlating them thematically, form the structural unity of the play. The first examines all the dramatic action from the human point of view, or, in other words, from the relationship, symbolized in the Cross, of all characters with God. The second perspective alters radically the first approach, enriching our appreciation of the dramatic action by allowing us to see that the devotion of (not "to") the Cross symbolizes the profound divine love for humankind. We need not choose between the two perspectives. It is sufficient to understand that the confluence of the two resultant interpretations constitute the structuralizing idea of the drama.

Devoción is replete with miracles that constantly call our attention to the existence of two planes of reality. Ordinarily we accept these planes as distinct and often separate. Nevertheless, the presence of so many miracles attests to the interaction between the human and the supernatural planes artificially divided by sin. Perhaps the Cross symbolizes as no other object the mediation between God and humankind, the latter having been separated from the Creator by the sin of Adam and Eve. Thus the Cross symbolizes not only divine love for man and woman but also represents their eternal destiny, the fruit of that love.[36]

At the beginning of the drama Eusebio did not know who he was, but at the denouement he discovers three important facts about himself: 1) his real father is God; 2) his identity is based on the fact of being God's son; 3) his true destiny is heaven, the only permanent inheritance of value. The drama also focuses on Julia, as the pattern of supernatural concern for man and woman becomes clearer. After having been subjugated to the constant rigor of her father, Julia likewise learns that she has another father, God, that she is His daughter and bride, that her identity is founded on that relationship, and that her destiny is also heaven. On returning to her convent as if by flying, Julia is liberated from the oppressive weight of the code of honor and from the rigors of a tyrannical father who never was able to appreciate her true value. At the conclusion she experiences, just as her twin brother, the clement reality of "God with us."

For these reasons Eusebio and Julia are twins, not merely in their carnal relationship, but in view of their supernatural lineage and inheritance: the two are recipients of the miraculous and unconditional love of God who predestined them to heaven. The great and profound Christian myth that *Devoción* places before us does not depend so much on the miracles that we read on some pages or that we see on the boards, but on the miraculous nature of divine love that informs the world and suffuses it with meaning and permanence. This is the world disclosed by *Devoción*.[37]

Notes

1 All biblical references, unless otherwise indicated, are from *The Jerusalem Bible* (Garden City, N.Y.: Doubleday, 1966).

2 Calderón de la Barca, *Comedias religiosas: La devoción de la Cruz y El mágico prodigioso*, ed. Angel Valbuena, 3 ed. (Madrid: Espasa-Calpe, 1963). All references to *Devoción* are from this edition.

3 *This Time of Salvation*, tr. Arlene Swidler (New York: Herder and Herder, 1966), p. 229.

4 See the introduction to *Basic Writings of Saint Augustine*, ed. Whitney J. Oates (New York: Random House, 1948), I, xxvii.

5 *The Courage To Be* (New Haven: Yale UP, 1968), p. 50.

6 "Icaro seré sin alas, / sin fuego seré Faetón" (ll. 1411-12).

7 See Richmond Y. Hathorn, p. 316.

8 *The Enchiridion on Faith, Hope and Love*, in *Basic Writings of Saint Augustine*, p. 685.

9 See *A Catholic Dictionary*, ed. Donald Attwater, 3rd ed. (New York: Macmillian, 1958), s.v. "Providence, Divine. St. Thomas teaches (I, xxii, 1) that the ordering of things to an end is in God called Providence. . . . The presence of evil in the world is no conclusive argument against divine providence. Circumstances which are adverse to individuals are often for the common good; or they may be the punishment of sin or the testing of the just. Moreover, the world is not a place of rest, but one of trial, a place in which we have to win eternity." Tillich provides another formulation of providence that, though compatible with the one above, is more modern. "The courage of confidence takes the anxiety of fate as well as the anxiety of guilt into itself. It says 'in spite of' to both of them. This is the genuine meaning of the doctrine of providence. Providence is not a theory about some activities of God; it is the religious symbol of the courage of confidence with respect to fate and death" (p. 168).

10 Francisco Ruiz Ramón, in *Calderón y la tragedia*, examines "el Hado" as a characteristic of a type of tragedy he labels "the conflict of freedom/destiny." While in the other model of Calderonian tragedy, that of honor, he does not deal with fate, he imbues time with properties related to fate (p. 178).

11 See Häring, p. 224.

12 For example, throughout the play key phrases are repeated, such as "la estrella. . . enemiga" (ll. 252-53), "estrella cruel" (l. 456), and "la rigorosa estrella" (l. 1055). This "fatalistic" tone is found also in *Médico*.

13 *The Jersualem Bible* contains the following note to Rom. 5:12: "Sin divides man from God. This separation is 'death', death spiritual and eternal; physical death is the symbol of it. . . ."

14 John Steinbeck, *The Winter of Our Discontent* (New York: Viking P, 1961), pp. 69-70, writes: "A man who tells secrets or stories must think of who is hearing or reading, for a story has as many versions as it has readers. Everyone takes what he wants or can from it and thus changes it to his measure. Some pick out parts and reject the rest, some strain the story through their mesh of prejudice, some paint it with their own delight. A story must have some points of contact with the reader to make him feel at home in it. Only then can he accept wonders." Curcio's tragedy is that he cannot accept wonders; his hell is having no meaningful contact at the end of the play with the stories of his very own children.

15 See the generic studies of Northrop Frye, *Anatomy of Criticism*, and Ruiz Ramón's observations in *Calderón y la tragedia*.

16 Other examples of this structural characteristic of Calderonian works, of side-

stepping a conclusive and final solution at the denouement of a serious play, are found in *Médico* and *Vida*.

17 "On the Tragic," in *Tragedy: Vision and Form*, ed. Robert W. Corrigan (Scranton, PA: Chandler, 1965), pp. 7-8. Jaspers, in the same volume, says that "*There is no tragedy without transcendence*," in "Basic Characteristics of the Tragic," p. 43.

18 Curcio says "Muerte de amor son los celos" (l. 1309) on describing the Rosmira episode.

19 *The Comic Hero* (Cambridge: Harvard UP, 1978), p. 22.

20 See Frye, p. 215.

21 See Elder Olson, *Teoría de la comedia*; B.W. Wardropper, *La comedia española del Siglo de Oro* (Barcelona: Ariel, 1978).

22 See "Religious and Poetical Speaking," in *Myth, Symbol and Reality*, pp. 96-97.

23 *The Seven Storey Mountain* (New York: Harcourt, Brace, 1948), pp. 23-24.

24 *The Restoration of the Self* (New York: International Universities P, 1977).

25 See Tillich, p. 42.

26 Merton says of himself: "I was entering into a moral universe in which I would be related to every other rational being, and in which whole masses of us, as thick as swarming bees, would drag one another along towards some common end of good or evil, peace or war" (p. 12).

27 For Antonio Domínguez Ortiz, *La sociedad española en el siglo XVII*, vol. II, *El estamento eclesiástico* (Madrid, 1970), p. 176, the sexual taboo was at the center of moral problems in seventeenth-century Spain.

28 See Gilson's remarks on "Nisi credideritis, non intelligetis," in Oates's introduction, p. xxv.

29 See Oates's comments on the Augustinian doctrine of grace, p. xxx.

30 *De moribus Ecclesiae catholicae*, lib. I, cap. XV; *PL* 32, p. 1322. Quoted in Häring, p. 84.

31 Such descriptions of love are common in Calderonian theater, representing the true battle between love as respect and love as lasciviousness.

32 *Go Down, Moses* (New York: The Modern Library, 1955), p. 286.

33 See St. Augustine p. 729, where he explains that for those who have received the grace of regeneration, death no longer retains dominion over them.

34 *Man in the Modern Age*, tr. Eden and Cedar Paul (New York: Anchor Books, 1957), p. 159.

35 Another explanation of the matter at hand is that the world of honor as depicted in the play is totally incompatible with love as represented by the Eucharist. Therefore, its presence did not fit into the emotional and intellectual world of the play. Since forgiveness is the dominant theme of the work, the sacrament of penance is the appropriate symbol of divine mercy and love.

36 "pues los cielos / me han señalado con ella, / para públicos efectos / de alguna causa secreta" (ll. 335-38).

37 See Palmer, p. 133.

IV The Mythic Aspects of the Code of Honor

> An honourable murderer, if you will;
> For naught I did in hate, but all in honour.
> *Othello*, V.ii, 294-95

> The meaning of words had no longer
> the same relation to things, but
> was changed by them as they thought proper.
> Thucydides III, 82

> una infelice mujer
> perseguida de su estrella
> Coquín, regarding Mencía, III, 712-13[1]

El médico de su honra

La devoción de la Cruz moves from a human plane, in which the tragic tone dominates the action, to a supernatural one, in which tragedy itself is transcended by the beneficent effects of divine providence. Since tragic action is normally seen as conclusive, *Devoción's* dramatic form becomes a hybrid product characteristic of religious drama and the *auto sacramental*. Where tragedy is the raw material of triumph, we find ourselves in a "christianized" world. Viktor Frankl captured the human essence of this process when, speaking on his eightieth birthday, he remarked: "Even when confronted with a hopeless situation, you still have a chance to make life meaningful . . . in turning personal tragedy into a triumph or by transforming your predicament to an accomplishment."[2] The world of *Médico* does not depict this possibility, and in fact the Christian world view has in effect been bracketed by the author. Though there is rhetorical allusion to God, the scope of divine action is significantly reduced. What we encounter is the secularized world of Gutierre Alfonso Solís, described by Leonor as a man "sin fe, sin Dios y sin ley" (I, 1009).

Nowhere is the difference between the worlds created by *Devoción* and *Médico* seen more clearly than in regard to the role of death in both plays. *Devoción* contains the full Christian vision of death as freedom, for St. Paul writes that "We know that in Christ we will gain more than we will lose through death. So, life after death means freedom in life before death" (I Cor. 15:55). *Devoción* displays the growing freedom of Eusebio and Julia, whereas *Médico* depicts the narrowing of Gutierre's and Mencía's freedom. *Devoción's* world flowers outwardly to encompass almost all the main characters; *Médico's* restrictive environment and centripetal movement narrow choice to the point where it appears to be necessity. Calderón's great artistry is evident in his unflinching portrayal of the code of honor in its most extreme and degenerate state. Gutierre, though a good man, becomes, through his exclusive dedication to honor's tenets and demands, an automaton bereft of human compassion. *Médico's* world is one of masculine concern, and women are appendages to it; when they become obstacles clouding honor's brilliance, they are eliminated by whatever means available.

Though Calderón has been portrayed as a champion and apologist of imperial Spain and militant Catholicism, this jaundiced view may blind us to the "liberating" qualities of his theater. In *Médico* we discover what Ricoeur, in "Hermeneutics and the Critique of Ideology," has called "an act of defiance, a critical gesture, relentlessly repeated and indefinitely turned against 'false consciousness,' against the distortions of human communication which conceal the permanent exercise of domination and violence" (p. 63). *Médico* foregrounds masculine domination of women and underscores, both in Leonor's and Mencía's cases, how readily violence is done to them. Through this abuse of authority the honor code and its tenets shift from being the mainspring of the play's action to becoming its theme.

"Médico" and Its Embryonic "Comedy"

Following in broad outline the ideas of Bruce W. Wardropper, Robert ter Horst has elaborated on the manner in which tragedy grows out of comedy in Calderonian theater.[3] He states that "Calderón's great technical achievement in the three [honor] tragedies is to warp comedy into a vessel for tragedy" (p. 198). "The embryonic comedy," he observes, "miscarries" (ibid). What was the nature of the *comedia* that miscarried, producing *Médico's* action?

It is obvious that *Médico's* pre-history is not comic in the usual sense of that term. The events that lead to Enrique's arrival at Mencía's *quinta* have not contributed to love's triumph; if they have been comic in any sense at all, they bear witness to a truncated comedy that has sown bitter seeds that will produce tragic fruit. If comedy has miscarried, it has done so in two separate instances. First of all, Mencía and Enrique were deeply, though impossibly, in love. Their case, viewed through the action of Vélez de Guevara's *Reinar después de morir*, demonstrates just how impossible it was, for misalliance amongst royalty is not a personal affair, but a matter of state. Secondly, only after the revelation to the public of Mencía's continuing love for Enrique does Gutierre's affair with Leonor come to light. If an epigramatic description of comedy is *omnia vincit amor*, then it is not applicable to *Médico's* pre-history. When Leonor appears on stage we realize how little was settled at the end of the two distinct pre-play "comedies." Loose ends abound that, when finally tied, will result in a tragic knot. Though both couples were deeply in love, that was not sufficient to overcome the many obstacles in their paths to happiness. Enrique's violent intrusion into Mencía and Gutierre's home sets in motion new forces emanating from past conflicts. After his departure we discover that all is not harmonious – for Gutierre, there is his past, and yet unresolved, relationship to Leonor; for Mencía, there is her unresolved passion and ambivalent feelings toward Enrique. In Act II Mencía provides a beautiful, even prophetic, image of love:

> Dicen que dos instrumentos
> conformemente templados,
> por los ecos dilatados
> comunican los acentos:
> tocan el uno, y los vientos
> hiere el otro, sin que allí
> nadie le toque; y en mí
> esta experiencia se viera;
> pues si el golpe allá te hiriera,
> muriera yo desde aquí.
>
> (II, 195-204)

Unfortunately, this harmonious image does not represent the play's reality.

The two principal forces that, according to ter Horst, characterize comedy are the lovers' "socially acceptable desire to marry and time as an agent of overcoming the obstacles to marriage" (p. 186). Wardropper had shown earlier that the profanation of the sacrament of marriage provided the tragic potential of the *drama de honor*.[4] While these observations assist us in comprehending Calderonian comedy and tragedy, there is another important aspect to consider. Whereas *Devoción* manifests providential success, in *Médico* providence proves to be ineffectual. In non-Christian terms, it would be easy to attribute the underlying force in the play to malign fate, but I believe this to be a fundamental misconstruction, especially if we take fate in the traditional pagan sense of the term. Throughout the three acts there are constant references to *Jesús, cielo(s), Dios*; but such rhetorical reminders of the Christian *Weltanschauung* serve only to highlight the loss of its beneficent presence.

What the contrast of the worlds created in *Devoción* and *Médico* discloses is two distinct views of divine providence. In Christian terms we cannot accept the Greek notion of fate that the *Dictionary of Theology* defines as follows: "A Greek concept according to which everything, and especially the course of each man's life, would have been previously determined by an impersonal law superior to that of the personal gods."[5] Fate, in its Christian sense, has been defined in *A Catholic Dictionary* as follows: "Fate (Lat. *fatum*, a prediction). In its Christian sense the ordering of secondary causes by God so that they produce their effects in accordance with the divine providence." If we may use fate in this latter Christian sense, then *Devoción* depicts the action of fate, Christian fate or divine providence, whereas *Médico* is a play that reveals its absence. Calderonian tragedy is, therefore, the Christian world without its informing principal, divine providence; it is a narrative of loss, a lament for the mysterious disappearance of providence's individual and particular concern for man and woman. Thus fate in *Médico* is the negative image of providence encountered in *Devoción*. What has in fact negated providence's role in the former play is the unusual adherence to the demands of a degenerate code of honor.[6]

There are traces of an injustice in the play that cry out for satisfaction. Leonor's soliloquy at the end of Act I reminds us that there was no comedic solution to the Gutierre-Leonor affair, and her "venganza me dé / el cielo!" (ll. 1011-12) sets the tone for the remaining two acts. Her cries for blood ("y a ver / llegues, bañado en tu sangre, / deshonras tuyas" [ll. 1013-15]) are echoes of a pagan past. If we truly accept that providence plays a role in the affairs of humankind, then, in this instance at least, providence appears to operate in accord with Leonor's wishes.

In Act II there is further evidence that the confluence of injustice to Leonor and Gutierre's ruling temper contributes to the tragedy we are witnessing. In speaking to Leonor, Arias observes:

> En mi vida he conocido
> galán necio, escrupuloso
> y con extremo celoso,
> que en llegando a ser marido
> no le castiguen los cielos.
>
> (II, 793-97)

If this be an accurate description of the action of providence, that it demands the death of an innocent woman, then the "truth" of *Médico* would be a horrible one indeed. Such would be the vision of the play were it not for two further scenes that remind us that it is Gutierre's blind adherence to what he believes to be honor's dictates that checks providence's role in the play. As Mencía revives from her faint, having been discovered by Gutierre in the act of writing to Enrique, she cries out in fear: "¡Señor, detén la espada, / no me juzgues culpada: / el cielo sabe que inocente muero!" (III, 432-34). Since this plea takes place after Gutierre's departure, Ludovico, in his account to King Pedro, emphasizes that Gutierre witnessed Mencía's incessant claims of innocence: "'Inocente muero; / el cielo no te demande / mi muerte'" (III, 640-42).

There is one instance in the play when providence proves to be effectual, for at that time Gutierre heeded its promptings. As he leads a blindfolded Ludovico through the streets of Seville, intent on killing him and sealing thereby the secret murder of Mencía, he comes upon King Pedro and Diego. Gutierre interprets correctly the meaning of this encounter: "*[Ap.]* ¡Que así me ataje / el cielo, que con la muerte / deste hombre eche otra llave / al secreto!" (III, 601-4).

Médico's narrative reveals how Gutierre thwarts the action of providence, for he has interiorized what we may call a *fateful direction* to his life. Thus fate is the underlying myth of *El médico de su honra*, but not in the pagan sense of an impersonal law superior to the gods that determines the lives of the characters. Through his adherence to the exaggerated demands of the honor code, Gutierre has internalized a code of action that effectively determines his choices in all situations in which honor is involved. Fate is a force in the play, but one motivated by fear and determined by exterior factors. Gutierre has surrendered his freedom by accepting the code of honor as his *raison d'être*. Providence is largely absent from *Médico's* action because it is absent from Gutierre's life.

At the outset of the play Gutierre is an admirable personage whose positive qualities far outweigh his negative traits. The tragic dimension of the play highlights how he loses control of his life as events overwhelm him, as if he were caught in a maelstrom. His family life, his true honor, his love of Mencía, his respect for the king, his humanity—all are sacrificed for a sense of honor that is not inner directed but outer regarding, preoccupied as it is with the famous *¿qué dirán?* What causes us to wonder is the almost total absence of providential concern for Gutierre and those with whom he comes into contact. Left to their own devices, their choices are inevitably the wrong ones, their goals are assuredly shortsighted, and their fates are ineluctably tragic. The play has the courage to face the awesome reality of human existence enslaved in its own narrow perspective and the integrity necessary to follow it through to its inevitable and tragic conclusion.

Tragedy and Sin

Tragedy always exhibits the *ethical* dimension of a life, for it usually demands a superior individual's fall from a state of happiness to one of misery. Christian tragedy may emphasize the moral aspects of that fall, and such is the position of this honor play. But whereas so often the tragic hero suffers due to his efforts, in the honor tragedies the principal sufferer, and victim, is the hero's spouse. At the core of this tragic vision is the Christian notion that sin, though personal, is also social since it inevitably has social ramifications. As grace has its social impact in *Devoción*, so too sin has its social impact in *Médico*.

In spite of the jaundiced view held of her, Spain lived a split-personality existence, especially in the area of honor. Martín de Azpilcueta, in *Manual de confesores y penitentes*, highlights the conflictive tension that existed between Christian morality and secular law: "We add however (because we are told that we should) one clear thing, namely: that the husband who kills or wishes to kill his wife having found her in adultery, sins mortally, although by law he receive no punishment therefor."[7] What Calderón has accomplished in *Médico* is a narrative of the abuse of freedom, personal sin, in its most harrowing social implications.

Gutierre's personal tragedy is having forgotten that honor, according to Aristotle, is grounded in virtue.[8] As honor becomes an end in itself, Gutierre fails to appreciate its truly superficial nature, depending, as it does, "On those who confer it more than on him upon whom it is conferred." Aristotle further pointed out that the primary motive in the pursuit of honor appears to be to assure oneself of one's own merit through its acknowledgement by others; the motivating factor evidently is a lack of self-confidence. Gutierre's pursuit of honor above all else is a travesty of the dynamics of honor, "for honour is the due reward of virtue and beneficence" (VIII, xiv. 2). For him honor results from what may not be to him a crime, but is definitely a sin.

The *katharsis* we readers or viewers experience depends fundamentally on the force of emotion felt and the learning subsequently derived from it. James M. Redfield writes that "*pathē* and learning constitute the characteristic value to us of a well-made narrative. I suspect that Aristotle meant by *katharsis* exactly this combination of emotion and learning."[9] It has been debated by critics whether Gutierre experiences *desengaño* in its full sense. Obviously he suffers greatly, but I doubt he ever learns the lesson of Mencía's death. He could very well repeat Othello's famous phrase: "An honourable murderer, if you will; / For naught I did in hate, but all in honour." The character who truly experiences the *katharsis* of the play's action is King Pedro, who, as our surrogate, fully understands what has occurred. Roland Barthes wrote that "Tragedy is but a means of recovering human misery, of subsuming it, hence of justifying it in the form of a necessity, a wisdom, or a purification. . . nothing is more insidious than tragedy. . . ."[10] Such a description is not applicable to *Médico*, because Gutierre lacks insight into his participation in the tragic action. His final tragedy is the lack of sensitivity to the enormity of his sin. For us *Médico* neither recovers, nor subsumes, nor justifies Gutierre's brutality; the play foregrounds it. Further, there is no necessity, no wisdom, no purification, only the loss of human life and dignity.

The Literary Function of "El médico de su honra"

I take it as axiomatic that the function of a literary work is to make problematic the lived experience of a culture (Ricoeur, *Time and Narrative*, p. 243 *n* 45). In the particular case of *Médico*, there is a wide field that falls under its sweep: the nature of honor, its conflictive relationship to love, masculine-feminine relationships, the role of men and women in society, the sense of duty and mutual obligation. But whether we pertain to that particular cultural tradition or not, it is the nature of literature to transcend its own limited psycho-social conditions, spanning both time and culture, as it speaks to us in the here and now. There is no way that we can enter the experiential framework of seventeenth-century Spain, at least as direct participants. Nevertheless, we are able to recapture *Médico's* experience from the perspective of our own time and history. What makes great literature is its ability to speak to us now, to address our concerns today, and to provide insights into our own world.

We tend to view the structures of literary works as fixed, perhaps due to the all-pervasive influence of structuralism. When we assume the viewpoint of the author, we realize that mimetic activity is an operation that involves selecting and ordering events of the plot. Ricoeur has shown that "emplotment," or *muthos*, concerns the re-configuration of "our confused, unformed, and at the limit mute temporal experience" (*Time and Narrative*, p. xi). Narratives explain who we are, what we are doing, why we are doing it in that way, and the consequences thereof. Time has a way of blurring our perceptions and our sense of participation in the events that form our world. Both the historian and the writer, through narrative, order events in such a way that the pattern of experience thus created becomes meaningful.[11] As a result of encountering a narrative sequence, we are potentially capable of seeing our own world differently, evaluating our own experiences in other ways, and finally acting otherwise than if we had not confronted that specific series of events organized in that particular manner. Since narratives articulate experience, they do so in such a way as to allow us to perceive the significance of our own unarticulated temporal experience. All human experience is temporal, and it is well for us to ponder Ricoeur's insight into the relationship of time and narrative: "time becomes human time to the extent that it is organized after the manner of a narrative; narrative, in turn, is meaningful to the extent that it portrays the features of temporal experience" (*Time and Narrative*, p. 3). In sum, *muthos* links our temporal experience in the here and now with that of other places and other times, bridging what otherwise would have been temporal and cultural alienation.[12]

Inherent in the character of temporal experience is a blindness to its ideological nature. Through ideological codes we develop our consciousness.[13] Ideology is two-fold in its relation to those who live in a particular culture: on the one hand, we experience a sense of belonging to what is our own world; on the other hand, that limited world leads to dissimulation and distortion by allowing us to believe that what is uniquely our own is what is or ought to be for all. In this regard the ideological nature of culture narrows our field of perception, and consequently our interpretative capacity is further restricted by our familiarity with limited cultural models that may become for us paradigms for all experience. The limited nature of one's cultural experience also tends to contribute to ideological closure, a state combated by the masterworks of literature.

El médico de su honra reveals to what extent power distorts communication. It is highly significant that the play has an unusual number of asides occurring in each act, reaching almost thirty in Act II. By limiting the range of discourse, *Médico* emphasizes the imprisoned state of consciousness within the obligations of the code of honor. Act II, if we remember Lope's advice in the *Arte nuevo de hacer comedias*, complicates the events of the plot set out in Act I. At the end of Act II there is an opportunity for real communication between Gutierre and Mencía, but it is foreclosed as he seals himself up within his own fears and insecurities. As Gutierre's silence makes clear, the institution of power, such as that found in the code of honor, is rooted in distorted or incomplete communication. After Gutierre's allusion to the wind that could snuff out Mencía's flame at the same time as it gives light to his, she responds: "Parece que, celoso, / hablas en dos sentidos" (II, 995-96). Gutierre begins his response in an aside, but on repeating the word "celos" he erupts into his famous tirade on jealousy, with its violent and bloody imagery. At this point there is still an opportunity for communication, but honor's obligation shall seal all suspicion in the cold tomb of silence and death.[14] *Médico* depicts how effectively the honor code controls discourse and reinforces institutionalized power through the distortion of communication. All the characters are imprisoned within a consciousness defined by honor. Notwithstanding this implicit violence to the individual, such repression is not complete—the evidence of the resultant psychological distortion is found in asides, soliloquies, and other expressions of honest experience. *Médico* makes a bold statement about the eventual cost such distorted communication may exact—the life of an innocent woman.[15]

From Ideology to Theme: Honor's Movement in "El médico de su honra"

James Hillman has observed that

Fictions are not supposed to have great explanatory power, so they do not settle things for a mind searching for fixity. But they do provide a resting place for a mind searching for ambiguity and depth. In other words, fictions satisfy the aesthetic, religious, and speculative imagination more than they do the intellect.[16]

It is clear from the above that *Médico* explains little while intimating a great deal. It is the object of criticism to bring to discourse the suggestive possibilities the text offers. One point in particular requires close scrutiny: *Médico* dramatizes a breakdown of the ideology of honor; opinions about honor become suspect, thought begins to regain vigor, thus reducing the social efficacy of the code of honor. The system of belief inherent in the code of honor is presented as reverting to a system of thought. In consequence, the idealized image of the "man of honor," established through the praxis of honor's extreme demands, becomes tarnished. The existence, therefore, of the class "honorable men," as represented in its idealized image, becomes problematic, necessarily implying the problematization of the interpretative code of honor itself. Through the dramatization of Gutierre's case, the interpretative code of honor, which under normal circumstances is operative, becomes thematic. In other words, Gutierre thinks too much about honor and its obligations. Honor, rather than operating from behind his back, so to speak, appears as a theme before his eyes. Ricoeur has written that the mutation of a system of thought into a system of belief, such as the honor code, is the very essence of the ideological phenomenon (*Hermeneutics*, p. 226). A corollary of the movement from thought to belief is that through an idealized image a group represents its own existence and reinforces its interpretative code. The revolutionary stance of *Médico* reverses this entire process, forcing upon us the onus of honor.

As the ideology of honor becomes thematic, the interpretative code, which has also set its basic premises before our eyes, is scrutinized for its elementary concepts and assumptions. We too are forced to confront the value of life, the place of love and home in one's life, the weight of opinion on our decisions. We experience, as Gutierre does, a distanciation from the code of honor, a process which Ricoeur has posited as the condition of understanding (p. 144). In a play such as *Médico*, the critique of ideology is a necessary detour which forms part of the process of understanding. The text provides us with an extreme imaginative variation of the ego, in which the honor code's unequivocal premise, that honor is more valuable than life, is brought to its logical conclusion. The reader or spectator is obliged to confront his own illusions in this regard, and from that confrontation understanding develops.

El médico de su honra is a Utopian document that explodes its own reality. Ideologies look backward, accommodating themselves to an already-given reality. *Médico's* Utopian stance looks forward to a new reality, a new possibility of being. As ideologies dissimulate their social realities and thereby justify them, so Utopias directly attack and explode them (Ricoeur, p. 240). The play does not present us with a definitive solution to the problem raised; it explores its nature, bares the motivational mainspring of its action, and suggests that the images of man and woman may be out of focus. As honor cuts short communication between men and women, it hints *soto voce* that if honor prevents frankness between those who through marriage are one, ("si en vos / quedo yo, y vos vais en mí" [I, 551-52], according to Gutierre), then exaggerated honor is divisive of the very basic unit of society. What binds us together is free and open communication in which domination and violence have no place. The subversive power of *Médico's* discourse enables us to refigure reality founded on the insights it has allowed us to glimpse.

The Code of Honor and the Structuring of Personality

C. S. Lewis has observed that "there is, hidden or flaunted, a sword between the sexes till an entire marriage reconciles them."[17] What our play clarifies, at least as far as honor is concerned, is to what extent the code of honor exacerbates this conflictive relationship and inhibits the healing process. There is no reconciliation in *Médico*, and even the tentative steps taken at the denouement are fraught with danger and threats. Contemporary theology of marriage stresses that, for the married couple, grace, God's gift of friendship, is an empowering gift to live God's own life. Since the Christian concept of the Trinity concerns the relationship of three persons within one godhead, God's own life is relational.[18] But *Médico* portrays how relationality is thwarted by setting up a counter movement checking the positive and curative properties of marriage. What transpires is violence to the personality and a warping of marriage's wholeness.

The code of honor is an unwritten but powerful set of normative guides to conduct. What Calderón has achieved in a masterful way in this tragedy is to dramatize the effect of internalizing norms which, in their exaggerated form, establish personality structures.[19] We shall examine how these personality structures, reflecting honor's norms, are dehumanizing and anti-vital for all concerned.

R. D. Laing has remarked that "The characters in Shakespeare 'seem' in order to further their own purposes. The schizoid individual 'seems' because he is frightened not to seem to further what he imagines to be the purpose that someone else has in mind for him."[20] Gutierre is a schizoid personality who, to further his own interests, has killed his wife and is disposed to killing his new fiancée. What is most significant about the murder of Mencía and the horrific marriage to Leonor is the betrayal of marriage's essence. Before this stage, however, Gutierre had to arrive at full consciousness of the claims of honor and to accept them as his own. Before this tragic acceptance of honor's extremes, Gutierre operated from its principles without full awareness of their implications. But after his long soliloquies and clear recognition of honor's ultimate demand, the surrender of his selfhood, he has lost innocence and naïveté. His tragedy is completely *self-conscious*! He is, however, as much victim as victimizer, and in this double sense we are able to commiserate with his loss. We too fear that we could become victims of an ideology's dehumanizing claim. Though knowledge is always in the process of tearing itself away from ideology (Ricoeur, p. 246), Gutierre's discovery of honor's claim has not freed him from its clutches.

At this point we see clearly how all was presaged in the embryonic "comedy" when Gutierre sacrificed Leonor to his honor. Ricoeur has written, though in a different vein, that "He who is unable to reinterpret his past may also be incapable of projecting concretely his interest in emancipation" (*Her-*

meneutics, p. 97). This, indeed, is Gutierre's blindness and his loss. At the end of the play he once more declares his willingness, rather his determination, to sacrifice Leonor if called upon to do so. In this way "comedy" is truly turned into tragedy, for in an age that had ceased to live in accord with its own beliefs, Gutierre anachronistically and insanely endeavors to uphold them in practice. He is not capable of defying society's values because they have become his own.[21]

Gutierre is a proud man whose pride is founded on a jealous regard for all that affects him. But *celos* are fatal. In *Devoción*, Curcio reminds us that "Muerte de amor son los celos" (l. 1309). As Gutierre internalized the norms of conduct demanded by honor, he effectively reduced his capacity to love. This statement does not imply that Gutierre does not suffer as he accedes to honor's call. He suffers greatly, and his suffering is all the greater as he recognizes that he cannot forgive Mencía her indiscretions nor live with Enrique's threats to his honor. The theologian Reinhold Neibuhr calls forgiveness "the final form of love."[22] Because Gutierre has not been able to forgive, he eventually loses his capacity to love. This is the horror of the last scene of the play. Euripides's Medea sums up the plight of women in these terrifying words:

> Men choose their wives, and when they
> are tired of them find other women. A
> woman can neither choose nor reject
> the possessor of her body. We are the
> most wretched of all creatures; if
> marriage is unhappy, death is better.[23]

Leonor's marriage to Gutierre Alfonso Solís promises no happiness–only death.

The denouement of *El médico de su honra* shocks our notions of justice, poetic or otherwise. The joy and serenity of marriage have been shattered by Mencía's death, and marriage's power as a socially restorative process has been challenged, indeed fundamentally shaken, by Leonor's marriage to Gutierre. A literary convention of comedy is turned on its head, thus becoming a means for real insight into Calderón's poetic conception of *Médico's* world. There is no serenity, no calm; the great chain of being is shattered. The dialectic of the *comedia* fails in this *drama* to reduce multiplicity to unity and to dispel contradiction. In fact it underscores the contradictions of the poetic world thus conceived. In life the discordant overthrows the concordant; in tragic art, however, this is not the case.[24] On following the narrative line of *Médico's* discourse, we begin to see the forces at work in our world that thwart life's essential goodness.

In the murder of Mencía and the marriage to Leonor, Gutierre denies the sacredness of feminine life. Eliade has described it as "the mystic unity between life, woman, nature and divinity" (p. 217). In rejecting this sacred

element in others he suppresses it in himself. Leonor's role in *Médico* is that
of the suppliant, whom Frye has described as "the character [in tragedy],
often female, who presents a picture of unmitigated helplessness and destitu-
tion. Such a figure is pathetic, and pathos, though it seems a gentler and
more relaxed mood than tragedy, is even more terrifying" (p. 217). In fact she
has been excluded from society because she has lost her honor to gossip and
innuendo. Though she loved Gutierre, he rejected her based on suspicion of
infidelity. As he stated it to King Pedro:

> si amor y honor son pasiones
> del ánimo, a mi entender,
> quien hizo al amor ofensa,
> se le hace al honor en él. . . .

(I, 927-30)

Though Gutierre has renounced any claim to Leonor's affection, he continues
to control her life through his absence. For this reason she seeks legal assistance first, and lastly the intervention of the king to sustain her in a convent, a
living symbol of death within her society. Leonor is a picture of pathetic des-
peration caused by her acceptance of the honor code's obligations. She, too,
has internalized its norms, lived up to its demands, and suffered as a result of
her obedience. Her tremendous words at the play's conclusion, "Cura con ella
/ mi vida, en estando mala" (III, 900-1), depict the suppliant's wholehearted
acceptance of honor's terrible burden, the price of the modicum of integrity
the code of honor allots her.

Mencía is also doubly victimized by the play's action. Since she could not
marry Enrique, she must have someone to protect her honor, and therefore
her father arranged her marriage to Gutierre. Though she loved Enrique
deeply and passionately, she had to deliver herself up to another. At her
death, she makes the ultimate sacrifice to honor, though not willingly. In
these women's cases we have seen how honor aggravates the conflictive
nature of the male-female relationship, something marriage should lessen
and heal. Women are scapegoats in *Médico*, and, following René Girard's
lead, it behooves us to explain how this is so. First of all, Leonor appears clan-
less, without males to protect her interests and to avenge wrongs done to her.
Secondly, Mencía's family is bracketed by the plot, effectively leaving her in
Gutierre's hands. Only in this condition of clanlessness do they become scapegoats, so that their sacrifice does not provoke vengeance, at least not immediately. Just as there was a pre-play action, there is also a post-play action — but
the process of scapegoating fails as the history of Montiel overshadows the
personal tragedies of these characters. In this post-play action Gutierre is the
katharma, the evil object to be ritually purged by the blood of history. We the
spectators are purged, in turn, of our *anti-feminine passions*, through an individual and collective *katharsis*.[25]

Conclusion

El médico de su honra makes explicit the implicit mythic aspects of the code of honor as lived in its most extreme and degenerate form. Through Gutierre Alfonso Solís's story, the particular organizing and explanatory principles of that code are dramatized in a limit situation. The narrative expresses "in imaginative form a belief about man, the world or deity which cannot be expressed in simple propositions" (Sharpe). Man's purpose is to gain and maintain worldly esteem and standing, no matter what the cost. The world is not a place of trial or a proving ground for the hereafter, but rather a solipsistic universe in which each one must jealously guard one's own. And the deity is a transcendent power with no consistent and effectual presence in the affairs of men and women. Gutierre's "cristiana eres, salva el alma" (p. 103) acknowledges the existence of a Christian universe that his actions boldly negate. What *Médico* establishes is not an atheistic world, but one much more perverse and perverted—a world in which there is no need nor place for God.

Notes

1 All citations from the text of *El médico de su honra* are from Calderón de la Barca, *Dramas de honor: El médico de su honra y El pintor de su deshonra*, ed. Angel Valbuena Briones, Clásicos Castellanos (Madrid: Espasa-Calpe, 1965), II, 11-118.

2 See *Christopher News Notes*, No. 283, May 1985, "Life: There's Nothing Like It."

3 "From Comedy to Tragedy: Calderón and the New Tragedy," *MLN*, 92 (1977), 181-201. I have taken part of the title of this section from ter Horst's study (p. 198). For his fully elaborated view of honor in Calderonian theater, see *Calderón: The Secular Plays*, especially Chapter 2, pp. 69-170.

4 "Poetry and Drama in Calderón's *El médico de su honra*," *Romanic Review*, 49 (1958), 3-11.

5 *Dictionary of Theology*. ed. Louis Bouyer, tr. Charles Quinn (New York: Desclee, 1965), s.v. Fate.

6 See Peter N. Dunn's "Honour and the Christian Background in Calderón," ed. B.W. Wardropper (New York: NYU P, 1965), pp. 24-60 for background on the relation of honor to Christian faith.

7 See *The Literary Mind of Medieval and Renaissance Spain: Essays by Otis H. Green* (Lexington: UP of Kentucky, 1970), p. 12.

8 See Aristotle, *The Nicomachean Ethics*, tr. H. Rackham (Cambridge, MA and London: Harvard UP and W. Heinemann, 1975), I, V. 4-5.

9 *Nature and Culture in the Iliad: The Tragedy of Hector* (Chicago: U of Chicago P, 1975), p. 67, quoted in Paul Ricoeur, *Time and Narrative*, tr. Kathleen McLaughlin and David Pellauer, vol. I (Chicago: U of Chicago P, 1984), p. 240 *n* 30.

10 *Critical Essays*, tr. Richard Howard (Evanston: Northwestern UP, 1972), p. 92.

11 In his *Philosophy of Symbolic Forms*, Cassirer has shown that "symbolic forms are cultural processes that articulate experience" (*Time and Narrative*, p. 57).

12 C. S. Lewis, in *Surprised by Joy* (New York: Harcourt, Brace, 1955), p. 177,

makes the following observation: "What I like about experience is that it is such an honest thing. You may take any number of wrong turnings; but keep your eyes open and you will not be allowed to go very far before the warning signs appear. You may have deceived yourself, but experience is not trying to deceive you. The universe rings true wherever you fairly test it."

13 The present discussion depends on Ricoeur's *Hermeneutics*, p. 228.

14 Robert ter Horst significantly titles his second chapter of *Calderón* "The Idioms of Silence."

15 For further comments on the relationship of power to distorted communication, see McCarthy, p. 86.

16 *Re-Visioning Psychology* (New York: Harper and Row, 1975), p. 151.

17 *A Grief Observed* (New York: Seabury P, 1961), p. 40.

18 See David M. Thomas, *Christian Marriage: A Journey Together* (Wilmington, Del.: Michael Glazier, 1983), pp. 201-2.

19 See Habermas, p. 92.

20 Ronald D. Laing, *The Divided Self* (New York: Pantheon Books, 1969), p. 105.

21 See Robert M. Torrance, p. 145.

22 *Christopher News Notes*, no. 282, "'I Love You': Charity in the Home."

23 Quoted from Vellacott, *Ironic Drama*, p. 143.

24 See *Time and Narrative*, p. 43.

25 See René Girard, *Violence and the Sacred*, tr. Patrick Gregory (Baltimore and London: Johns Hopkins UP, 1977), pp. 12-13 and p. 290. For Don Arias's role in the "regeneration" of Enrique, see Dian Fox, *Kings in Calderón: A Study in Characterization and Political Theory* (London: Tamesis, 1986), p. 78. Fox's conjectures about Don Arias as a man of honor and Enrique as a future responsible king ignore *their* participation in and responsibility for Mencía's death. Their rebellion smacks more of vengeance than the search for justice. In Part II I shall demonstrate how vengeance is viewed in Calderonian theater.

Part II

V Myths of Masculine Sexuality and Maturation

A. Fortunas de Andrómeda y Perseo

> Pues a quien se hace por sí
> su fortuna, es a quien vi
> dar mayor estimación;
> que hijos de sus obras son
> los hombres....

(1652a)[1]

As Act III of the play opens, Bato, Perseo's servant and the play's *gracioso*, characterizes their wanderings thus: "caminamos hechos libro / de caballeros andantes" (1669a). Indeed we are in the mode of romance, where the fantastic is norm and all's well that ends well. But if our identification of the play's mode lulls us into a critical somnolence, we run the risk of missing the philosophical and dramatic richness of both design and execution that is the hallmark of Calderonian drama. There have been some very elaborate allegorical readings of *Fortunas*[2] that assist us in placing the work within the allegorical tradition and the allegorized circumstances of its first performance. But as I insist throughout this study, such historically oriented approaches are only first steps in the process of understanding the play's significance. In his commentary on Calderón's bipolar use of classical myth,[3] Sebastian Neumeister states the following:

Según el criterio de una poética del drama, fiesta y auto, fábula y alegoría ocupan posiciones opuestas en la obra calderoniana. En sus autos mitológicos Calderón deforma el mito en alegoría. En sus fiestas mitológicas, en cambio, el mito sigue siendo el núcleo del drama y de la acción.

Thus, while allegory permits the alloying of pagan myth and Christian truth in drama, myth stubbornly maintains its polyvalence, pointing towards those situations Ricoeur has denominated the *aporias* of human existence. Allegorization, furthermore, tends to destroy myth's potential for confronting the fundamental issues of existence by converting a searching probe into a dogmatic response. Calderón's use of myth demands more of us than catechetical repetition.

Both *Fortunas* and *Eco y Narciso* deal with myths of masculine sexuality and maturation, but from distinct perspectives. In the former we witness a positive outcome to physical growth and chronological maturity, whereas in the latter the blocking of these forces leads to immaturity and death. Our approach to *Fortunas* will be from the perspective of an initiation myth, characterized by Richmond Y. Hathorn as "inducting a male into the life of full sexuality and full communal activity" (p. 26). In addition, initiation rites accompany a basic transition "from an old order of nature to a new nature that transcends the old" (p. 26). The stories of Perseo and Andrómeda dramatize the transition from childhood to manhood, but to a manhood marked by feats that will reveal him as a *hero* in the full sense of that term.

The Divine Background to Human Action

The process of Perseo's becoming a hero is set against the divine background of disharmony among the gods and goddesses, symbolized by Discordia's presence and caused by the sexual exploits of Júpiter, which provoke Juno's jealousy. Juno prevents Danae from informing Perseo of his origin, thus precipitating a crisis for the young man. Mercurio and Palas set out to thwart their stepmother's "siempre sañudo ceño" (1646b), because Perseo is their brother. The principal divine interveners are surrogates of Júpiter and Juno. The former has surrendered to lust, and his fear of discovery makes him virtually impotent in assisting his human son. As a result Perseo experiences a living death in his "rústicos sayales" (1646b) that mask his true identity and frustrate his heroic desires and impulses.

The forces tugging at Perseo represent a split in the celestial chorus. Juno is the vengeful pursuer of her husband's lovers (victims?) and bastards, commanding Discordia to convey to the Furies the following message: "di que dispongan / de Danae y Perseo la persecución" (1661a). Her agents are the negative forces of life that thwart the good that is in Perseo. Discordia requests that the Furies "me ayudéis a que deshaga / de Perseo las fortunas, / que ya su gran nombre ensalzan" (1662a). His "fortunas" will be, in fact, the realization of his royal and celestial potential, the inheritance of Danae and Júpiter. Since Júpiter, as "padre / de los hados" (1645b), is unable to provide any assistance, Perseo is dependent on the intervention of Mercurio and Palas. His divine siblings ensure that he not become a victim of Discordia's fury and that his path to fame and fulfillment be straight and true.

At the end of Act II, Mercurio hands Perseo his caduceus, and Palas, her transparent shield, instruments necessary in the conquest of Medusa (1668a). In telling fashion, the play's denouement underscores the central roles of Mercurio and Palas. As Juno and Discordia admit their defeat, the latter attempts to mitigate it by claiming:

> porque trató de impedirlos [efectos]
> el gran Júpiter supremo;

> que de Mercurio y Palas
> poco importara el esfuerzo.
>
> (1679a)

Palas immediately retorts:

> No importara sino mucho,
> pues escudo y caduceo
> fueron de su triunfo causa.

In summary, the celestial protagonists are Mercurio and Discordia, representatives of the opposing forces of good and evil. We have in Mercurio a force analogous to that of divine providence as seen in *Devoción* that "manipulates" the action in such a way "que anden mis favores / delante de sus venganzas" (1661a).

The Masculine World of Violence and the Victimization of Women

At the core of *Fortunas de Andrómeda y Perseo* there are two distinct notions of time that characterize tragic and comedic world views. On the one hand tragedy results from time viewed as cyclical, in which history repeats itself from generation to generation. Such a tragic view underlies the generational revolts of Cronus against Uranus, and Zeus against Cronus, and even Perseo's fledgling outburst against his father on discovering the rape of Danae. On the other hand comedic, or in this case "romantic," outcomes are possible only where that cycle is superseded by a teleological sense of time in which one is able to escape the restrictions of heredity and the limitations of circumstance. Discordia seeks to entrap Perseo and Danae in the events of the past, whereas Mercurio and Palas point the way out of that morasss. Discordia is past time devouring the present and foreclosing on the future; Mercurio and Palas represent hope in the present and a better world in the future.

Though we traditionally associate physical violence with the masculine sphere of action, forcefully suggested by Júpiter's ascension to supreme power in heaven, we frequently forget or overlook that all too often the object of that violence is woman. *Médico's* conflict between males was partially resolved through the death of Mencía. The theme of woman as victim is a constant one in Calderonian drama, and nowhere is its very nature underscored as well as in *Médico* and *Fortunas*. Commenting on Casiopea, Andrómeda's mother, Fineo remarks: "que las infelicidades / son lunar de las bellezas" (1649a-b). Lidoro provides a striking depiction of a beautiful woman's fate when, narrating Medusa's history, he states: "que es más su hermosura / cuanto es más triste su estrella" (1651a). A woman's great beauty is a prophetic sign of her fate. In this manner Andrómeda is associated with the play's other female victims, and only by the cojoining of her fate with that of

Perseo will she be saved from becoming yet another victim in the long history of female victimization. The difference between Perseo and the rapists, Júpiter and Neptuno, lies in the young man's discovery of what Eliade has termed "the revelation of the feminine sacredness, i.e., of the mystic unity between life, woman, nature and the divinity" (p. 217). This discovery is part and parcel of his rite of passage to a higher consciousness as well as to an extended sphere of action. Indeed, that discovery will channel his heroic efforts.

In examining the three principal female human characters, we see how women become victims of male violence. From her youth Danae lived under an ill-fated star that constantly threatened her. Her father Acrisio unjustly imprisoned her after an oracle's prediction that his death would come about through the agency of a grandson, the son of Andrómeda. As Segismundo of *La vida es sueño*, Danae complains rhetorically:

> ¿Qué delito cometí
> para que tan riguroso
> mi padre me lo castigue?

> (1655a)

In spite of the extreme measures employed by Acrisio to prevent Danae's pregnancy, she is raped.

Perseo is the product of this brutal rape, and the manner of his conception undermines the traditional allegorical approach to the play. Rape represents such basic evil in the theater of Calderón that the notion of a "heroic" rape finds no place therein.[4] In Morfeo's grotto Perseo witnesses the unfolding of events that will disclose his identity. Danae is locked up with her ladies, but, appearing as Cupido seated upon an eagle,[5] Júpiter circumvents Acrisio's guards. In Renaissance painting Danae surrenders her virtue for gold; in Titian the golden rain is a shower of coins and in Van Dyck, of coins and jewelry. By omitting the gold entirely Rembrandt reaffirms Danae's virtue.[6] In *Fortunas* only the ladies in waiting gather up the gold, stressing Danae's innocence and virtue as well as Júpiter's cynicism. As he appears dressed in the symbols of love and power, his musical *letra* emphasizes a cynical realism:

> *El que adora imposibles*
> *[que] llüeva oro:*
> *sin él nada se vence,*
> *y con él todo.*

> *(1655a)*

Explaining the symbolism of his appearance, Júpiter elaborates on the implications of Apolo's metal:

> si bien solo este bastara,

> que para llegar airoso
> a los ojos de una dama,
> no hay más gala que el soborno. . . .

> (1655b).

This "practical" view of matters of the heart reveals Júpiter's essential hollowness and his total lack of respect for women. His words, though flattering and reassuring, are empty; his promise to protect her proves to be a lie. As Júpiter grabs her by the hands, Danae cries for help; but he drowns her out with music. She screams in fright:

> ¡Cielos, piedad! ¡Favor, cielos!
> ¡Socorro, dioses, socorro!

> (1656a)

This ironic cry for help, with the supreme power in the heavens her attacker, highlights Danae's helplessness and destroys Júpiter's justification for what some have called a "heroic rape." We are encouraged, however, to view the scene in more critical terms by Lidoro's earlier observations on Neptuno's rape of Medusa. His lust is "codicia necia" (1651a). As a god he has recourse to his majestic power:

> Amante pues suyo, no
> se valió de las finezas
> de rendido; que el amor
> de un poderoso no ruega,
> cuando puede la caricia
> valerse de la violencia.

> (1651a)

Here we have the basic coordinates of male-female relations: "las finezas de rendido" or "la violencia." The gods use violence and rape those they presume "to love"; Perseo will employ *finezas* and win Andrómeda's love.

Rape, as traditionally viewed in allegorical terms, was an ambivalent act. It could, as in Neptuno's rape of Medusa, destroy the *concordia discors* by dividing the soul from wisdom, or, as in Júpiter's rape of Danae, produce the ideal balance in the human soul symbolized by Perseo. Instead of negating divine justice, rape actually presages it.[7] While these allegorical interpretations indeed form part of the intellectual background to plays such as *Fortunas*, Calderón's depiction of the rape of Danae fundamentally challenges such an allegorical scheme. Perhaps the realization of the horror of rape prevents, or forecloses on, the textual harmony that such allegorical interpretations set as their goal. There could be no heroic dimension to rape, and for this reason the allegorized approaches to the play fail to come to grips with *Fortunas's* inner dynamics. Thus, when Júpiter appears at the play's finale to acknowledge his son, his reference to *finezas* can be viewed only as an ironic example of contradiction and textual disharmony:

> Yo, el festivo parabién
> de vuestro aplauso agradezco,
> y en el traje de Cupido,
> que fue mi disfraz primero,
> le recibo, por hacer
> de mis finezas acuerdo,
> como al fin primera causa
> de tan gloriosos efectos.
>
> (1680a-b)

Júpiter's claim to "finezas" rings hollow in light of Perseo's demonstrated "finezas de rendido." And again, the crucial factor that discriminates between the father's and the son's exploits is how each one treated women – violence (rape) or love, beneficence, and expressions of high regard (*finezas*).

In Act I Danae could not reveal to Perseo his identity "porque sellan mis labios / de Juno celos y de Jove agravios" (1648a). This bimember phrase summarizes the plight of Danae: she lives with the results of Júpiter's injuries and constantly fears the threat of Juno's jealousy. Like Juno, Minerva is offended by Medusa's rape, and, furthermore, Venus is insulted by Casiopea's imprudent extolling of Andrómeda's beauty. In each case a goddess's pride is injured by the actions or words of other gods or mortals. The chain of offense-vengeance seems to be an eternal norm for the conduct of gods and goddesses, and only Perseo's heroic exploits will supersede this chain as well as break the cyclical rhythm of victimization.

Medusa's sad history uncovers another horrible aspect of the constant victimization of women. Like Danae and Andrómeda, she was beautiful, and "es más su hermosura / cuanto es más triste su estrella" (1651a). Incited by her beauty, Neptuno rapes her producing a change in her nature. This violent act is explicitly denied the appellation love:

> por fuerza logró su amor . . . .
> Mas miente, miente mi lengua;
> que aunque consigue, no logra
> el que consigue por fuerza.
>
> (1651a)

The rape occurred in the temple of Minerva, and the goddess, unable to avenge this sacrilege on the god himself, decides to punish Medusa by converting her beautiful hair, which originally attracted Neptuno's attention, into writhing serpents. Rape is the negation of a woman's personhood and being, and the consequences for Medusa are horrendous. She is transformed or metamorphosed into a monster, the "bandolera de Africa" who in fact is a "bandolera / de las vidas" (1651b). The serpents' poison acts through her eyes, changing rational men into trunks of wood; the sign of her degradation is the writhing presence of snakes on her head. This portrait could not be more dehumanizing, and thereby Calderón emotively conveys the consequences of this and other rapes. Whereas Danae does not appear on stage during the second half of the play, Medusa's presence is necessary for the solution of Andrómeda's fate: "'De la sangre de Medusa / uno y otro alivio espera'" (1657b). Thus Medusa becomes the tragic figure who in life suffered violent abuse and in whose death, at least, another fellow sufferer may find solace.[8]

On examining Andrómeda's victimization, we enter the world of feminine jealousy and revenge. Like Danae and Medusa, Andrómeda is the scapegoat for another's injury to Venus and the Nereids. Casiopea, the queen of Trinacria and mother of Andrómeda, extolled the beauty of her daughter, declaring her to be even more beautiful than the goddess of beauty, Venus. As punishment for this insult, a marine monster devastates the region of Trinacria. Fineo learns from Júpiter's oracle that the only way to free his country from the monster's ravages is through the sacrifice of Andrómeda: "'Ofrecida al monstruo muera / Andrómeda'" (1657b). Once again fate threatens the life of an innocent woman. Helpless in her isolation, Andrómeda will be the scapegoat that liberates her homeland. She complains of her fate, communicating the emotive significance of her sacrifice as victim:

> que el que culpado se angustia,
> en la culpa que comete
> halla honestada la injuria;
> mas quien la padece (¡ay triste!)
> sin cometerla, es locura
> persuadirse a que es consuelo
> el fracaso a que se ajusta.
>
> (1674b)

In the cases of Medusa and Danae there is no solution. But for Andrómeda's fate, brought to Trinacria's attention by a jealous Fineo (1667a), indeed there is hope in Júpiter's oracle: "De la sangre de Medusa / uno y otro alivio espera" (1657b). Perseo will save her from death, and the mode in which he does so constitutes Calderón's original interpretation of the myth.

There is a dual aspect to fate in the play. On the one hand, fated women are cut off from family and society, as are Leonor and Mencía of *Médico* and Danae and Medusa of our play. And even Andrómeda is "La que nace para ser / estrago de la fortuna" (1674a), on becoming the scapegoat of her country's ills. But for a man like Perseo, on the other hand, fate involves not knowing his paternal identity, a situation similar to Eusebio's fate in *Devoción*. Perseo seeks to discover his fate (1646b), and Palas and Mercurio will assist *"a decirlo, sin decirlo, / y a saberlo, sin saberlo"* (1646a). As Eusebio learns that he has a higher destiny than that inherited from Curcio, so too Perseo discovers that his destiny transcends mere knowledge of his origin. When Mercurio points the way by singing

> *Ama, espera y confía;*
> *porque no puede*
> *el que vence sin riesgo,*
> *decir que vence.*

(1667b)

he intimates that Perseo's purpose in life is not only to know, but more importantly to love, the true life of the soul. And only through love will Perseo conquer his and Andrómeda's fates.

The Problem of Identity: Perseo as Hero

Perseo's development as a masculine hero is set against the negative background of the normal male world of violence. Calderón's version of the myth of Perseus unfolds the latter's initiation into what it is to be a man, and the essence of the myth resides in that process. The drama examines the nature of the hero, i.e., his qualities, personality, and mode of being in a hostile world, but in a positive light that sharply contrasts with those of Neptuno and Júpiter.

Generally speaking a hero knows who he is or, rather, has a solid foundation upon which he actualizes his heroic potentiality. But in the case of Perseo, his identity, his paternal origin, is in question. The theme of ¿quién es? reverberates throughout the play, predominately affecting Danae and Perseo. The shepherds of Acaya know more of his past than does the future hero, and one of them even reproaches him with its secretive nature:

> ¿qué te persuade a pensar
> que eres más que un extranjero,
> advenedizo pastor,
> hijo vil de un adulterio,
> u de otra traición?

(1643b-1644a)

In his first appearance on stage, Perseo comports himself with an arrogance which profoundly disturbs his companions. Suddenly the haughty youth has to confront the troubling doubts provoked by the revelation that he is not Cardenio's grandson. Though Act I begins with a conventional hunt scene, instead of seeking *fieras*, Perseo finds himself forced to discover his identity.

Act I contains some indications of the young man's identity. He feels a profound and inexplicable reverence toward Júpiter:

> yo no sé por qué secreto,

> aun más que todos adoro,
> más que todos reverencio.
>
> (1642b)

And later when he mentions the word "padre," he is profoundly moved:

> ¡Oh gran Júpiter, oh padre
> de los hados!.... Mas, ¿qué es esto?
> Al decir padre, no sé
> qué no usado, qué violento
> impulso me alborozó
> el corazón acá dentro....
>
> (1645b)

The disclosure of his identity does not frighten him as long as he is not revealed as a *villano*. For him all is pardonable except a non-illustrious heritage. Furthermore, Calderón almost imperceptibly changes this question of the young man's origin by linking it with the resolution of the problems provoked by Medusa and the marine monster. Perseo, apparently in a temerarious fashion, believes that only he can conquer them. But he is suddenly paralyzed by doubts concerning his origin. At the height of indecision, he rejects his inner doubts so as to affirm a surprising truth:

> Pues a quien se hace por sí
> su fortuna, es a quien vi
> dar mayor estimación;
> que hijos de sus obras son
> los hombres.
>
> (1652a)

Calderón apparently emphasizes an anti-nobiliary principle. However, the play's action furnishes us with a broader view of the topic, that a man is not merely what his blood has made him, but rather what he makes of himself. In consequence, if man is his actions, then in this drama Perseo will disclose to us in a most positive manner what constitutes a true man, a hero.

With the assistance of Mercurio and Palas, Perseo discovers that he is Júpiter's son and is thus freed to follow his heroic inclinations. And yet the hero's deeds in themselves are not significant; what is of supreme importance is the motivation behind them. An arrogant and haughty young man in Act I, Perseo finds sense and purpose for his heroic impulses on loving Andrómeda. Before realizing this mutual and passionate love, however, the young man will have to face first the dangerous Medusa and second the monster that devours the region of Trinacria and threatens Andrómeda's life. Thus Perseo's life is intimately linked to the women of the play, and this relationship discloses the universal significance of the drama.

From the petulance of a troubled adolescence Perseo evolves to the assurance of self-knowledge and the affirmation of mature masculinity. That Perseo is very different from his father reveals a dual transition from the old order of nature to a new one that transcends the old. First of all, there is his physical maturation during which he develops into a model of masculinity. Secondly, instead of repeating the cycle of rebellion and violence, Perseo symbolizes a new order, a new paradigm for sonship. Júpiter obtained his status and supremacy in the heavens through rebellion against Cronus/Saturn, just as Cronus had achieved his station through the violent and bloody castration of his father Uranus. Perseo passes through a natural but less violent rebellion, providing us with a broader perspective on the process of maturation. Early in the play the young Perseo is depicted as experiencing a powerful, though secret, reverence toward Júpiter on referring to him as "padre / de los hados" (1645b). But in Act II, after witnessing the violent rape of Danae, he ardently desires to avenge this wrong done to his mother, although he cannot bring himself to say the word "rape":

> que aunque seas poderoso,
> Júpiter, vengaré en ti
> de mi madre....
>
> (1656a)

For Perseo, Júpiter's rule is fraught with transgression and severity, and the young man is inevitably caught in the web of his father's crimes.[9]

The problems provoked by Júpiter's wanton actions are not directly addressed in the play. Perseo is indeed the son of Júpiter, but his search for identity and meaning will elevate him above the personal confrontational level with his violent, brutal, and rigorous father to a symbolic plane where the cycle of violence and rebellion is not so much broken as transcended by the power of heterosexual love. Mercurio reveals to Perseo that his road to integrity, though it travels through the two monsters, will actually be an inner journey, a psychomachy of the highest order.[10] When Perseo can find no solution to this personal and heroic impasse, Mercurio declares in song:

> *Ama, espera y confía;*
> *porque no puede*
> *el que vence sin riesgo,*
> *decir que vence.*
>
> (1667b)

Perseo will assume personal risk and confront the horrible monsters; but they are also symbols of his interior conflicts. Medusa allegorically represents sensual delights, according to Valbuena Briones (p. 101). More significantly she represents the deadly effects of jealousy on love just as the marine monster symbolizes the devouring potentiality of fate and death on life.

Once Pereso meets Andrómeda he discovers in her a *telos* toward which he can direct his efforts. Since she needs a champion to defend her from the monster, Perseo discovers a purpose for his heroic impulses at the same time as he discovers the stirrings of love. And Perseo's love of Andrómeda establishes a very telling contrast with the way Júpiter and Neptuno "loved" Danae and Medusa. Perseo wins his love through heroic deeds, the epitome of *finezas*, while the two gods obtain theirs through force.

The two obstacles, Medusa and the marine monster, symbolically exemplify the obstacles that each person must conquer before attaining love's plenitude. For example, jealousy, in various guises, plays a crucial role in the plot. Medusa's sisters sing the following:

> *Pisa, pisa con tiento las flores.*
> *Quedito, pasito, amor; que no sabes*
> *en cuál de ellas se esconden los celos;*
> *y puesto que son de tus flores el áspid....*
>
> (1671a)

In this *letra* jealousy is associated with an asp, symbolizing jealousy as a poison that destroys love. Perseo must first conquer Medusa, or jealousy, before realizing his love for Andrómeda.

In Calderonian drama jealousy plays a significant and prominent role. In the honor dramas, jealousy is an antivital force that destroys all in its path. Nathaniel Hawthorne, in *The Scarlet Letter*, writes: "Let men tremble to win the hand of women, unless they win with it the utmost passion of her heart."[11] Due to Juno's jealousy, Perseo is in danger, a danger so great that his mother refuses to tell him who he is: "Por guardar tu vida" (1645a). In addition Fineo, Andrómeda's suitor, twice tries to kill Persco because of jealousy. This passion is so strong that he will even prefer the death of his beloved rather than see her love of Perseo fulfilled:

> Y pues que en llegando a cclos,
> no hay pundonor que no cese,
> pues el que siente más noble
> es quien más infame siente,
> civilmente de los dos
> mis sinrazones me venguen.
>
> (1667a)

Jealousy is not merely antivital but also antirational, destructive of one's natural nobility of character. Juno acknowledges "la necedad de los celos" (1679a), but such a discovery does not lead in any way to insight and self-control. To emphasize the perniciousness of jealousy, Calderón has Lidoro comment immediately after saving Perseo's life:

> Ya con esto te he pagado
> aquella fineza, puesto
> que si mataste una hidra
> que tenía en el cabello
> los áspides, yo maté
> a quien los tenía en el pecho,
> no siendo menos rabiosos
> los áspides que los celos.

(1679b)

At the end of Act II, Perseo is at a loss as to what to do after Fineo reveals that Andrómeda's fate is to be the victim sacrificed to the monster. With his beloved at the point of death, the hero finds himself in a labyrinth of confusion. Mercurio appears with the key to a final resolution of his difficulties: *"Ama, espera y confía"* (1667b). The play forcefully suggests that love is the only positive force capable of confronting and conquering the evil effects of both fate and jealousy. With Palas and Mercurio's aid, as they provide him with a shield and the caduceus, the hero undertakes the adventure that will end with the Gorgon's death. The shield of arms that he symbolically bears represents love, a most powerful impulse.

The death of Medusa and the subsequent death of the marine monster represent dual victories for love. The first represents love's victory over jealousy and the hatred it produces. The second victory of love, the defeat of the Monster, represents love's conquest over fate or ill-starred fortune. At the conclusion of Act II all the inhabitants of Trinacria cry out for Andrómeda's death in order to escape the destruction threatened by the Monster. All view her destiny as one imposed by hostile fate:

> And. ¡Suerte injusta!
> Rey.   ¡Triste hado!
> And. ¡Fiera pena!
> Rey.   ¡Estrella fuerte!

(1667b)

After his victory, Perseo expresses the symbolic purport of his adventure:

> Mas ¿qué mucho facilite
> más que el hado dificulta,
> amor, que en estas finezas
> todos sus méritos funda,
> para arrojarme a tus plantas?

(1678a)

Such a declaration from the astounded hero leaves no doubt about love's power. In this way we grasp the true meaning of *finezas* and the heroic dynamic that produces them.

Perseo's Rite of Passage

After the victory over the Monster, Perseo and Andrómeda marry, as is to be expected at the conclusion of a romance. We should note, however, that this union is not purely conventional, or at least its significance is in no way conventional.[12] The young adventurer, representative of the perfect hero, has just passed through various dangerous trials, trials which represent the proof of his masculinity and of the inner harmony of his being. Rites of passage signal ontological mutations that accompany birth, initiation, sexuality, marriage, and death (Eliade, p. 116). Perseo has passed his initiation trials and is now prepared for the wise exercise of his sexuality in conjugal union with Andrómeda.

As dramatic experience, *Fortunas de Andrómeda y Perseo* represents quite clearly the three distinct phases of a typical initiation myth.[13]

1. Perseo's supernatural birth presages his divine destiny. His life communicates the vital and dynamic force that emanates from true love.

2. His departure from Acaya and his duels with Medusa and the Monster represent the death of his infantile and puerile nature. Through his heroic deeds, the meaning of *finezas*, the willingness to sacrifice or to risk one's life for another, takes on clearer focus and contrasts sharply with the phantom exploits of Júpiter and Neptuno.

3. His encounter with Woman, or Andrómeda, represents the beginning of his mature sexual life. In *Médico* the murder of Mencía is a fundamental denial of something sacred. In *Devoción* Eusebio's refusal to rape Julia is due to the recognition of this mysterious feminine quality. As Eliade has pointed out, "It is the *access to the sacred*, as it reveals itself upon assuming the condition of woman, that constitutes the aim and objective, both of the initiatory rites of puberty and of the feminine secret societies" (p. 209). Persco's marriage further symbolizes what Frye has called the apocalyptic conception of human life, for Perseo's fulfilment as a human being is threefold: individual, sexual, and social. His new self corresponds to the inauguration of a new life.

Conclusion

Perseo's heroic deeds, his *finezas*, demonstrate how love shatters the pernicious pattern of fateful heredity and paternal tyranny. *La vida es sueño* suggests forgiveness as the solution to the direct confrontation of father and son. In *Fortunas* love is a transformational force moving the question from its conflictive potentiality to redemptive opportunity: *"Ama, espera y confía"* (1667b). But there is also another significant pattern broken by Perseo's deeds, the pattern of one generation's having to pay for the misdeeds of another. This situation is so obvious in the case of Perseo that we may easily overlook its relevance to Andrómeda's. Pérez de Moya has emphasized this point as follows:

El pagar Andrómeda el pecado que cometió su madre, avisa que muchos suelen pagar el pecado ajeno o que la justicia injusta siempre hace efeto en las cosas flacas, e inocentes, o que suelen los hijos pagar los pecados de los padres, y a la contra (II, 173).

In chapter 46 of *The Enchiridion*, St. Augustine presents a Christian view on the same matter:

there are other sins of the immediate parents, which, though they have not the same effect in producing a change of nature, yet subject the children to guilt unless the divine grace and mercy interpose to rescue them (I, 685).

When Andrómeda is at a loss to explain why she must pay for her mother's boastful extolling of her beauty, we finally come to understand how the fates and fortunes of Andrómeda and Perseo are joined, and how only through their mutual love can both be saved. Divine grace and mercy may be seen by analogy in Mercurio and Palas's championing of Perseo's cause. But we should not stop there, for *Fortunas de Andrómeda y Perseo* strongly suggests that human, sexual, and mutual love is the natural counterpart to "divine grace." Love is a power infused in human nature that frees both man and woman from the pernicious influence of heredity. The true fortunes of Perseo and Andrómeda are to have found that power in one another.[14]

Notes

1 All quotations of *Fortunas de Andrómeda y Perseo* are from *Obras completas: dramas*, pp. 1639-80, cited by page and column.

2 See C. A. Merrick, "Neoplatonic Allegory in Calderón's 'Las fortunas de Andrómeda y Perseo,'" *MLR*, 67 (1972), 319-327 and A. Valbuena Briones, "La construcción artística de *Fortunas de Andrómeda y Perseo*," *Homenaje a José María Solá-Solé* (Barcelona: U of Texas at Austin and Puvill, 1984), pp. 91-102.

3 "Calderón y el mito clásico (*Andrómeda y Perseo*, auto sacramental y fiesta de corte)," *Calderón: Actas*, II, 721. See also Blue's comments on allegorical readings of the myth plays, in *The Development of Imagery in Calderón's 'Comedias,'* p. 126.

4 See Merrick, p. 323, where a distinction is established between Júpiter's rape of Danae and Neptuno's rape of Medusa.

5 See Phyllis Dearborn Massar, "Scenes for a Calderón Play by Baccio del Bianco," *Master Drawings*, XV, No. 4 (1977), 365-75 and plates 21-31. This particular scene is represented in Plate 26.

6 See Hathorn, p. 27.

7 See Merrick, p. 323.

8 I have followed in broad outline here and elsewhere the ideas already expressed in my "Violación, amor y entereza en *Fortunas de Andrómeda y Perseo* de Calderón de la Barca," *Homenaje a Gonzalo Torrente Ballester* (Salamanca: Biblioteca de la Caja de

Ahorros y M. de P. de Salamanca, 1981), pp. 573-82.

9 See my article, "The Father Figure in *Fortunas de Andrómeda y Perseo*: A Comment on the Father-Son Motif in Calderonian Drama," *Proceedings of the Fifth Annual Golden Age Spanish Drama Symposium* (El Paso, TX: U of Texas at El Paso, 1986), pp. 29-35.

10 See Ignacio Elizalde, "El papel de Dios verdadero en los autos y comedias mitológicos de Calderón," in *Calderón: Actas...*, II, 1008.

11 *The Scarlet Letter* (Boston: Houghton, Mifflin, 1889), pp. 212-13.

12 To realize the significant changes made in the Perseus-Andromeda myth, see H. M. Martin, "The Perseus Myth in Lope and Calderón with Some Reference to their Sources," *PMLA*, 46 (1931), 450-60 and Juan Pérez de Moya, *Philosophia secreta*, 2 vols., ed. Eduardo Gómez de Baquero (Madrid, 1928), II, 160-73.

13 See Hathorn, p. 26.

14 Hester Prynne, of Hawthorne's *The Scarlet Letter*, anticipates a future in which "sacred love should make us happy, by the truest test of a life successful to such an end!" (p. 311). While verily we fear for Gutierre and Leonor at the denouement of *Médico*, we have no such foreboding at *Fortunas's*, for in Hester's own words: "She assured them [wretched women], too, of her firm belief, that, at some brighter period, when the world should have grown ripe for it, in Heaven's own time, a new truth would be revealed, in order to establish the whole relation between man and woman on a surer ground of mutual happiness" (p. 311). Calderón's *Fortunas* imaginatively anticipates that same brighter period.

B. Eco y Narciso

> *Si en los que bien quieren*
> *todo es padecer,*
> *y no hay dicha alguna*
> *en el bien querer,*
> *¡fuego de Dios en el querer bien!*
> *¡Amen, amén!*
>
> Eco and Narciso, (1930a)[1]
>
> que un día todo es amar,
> y otro día aborrecer.
>
> Narciso, (1930b)
>
> pues ruina de entrambos fueron
> una voz y una hermosura. . . .
>
> Liríope, (1940b)

The structuring of *Eco y Narciso* and *Fortunas de Andrómeda y Perseo* along the broad lines of initiatory myths and the similarity of motifs developed in each play immediately catch our attention. The problem of identity, the ¿quién es? theme, reverberates from mother to son, from Liríope to Narciso, just as it did from Danae to Perseo. Feminine beauty as a source of unhappiness finds similar treatment in *Eco y Narciso*. Liríope reminds us from her bitter experience "que no vio el sol / una hermosura feliz" (1913a). Such observations are ominous, for Eco is "zagala la más bella / que vio la luz de la mayor estrella" (1906a). A new twist to this oft-repeated motif involves Narciso's reaction to discovering his own beauty reflected in the fountain: "¿Quién vio / jamás igual hermosura. . .?" (1932a). His fate is inexorably linked to his own remarkable beauty. Once again the violent and fearful abduction and rape of Liríope by her frustrated suitor Céfiro precipitate Liríope's and Narciso's misfortunes. And lastly, while Perseo's formative years were spent in community with normal relationships as guide for his own development, Narciso will mature in a truncated and suffocating environment dominated by his mother's fears and forebodings.

Eco y Narciso, though it repeats some of the situations found in *Fortunas's* world of romance, embodies a tragic world view. We are not in the world of monsters and wondrous deeds but rather in the narrow confines of the inner worlds of the characters. Divine intervention is absent from the affairs of men and women, and, although this dramatic world is not deterministic, the influence of fate is oppressive.

Eco y Narciso contains the broad outline of a typical initiation myth, but one with a tragic issue. What originally led to the combining of the stories of Echo and Narcissus, either by Ovid or some predecessor, was what Hathorn has termed "the associated ideas of sound-reflection and sight-reflection" (p. 106).

While this observation helps us grasp the commonality of their fates, it may lead us to overlook the more fundamental bonds that link them together. As Perseo, the hero, meets Andrómeda in the form of Woman as Death, the Bride of Death motif, so Narciso meets Eco. But what *Eco y Narciso* adds to this one-sided perspective of *Fortunas* is the masculine counterpart to the Bride of Death motif, the depiction of the male as an Agent of Death (Hathorn, p. 99).

Fate and Tragedy: Providential Absence

In analyzing *Fortunas*, a great deal of time was spent clarifying the divine background to the human action. In *Eco* we must explain the absence of the gods and goddesses from the play's action. The environment of *Eco y Narciso* is similar to that of *Médico* in which the characters, cut adrift from any providential concern for their welfare, are left to their own devices. The dramatic world of *Eco* is truly one of absence, a universe without a center, in which the children do indeed pay for the deeds and crimes of their parents. As Febo reminds us on referring to Eco's birthday, time is cyclical and wears down every human being including Eco: "cada año más es una gracia menos" (1906b). Time also bears down on the inhabitants of Arcadia, underscoring the recurrent theme of victimization of the lowly and weak by the mighty and powerful. The only suggestion of a larger context for the action occurs when, as Liríope claims to be innocent of the plights of Eco and Narciso, Febo avers:

> pues ese efecto
> es venganza de los dioses,
> que en él tus atrevimientos
> han castigado.
>
> (1939a)

But her case is very different from that of Basilio in *La vida es sueño*, in that Liríope is caught up in a series of events that overwhelms her strength and outdistances her powers and wisdom. Though she learned her magical arts from Tiresias, they were never practiced outside of the narrow confines of her prison and mountain retreat. Júpiter punished her tutor for trying to equate himself to that deity, and as a result kept the magician "ciego y preso" (1914a) in that wilderness until his death. Whatever the divine presence in this play, it is basically a vindictive one. The gods are far removed from the concerns of Arcadia's inhabitants, and their activity is limited to a punitive function. As Céfiro, Narciso's father, appears to be indifferent to his son's fate, so too the gods are acknowledged powers that disdain the puny world of mortals.

Arcadia: The Valley and the Mountains

The action takes place in Arcadia, that idealized land of innocence and joy. The luxurious sets accompanying these courtly productions were spectacles for the eyes. In the very staging of the play Calderón visualizes a favorite Baroque theme, the opposition of reality and appearance. Arcadia projects the beauty of nature and appears to rest securely upon the harmony of its various elements. We soon learn that Eco is about to celebrate her birthday, and all the inhabitants of this happy and blessed land turn out for the joyous occasion. But in the midst of rejoicing there is one constant and dissident voice, that of Sileno, who laments the loss twelve years ago of his daughter Liríope. He reminds us:

> pues el día (¡suerte dura!)
> que cumple años tu hermosura
> cumple mi desdicha años.
>
> (1907b).

We catch another hint of Arcadia's disharmony in the words of Febo, a shepherd, reminding us that nothing is capable of withstanding the onslaught of time, for even in Eco "cada año más es una gracia menos" (1906b). Moreover, the development of the motif of truth and reality versus falsehood and appearance leads us to probe more deeply into the scenes which are about to pass before our eyes. We realize that there are two basic locales for the play's action, the valley and the mountains. The valley represents civilization and the benefits it brings to humankind, for the pastoral life is abundant both in the fruits of nature and in the leisure it affords its followers. The mountains do not participate in the joy of the valley, for they contain a cave in which two humans make their miserable abode. This cave serves as a prison for Narciso who yearns for the experiences of the outside world. The mountains also provide an ideal place in which to hide one's *delitos*, and Liríope, Narciso's mother, finds herself to be as much the mountain's prisoner as she is her son's jailor. The movement to and fro, from valley to mountains and back again, is fundamental in the play's structure, representing as it does the cyclical nature of time that undergirds the play.[2]

Appearance, change, and time all bear down on the inhabitants of Arcadia, and Calderón beautifully reminds us of this fact in the following sonnet found in Act II:

> Apenas el invierno helado y cano
> este monte de nieves encanece,
> cuando la primavera le florece,
> y el que helado se vio, se mira ufano.
> Pasa la primavera, y el verano
> los rigores del sol sufre y padece.

Llega el fértil otoño, y enriquece
el monte de verdor, de fruta el llano.
Todo vive sujeto a la mudanza.
De un día y otro día los engaños
cumplen un año, y este al otro alcanza.
Con esperanza sufre desengaños
un monte, que a faltarle la esperanza,
ya se rindiera al peso de los años.

(1920a-b)

Reciting this sonnet, Febo laments his inability to move Eco to love him. But there is more than a character's sorrow therein, for the poetry reminds us that hope is essential for those caught in the tides of time. The changes produced in Nature are cyclic, and so too are the joys and misfortunes of men and women. Calderón is subtly undermining the visual impact of the stage by introducing the note of decadence which is inevitable in all subject to time. This Arcadia is not the Garden of Eden, and its characters do not live in a Golden Age of innocence and freedom. Time, change, and deceit are part and parcel of the ambiance, and Sileno's sorrow hints at unresolved problems and new misfortunes to be faced by the dwellers of Arcadia. We are about to witness a new cycle in which the tragedy of one generation will be visited upon the next.[3]

Liríope: Victim and Victimizer

Liríope is one of the many women in Calderonian theater victimized by an impatient and rapacious male. Her story, though not at all the center of the dramatic action, is nonetheless at the heart of the tragedy we witness. Her misfortune repeats the sad tale of many a beautiful woman, because her beauty was the prime mover in her tragic undoing. She is, as we have already indicated, her son's jailor, and her story explains their strange presence in the mountains and the odd relationship she has established with him. Dressed in animal skins, she truly appears to be a "monstruo cruel" (1913a). Nevertheless, her self-characterization reinforces the pitiful figure she actually strikes: "soy / una mujer infeliz" (1913a).

As a young girl Liríope attracted the attention of Céfiro, the son of the wind, who burned with passion for her until he could bear no more the torment of having to do without her. In order to enjoy this maiden, Céfiro abducted her to the mountains where he violated and then immediately abandoned her. Céfiro is another of the seemingly unending line of rapists Calderón has seen fit to depict, such as Júpiter and Neptuno of *Fortunas* as well as Amón of *Los cabellos de Absalón* and the Captain of *El alcalde de Zalamea*. This brutal and violent rape of an innocent young girl produced repercussions beyond the personal horror of that ignominious act. The most understandable, though not justified, reaction in any woman stripped of her dignity is a profound sense of shame. Liríope remained in the mountains to hide herself and her child from the sneers and jeers of the sanctimonious. Calderón understood this human reaction, and the word *vergüenza* echoes through this play and others, such as *El alcalde de Zalamea*. Isabel, the victim of the heedless Captain, repeats this word several times during her soliloquy as she seeks to flee from the light which would reveal the extent of her dishonor and shame. Metaphorically her lines, "de vergüenza cubro el rostro, / de empacho lloro ofendida" (562a), are translated into a reality by Liríope as she seeks to hide her sad story from the world. Céfiro abandoned Liríope, yet he did not fail to provide some way of covering his treachery, for Tiresias was to be her mentor and jailor. Calderón's depiction of cyclical tragedy becomes more evident when we examine this situation. Tiresias, punished by Júpiter with imprisonment in the mountains, assists Céfiro by becoming Liríope's jailor. As death approaches this old magician, he issues a prophecy for the child Liríope is about to bear, which serves as a powerful restraint on her freedom. With the birth of the child, Liríope in turn becomes the jailor of her son and thus the guardian of her shame and Céfiro's perfidy. The wrenching of her freedom from Liríope contributes to her ill-advised treatment of Narciso, now a prisoner just as his mother surely was and remains.

We should underscore at this point the duality of reaction produced by rape. For the woman, shame is dominant, so much so that it can produce some bizarre courses of action, from outright denial to justifiable fury. But on the part of the male the rejection of the woman he has raped is predominant. Rape brings to the fore those feelings of contempt and disgust that characterize the rapist's attitude toward women. Liríope's shame is so great, moreover, that she cannot denominate its source as rape. Neither can Isabel of *Alcalde*. What links Perseo to the sufferings of raped women is his inability to say "violación" as he swares to avenge his mother (1656a).

It is ironic that as part of the joyous festivities in honor of Eco's birthday, Anteo captures this mountain dweller Liríope and returns her to the valley and its light. This situation is doubly ironic because in mythology Anteo is the son of the Earth, and it appears that the earth's forces are joined in an effort to force Liríope to face squarely her shame and the brutal reality of her response to it. Everett W. Hesee has written at length about the question of Liríope's responsibility for the strange upbringing of Narciso, and he finds the dominant mother, the "terrible-mother image," to be the play's lesson for modern readers.[4] I find his treatment of Liríope to be incomplete. The precipitating action of this tragedy, as in many Calderonian tragedies, involves the violent rape of a woman. Moreover, where is the father who shared in the procreation of this boy? Before we can adequately understand Narciso's plight, I believe that we must come to grips with Liríope's. She puts her finger squarely on the point when she rejects Céfiro's attempt to justify his actions "honestando la traición / con la disculpa civil / de amor" (1914a). Narciso is a child of violence, not of love, and this violence, perpetrated on an unsuspecting and innocent woman, molds her and her offspring.

Liríope, a young girl of perhaps thirteen years, alone on a remote mountain top, chose to live in seclusion with a child forced upon her by a vicious and frightening rape. She brings the boy up in almost total ignorance. Calderón examined in many plays, particularly in *La vida es sueño*, the question of the education of children, and in each we encounter a complex motivational pattern. In *Eco y Narciso* we find shame and fear intertwined with love and care. This mother sets a goal which we may find absurd: to bring up her child in almost total ignorance of the world in which he lives. Moreover, she sets up what the Greeks would call an *eidolon*, or a phantom reality—a phantom house, or a seeming home, in which Narciso will have no female contact save her own. She fails miserably to avert her son's fate, for in Calderonian drama, only with knowledge and love may a character overcome ignorance and hostile fate, and only with freedom and experience may one conquer the forces opposed to life. Liríope abuses her authority with the limiting and restricting education she provides for Narciso, and his lack of experience and inability to reason properly will lead to his undoing.

Indeed, she may be seen as the source of Narciso's tragedy, for she is, in many ways, a lamia, a destroyer, robber of children, and man destroyer.[5] But such a unidimensional view reinforces misogynous tendencies rather than examines the details of *Eco*. Like Oedipus or Basilio of *Vida*, Liríope fulfills her son's fate by attempting to run from it or to control it. In this process she relies on the magician's arts rather than on knowledge and love. When Liríope says "aprovechémonos, pues, / del saber" (1930b), she is calling upon her past experience to deal with the present crisis. Victimized by Tiresias's arrogant "saber," she judges and interprets the *vaticinio* to refer exclusively to Eco (1930b). Liríope, confident in her knowledge and magical powers, is tragically led into error by her fears and imperfect knowledge. Her interpretation of the *vaticinio* is faulty, though her motives are good. We are truly in the world of tragedy when every action taken on her part appears to seal more securely the fate of her son.

Narciso's Fate

Tiresias, the seer and magician, discloses to Liríope what his studies indicate her child's fate to be:

> En cinta estás. Un garzón
> bellísimo has de parir.
> Una voz y una hermosura
> solicitarán su fin
> amando y aborreciendo.

Guárdale de ver y oír.

(1914b)

This prophetic utterance includes Tiresias's advice to Liríope: "Guárdale de ver y oír." It is tempting to speculate on what would have happened to Narciso without this pronouncement. Tiresias, a learned man, urges Liríope to do precisely what she did: to bring up Narciso in such a way as to hinder his opportunity to see and hear, in other words, to restrict his natural development. Once the prophecy is seen in this light, and once we understand Liríope's response to it, she seems to be less "terrible" than before.

Liríope's response to Tiresias's prophecy is motivationally complex. In the birth of Narciso and in his great beauty, she finds a firm indication of the *vaticinio's* misleading truth. As always, Calderón underscores the role of interpretation in relation to the manner in which the prophecy will eventually be fulfilled. This concerned mother interprets the adivination to mean that external forces will threaten her son with doom, so she "logically" sets out to cut him off from all that could be considered potentially injurious. Liríope molds her son not through love, as is the case in normal child-rearing situations, but through love and fear. She describes her parenting technique as follows:

> criándole, sin que llegase
> a saber ni discurrir
> más de lo que quise yo
> que él alcanzase, y en fin,
> sin que otra persona viese
> humana, sino es a mí.

(1914b)

Tiresias states Narciso's fate in a most curious fashion: a voice and a beauty will seek his demise loving and hating. A first reading of this enigmatic prophecy would naturally lead one to suppose that the beauty and the voice would refer to one person's voice and beauty. Most commentators have interpreted the prophecy in this manner. But the *desenlace* of the play demonstrates that the voice referred to is Eco's, for she loves Narciso up to the moment of her death; her frustrated love spells her death. The beauty referred to is Narciso's, for he hates the nymph up to the moment of his death. In the disharmonious process of loving himself and hating Eco, Narciso falls victim to suicidal self-love just as Eco consumes herself in suicidal self-hate. Instead of viewing the prophecy as a potential warning against destructive forces we all carry within our being, Liríope sees it exclusively as an admonition against external sexual influences to which we are all subject. Liríope's past experience has affected her judgment and dictates her present course of action. Narciso will, in her fondest hopes, not turn out to be like his father nor like his mother, neither victimizer nor victim. Ironically he turns out to be like both.

To prevent Narciso's perdition, Liríope destroys Eco's voice, thus causing, in her thinking, the nymph's beauty to be imperfect and less seductive for Narciso. She destroys Eco as a whole person and thereby ultimately prevents the nymph from revealing to Narciso in a timely fashion that the image reflected in the pool is his own. Though Liríope eventually recognizes her part in Narciso's death (1938b and 1940b), she never realizes that her son's salvation lay precisely in his being able to go out of himself, in being able to extricate himself from the death-in-life condition of his upbringing and its narcissism. If Narciso could have continued to relate positively to the world and to love's promptings, he would not now be dead.

Marilyn DiSalvo elaborates on Narcissus's love instinct, an infantile mode of love, as follows:

In his *figurae*, Ovid presents the love instinct itself, transformed and distorted through myriad metamorphoses. In Narcissus, we see the most archaic shape of love, yearning to blossom, to find an object apart from itself, and the agony and rage which result from failure. We see how the urge to love, cut off from a real object, creates in its loneliness a fantasy reality so beautiful and so vivid that it eclipses the reality of the natural world.[6]

This love instinct is in itself naturally good and leads Narciso to his encounter with Eco. The youth is attracted by the shepherds' music that forcefully stirs him, but Liríope's fear of the prophecy blocks his natural inclination to follow their melodious accents: "porque los hados han puesto / tu mayor peligro en ellas [voces]" (1908b). As Narciso hears Eco's voice, he is profoundly affected by it. Only when both mother and son are brought from the mountains to the valley, does Liríope fully inform Narciso of his fate, a process begun in Act I (1909b) and completed in Act II. Narciso responds to what his mother has just revealed thus: "en la memoria lo tengo / y en el corazón escrito" (1920b). He summarizes his birth and upbringing as follows:

> todo para en que yo tengo
> en las estrellas previsto
> que una voz y una hermosura,
> con dos efectos distintos,
> amando y aborreciendo,
> son mis mayores peligros.
>
> (1920b)

For him, as for Liríope, the voice and beauty belong to Eco, since she has stirred Narciso's passion. Being an obedient child, he follows his mother's advice and flees from the young woman:

> Como habiendo sido
> una voz y una hermosura
> mis dos mayores peligros,
> y concurriendo en ti entrambos,
> el huir de ti es preciso;
> que es un encanto tu voz
> y tu hermosura un hechizo.
>
> (1922b)

Only too late in the play, when the destructive forces are already at work, does Liríope recognize that Eco's beauty and voice, offered in love, presented no threat to her son. The beauty alluded to in the prophecy referred to Narciso's great physical beauty, and the voice, to Eco's melodious and captivating song:

> ¡Oh qué en vano los mortales
> quieren entender al cielo!
> todos los medios que puse
> para estorbar los empeños
> hoy de su destino, han sido
> facilitarlos más presto;
> pues la voz de Eco la aflige,
> y por venir de ella huyendo,
> muerte le da su hermosura:
> con que ya cumplido veo
> que hermosura y voz le matan
> amando y aborreciendo.
>
> (1938b)

Liríope fully understands that her son's fate was not determined by powers and influences outside himself, but by the confluence of external and internal factors. She reminds us that one's destiny is not isolated from that of others but rather intertwined like the individual strands that go to make up one cord. What Tiresias did not read in the stars was the fact that two deaths were implicated in the events we witness on stage. Together, Eco and Narciso would have found true love and a fulfilled life like Perseo and Andrómeda. But alone, Eco could only lament her isolation and rage against her unfulfilled love, ultimately hating herself because of it. Narciso, whose passion created a beautiful illusion of the other, could only discover himself in his futile surrender to an unresponsive phantom, a self-giving that ultimately produces radical alienation. Both conditions lead to death. Eco and Narciso could have found life only in each other; but this mutual dependency was not revealed in the stars, or Tiresias was truly blind in not discovering it along side the fateful words that doomed Narciso, and implicitly Eco too.

The Problem of Identity: Narciso as Tragic Figure

Eco y Narciso dramatizes how the pathetic attempts of a fearful and lonely woman to isolate her son from the world create the conditions for his destruction. From the very first, Narciso seeks to find out who he is and why he is brought up in this harsh fashion. The theme of *¿quién es?* underscores Narciso's search for identity throughout the play, and its repetition, from his first appearance to the discovery of the identity of the image reflected in the pool, highlights the importance of self-knowledge in the process of survival. Narciso is doubly a prisoner, living in ignorance of himself and of his world. He thirsts for knowledge and experience, but is constantly thwarted until finally his mother realizes that he no longer can be put off. At this point Anteo, who has come to the mountains in search of the monster, carries Liríope off to the valley. On hearing Liríope's woeful story, the Arcadians, accompanied by music and song, set out for the mountains in search of Narciso. This confused lad is moved by their joyous music, and Eco's voice attracts him. These elements lead him to an encounter with Eco, a tender moment in which two young people are naturally and beautifully drawn together. The situation reflects again the theme of *¿quién es?* for Narciso asks this very question of Eco, who replies: "Una mujer" (1918a). Narciso's natural and healthy inclinations, which lead to wholeness and love, come to the fore. Such affection normally leads to a love that draws one out of oneself. But when Liríope's brusk intervention forecloses on this love, Narciso's inchoate growth stops. In fact Calderón describes how negative forces have once more been set in motion.

In Act II (1920b) Liríope admonishes her son to *guardarse* and to *vencerse* in Act III (1930b), and Narciso ultimately follows her advice by rejecting Eco and her love as the source of his doom. But his nature keeps drawing him back to the nymph with an irresistible force that he does not understand. In Eco he too believes he has found the *voz* and the *hermosura* of the prophecy (1922b), but fails to perceive that they are joined in love, a love freely offered to him. Eco overcomes her natural embarrassment at having been rejected by this beautiful youth in offering herself in marriage, only to be rejected again. This is one of the most remarkable scenes in Golden-Age theater. Suppressing her natural shame, Eco confesses in song her love of the beautiful youth:

> Eco soy, la más rica
> pastora de estos valles;
> bella decir pudieran
> mis infelicidades.

> (1925a)

Boldly she speaks to Narciso: "Todo a tus pies lo ofrezco" (1925b), but only in marriage. Her declaration of love is tender, profoundly moving in its intensity.

Prophetically she avers that, if rejected, "Eco enamorada" will be converted into air.

In Act III, nature almost triumphs as Narciso is drawn by Eco's voice to be what he is, a youth in search of love. Liríope's intervention here is decisive, for she forcefully restrains her son from responding to the plight of the scorned nymph. Rejecting a love which induces one to go outside of oneself and relate to the other, Narciso symbolically turns within searching for the affection he cannot find any other way. Before encountering the pool, Narciso laments, "¡Oh, qué ignorante nací! / ¡Oh, qué necio me crié!" (1932a). When he sees his own image reflected in the pool, he says "'quiérote como a mí'"(1932b). But as Eco is about to inform Narciso of his mistake, Liríope's poison takes away her voice. Communication is brutally truncated, knowledge is tragically denied Narciso—we witness the alienation of a man and a woman who, in other circumstances, would have been made whole by their mutual love. And Narciso, through the silencing of Eco, is denied the discovery of who he is.

The ¿quién es? theme now takes a curious twist, for Narciso wants to know the image's identity. Narciso cannot recognize himself in the visage reflected in the pool. He does not know who or what he is. When Liríope at last informs him that he has fallen in love with his own self-image, calling this act "tu amor locura" (1938a), he recognizes that the prophecy has been fulfilled: "'muero / aborreciendo y amando'" (1938b). Self-love has brought about his ruin.

While Narciso and Segismundo of *Vida* share feelings of estrangement and derealization, their stories are vastly different. Segismundo exhibits the "normal" schizoid reaction to threatening experiences, whereas in Narciso's case the schizoid reaction becomes the abiding mode of his being-in-the-world.[7] Narciso's isolation in the mountains is a symbol of his alienation from others, especially from those of the other sex. The schizoid individual is "self-conscious," and as such "he turns the other person into a thing, and depersonalizes or objectifies his own feelings toward this thing, or he affects indifference.... The depersonalized person can be used, manipulated, acted upon" (Laing, p. 79). Without knowing who he is, Narciso is incapable of recognizing Eco as another person; without experience of how men are to act in the world, he is also incapable of relating to her as a woman. After his mother's capture by Anteo, Narciso, alone in the world, laments his plight, exclaiming:

> ¡Ay de mí!
> ¡Qué he de hacer sin ti en aquestas
> montañas solo, ignorando
> quién soy, y qué modo tengan
> de vivir los hombres, pues

nada sino a hablar me enseñas?

(1911a)

In short, Narciso's upbringing contributes to his schizoid state, the result of a precariously structured personality whose hallmark is its insecurity. Narciso's love of his own self is the symbol of his withdrawal into a self threatened by the outside world. Laing has commented on this situation: "But the tragic paradox is that the more the self is defended in this way, the more it is destroyed" (pp. 80-81). That is why Narciso's desired union with his other "self" is a union that signals death, that symbolizes the derealization of Narciso in schizophrenia.

Eco and Narciso: Mutual Destruction

As Narciso's case depicts the destruction wrought by self-centered love, Eco's will reveal the damage produced by love's rejection. From the start we are made aware of her great beauty, often the portent of misfortune, as in Liríope's case: "que no vio el sol / una hermosura feliz" (1913a). Early on in Act II, Eco sings prophetically about her own particular doom:

> Solo el silencio testigo
> ha de ser de mi tormento,
> y aun no cabe lo que siento
> en todo lo que no digo.

(1917b)

Silivo, one of the shepherds seeking her hand in marriage, further heightens the aura of doom surrounding her with his curse: "que de quien amas te veas / quejosa y aborrecida!" (1923b). Some feel that there is poetic justice in Eco's frustrated love precisely because of her previous rejection of Silvio and Febo.[8] Eco and Narciso play a much more significant part in Calderón's view of the tragic nature of this world, for both characters seem destined to die frustrated in their search for love and happiness. Eco phrases it well when she says that "vienen a ser nueva historia / del mundo Narciso y Eco" (1919a). This "new history" involves Calderón's original interpretation of the myth, one which clearly manifests the two fundamental ways in which human beings destroy themselves. Eco's manner is fairly obvious: she suffers profoundly from Narciso's rejection of her and is thrown into paroxysms of jealousy. Fleeing from all, less a person than before with the loss of *her ability to communicate*, she declares a rabid self hate that leads her to suicide: "que yo, de mí aborrecida, / de mí en mí vengarme intento" (1939b). Narciso dies loving himself: "que yo, de mí enamorado, / moriré de mi amor mesmo" (1939b): but the manner of his death also involves suicide. Calderón appears to have intuited what modern psychoanalysis has just come to fathom, that is, that "self-love" is a masked form of self-hate.[9] *Eco y Narciso* ends with the suicide of both principal characters, suggesting that the end of "self-love" and self-hate is the same: self-destruction. However, Narciso's fate is not isolated in the terms of its fulfilment, for it involves his mother, and it also brings about the tragic doom of Eco. Calderón shows that their fates are mutually dependent.

The Gracioso's Last Words

At the play's close the *gracioso* seems to undermine the serious nature of the action by remarking:

> ¡Y habrá bobos que lo crean!
> Mas sea cierto o no sea cierto,
> tal cual la fábula es
> esta de *Narciso y Eco*.
>
> (1940b)

This comment follows immediately after the metamorphosis of Narciso into a flower, and in that context its scope is limited to that metamorphosis. It undercuts the mitigating effect of that transformation by revealing its problematic and illusory nature. The powerfully visual nature of the scene could lead to one's forgetting that the action depicted was tragic and that its message, though found in traditional material from the pagan past, nonetheless possessed universal validity.[10] This more restricted view would appear to be in accord with a similar but more straightforward statement found at the end of *El hijo del Sol, Faetón*, given 1 March 1661 in the Buen Retiro:

> Con que los bobos
> lo creerán, y los discretos
> sacarán cuán peligroso
> es desvanecerse, dando
> fin *Faetón, hijo de Apolo*.
>
> (1902b)

Performed four months before *Eco y Narciso*, *El Faetonte* reveals in these departing remarks the antagonistic relationship between the material and its message, between the poet and his medium. By indicating this relationship, Calderón warns us not to be so foolish as to accept a literal interpretation of the myth, for myth, by its very nature, requires symbolic thinking. Narciso was conceived in violence, and this violence led to his undoing. No matter how brilliant the concluding metamorphosis, we cannot escape the fact that, in Panofsky's words, "the birth of a beautiful flower signifies the death of a beautiful human being" (p. 244).

The Social Context of Tragedy

Eco y Narciso is not a realistic work, nor was it ever intended to be one. For Calderón's audience, accustomed to his allegorical *autos*, the point need not be belabored, but it should be emphasized for a modern audience. Narciso is not Everyman, though he could stand for many a man and woman caught up in the egocentricity of contemporary living. Narciso's tragedy is a poignant portrayal of his frustrated search for wholeness. Narciso's and Eco's searches ended with their defeat by the forces of divisiveness that they carried within their very beings as well as by those constantly at work in the world. More-over, Calderón underscores the social context of their tragedy, for in Narciso's fate, Eco's was intertwined.

"No man is an island, entire of itself;" we are inevitably affected by what others do, just as we influence those with whom we come in contact, both directly and indirectly.[11] Céfiro set in motion the destructive forces which directly impinged on Liríope and then indirectly on Narciso and Eco. We witness the efforts of many to make their wills the hub of the universe, into which all is channeled and from which all flows. Egocentricity is at the heart of Calderón's tragic world, and *Eco y Narciso* places his insight in a universally valid context. Tirso de Molina conveyed a similar truth in his magnificent *El condenado por desconfiado*, where Enrico and Paulo begin the play as remarkably similar characters in their egocentricity, though divergent in outward appearance. Paulo is completely given to himself, whereas Enrico has one positive force moving him outwardly, the love of his father. Paulo never overcomes the negativism of his self-centeredness and thus falls easy victim to the devil's wiles. Enrico, on the other hand, moved by the love of his father, is capable of rejecting his self-centeredness and placing God as his first concern. Though *Eco y Narciso* does not incorporate this theological dimension, it proceeds from a similar awareness of the interplay of love, wholeness, and completion on the one hand, and egocentricity, scission and destruction on the other. *Eco y Narciso* is a tragedy of love's failure, and Calderón has seen fit to repeat this failure under various guises in many of his plays. What this work stresses with particular insistence is how the destinies of Eco and Narciso were bound as in one knot: "pues ruina de entrambos fueron / una voz y una hermosura" (1940b).

Narciso's and Eco's Rites of Passage

Pérez de Moya writes of Tiresias's prophecy in terms different from those used in *Eco y Narciso*: "dijo que sería hermoso y que tendría larga vida si se conociese" (II, 262). While Calderón does not follow the moralizing interpretation of Narciso as a vainglorious and presumptuous youth whose self-love causes his perdition, he does dramatize the implications of the absence of self-knowledge for those who fail to reach out and to love. The paradox of love is that only in loving another can one truly know oneself. DiSalvo explains this point as follows:

Authentic self-knowledge requires experience of, and reflection of, a tangible reality clearly distinguished from the self; just as love, if it is to be healing, not deadly, requires the experience of a substantial other, and not merely a flattering reflection of an idealized self. In healthy love, the real other becomes a true reflection and guide to self-knowledge. The beloved, as Socrates says to Phaedrus, sees himself in his lover "as in a mirror" (p. 23).

Though Calderón did not choose to express Narciso's fate in terms of self-knowledge, he nonetheless included this aspect as a vital part of his fate. Because Narciso could not love Eco, he never learned who he was. Narciso's narcissism symbolizes his inability to accept love and thereby his failure to rise to a higher level of being. In his personal vacuity lies the source of his psychological suicide. This insight reminds us of the mirror scene in *El príncipe constante*, where Fenix's narcissism prevents her from rising to a higher level of existence through her refusal to recognize Fernando's superior system of values. We find therein a spiritual vacuity.

Narciso is at a crossroads in his life. His encounter with Eco is similar to Perseo's encounter with Andrómeda; both meet Woman as Death—i.e., she represents the death of their infantile and child-like natures as requisite for their rebirth as men, the positive counterpart of the experience as a whole. This passage from child to man represents a discovery of a deeper, more profound knowledge of one's self and one's potential. Perseo's triumph results from his fearless passage from child to man; Woman as Death is only the negative side of his rite of passage to fuller being-in-the-world. It broadens his sphere of activity as he becomes a full-fledged member of the community which he saves. Narciso's tragedy, on the other hand, results from his fear of fate and his refusal to undertake the journey from childhood to manhood; for him Woman as Death becomes a terrible image of his failure in his rite of passage, for without growth there is no stagnation, only death.[12] For this reason he cannot be integrated into Arcadian society.

Similarly, Eco's tragedy is linked to another rite of passage. To the extent that woman represents the death of the boy's infantile nature, so too man represents the death of the girl's child-like nature. Hathorn observes that "To the female even more than to the male the loss of virginity means the passing away of a former life of simplicity and its replacement by a life of potential motherhood. So to every female the male is an agent of death" (p. 99). In Act II Eco's offer of herself in marriage to Narciso is a most remarkable scene. She is conscious of the implications of her words, and for this very reason she says: "Amor sabe con cuánta / vergüenza llego a hablarte" (1925a). For Andrómeda, Perseo was an Agent of Death, negatively the agent of her loss of innocence and virginity, and positively the agent of the full flowering of her womanhood into motherhood. Their descendants were called the Persides, one of whom was to be Heracles, the greatest hero of all Greece.[13] But for Eco, Narciso ceases to be a symbolic Agent of Death, becoming instead a terrible image of failure in her rite of passage. Narciso's rejection of her, not once but several times, frustrates what would have been under normal circumstances an easy transition to a new and fuller being-in-the-world.

Conclusion

The metamorphoses that conclude the play are not so much spectacular symbols of altered natures as they are brilliant reminders of Eco's and Narciso's tragedy. Nature responds to their deaths by casting a somber shadow over all: "En cuyas obsequias hacen / cielo y tierra sentimiento" (1940a-b). Neither has passed to a higher state of being; neither has entered into full participation in Arcadia's communal life. The echo and flower symbolize their solitude and their loss.

Eco y Narciso is the negative version of the dramatic world depicted in *Fortunas de Andrómeda y Perseo*. Through these works which contrast the paths open to and the consequences resulting from rites of passage, we become more cognizant of this significant period in everyone's life. For on the outcome depend who we are and what we shall become. For Perseo love represents the healing of past wounds, the promise of present happiness, and the guarantee of future fame. For Narciso, on the other hand, love rejected opens past wounds, thwarts present happiness, and ensures a tragic issue. There are only two paths coming out of the rite of passage: one leads to wholeness and life, while the other, to imperfection and death.

Notes

1 The text of *Eco y Narciso* employed is that of the Valbuena Briones edition, cited above, pp. 1903-40.

2 The valley, with its pastoral life, represents the hopes and dreams of civilization. The mountains, with their wildness, represent the threats posed by uncontrolled nature. In *As I Lay Dying*, William Faulkner writes about circumstances similar to those found in *Eco*: "Life was created in the valleys. It blew up onto the hills on the old terrors, the old lusts, the old despairs. That's why you must walk up the hills so you can ride down." Quoted from *William Faulkner, Eugene O'Neill, John Steinbeck* (New York and Del Mar, California: Alexis Gregory and CRM Publishing, 1971), p. 92. This section, as well as many of those that follow, first appeared in outline form in my article "On Love and the Human Condition: A Prolegomenon to Calderón's Mythological Plays," *Calderón de la Barca at the Tercentenary: Comparative Views* (Lubbock, TX: Texas Tech P, 1982), pp. 119-34.

3 See Erwin Panofsky, "*Et in Arcadia ego*: On the Conception of Transience in Poussin and Watteau," in *Philosophy and History: Essays Presented to Ernst Cassirer*

(Oxford: Clarendon P, 1936), pp. 223-54, for the importance of Arcadia as the setting for the play's action and of the principle of metamorphosis.

4 See Everett W. Hesse, "The 'Terrible Mother' Image in Calderón's *Eco y Narciso*," *Romance Notes*, 1, No. 2 (1960), 1-4 and "Estructura e interpretación de una comedia de Calderón: *Eco y Narciso*," *Boletín de la Biblioteca de Menéndez Pelayo*, 39 (1963), 61-76. See also Stephen H. Lipmann, "Sobre las interpolaciones en *Eco y Narciso* de 1674," *Segismundo* 27-32 (1978-80), 181-93.

5 See Carl G. Jung's comments in *Symbols of Transformation: An Analysis of the Prelude to a Case of Schizophrenia*, Bollingen Series XX, tr. R. F. C. Hull (New York: Pantheon Books, 1956), p. 298: "The young, growing part of the personality, if prevented from living or kept in check, generates fear and changes into fear. The fear seems to come from the mother, but actually it is the deadly fear of the instinctive, unconscious, inner man who is cut off from life by the continual shrinking back from reality. If the mother is felt as the obstacle, she then becomes the vengeful pursuer. Naturally it is not the real mother, although she too may seriously injure her child by the morbid tenderness with which she pursues it into adult life, thus prolonging the infantile attitude beyond the proper time. It is rather the mother-imago that has turned into a lamia."

6 "The Myth of Narcissus," *Semiotica*, Special Issue "Signs About Signs: The Semiotics of Self-Reference," 30-1/2 (1980), 22-23.

7 See Ronald D. Laing, pp. 82-83.

8 See William R. Blue, "Dualities in Calderón's *Eco y Narciso*," *Revista Hispánica Moderna*, 39, No. 3 (1976-77), 116.

9 See Shirley Sugerman, *Sin and Madness: Studies in Narcissism* (Philadelphia: Westminster P, 1976), and Ronald D. Laing, *The Divided Self*.

10 For some interesting, though different, perspectives on the dramatic nature of *Eco y Narciso*, see *Eco y Narciso*, ed. Charles V. Aubrun (Paris, 1961 and 1963), and Pierre Groult's review in *Lettres Romanes*, 16 (1962), 103-13. See also Aubrun's "*Eco y Narciso*," *Homenaje a William L. Fichter*, eds. A. David Kossoff and José Amor y Vázquez (Madrid: Castalia, 1971), pp. 47-58, and Edmond Cros's "Paganisme et Christianisme dans *Eco y Narciso* de Calderón," *Revue des Langes Romanes*, 75 (1962), 39-74. In *The Development of Imagery*, Blue examines the play (pp. 163-71). Cascardi's analysis (pp. 130-41) has little new to say about it, and in fact he considers the play to be more lyric than dramatic.

11 See A. A. Parker, "Towards a Definition of Calderonian Tragedy," *Bulletin of Hispanic Studies*, 39 (1962), 227-37.

12 Sugerman notes that "Narcissistic disturbances are seen to be the response to the poisonous, destructive containment of negative feelings related to frustrating maturational factors, rather than repressed sexual feelings associated with the oedipal disorders" (p. 140). Narciso's tragedy is not so much due to the repression of sexual feelings and desires as to the violent repression of natural maturative processes. And only in this latter regard are we able to speak of sexual repercussions to the process as a whole.

13 See Jay Williams, *Medusa's Head* (New York: Random House, 1960), p. 53.

VI   Myths of Masculine Power: Domination and Violence

A. El laurel de Apolo

> Dafne. Fuera de que si al Amor
> vencer, Apolo, pretendes,
> no se vence Amor amando.
> Apolo. ¡Ay, que ya no es amor este!
>
> (1756b)[1]

There is a great deal of confusion surrounding the text and first performance of *El laurel de Apolo*, which leads one to mistrust the texts commonly available for our perusal. There were two important state performances of the play: the first took place on 4 March 1658 in the Real Coliseo of the Buen Retiro to celebrate the birth of Felipe IV and Mariana de Austria's son, Felipe Próspero, which took place on 20 November 1657. The second performance celebrated the name day of King Carlos II, and we have no information as to the year of this performance.[2] As a result of these separate performances, there are two distinct dramatic texts. Whereas the Valbuena Briones edition has eliminated the *loa* to the 1658 performance, it includes the *fin de fiesta* that celebrated Carlos II's name day. Other texts include both the *loa* and *fin de fiesta*, bearing witness thereby to the recycling of dramatic texts.[3] In addition to problems involving the *loa*, *fin de fiesta*, emendations, accretions, and deletions of portions of the text, at times entire scenes are dropped or added.[4] We need be wary of the text consulted, for it may incline us to a view of the play that may be inadequate.

The *loa* is missing from the standard version of the play in spite of the fact that it forms an integral part of the performance text. Valbuena Briones most likely eliminated the *loa* due to the textual disharmony resultant from allusions in the *loa* to Felipe Próspero and in the *fin de fiesta* to Carlos II. The *loa* begins as follows:

> Todos hoy se alegren, pues
> hoy, con *próspero* arrebol,
> para todos nace el sol.
>
> (188a; emphasis added)[5]

In turn the continents of Asia, Africa, America, and Europe, represented by a troop of Spaniards, pay obeisance to the infant prince. What began as a joyous courtly celebration of the birth of an heir, now turns into a hybrid celebration as the *pueblo*, represented by the rustic personage Zarzuela, joins the festivities. In unmannerly style, she explains her strange presence in the

Retiro:

> no sé qué aldeana fiesta,
> que tenía prevenida,
> viendo las carnestolendas
> tan dentro de casa ya,
> o tarde o temprano sea,
> por no esperar a otro año,
> obligándome grosera
> a desear no sea lo mismo,
> vengo al Retiro con ella;
> y aunque pese a todo el mundo,
> pardiez que tengo de hacerla.

(191r)

The text underscores the discordant tension of this particular *fiesta de zar-zuela*, rustic entertainment suddenly transferred to the regal Retiro, a hybrid-ization that will be reflected in all other areas of the dramatic action.

Zarzuela now proceeds to criticize the "señas / de idólatras, ni gentiles / ritos" (191r) due to the fact that Felipe Próspero

> Católico Príncipe es
> el que nace a ser defensa
> de la cristiana milicia.

(191r)

While such emphasis on duty routinely appears in court theater, it correlates well the prince's duty to the action of the play proper, for Fitón is described as issuing from a divine punishment of the people's neglect of the worship due to Apolo and Venus. They were led away from their religious duty by the magi-cian Fitón, who, through his "diabólicas ciencias" (1742b), mesmerized the *pueblo*. The allusion to heresy requires no further comment, but the reminder that a prince should be a Defender of the Faith underscores again the serious responsibilities of the ruler.

Zarzuela's intervention primarily stresses, however, the novelty of the dra-matic form to be presented:

> No es comedia, sino sólo
> una fábula pequeña
> en que a imitación de Italia
> se canta y se representa;
> que allí había de servir
> como acaso, sin que tenga
> más nombre que fiesta acaso.

(191r)

The Calderonean *zarzuela* was inaugurated 17 January 1657 with *El golfo de las Sirenas*, and it was truly an experiment combining music and declamation that would eventually evolve into the operas *La púrpura de la rosa* and *Celos, aun del aire, matan*. In both *zarzuelas* and *óperas* the role of music and dance was stressed, leading to the dramatic text's apparent "devaluation." These *zarzuelas'* consciousness of themselves as innovations in court theater did not preclude a more ironic view of these very same efforts. What suffuses *Laurel* is its ironic tone, a tongue-in-cheek attitude that masks the text's exposure as a novelty. The ironic stance is in fact a defense mechanism by which the text asserts its difference at the same time as it acknowledges its hesitancy to full commitment.

El laurel de Apolo is not great drama though its significance as an experiment in musical theater should be acknowledged. We encounter familiar motifs such as the love-hate dynamic, the offense-vengeance mechanism, the importance of jealousy as an antivital force, the role of fate and prophetic dreams, the use of force and violence against women—all are contained therein, but they lack coherence and conviction. Perhaps this weakness is partly due to the text's inability to claim a unified control of the disparate elements that compose it. The *fiesta* tends more to spectacle than to drama, and its ironic tone, self-consciously acknowledged, betrays the text's lack of confidence.

Nonetheless, Calderón's dramatic genius was able to integrate the play's novelty into the thematics of the mythological story. Bata, the *graciosa*, tells us that one may identify the gods as follows:

> Con tan dulce melodía,
> tan süave consonancia,
> que siempre suena su voz
> como mósica en el alma:
> y así, en oyéndole, que hace
> gorgoritas de garganta,
> cátate dios.

(1747a)

Curiously, as Apolo experiences the debilitating effects of passion, he abandons the grand "operatic" style in his *suasoria* or courting of Dafne in favor of a more hybrid form of declamation and song, characteristic of the *zarzuela*:

> Si me temes
> como a deidad ofendida,
> yo sabré, por complacerte,
> que el estilo de deidad
> con el de mortal se mezcle,
> hablando en ambos estilos.

(1755b)

And when he completely abandons his harmonious song for straight declamation, it is due to the disharmony ruling his very soul:

> ¿Cómo quieres,
> destemplado el corazón,
> que la voz no se destemple?

(1757b)

Ascendant passion strikes at the core of Apolo's being, stripping him of his
god-like bearing and being, as his once harmonious voice is reduced to common prattle, symbolizing the negative effects of lust on his person.

The Dualistic Structure of "El laurel de Apolo"

The *loa* begins in a bimember fashion with Iris's and Eco's celebrations of
the "Felice natal de España" (189v), the birth of Felipe Próspero, and continues with the obeisance of the continents until Zarzuela's arrival. At this
point the piece bifurcates into a rustic celebration of the same event, ending
with traditional allusions to Felipe IV, Mariana de Austria, María Teresa, and
Margarita. On the one hand, there is the elegant and literary portion worthy
of a great court (Retiro), while on the other the rustic celebration–"Con grita
de villanos, suenan dentro instrumentos rústicos" (190v), as the *acotación*
reads–reflects the appropriate atmosphere of an entertainment designed for
the Zarzuela. As Zarzuela, the personification of the rustic palace, says:

> Que venga al Retiro
> también la Zarzuela,
> porque alguien que puede,
> la manda que venga.

(192r)

The *zarzuela* proper continues the dualistic pattern already set by the *loa*.
First there is a courtly dimension to the play, reflected both in terms of structure and language. Céfalo and Silvio have just saved Dafne from Fitón the
horrible serpent. Dafne, who loves Céfalo but disdains Silvio, is at a loss as to
whom this *fineza* belongs:

> dudo cuál primero
> lugar en mi riesgo adquiere,
> quien logra lo que me quiere [Silvio]
> o paga lo que le quiero [Céfalo].

(1741b)

All the action involving Céfalo, Silvio, and Dafne reflects a *certamen poético*,
but *a lo dramático*. In order to resolve this thorny problem, Dafne decides to
request a special *fineza* from each suitor. Céfalo, who has disdained Dafne, is

now to pretend that he ardently loves her. Silvio, who has passionately loved her, is now to feign disdain. Only in this manner will Dafne be able to decide to whom to be thankful for saving her life:

> he de ver quién hace más
> en servicio de una dama,
> quien lo que ama disimula
> o finge lo que no ama.

(1744b)

This courtly atmosphere of a *certamen* dominates much of the action in Act I.[6] Dafne's dilemma revolves around which action that she requests of her suitors, to dissimulate love or hate, is the greater *fineza*, since Silvio has earned her obligation just as Céfalo has earned her gratitude.

The hybridization of the play's structure stands out more clearly as the elevated poetic style contrasts with *Laurel's* rustic atmosphere and remote locale. We are not in some Edenic Paradise, but in an agonistic world similar to that encountered in *Fortunas*, where beasts freely roam devastating both the environment and its inhabitants. Fitón, the greatest of the *fieras* set loose among the wayward populace, ravages Tesalia, and Dafne has just escaped its clutches. At this point the chorus of *zagalas* returns from Venus's temple, concurrently with that of *zagales* from Apolo's, joyously announcing that Amor (Cupid), dressed as a *pastor*, is to be sent by Venus to rid the land of Fitón. Apolo sends word that he himself will undertake the feat disguised as a *cazador*. The agonistic structure of the universe, reflected in the *zarzuela's* dualistic structure, is again underscored. The sinful people's salvation lay securely in their return to the old religious rites at Venus's and Apolo's shrines. But in their very supplications to the gods, another type of plague is let loose among the people, rivalry among the gods themselves. Once more we find ourselves in a masculine world of competition, analogous to that of *Médico*, in which a woman will lose her life so that a masculine sense of honor may be upheld.

There are, therefore, two distinct planes of action that are interrelated in diagram form as follow on p. 124. The nexus between the human and divine planes is Dafne. On the human plane Silvio and Céfalo compete for the honor of having saved Dafne's life. Though they experience opposing emotions of love – disdain (hate), their masculine pride is piqued by Dafne's request that they each exhibit the characteristics of the contrary passion. On the divine plane Amor as a shepherd and Apolo as a hunter both seek the glory of ridding Tesalia of Fitón. But as Apolo disparagingly remarks to Amor, "Porque no sé que se hiciesen / para los montes tus armas" (1748a), he underscores in song a more traditional view of Cupid's field of action:

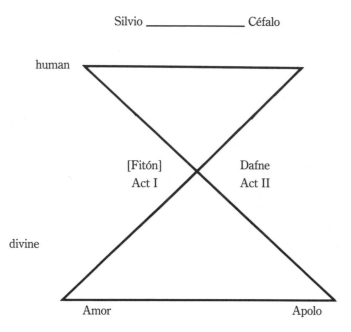

No desdores, Amor,
tu arco y tus flechas;
que es desaire de hermosas
que maten fieras.

(1748a)

To which Amor retorts:

Antes quiero que vean,
sagrado Apolo,
que del Amor las armas
lo rinden todo.

(1748a)

After further taunts from Apolo, Amor observes: "¿Quién habrá, sin ser loco, / que a Amor compita?" (1748a). Thus when Amor runs from the sight of Fitón, dropping both bow and arrows, and Apolo dispatches the beast, Amor swears vengeance by *using* Dafne as the means of Apolo's downfall. Whereas in *Médico* Mencía was the direct source of rivalry between Gutierre and Enrique, in *Laurel* Dafne becomes the means of Amor's vengeance on Apolo, for as the former states: "que no son brutos triunfos para mí" (1751a).

Furthering the dualistic structure of *Laurel*, comic scenes tend to alternate with more serious ones. We also acclimate ourselves to the alternation of declaimed verse, principally at the hands of the human personages, with the free recitatif associated with the gods. Every aspect of the play manifests a bimember nature, reflecting the discord at the heart of this universe that has not matured into *concordia discors*.

Vengeance: The Reflex Passion

Tesalia is a world suffused with unresolved problems, at whose heart lies what I have called the offense-vengeance mechanism. The cyclical nature of this reflex passion mirrors the cyclical nature of time that undergirds the *zarzuela* and its dramatic world. In Act I Dafne narrates the pre-dramatic action that created the conditions the characters now must confront. As has been mentioned earlier, Fitón the magician led the people away from their traditional religious rites, celebrated at the temples of Venus and Apolo, through his dazzling use of "diabólicas ciencias" (1742b). The gods punished the inhabitants of Tesalia with damaging floods. The people quickly repented their heresy and killed Fitón. But fickle as the *pueblo* is wont to be, they soon missed the magician's arts and complained of his loss rather than amend their faults. A second punishment by the gods descended on Tesalia in the form of "inmundos monstruos" (1743a), the most frightening and terrible of which was a serpent who took up residence in Fitón's cave. Superstition led the people to call it Fitón's ghost. Thus we have the situation in which an offense leads to vengeful punishment of the offending party, a pattern characteristic of Calderonian drama.

Towards the end of Act I, Amor flees from Fitón, leaving the field open to Apolo. Once he kills the beast, the people rejoice at their liberation, and the god states:

> y aunque quiso el Amor
> conmigo competir,
> el triunfo ha sido mío.

> (1749b)

But instead of rejoicing in their deliverance from the *fiera*, the people begin to mock and insult Amor:

> Rústico.   ¿qué había de hacer
>   un niño sino huir
>   del coco?

> (1750a)

> Rústico.   dando la *vaya* a Amor,
> y el triunfo a Apolo.
>
> (1750b; emphasis added)

And both Rústico and the *pueblo*, alluding to Amor's "tiritando de temor" (1751a), sing and dance to the following refrain:

> Titirití, que de Apolo es el día,
> titirití, que no del Amor.
>
> (1751a)

Crestfallen and shaken by the turn of events, Amor swears vengeance on Apolo:

> Pues que de celos muero,
> nunca más Amor fui;
> pero de mi venganza
> presto llegará el fin.
>
> (1750b)

The poisonous effects of *celos* are once more set in motion, for, though Apolo has vanquished the serpent Fitón, there are greater and more terrible beasts to be conquered, as Dafne reminds him:

> si el Amor ofendido
> contagio del aire ha sido,
> advierte que a tu poder
> mayor monstruo que vencer
> le queda que el que ha vencido.
>
> (1752a; text altered)

Amor's vengeance follows the traditional lines of the Daphne-Apollo myth. The god of love prepares opposing shafts, the gilded arrow of love for Apolo and the leaden arrow of hate for Dafne. This action takes place within a larger scheme in which characters from the *loa* appear to side with the competing deities: 1) Eco and her chorus of love appear to chant "Amor"; 2) Iris and her chorus of forgetfulness arrive to chant in counterpoint "Olvido" (1752b-1753). Amor's designs are to demonstrate "que no son brutos triunfo para mí" (1751a). Amor's vengeance forms part of a larger pattern that exists in function of corresponding dualities: 1. First of all, Eco and Iris with their choruses chant in counterpoint "Amor" and "Olvido." 2. The fundamental opposition continues between Amor and Apolo, with the latter refusing to recognize Amor's powers and providence. 3. Silvio and Céfalo have now reversed roles, since their role-playing has produced the states they set out to feign. Céfalo is now madly and passionately in love with Dafne, his *burlas* having become *veras*. Silvio now experiences the lessons of his feigned hatred of Dafne, having become disdainful of the nymph; once more *burlas* become *veras*. 4. Once Amor has let fly his contradictory shafts, Apolo becomes the *enamorado* at the same time as Dafne becomes *esquiva*. As part of this punishment of Apolo's arrogance, the god progressively descends from singing to mixed singing and declamation to finally straight declamation. 5. In burlesque fashion, Bata, who loved Rústico, now forgets him as the latter experiences the first pangs of passion.

As the *zarzuela* moves towards the metamorphosis of Dafne into a laurel tree, it should be stressed that the opposing emotions induced by Amor's arrows are those of love and hate. Dafne becomes *esquiva*, cold to love's advances. But more importantly, she undergoes a pre-metamorphic change that presages her downfall: she experiences a profound hatred of all things, including herself (1758b). This once passionate nymph, who loved in turn Céfalo and Silvio, now seeks *soledad* like Eco and Narciso. This desire to flee from human company, to be alone with one's suffering, signals her imminent doom.

Apolo, who in Act I felt no desire for the nymph Dafne, becomes an ardent pursuer of her in spite of his proclaimed *blasón* of *olvido*. This most Greek of the Greek gods admits antirational positions that contradict his divine essence. As he courts Dafne the latter points out in song and verse:

> *Que dar un consejo* [olvido] *y sentir que le acepten,*
> *es formar un monstruo de opuestas especies.*
> Fuera de que si al Amor
> vencer, Apolo, pretendes,
> no se vence Amor amando.
>
> (1756b; text altered)

As Apolo ponders this contradiction, he tosses prudence to the wind in his headlong plunge into passion:

> ¡Con mi antídoto me matan!
> ¡Ay de mí infeliz mil veces!
> Gusano de seda he sido.
> Yo me he labrado mi muerte.
> Pero ¿qué importa, qué importa,
> ni que Amor de mí se vengue,
> ni que tú?
>
> (1756b; text altered)

He "reasons" as do the husbands of the honor tragedies once overcome with jealousy and passion, and their illogical behavior is precisely the next fall awaiting him. His *celos* produce Rústico's burlesque transformation into a tree. The god's wild, frenetic vengeance on its branches, on seeing Céfalo's *mote* carved thereupon, contributes to his degradation.

Apolo's *suasoria*, or passionate attempt to woo Dafne, reminds us of Febo's sonnet in *Eco y Narciso* (1920), in which the cyclical nature of time and events is acknowledged. In his arrogance he asserts in declamation and song:

> De este pues círculo entero
> del año soy rey, y de este
> compuesto triunfo de horas,
> días, semanas y meses,
> *el dueño serás, bella Dafne, si quieres*   *Canta*
> *feriarme a tan solo un favor tus desdenes.*
>
> (1756a; text altered)

Her flight from the god ends this first amorous encounter as the *villanos* enter acclaiming:

> ¡Viva Apolo, viva,
> pues solo puede
> vencedor llamarse
> quien al Amor vence!
>
> (1757a)

Frustrated, Apolo chases them away saying:

> que ya es baldón y no aplauso
> el decir que solo puede
> vencedor llamarse
> quien al Amor vence.
>
> (1757a)

At this point Apolo degenerates from the harmony of his beautiful singing to the out-of-tune speech common to mortals (1757b). Passion rules his life as he fully enters into the human world of contradiction symbolized by the dual emotions he experiences:

> no sé cuál más me ofende,
> o el que ama lo que amo,
> o el que lo que amo aborrece.
>
> (1760)

He has suffered a symbolic metamorphosis as he descends into the world defined previously by Céfalo and Silvio, a world of conflicting passions tinctured by *celos*.

The "Zarzuela's" Comic Perspective

Comedy plays a large role in *Laurel*, just as it does in *El golfo de las Sirenas*, and assists us in understanding the extent of Calderón's dramatic experiment in form. As entertainment to be performed in a rustic setting, the Palace of the Zarzuela, it is natural to have the presence of *villanos* stressed.[7] They provide a distancing perspective on the serious action we witness on the stage. The basic ingredient of this form of comedy is the *villanos'* simplicity, often manifested in their distorted speech. In this vein their distortions are disingenuously delightful: Faetón becomes Faraón; Fitón, figón (1745b); Venus, Veras; Apolo, Pollo (1746a); and even Cupido, Escopido (1747b).[8]

At the core of *Laurel's* comedic stance lies a burlesque treatment of the Daphne-Apollo myth, the transformation of Rústico, the *gracioso*, into a tree. Rústico is to spy on Dafne so that Apolo may know who are her suitors; his *celos* comically lead him to the misuse of his divine powers. Even the moment of the metamorphosis is used for the *zarzuela's* ironic comedy:

> ¡Valedme,
> dioses de mi devoción,
> pues que lo sois, Baco y Ceres,
> en este aprieto, en que ya
> mi pie en raíz se convierte.
> Mi pellejo una corteza
> es de la planta a la frente,
> troncos mis brazos y hojas
> mi melena y mi copete!
>
> (1758a)

The scene in which Lauro and Anteo exercise their skills with slings, at the cost of one of Rústico's eyes, and those in which Céfalo and Silvio inscribe their *motes* in his hide-bark—all provide great diversion for the spectator. Even Bata exhibits her two-faced sense of humor on requesting a loan of Apolo's bow and arrows to dispatch *dos dueñas*:

> Y solo pueden
> matar dueñas arpones
> que matan sierpes.
>
> (1757a)

The comic expressions reinforce the ironic perspective that imbues the play.

The Roles of Fate and Prophetic Visions

The Daphne-Apollo myth is tragic especially from the point of view of Daphne. She is the victim caught in the web of masculine competition and rivalry. In the Calderonian framework, and that of the *comedia* too, Dafne's beauty is at the heart of her personal tragedy. Céfalo, who was born more inclined to study than to love, discovered in his "judiciaria astrología"

> que había de venir a ser
> la beldad de una mujer
> su destrucción y la mía. . . .
>
> (1741b)

Though he fled his fate, he eventually was caught up in its announced doom. When he experiences the delirium of love, as does Apolo, all caution is abandoned:

> y pues tu *hermosura* adoro,
> a pesar de aquel temido
> hado, no tras ese fiero
> desdén vayas ofendida;
> que si él [Silvio] finge que te olivda,
> yo no finjo que te quiero.
>
> (1754a; emphasis added)

At the *zarzuela's* conclusion he confesses the truth of the prediction read in the stars:

> pues en mí el hado
> su influjo cumplió inclemente,
> y me ha de costar la vida
> quedar llorando su muerte.
>
> (1762b)

But what was unique in Céfalo's reading of his fate was the *duality* of the destruction awaiting him and Dafne. What Tiresias could not see in *Eco y Narciso*, Céfalo clearly saw but could not avoid in *Laurel*. It is all too patent that the fate of one individual is intertwined with that of another.

Even for the gods chance contains a predicative function reflecting their fates. As Amor boasts of his prowess and determination to kill Fitón, the *villanos'* voices interrupt him prophetically with their cries: "¡Ay qué terror! ¡Qué asombro!" (1748b). Shortly afterward, Amor will flee from the horrible visage of the monster. Indeed there is a ruling presence in these pagan myths that heeds neither god nor man, and Calderón could not entirely eliminate it from his dramatizations.

Once Apolo rids Tesalia of Fitón, the people celebrate their liberation.

Dafne, the daughter of Peneo, is about to crown the god with a garland of jasmine and rose when it suddenly falls from her hands, which are left resting on the god's head. Any *caída* in Calderonian theater bodes ill for the party involved, and Dafne is no exception. Immediately following the garland's fall Dafne explains to Apolo that she saw in a prophetic vision "que otra [guirnalda] de verdes hojas / flechaba contra mí / ardientes rayos" (1750a). Dafne then confronts her impending doom:

> parece que, animado
> tronco, el hado de mí
> va labrando una estatua.
>
> (1750)

Once Amor sends his conflicting shafts into Apolo's and Dafne's hearts, as the former burns with passion and the latter shivers from cold, Dafne remarks:

> Yo, que un pasmo me suspende
> tanto, que me obliga a que
> de aquel presagio me acuerde,
> pues si allí fui vivo tronco,
> muerta estatua aquí.
>
> (1755b)

What characterizes Calderonian tragedy is the absence or ineffectualness of provident intervention in the characters' lives. Céfalo's fate, tied to the beauty of some woman, signals both his and her doom. And she, though cognizant of what awaits her, is totally helpless to avert her death and his suffering.

Love or Lust?

When Dafne commented to Apolo that Amor is not conquered by loving, the god immediately retorted: "¡Ay, que ya no es amor este!" (1756b). This offhanded remark provides us with the proper perspective from which to view his attempted rape of Dafne. First of all, Apolo recognizes that the woman must first lose "estimación" (1760b) in the man's eyes, and Dafne's *desestimación* "facilita / la acción de quien se la atreve." When Dafne flees from the god's advances, she requests Amor to lend her his wings; Apolo only wonders how Amor could frustrate his own purpose. Dafne responds:

> Si atiende
> que es miedo el que a mí me valga,
> para que de ti se vengue.
>
> (1761a)

Apolo then clearly states the new impulse that spurs him to violence:

> Si es venganza tuya, ingrata,
> tu rigor yo he de vencerle,
> triunfando de él y de ti.
>
> (1761a)

He will dominate her, conquer her resistance, and have his way with her. She pleads for the gods' assistance, but Apolo has Iris drown out her cries with the chorus's melodies. Dafne begs Eco to carry her cries to heaven. As Apolo grasps at her, she runs off, begging divine protection against the brutal designs of "un tirano" and "un aleve" (1761b). Apolo now knows that Dafne's disdain is part of Amor's vengeance, and he seeks to conquer them both through rape. Only when she calls on her father, Peneo, reminding him that both his honor and hers are at risk, does she obtain assistance. She prefers death to dishonor. Her metamorphosis into a laurel tree saves her honor, but at a great price. Apolo interprets her deliverance as follows:

> ¡Hados! ¿Qué prodigio es este?
> ¡La beldad que a abrazar iba
> entre mis brazos, convierten
> en yerto tronco los dioses,
> que de su llanto se duelen!
>
> (1761b)

His tender yielding, idolatrous in point of fact, to the perpetual adoration of her beauty, "aun en su cadáver" (1762a), symbolizes a defeat similar to Hércules's at the conclusion of *Fieras afemina Amor*.

Dafne is the innocent victim caught in the web of masculine competition, rivalry, and jealousy. Amor, proud of his triumph over Apolo, acknowledging that his arms have no effect on beasts that feel not the effects of love, declares the significance of the action that has just transpired:

> y para que llegue a verse
> quién triunfa con más ventajas,
> quién más aplausos merece,
> quién vence fieras, o quién
> vence al dios que fieras vence. . . .
>
> (1762a)

Apolo accepts Amor's *baldón*, claiming it to be in fact the "blasón de mis hazañas; / que mi mayor triunfo es este / de saber amar" (1762a). This final scene of the *zarzuela* proper depicts the callous vengeance of Amor and the degradation and lack of insight on Apolo's part. Amor is unconcerned that he has dehumanized Dafne by using her as a means of revenge, thus a violation of the Kantian ethical maxim that persons are always ends. And when Apolo attempts to label an unsuccessful rape as an "hazaña," this self-centered and insensitive god stands before us starkly revealed. Dafne had no real value for either of them, being merely the means of satisfying cruel vengeance or base lust.

The *zarzuela* concludes with an encomium of Carlos II on the occasion of his birthday. Regaining composure, Apolo claims that he knows who is worthy of Dafne's laurel branches—the young King. But Amor once more upstages him by asserting that only he is worthy of bearing the triumphant laurel to the king, due to the fact "que el amor de los vasallos / patrimonio es de los reyes" (1763a). Their petty rivalry continues even after Dafne's death, and the award of her laurel to Carlos II is Amor's second triumph over Apolo.

Conclusion

For Pérez de Moya the myth of Daphne and Apollo celebrates the virtue of chastity (I, 220). Valbuena Briones states that "La moraleja de la obra indica que es más difícil vencerse a sí mismo que vencer un terrible obstáculo externo" (1740b). This view is supported by Dafne's words to Apolo:

> advierte que a tu poder
> mayor monstruo que vencer
> le queda que el que ha vencido.

> (1752a)

Apolo is not able to control his powerful lust, and therefore it becomes a *fiera* that dominates him and sets for him a course he would have otherwise never willingly chosen. But Dafne is perhaps the only principal character to recognize that she had acted foolishly as she observes: "que imprudente / amaba o aborrecía" (1760b). To trifle with amorous passion is to court destruction; but her suffering, death, and metamorphosis into a tree are in no way warranted by her imprudence. In Calderón's dramatic version of the myth, we view two gods, Apolo and Amor, who attempt to dominate others while lacking the knowledge and control of self necessary to act prudently. Amor did not recognize the limits of his powers and arms; Apolo did not realize the force and power of passion. What links them both is their immediate, reflex recourse to the use of violence, and the one who suffers from it is the nymph Dafne.

Though Apolo is not technically a rapist, his actions become explainable only in terms of the words he uses to describe his behavior, words that link him with Júpiter and Neptuno of *Fortunas* and Céfiro of *Eco y Narciso*. His "hazañas" are in fact pure and simple acts of violence; his claim "que mi mayor triunfo es este / de saber amar" (1762a) is fraught with contradiction and blindness. Violence is the sign of his lack of self-domination. Both Amor and Apolo have recourse to violence when they perceive their domination of circumstances and events to be slipping from their grasps. Creon of *Oedipus*

Tyrannus says: "Seek not control...in all things; the control that you did have broke before the end." As Kitto remarked on these lines, "Certainty, and control: both are illusory" (p. 179).

Our *zarzuela* is an innovative attempt at melding drama and music, comedy and serious action into one unified whole. The year before its performance Calderón wrote *El golfo de las Sirenas*, a one act "piscatory eclogue," in which the comic was intensified in the book-end pieces of the performance, the *loa* and *mojiganga*. Though there were still comic scenes in the *zarzuela* itself, serious action predominates. What *Laurel* sets for its goal is to balance the comic and the serious action by means of an internal dynamic that holds the performance together. This hot-cold rhythm unmasks the play's ironic stance, admitting the seriousness of the action that unfolds before us at the same time as it steps back in reflective observation of the process of artistic creation. It is only Calderón's great dramatic artistry that holds together these disparate, and apparently conflictive, forces and in fact transforms them into a dramatic whole. While *Laurel* does not move us powerfully like *Vida* or *Médico*, we come away from our experience of the text with a greater admiration for Calderón's dramatic versatility and artistic control.[9]

Notes

1 The text of *El laurel de Apolo* quoted is the Valbuena Briones edition, cited above, pp. 1739-63.

2 Angeles Cardona Castro, in her article "Función de la música, la voz humana y el baile a través de los textos de *El laurel de Apolo* (*Loa para la zarzuela* y *Zarzuela*) y a través de la loa *La púrpura de la rosa*," *Calderón: Actas*, II, 1080, states that *Laurel* was first performed in December of 1657, but fails to document this assertion.

3 See Everett W. Hesse, "The Two Versions of Calderón's *El laurel de Apolo*," *HR*, 14 (1946), 213-34, for pertinent information on the text's evolution. From a comparison of the 17th-century editions of *Laurel*, it is obvious that the *editio princeps* of 1664 and the spurious '1664' edition of the *Tercera Parte* are both truncated versions of the original text written by Calderón and performed on 4 March 1658. These 1664 editions do not contain the metamorphosis of Dafne into a laurel tree, the climax of both the myth and its dramatization. Though '1664' corrected some faulty passages and errata found in the *editio princeps* of 1664, it printed the amputated version found there. We cannot be certain about the extent to which the 1687 Vera Tassis edition of *Laurel* represents Calderón's revisions rather than Vera's creative editing. One fact, though, remains clear: the 1664 versions of *Laurel*, albeit the earliest versions known of the play, fail to reproduce the climax and denouement of the play. Whether this omission is due to negligence, or to a deliberate moral decision not to print the attempted rape of Dafne by the god Apolo, or to some other unsuspected reason, awaits further investigation. In addition, the original text was published without clear demarcations of the *loa*, the play proper, and the *fin de fiesta*, much in the manner of *El golfo de las Sirenas's* dramatic text, performed on 17 January 1657 and published in the *Cuarta Parte* of 1672. In Vera Tassis's *Tercera Parte, Laurel* was edited for the first time with two acts, though the *loa* was incorporated into the first one and not set apart. The Apontes edi-

tion of 1761, *Tomo Sexto*, and the Kiel edition of 1828, *Tomo Segundo*, follow the Vera Tassis version. A *suelta*, Num. 33, published in "Barcelona. Por Francisco Suria y Burgada, Impresor; calle de la Paja. A costas de la compañia" follows Vera's version. Valbuena Briones's edition basically reproduces the Vera Tassis version, but omits the *loa*. From Vera Tassis's edition on, the *fin de fiesta* that specifically refers to Carlos II has been incorporated into the *segunda jornada*.

4 See Hesse, p. 216, with reference to the two comic scenes involving Rústico and Bata, the slingshot and kindling scenes, the latter of which is not found in the Valbuena Briones edition.

5 The text consulted is that of the *Tercera Parte* of 1664, found in the facsimile edition of D. W. Cruickshank and J. E. Varey (London, 1973).

6 This role-playing aspect of the action reminds us of Amón's request that Tamar assume the role of his beloved in *Los cabellos de Absalón*.

7 See the analysis of *El golfo de las Sirenas*, the first *zarzuela* in the Calderonian corpus, in the chapter that follows.

8 In the latter case, Bata, who pronounced "música" as "mósica" (1747a) is at least consistent in her defamiliarizations.

9 For a comparative study of the sources used by Lope and Calderón in their plays on the Daphne-Apollo myth, see Henry M. Martin, "The Apollo and Daphne Myth as Treated by Lope de Vega and Calderón," *HR*, 1 (1933), 149-60.

B. 1. Los tres mayores prodigios

Jasón. ¡Qué trágico fin tuvieron
de Hércules las alabanzas!

(1589b)[1]

Los tres mayores prodigios is a dramatic experiment that was staged St.
John's Night of 1636 in the patio of the Buen Retiro. The *loa* acknowledges,
and even requests recognition of, its innovative format: "pues a la novedad /
algún aplauso debe" (256v).[2] The nymphs Pales and Flora compete to celebrate this entertainment designed for presentation at night. Pales is the goddess of farmhouses, villas, and country homes, such as Felipe IV's Retiro
palace, where "bucólica Talía / canta en mí rústicamente" (253r); Flora is
responsible for the flowers and fountains which abound in the Retiro's gar-
dens. Night has prepared a *fiesta* involving three of the greatest heroes of
antiquity, Hércules, Teseo, and Jasón. Hércules, in a frenzy, attempts suicide.
His loyal friends Jasón and Teseo restrain him, as he informs them of the
abduction of Deyanira by the centaur Neso. Tormented by the loss of his
beloved wife, Hércules exclaims:

> ved los dos cuán dignamente
> quieren los hados que yo
> me mate y me desespere,
> pues como amante y marido
> lloro esta ofensa dos veces. . . .

(255v)

The action is now set as the three heroes depart in pursuit of Neso and
Deyanira: Jasón searches Asia; Teseo, Europe; and Hércules, Africa. After
one year elapses, they will meet at Mount Oeta in Africa. The three *jornadas*
performed by three different theatrical companies will depict on three separate stages the exotic deeds of the three heroes. Act I could be labelled a
proto-*zarzuela* because it contains all the elements, except free recitatif, that
characterize such works as *El golfo de las Sirenas* and *Laurel*.

At first glance the linking of Jasón and Teseo to Hércules's loss of Deyanira
appears capricious. It must be remembered, however, that Heracles was one
of the Argonauts. Further, Medea's preparation of the poisoned robe for
Jason's proposed new wife Glauce reminds us of Heracles's death on donning
the centaur Nessus's poisoned robe. Jason's treachery and ingratitude also
bring to mind Teseo's betrayal of Ariadna in *Prodigios*. Theseus and Heracles
were at one and the same time rivals and friends: Heracles rescued Theseus
from Hades, whereas Theseus comforted Heracles after the violent death of
Megara and their three children. But what most links Theseus to Heracles is
the memory of Theseus's shame. He abandoned Ariadne on

Naxos because of the shame he thought he would experience among the Athenians on his return with a Cretan bride. In *Prodigios* Hércules experiences both shame and jealousy on appearing in public with his innocent, though in Hércules's eyes "dishonored," wife.[3] Therefore, we are in a world of masculine design, heroic exploits, and petty vanities and egos. What *Prodigios* highlights is the common thread which unites the three stories. Though at first each hero departs to search for Deyanira's abductor, we soon discover that beneath the surface glamor of heroic exploits there lies a turbulent world of human passion and frailty. While the former is normally for public display and consumption, *Prodigios* reveals the latter for our full inspection.

Prodigios's dramatic movement is from the world of chivalry and romance to that of tragedy. As we follow the deeds of Jasón and Teseo, which are depicted on the right and left of Hércules's central frame and lead up to the latter's own tragic passion and death, we realize that in these two earlier adventures the seeds of destruction were sown. In this fashion Hércules's tragedy serves as predictive for his two comrades. Jason would eventually witness the slaughter of his two children; as he pondered his loss in the shadow of the Argo, the rotting hulk of the ship would collapse crushing him. And Theseus would curse his son Hippolytus and bring about his doom in a frenzy of passion and vengeance. These are, nevertheless, the greatest heroes of ancient Greece. They stand as emblematic figures of virtue conquering lust and concupiscence.[4] But they are also men subjected to all the passions and ravages of human nature. In a world without provident efficacy even these great men are doomed to defeat by the human weaknesses that characterize existence. They are men of violence; they conquer horrible monsters, becoming benefactors of civilization. But the web of human emotions and passions will in due course entangle them, bringing about their doom. If Hércules, the hero above all other heroes, could not avoid his tragic fate, what hope would there be for Jasón and Teseo?

The Heroes' Stories

1. *Jasón and Medea*—Though Jasón, as the leader of the Argonauts, was a primary figure among the great heroes of Greece, the central personage of *Prodigios's* Act I is Medea. As a powerful witch, she is famous for her knowledge of nature's secrets (1549a), and her recourse to *encantos* is facile. In this way she is subtly linked to Deyanira, who will seek to regain Hércules's faltering affection through the use of *hechizos* contained in Neso's bloody tunic (1582 and 1585a). This motif of enchantments and magic charms highlights the feminine world where power is to be exercised unobtrusively, in contradistinction to the male world of fame characterized by boast and public exposure.

Medea is a social rebel, recalling in a different key the *bachillera* of the *comedia*. As the play opens she exhibits overweening pride, equating herself with godhood. Absinto her brother accuses her of going beyond reasonable limits, to the extreme of "negando a tu decoro / los reales blasones" (1549a). After listening to the history of Friso and Heles, and to the music that celebrates Friso's offering of the golden fleece to Marte, Medea erupts with passionate anger:

> ¡Que esto escuche! ¡Que esto vea!
> Por la boca y por los ojos
> áspid soy, ponzoña vierto;
> Etna soy, llamas arrojo.
>
> (1550b-1551a)

This extreme expression of jealousy, conveyed through the image of the asp, will be the very same one that Hércules will employ to describe his consummate *celos*: "Aspides tengo en el pecho" (1589a). Medea's vaulting pride drives her to excesses that include the deprecation of Marte's godhood. She claims that "no hay deidad que mayor sea" (1551a) than herself. Absinto reminds her of the god's power and her imminent punishment. The suggestion of her inferiority before the gods only incites her to insult Marte, Venus, and Amor. After a powerful exchange between Medea and her ladies, in which the former ridicules the power of the gods as the latter express fear for their mistress's *fuerza*, *hermosura*, and *altivez*, Medea challenges the gods:

> Pues muestre Marte el furor,
> Venus y Amor el rigor,
> que no hayas miedo que tuerza
> mi altivez, beldad y fuerza,
> por Marte, Venus ni Amor.
>
> (1551a)

Suddenly "tiros y armas" are heard offstage. In Calderonian theater these apparently chance occurrences invariably predict disaster. When Astrea interprets this event as the gods' intent to punish the beautiful witch, Medea once more expresses her excessive pride:

> Contra mí no tiene, no,
> fuerza todo el cielo. Yo
> su fábrica singular
> sola puedo trastornar.
>
> (1551b)

But when a clarion sounds within, Medea becomes *turbada*, a sign that she is quickly losing control of events.

Medea's pride (*soberbia*) is so excessive in its expression that punishment cannot be far away. While the offended gods do not appear on stage to swear vengeance, Jasón does land with the Argonauts. A sudden desire for the adventurer forces Medea to confront her *human* passion, a passion so strong that she will betray family, father, and homeland to satisfy it. The offense-vengeance mechanism that rules the lives both of gods, as seen in *Laurel*, and of men and women is set in motion.

The other characters also interpret the strange phenomenon of the Argo, a ship which to them successively appears to be a mountain, a cloud, a bird, and a fish, as the means of Medea's imminent punishment. But, undaunted in her defiance of the gods, Medea confronts Jasón and his men. More importantly, she herself begins to take cognizance of her own offenses as she addresses Jasón (1553a). The latter states that his mission is a peaceful one, having nothing to do with vengeance. Clearly, then, there are two planes on which the action advances: first, the human plane in which Jasón searches for Neso and Deyanira; and second, the divine plane in which the gods' designs are slowly advancing to their end.

The witch confronts the explorer/adventurer from Greece, the land of burgeoning science, the proof of which is his ship the Argo. Europe and Asia confront one another: Medea claims expertise in astrology, necromancy, and pyromancy before Jasón who stands for reason and science. Meanwhile Medea becomes ever more conscious of her guilt (1555a) and experiences sexual desire, the means the gods will employ in her humiliation (1555b). When we next encounter Medea she is totally engulfed in a passion for Jasón.

Medea, who was first associated with the solitary life dedicated to study of the stars and the occult sciences, must now reject solitude to satisfy her passionate desires. She proclaims "una academia de amor" (1558a) and invites Jasón and Friso as participants. Her remote and lugubrious palace becomes a sparkling court of gaiety and apparent frivolity. The question put to the two young men, Friso having received a *banda* from Medea, Jasón having been requested to hand one over to her, is: "¿cuál de los dos ahora fuera / (responded) el que estuviera / favorecido de mí?" (1558b). The competition of wit quickly turns into a physical confrontation between the two men. Though Medea reminds them that "Duelos del ingenio, no / el acero los lidió" (1559a), the rivalry suddenly coalesces around the golden fleece, with Jasón's promising to conquer it and Friso's swearing to challenge him if he does so. This stylization of passion recalls the dual structure that characterizes the human dimension of *Laurel*. In Act I of *Prodigios*, however, the woman is not the victim of masculine lust or rivalry; Medea provokes them in Jasón and Friso.

As the two gallants proceed from angry words to the threat of physical violence, Medea's pride and decorum are offended. She reminds them:

> Argüir y disputar
> no es reñir ni conquistar

el vellocino de oro.

(1559a)

Jasón quickly seizes on this subconscious suggestion, promising to conquer the golden fleece and to place it at her feet. Medea, losing control both of herself and of the situation, confesses to Jasón that she did not intimate that he undertake such an exploit on her behalf (1559b). Jasón's and Medea's fates are being intertwined. As Medea loses her self-control, self-reliance, and self-direction, so too Jasón is deflected from the expressed goal of his journey, having become entangled in a maze of passion and pride.

Act I comes to a rapid conclusion with Jasón's victory over the bulls and serpent that guard Marte's *vellocino de oro*. But was this prize won solely through his efforts? No indeed, for when the guard asks how the monsters were conquered, voices from within cry out: "Medea nos ha vencido" (1560a). As in *Fortunas* Mercurio and Palas's assistance was absolutely necessary for Perseo's successful expedition against Medusa and combat with the maritime monster, so too Jasón has to rely heavily on Medea's aid. This dimension of masculine exploits will receive further emphasis in Ariadna's and Dédalo's participation in Teseo's conquest of the Minotauro. Once Medea's part in the exploit is revealed, she rushes to Jasón requesting his protection. When Colcos's warriors enter to punish the two, Medea uses witchcraft to set them fighting amongst themselves as she and Jasón flee in safety.

What began for Jasón as an expedition undertaken for the sake of a friend, ends as a hurried flight from danger with Medea in his arms. Jasón is now caught up in a maelstrom of human passion that sets him on a course not of his rational choosing. And Medea, that proud and haughty woman who relished the *soledad* of her remote palace and her occult studies, is transformed from a *mujer esquiva* into a passionate and daring woman capable of betraying both family and homeland. Though the adventure of the golden fleece ends satisfactorily, it portends further strife, further violence. Two lives are joined; two fates are melded into one.

2. *Teseo, Ariadna, and Fedra*—Though Act I is the weakest of the three, being more an *exemplum* of the punishment of Medea's haughtiness than a dramatic narrative of Jasón's exploits, Act II is fine dramatic fare. Calderón has altered the mythological stories of the three, introducing Fedra into Teseo's adventure in the Labyrinth of Crete. This act focuses on the heroic deeds of Teseo, described as a *caballero* and "Centauro noble" (1562a), in contradistinction to Neso. Teseo describes his fleet steed as "sujeto a ley y obediencia" (1562a); but he too will be thrown into a world of passion and vengeance that will turn him from his avowed purpose.

The background stories of Pasifae and the Minotauro serve as a brooding presence that tinctures all that comes into contact with it. Pasifae's passion for the beautiful bull is described as abominable, barbarous, and irrational.

The birth of the Minotauro, the fruit of this beastly union, is viewed as a punishment of the gods (1564a). Minos requested that Dédalo design and build a labyrinth that would serve as "viva / sepultura a una honra muerta" (1564a), and in it human sacrifice is offered to the monster. The horrendous sacrifice required by Minos's lost honor subtly anticipates the future sacrifices of Hércules and Deyanira to the hero's shame, the result of the mistaken perception of his *honra muerta*.

Act II begins with Ariadna, Fedra, and Flora fleeing from a bear. Teseo valiantly saves their lives by dispatching the beast. In due course Teseo saves yet another life, Flavio's, which was to be sacrificed to the Minotauro. But his heroic deed has an unforeseen consequence since he and Pantuflo, the *gracioso*, will replace the victims thus freed. These actions introduce the motif of gratitude-ingratitude that directly relates to Hércules's own ingratitude toward Deyanira's heroic defense of her virtue in the face of Neso's amorous onslaughts. As the victims to be offered in sacrifice to the Minotauro are paraded before King Minos and his court, Teseo recognizes Ariadna and Fedra and pleads with them to intervene on his behalf. They ignore his requests for mercy because their own disobedience of Minos's command not to leave the palace walls might be discovered. Teseo claims not to feel his current plight as much

> como ver la ingratitud
> de aquellas raras beldades,
> que después desconocieron
> a quien las dio vida antes.

(1568a)

Although both ladies are not forgetful of the debt they owe to Teseo, Fedra chooses not to help Teseo in order to conceal her disobedience. Ariadna, conscious of her obligation to Teseo, seeks Dédalo's aid to free the hero from his doom. In characteristically courtly fashion, she asks him to undertake a *fineza* on her behalf (1567a). Dédalo assists Teseo by providing the counter-cipher to the labyrinth as well as instruments and poison with which to kill the monster. Ariadna expresses a hope that is destined to be dashed on the rocks of passion:

> Pues que yo tan atrevida
> de darte la vida trato,
> huésped, no me seas ingrato,
> que me costarás la vida.

(1568a)

While Teseo is undertaking his heroic exploit, Lidoro, Minos's captain general, is villainously planning to abduct Ariadna, the object of his passion. Recognizing that his entreaties are of no avail, he mistakenly believes that only through boldness can he obtain Ariadna's favors. Commingled with his unruly emotions are allusions to the violent rape of a disdainful woman. Under the pretext that "Amor es dios," he plans on abducting her to a remote region "y hacer que agravios consigan / lo que no pueden favores" (1572a). His conduct is exactly the same as Céfiro's, Liríope's rapist, in *Eco y Narciso*. Ariadna defends herself with his sword, swearing that she will kill him, when suddenly a voice from within shouts:

> Rompe
> su pecho al traidor, que así
> del Rey a la ley se opone.
>
> (1572a)

Lidoro exclaims "¡Ay de mí! Conmigo hablan" (1572a) as he hears his fate announced.

Meanwhile, Teseo has made his escape from the labyrinth and flees toward the mountains. First he kills Libio, the *alcaide* of the labyrinth and the executioner of hundreds of innocent victims who entered its precincts. Then he comes upon Lidoro in the act of abducting Ariadna. Once Lidoro recognizes that the *acaso* was provoked by someone else, he relaxes his guard, assured that his villainy has not been discovered. But Teseo kills Lidoro, who unwittingly provides the hero with a horse, the means of escape from Creta. For Teseo this provident occurrence is a sign of heaven's favor:

> el cielo
> ha querido que yo cobre
> aquese caballo mío,
> en cuyas alas veloces
> podré huir seguramente.
>
> (1573a)

Lidoro's death foreshadows Neso's at Hércules's hands, for both surrendered their reason to disordering passion and employed violence in the pursuit of their lust.

As Teseo prepares to depart, Flora arrives with the news that Minos, on capturing and imprisoning Dédalo, is about to punish his disobedient daughters. They beg Teseo to deliver them from his wrath. The Greek offers them his horse, promising to protect their escape. But Ariadna recognizes that they cannot control the brute: "que pasiones / arrastradas de un caballo, / ¿en qué poder será dócil?" (1573a). Teseo quickly sizes up the situation and determines to leave one behind. He chooses to flee with Fedra, but Ariadna reminds him that she helped liberate him from the labyrinth and begs him to take her. Teseo responds:

> Dices bien: primero son

> precisas obligaciones,
> que las pasiones del gusto:
> librarte mi honor dispone.
>
> (1573b)

Fedra then reminds him of his love for her. In Ariadna's words Teseo must choose between "ser vencido o vencedor" (1573b). The sisters summarize this conflict as either "¿Ser amante?" or "¿Ser honrado?" (1573b). Teseo does not hesitate:

> ¿Qué dudo? Que aunque me noten
> de ingrato, he de ser amante.
> Todo el pundonor perdone;
> que las pasiones de amor
> son soberanas pasiones.
>
> (1573b)

Teseo's excuse for his ingratitude comes down to a facile rationalization: those who love abandon obligation. Once again in dualistic fashion, similar to the *academia de amor* in Act I, Teseo chooses love over honor and duty. Though he recognized ingratitude in others (1568a), he cannot live up to the ideals of his own code of honor.

As Jasón of Act I was deflected from his goal of seeking Neso in Asia, now Teseo too is deflected from honor's obligation in Europe. Both experience the disruptive influence of passion on their lives, causing them to flee obligation as they pursue their own satisfaction. Teseo rationalizes a course of action that his sense of honor (his *pundonor*) cannot sanction:

> Acúsenme los atentos;
> que a mí me basta que tomen
> mi disculpa los que, amando,
> dejan sus obligaciones.
>
> (1573b-1574a)

This statement was very bold in Felipe IV's court, where the King, a conspicuous voluptuary, was noted for his disregard of royal duties.

Calling Teseo an ingrate, Ariadna laments the harsh treatment of her *finezas*, but jealously suffers more from the sight of the hero's and Fedra's flight to a more happy future. *Celos* produce in the spurned woman a vehement desire for vengeance, leading her to call Teseo *ingrato* and *aleve*, "el más traidor de los hombres" (1574a), and to curse him. Caught in the maelstrom of her own passions, on the edge of intense emotion where love and hate merge into one confused whole, she shouts:

> Si la quieres, te aborrezca:
> si te quiere, la baldones;

> con tus finezas la canses,
> y con las suyas te enoje;
> si tú la halagas, te olvide;
> si ella te halaga, la arrojes
> de tus brazos; y al fin nunca
> os miréis los dos conformes.
> En otros brazos la veas,
> contenta de otros amores.
>
> (1574b)

Battling conflicting emotions, she suddenly ceases to blame him for what is fate's design. Withdrawing her curses, calling him "feliz amante" (1574b), Ariadna now blesses him, even wishing that "sus finezas te diviertan, / sus halagos te enamoren" (1574b). But the violent emotions that dominate her being cause her to call for vengeance:

> Mintieron
> como aleves mis razones,
> como infames mis piedades,
> mis celos como traidores;
> que no he de ser noble amante
> con quien no es amante noble.
> Yo te seguiré, yo misma
> vengaré tus sinrazones.
>
> (1575a)

Ariadna will lie to her father, informing him that Fedra favored Teseo, and urge him to pursue the pair and avenge the wrongs done to him and Crete. As Act II comes to a close the terms *amante* and *noble* assume antithetical positions: the once noble Teseo abandons the obligations of *honor* for the pleasures of *gusto*; the once *amante* Ariadna, now frenzied with jealousy, casts aside her noble obligations in the pursuit of vengeance (1575b). Ariadna will be defeated in battle and appear toward the end of Act III as Teseo's captive. Within the heroic deeds of the valiant Teseo are sown the seeds that, with time, will produce bitter fruit indeed. What lurks in the future, however, is the ominous presence of Hippolytus who will be the undoing of this now happy couple.

   3. *Hércules, Deyanira, and Neso* – Heracles was the greatest hero of Greece, in Hathorn's words "the Hero above all other heroes" (p. 323). But his character contained a dual aspect that *Prodigios* exploits to the full, a strange combination of heroic impulse and bestial temperament constantly at odds. As Act III begins on the central stage, Hércules appears in frightening guise as the rustics flee in pell-mell fashion before him. He has to convince them he is human (1575a). This dual aspect of *hombre/fiera* is further underscored when

Hércules refers to his jealousy which was caused by Neso's abduction of Deyanira. As Act II ended with Ariadna's *celos* driving her to seek vengeance, so Act III begins with Hércules's *celos* tormenting him, urging him on to avenge Neso's wrong.

Deyanira is an admirable character. In spite of Neso's incessant pleadings, she has remained chaste during the year of her captivity. Neso has not raped her, as he attempted during the river crossing in the traditional story. Though driven by lust, he hopes to obtain through flattery and attentiveness what violence would otherwise gain him. Deyanira is, therefore, a model of wifely fidelity, due not just to virtue's promptings, but more importantly to her continuing love for her husband (1577b-1578a). There is, however, that fateful sign that portends her eventual doom, her great beauty (1583b).

Hércules's means of vengeance is premeditated, for he carries with him a poisoned arrow dyed in the Hydra's blood. The poison's hidden property converts any blood it touches into living fire. This arrow's secret virtue closely parallels the effect of *celos* on Hércules's life, for the hero too burns with a desire for vengeance, having had his blood figuratively turned into burning fire. This process of turning blood into fire is fully realized in Neso's means of posthumously avenging his death at Hércules's hands. Once the Centaur is shot by the arrow tinctured in the Hydra's blood, he recognizes its burning venom. Not informing Deyanira of its fatal effect on human flesh, he claims to hand over to her in his last *fineza*, the tunic, a love charm that will guarantee Hércules's affection for her. Hathorn reminds us that "an oracle had foretold that he [Heracles] would be slain by someone already dead" (p. 336). Vengeance calls for further vengeance, and as Hércules was caught up in honor's call to avenge Deyanira's abduction, so too he will be caught in the cycle of vengeance that only ends with his and Deyanira's deaths.

Neso has attempted every means to curry Deyanira's favor, but to no avail. Hidden in the forests at the foot of Mt. Oeta, he now abandons peaceful means for violent ones. He plans on raping her. Deyanira, like a Roman matron of legend, defends herself with a dagger, resolute in her determination to choose death before accepting dishonor. Faced with this choice, Neso desists, promising to return to love's conquest rather than rape's theft. At this point Hércules appears swearing vengeance. Neso grabs Deyanira and, using her as a shield, prepares to make his escape. Hércules is immobilized by this unexpected turn of events, not being able to avenge his honor without killing his innocent wife. Deyanira pleads with him to kill Neso even though it means her own death. She epitomizes the self-sacrificing attitude of the woman according to the honor code: "¿Qué importa que muera yo?" (1580b). She is his wife; his vengeance is hers also. In a frenzy of illogic she begs him to take her life, a life she was disposed to sacrifice herself:

sé tú mi homicida,

> pues importará mi vida
> mucho menos que tu agravio.
>
> (1580b)

Here in capsule form we find summarized the motive of the wife-murder dramas, but coming from the mouth of the woman herself.

Although Deyanira was disposed to accept death to preserve Hércules's honor, he cannot kill her since he is obligated to be grateful for such feminine heroism. Once again in dualistic fashion, Hércules recognizes that he cannot take the life of the very one who has upheld and preserved his honor. He is suspended between his love for her and what his *celos* demand – vengeance. Recognizing that Deyanira's innocence assures her life, Hércules finds himself in an agonistic world whose demands are contradictory. While Deyanira's *honra* guards her life, Hércules suddenly and unexpectedly exclaims: "es tu vida mi deshonra" (1581a). This totally illogical conclusion sets Hércules on the road to vengeance that implicitly requires his own life also.

As Neso flees with Deyanira, Hércules reveals the transformation he is undergoing:

> No sé
> quién soy, porque en esta hora,
> ajeno yo de mí mismo,
> aún no sé si soy mi sombra.
>
> (1581)

The situation has begun to define Hércules's very personality. Though continuing to recognize Deyanira's innocence, Hércules nevertheless chooses vengeance over love: "que hoy me vengo, aunque sea a costa / de mi amor" (1581b). He sinks to the level of the husbands of the honor tragedies as he pronounces: "harto dilaté tu muerte; / mas ya tu vida, ¿qué importa?" (1581b). Life is to be sacrificed for honor, for what others believe him to be.[5]

Once more a woman is caught in the deadly rivalry of two violent men. First, Neso abducted Deyanira, claiming priority over Hércules in his love of her. Second, Hércules risks her death to obtain vengeance on Neso. Hércules *chooses* vengeance over love, for in his value system a woman may have to be sacrificed to honor's demands. His vengeance is more precious to him than Deyanira's, or his own, life. Teseo chose love over honor on rescuing Fedra; conversely, Hércules chooses honor's demands, vengeance, over love. In both cases the heroes choose poorly, following the urgings of passion rather than life's imperatives. *Prodigios* brings us into the very heart of the dynamics of passion.

Though Neso fled with Deyanira across the water, Hércules comes upon his wife after shooting the Centaur. But he shrinks back at the sight of her. In spite of Deyanira's declaration of innocence and honor preserved, he is now attacked by a different form of jealousy. He experiences shame on being in her presence and fears what others will think and say of him, for "donde acaba / una duda, empieza otra" (1583b). Hércules now begins to manifest what A. I. Watson has characterized "moral cowardice,"[6] as he seeks convenience over conscience in his dealings with his wife. Jasón and Teseo are not so much procurers of Hércules's honor as, in the hero's warped mind, proclaimers of his *deshonra*. With heroic stature in the balance, he chooses the path of least resistance: he will not kill Deyanira nor return with her to civilization, but allow others to believe her dead as she assumes the disguise of a *villana* living in Oeta's shadows.

Deyanira perceptively identifies her husband's weakness as insecurity:

> ¿Tan poco
> fías tú de ti, que pongas
> duda en tu honor, fomentando
> malicias escrupulosas?
>
> (1584a)

Putting her finger in honor's wound, she asks why anyone would believe that Hércules has allowed "ensanchas a tu deshonra" (1584a). Furthermore, she reminds him: "porque si tú tu honra dudas, / ¿quién ha de creer tu honra?" (1584a). In spite of convincing arguments and declarations of innocence on Deyanira's part, Hércules yields to honor's promptings:

> Nada me respondas;
> que no seré yo el primero,
> Deyanira, que conozca
> que no esté agraviado, y tome
> satisfacción; porque importa
> la satisfacción ajena
> a veces más que la propia.
>
> (1584)

Hércules's weakness is his excessive dependence on the opinion of others, and his irrational fears are due to the suspicion of what others might say. This lamentable situation is all the more heartrending in the face of Deyanira's oft-expressed total subservience to Hércules's needs.

Hércules experiences terrible feelings of shame, which link him to Minos's *honra muerta* of Act II, for Hércules reads his *honra muerta* in the faces of others, or rather *imagines* his dishonor in their visages. Unlike Minos, he cannot incarcerate his "dishonor" in an external labyrinth of somber intricacy but rather interiorizes it in his own tortuous heart. His "public" shame is exacerbated by the presence of his dutiful and heroic wife, the contemplation of whom produces that schizophrenic reaction so usual with the husbands of the honor tragedies. On the one hand he publicly honors Deyanira, while on the other he privately shuns her very sight, sickened by his sense of shame:

> (*Ap.*) Vergüenza tengo de que
> me vean. ¡Qué escrupulosa
> la conciencia es del honor!
>
> (1584b)

In a series of asides, Hércules expresses his mental deterioration and emotional turmoil as his life of imagined dishonor becomes a living hell.

No matter how hard Hércules tries to dissimulate his anguish with flattery, Deyanira perceives the interior struggle that bodes ill for her. Consequently she decides to use Neso's love charm to win back her husband's favor. Her plan is simple: since Hércules will have to wash himself before offering ritual sacrifice to Júpiter, she enlists Licas's assistance to substitute Neso's *vestidos* for Hércules's own, for "siempre él gusta de traellos / manchados por vanagloria" (1585b). Deyanira identifies the fundamental personality flaw in Hércules's character that has led to his sense of shame and rejection of her. Hércules's extreme pride in his exploits reveals the inner motivation of his labors — he has undertaken his valorous deeds in search of that public acclaim that the weak personality requires to assure itself of its own self-worth.

Hércules next appears dressed in Neso's skins about to offer sacrifice to his divine father, when Jasón and Teseo arrive bringing their triumphs with them from Asia and Europe. But instead of rejoicing in the victories of his friends, he burns with a strange admixture of jealousy, fear, and shame. The other heroes proudly parade their conquests before the assembly's eyes: Jasón has conquered the golden fleece and the heart and affections of Medea; Teseo has brought along the *despojos* of the Minotauro and is accompanied by Fedra, his wife, and Ariadna, his slave. As Jasón conquered his adversaries Friso and Absinto, so too Teseo has overcome the armies of Minos and Ariadna that pursued him and Fedra. As the three stages are joined, Hércules experiences a furor tearing at his very being:

> ¡Ay de mí! ¡Todo soy fuego!
> ¡Ay de mí! ¡Todo soy rabia!
>
> (1588b)

He is engulfed in the invisible flames of Neso's vengeful tunic, and his friends are not able to help him. Deyanira confesses in asides her fears that she has killed her beloved husband. Hércules rushes off stage to immolate himself on the sacrificial pyre prepared for the offerings to Júpiter, for only death quells the agony produced by the Hydra's poisonous blood. But this external garment is merely the visual manifestation of what has been consuming him from within:

> Aspides tengo en el pecho. . . .
>
> (1589a)

After Hércules's suicide, Deyanira confesses her guilt, like Liríope of *Eco y Narciso*, for all her good intent has proven to be vain hope:

> Yo a mi esposo di la muerte
> por dar vida a mi esperanza;
> pero yo me vengaré
> con la más noble venganza.

(1589a)

She too throws herself into the same fires that shortly before consumed her husband. Teseo comments positively on her tragic end: "Fenix será de su fama" (1589b). Jasón, in bewilderment, declares more ambiguously: "¡Qué trágico fin tuvieron / de Hércules las alabanzas!" (1589b).

The Mythic Pattern of "Los tres mayores prodigios"

Gwynne Edwards has pointed out some remarkable analogies between *Prodigios* and *El pintor de su deshonra*.[7] Whereas Edwards's purpose is to demonstrate that the world views underlying both plays are essentially the same, he is more concerned with establishing the congruence of the *Prodigios's* structure with that of *Pintor* than with the basic mythic pattern underlying the former. As a result of his comparative approach, though it produces significant results, he tends to distort *Prodigios's* "mythic" perspective in favor of *Pintor's* critical idiom. For instance, Edwards views Act II as central to the play since it contains a primary image in Calderonian theater, the labyrinth (p. 332). This *literary* perspective distorts *Prodigios's* dramatic nature as a narrative that, in Ricoeur's terms, reveals the temporal character of human experience. For Watson Act III is central, and he even regards the play as a kind of triptych (p. 774). Hércules's story is central both in terms of the innovative dramatic experiment that placed Jasón's and Teseo's stories to either side of the hero's and in terms of the visual impact such an arrangement would have on the audience. In this regard Watson's *visual* perspective is more in tune with the play's dramatic structure.

Acts I and II embody yet again rites of passage in which the heroes must face death in the form of the monsters that guard the golden fleece and the Minotauro. Hathorn has observed that "The voyage of *Argo* is the hero's expedition into the world of death" (p. 297). But at the end of Jasón's journey there awaits Woman, who signals death to the old self as a new self emerges to replace the old. Likewise, the Minotaur "is the symbol of death overcome by the hero" (Hathorn p. 312). And again the Woman-as-Death motif symbolizes the transition to a higher level of existence. What Act III forces upon us, and for this reason it is the interpretative key that allows us "to read" well Acts I and II, is a *temporal dissonance* that permits us to examine Jasón's and

Teseo's heroic exploits in terms of Hércules's tragic experience. The fact of their heroic and external deeds in no way assures domination of the inner passions that led to Hércules's tragic death. Indeed, Hércules's inability to overcome his *hamartia*, his vainglory, his sense of honor and shame, demonstrates that his exterior domination of beasts through violence has not translated into inner peace and harmony that lead to a fullness of life. Hércules's more advanced story, in its *temporal dimension*, induces us to reexamine the deeds of Jasón and Teseo. They were deflected from their expressed goal of searching for Neso and Deyanira by their unruly passions, which they have not been able to dominate as they have, by violence, the monsters that face them. What *Prodigios* strongly suggests is that public deeds, such as the exploits of the three heroes, do not necessarily symbolize self-domination and self-control. As Ariadna stated the options for Teseo:

> Mira
> ¡cuál trae aplausos mayores,
> ser vencido o vencedor!

> (1573b)

Hércules may have vanquished death in variegated forms, for "all Heracles' Labors are victories over death" (Hathorn, p. 325). But on his journey to public acclamation and fame as the hero above all other heroes, he failed to dominate his own passions, and that was his tragedy. Though he imagined himself to be *vencedor*, in fact he was *vencido* by unruly passion.[8]

The Cyclical Nature of Time and Its Predictive Function

As Neso ensconces himself in the forest prior to his attempted rape of Deyanira, he recites to her a sonnet that, with slight variations, would reappear twenty-five years later in *Eco y Narciso*: "Apenas el invierno helado y cano" (1579a and 1920). The sonnet's acute sense of time, with the cycle of the seasons as its imagistic conveyor, reminds us of the cyclical nature of time at the core of Calderonian tragedy. *Prodigios*, with its temporal dissonance, attempts a bitemporal view of the process by which a man acquires fame and public regard for his heroic deeds and exploits. Though Acts I and II stress what must be called rites of passage, Act III moves the question of how a man becomes a hero to the quality of a hero's life once that status has been attained. In this manner *Prodigios* encapsulates a cyclical view of the process, emphasizing the early stages and the final stage of the entire process, not in one life, such as in a chronicle, but in several lives, allowing a simultaneity of focus not otherwise possible. In the deeds of the great heroes are sown seeds that, with time, will bring about their eventual downfall. As Hércules's story draws to a conclusion, with his acute sense of shame, jealousy, and honor overpowering and defeating his noble and heroic character, we suddenly real-

ize that the stories of Jasón and Teseo are in earlier phases of that same cyclical process.

In Act II we come across the two basic possibilities of *Dasein*, being-in-the-
world. As Teseo kills the traitor Lidoro, he recovers his horse, thus permit-
ting a timely escape from his pursuers. He stresses a provident concern for
his welfare by outside forces as follows:

> el cielo
> ha querido que yo cobre
> aquese caballo mío,
> en cuyas alas veloces
> podré huir seguramente.
>
> (1573a)

But he does not immediately flee, for suddenly he becomes more entangled in
the affairs of Ariadna and Fedra, who also must flee from their excessively
jealous father. Once Teseo chooses Fedra and spurns Ariadna, the latter
expresses in a moment of calm reflection another possible world, but one
where human freedom is reduced by the designs of an overriding fate: "Que
tú no tienes la culpa / de lo que el hado dispone" (1574b). While in the narratives of Jasón's and Teseo's deeds there does appear to be a provident concern
for the two heroes, it is only with Hércules's story that we begin to see a
broader pattern in which provident concern and fate are at loggerheads.
What frustrates "providence" is the chaos of passion running amuck in the
affairs of men and women. It is not so much that fate directs their lives as
they are ruled by unpredictable passions. In this sense, fate is a term by
which we designate the surrender of free will and self-direction to passion's
capricious and deadly influence. What makes their doom appear inevitable is
not so much that the stars determined their lives as that they allowed their
passions to place them on a bearing whose journey's end was destruction.[9]

Conclusion

Prodigios's dramatic structure sharply contrasts with *Fortuna's* positive
appreciation of how one becomes a true hero. The latter play deliberately
places obstacles in Perseo's path that are symbols of the passions the hero
must overcome to realize the fruits of his exploits. Perseo conquers the pernicious influence of *celos* and the malign effects of fate. The play neatly balances the accomplishment of exterior deeds with Perseo's psychomachy. It is
precisely this latter ingredient that is missing from *Prodigios*.

Both *Laurel* and *Prodigios* dramatize that masculine power does not solely
depend on the manifestation of strength and daring, but on the balancing of
great feats of boldness with the inner domination of those destructive tenden-

cies we all carry within us. *Laurel* depicts the tragic result of Apolo's lack of self-domination as the play's violence centers more and more on the hapless Dafne. At the play's conclusion, neither Apolo nor Amor has a valid claim to the status they both seek. Powerful though these two gods be, their inner flaws undermine their divine essence. In the world of men, in that of *Prodigios*, we discover a similar process at work: great though the deeds of these heroes may be, their lack of self-domination eventually undermines and vitiates their heroic status. In fact, these plays reveal a *demythologizing* stance that reaches full maturity in our next play, *Fieras afemina Amor.*[10]

Notes

1 The text of *Los tres mayores prodigios* cited is the Valbuena Briones edition, pp. 1547-89.

2 The *loa* consulted is from the *Segunda Parte* of Calderón's works (Madrid, 1641).

3 For background information on these heroes, see Hathorn, pp. 295-338.

4 See Pérez de Moya, II, 125-27, 145-49, and 235-36.

5 Although ter Horst states that the mythological plays are not truly tragic (*Calderón*, pp. 5-6), nonetheless he classifies *Prodigios* as "a mythological tragedy of honor" (p. 50).

6 "Hércules and the Tunic of Shame: Calderón's *Los tres mayores prodigios*," in *Homenaje a William L. Fichter*, eds. A. David Kossoff and José Amor y Vázquez (Madrid: Castalia, 1971), p. 783.

7 "Calderón's *Los tres mayores prodigios* and *El pintor de su deshonra*: The Modernization of Ancient Myth," *BHS*, 61 (1984), 326-34.

8 Frederick de Armas's view of the play as a subversion of heroic adventures (p. 159) is similar to my own. See pp. 149-63 of *The Return of Astraea* for his analysis. Cascardi finds that Hércules's adventures cause us "to question any wholesale trust in the powers of the mind" (p. 95).

9 Though Hércules's death at the hands of someone already dead does not form a highly visible part of *Prodigios's* plot, it most surely was in the minds of those familiar with the great hero's story. To predict the future does not translate into the ability to determine what will occur there. One who is able to foresee where the confluence of character and circumstance will lead is thus able to read or to predict the future.

10 For a study of a possible source for *Prodigios*, see Clark Colahan and Alfred Rodríguez, "*El Hércules* de López de Zárate: Una posible fuente de *Los tres mayores prodigios* de Calderón," *Calderón: Actas*, III, 1271-76.

B. 2. *Fieras afemina Amor*

> Que él quiera y que no sea
> querido es lo que quiero:
> hállase más burlado
> cuanto más satisfecho.
>
> Cupido on Hércules. (2053a)[1]

Fieras afemina Amor is a play about love, disdain, and vengeance, a *fiesta de espectáculo* written to celebrate the birthday of Queen Mariana de Austria in December of 1669 that had to be postponed until January of the following year.[2] The January performance served a double purpose for, in addition to Mariana's *años*, the festivity celebrated the birthday of María Antonia, the granddaughter of the Queen and daughter of the Spanish *infanta* Margarita and the Emperor Leopoldo I (Wilson, p. 183). The play was a courtly spectacle on a grand scale, distinguished by the great detail with which Calderón described the staging of the entire *fiesta*, from *loa* to *fin de fiesta*. It was lavish both in praise of the Hapsburgs and in celebration of their personal/state occasions.

But my approach will rely not so much on the motive for the play's presentation as on the inner dynamics that uniquely structure the work.[3] The *loa's* introductory *acotación* delineates what the entire *fiesta* purports: "Todo este frontispicio cerraba una cortina, en cuyo primer término, robustamente airoso se veía Hércules, la clava en la mano, la piel al hombro, y a las plantas monstruosas fieras, como despojos de sus ya vencidas luchas; pero no tan vencidas que no volase sobre él en el segundo término Cupido flechando el dardo que en el asunto de la Fiesta había de ser desdoro de sus triunfos."[4] The demythologizing dimension of the text is clearly announced, and the inscription underscores it:

> Fieras afemina Amor.
> Omnia vincit Amor.

As the *loa* begins, the traditional competition over who will celebrate the *fiesta* breaks out between Fénix, a symbol of love, and Pavón, a symbol of vigilance. They are accompanied by the months of the year, representing the earth, and the signs of the zodiac, representing the heavens. Aguila, the symbol of the Hapsburg dynasty, mediates their discord, restoring harmony to all the participants in view of the courtly purpose of the *fiesta*:

> y todos digáis en voces diversas
> que Carlos Segundo ofrece a su madre,
> pues ella admitió de sus años fiesta,
> esta fiesta también a sus años,
> que cumplan y gocen edades eternas.

As is to be expected in the competition between the months (twelve young men) and the zodiacal signs (twelve nymphs), December wins the garland because Mariana was born on 22 December. It is at this point that courtly economy acknowledges that, since *Fieras* is to be staged in January, one celebration may admit two different, though related, events.[5]

Valbuena Briones writes that Calderón "Escogió un episodio para presentar al aclamado héroe en un instante de debilidad" (2024a). It is precisely this weakness on the part of the hero that relates *Fieras* to *Laurel*. Repeated from *Laurel* we encounter Amor's contradictory shafts, the gilded one inciting Hércules's love, but not causing it as in Apolo's case, and the leaden arrow confirming Yole's hatred of the hero, but not producing it, as occurred with Dafne. Thus these two plays portray the downfall of a god and a hero before Amor's seemingly omnipotent power. But as we discovered that *Laurel's* critical perspective included a broader field of commentary than Apolo's hubris, so too *Fieras's* narrative will treat us to a penetrating analysis of Hércules's flaws as well as those of the other characters. We find ourselves in a world in which blindness leads to error that leads to offensive behavior that results in vengeance that supposedly ends the chain of events. Nevertheless, *Fieras's* critical perspective is more complex than the simple allegory announced in the theater's frontispiece.[6]

Prodigios deals with marital honor, a fact that relates it closely to Calderón's wife-murder dramas, such as *Pintor*. *Fieras* resembles, in N. Erwin Haverbeck Ojeda's terms, "los rasgos de la comedia de enredo de tipo palaciego."[7] Thus the two works on the Hércules figure in Calderonian drama represent not so much two different appreciations of the hero as two distinct generic designs that call for different outcomes. The marital-honor play normally calls for the death of the female protagonist; in *Prodigios's* case it demands Hércules's death in addition to Deyanira's. *Fieras*, as it relies on a more comedic mode, demands a marriage that in the ordinary *comedia palaciega* would resolve all the problems the plot could contrive. But Hércules's proposed marriage and subsequent subjection of Yole to his lust only provide further complications. Though Calderón has been accused of using formula writing to provide the court with plays, works such as *Fieras* demonstrate how ingeniously he manipulated the *comedia's* basic forms and problematized our expectations. His critical view of Hércules as a figure of masculine excellence suffuses both works while at the same time respecting, though transcending, the demands of the respective genres.

In structuring *Fieras*, Calderón blended and adapted several episodes from Hércules's life story. Whereas in the classical myth Dejanira employs the poisoned tunic to win back her husband who has become enamored of Iole, the latter does not appear in *Prodigios*. The elimination of Yole from this narrative centers our attention on Hércules's irrational fear of public opinion, provoked by his exaggerated sense of honor and its consequent feelings of shame. *Fieras* combines the eleventh Labor, the Apples of the Hesperides, during which the wrestling match with Antaeus occurs, with Hércules's passion for Yole. Placing the episode in which Hércules dresses as a woman, which occurred during his servitude to Omphale, within his amorous adventure with Yole, focuses the narrative on Hércules's disordered life.

Whereas *Laurel* exposes those aspects of Apolo's and Amor's characters that betray their divine essence, *Fieras* will demonstrate how the disregard of fundamental ethical principles permeates Libia and dehumanizes her inhabitants. Hércules is not the only one in the play who betrays himself through surrender to passion or disregard of reason. For instance, Yole unwittingly reminds Aristeo of what she will eventually disregard in her desire to avenge her affront at Hércules's hands:

> no digan
> que te vengaste, supuesto
> que tomó mejor venganza
> quien no se vengó pudiendo.
>
> (2051a)

Both Amor and Yole fail to heed the advice that Hércules himself rejects to his peril. There is a profoundly ironic double standard in the play's narrative structure that defines the world of hypocrisy that *Fieras's* critical insight lays bare.

"Fieras's" Narrative Dualities

Fieras afemina Amor is structured on a bilevel plot principle involving the actions of the gods, Amor and Venus, and the actions of men and women. Hércules provokes the anger of Cupido by deprecating the god and his place in the order of the universe. Hesperia reminds Hércules that "Alma del alma le llaman" (2031a), for the hero has claimed:

> Amor
> no es deidad, sino quimera
> que inventaron las delicias
> para honestar las flaquezas.
>
> (2031a)

From the start Hércules does not comprehend the opposing qualities of love, often represented by Cupid and Anteros, that are at one time called lust and love and at another love requited and love unrequited. Hércules calls Amor "fiera de fieras" (2048b), thereby placing him safely within an environment familar to the hero. But as the *loa* reminds us, Cupido is a "monstruosa fiera" who will prove to be more powerful than Hércules. Though he may conquer the wild beasts that populate the earth, Hércules fails to understand the real world in which he lives, preferring instead an illusion that adulates his pride and sense of self-esteem. Hércules chooses not to vanquish the monster guarding the golden apples for the following reason:

> que hago en no vencerle más
> que lo que en vencerle hiciera,
> pues vencería allá su furia,
> y aquí venzo la mía mesma.

(2031a)

Hércules's belief that he has already conquered passion (*vencerse a sí mismo*), when, in fact, he has never experienced it, leads to his blindness and eventual downfall. Hesperia regretfully leaves the hero commenting: "¡plegue a Venus que Amor / no vengue en ti sus ofensas!" (2031a), a refrain that is subsequently repeated musically (2031b and 2032a).

As Hércules sleeps, Venus and Amor appear overhead swearing vengeance. Amor states that:

> Ese humano fiero monstruo
> mi absoluto imperio niega;
> pues niega que amor es el alma del alma,
> y todo con él respira y alienta.

(2032a)

Through his ignorance and pride, Hércules extolls the more beastly aspects of his nature as he suppresses all that goes contrary to his flattering self-image. The gods' vengeance follows a predictable course: the contradictory shafts for the hero and Yole, who now appears to him as a phantasm. The offense-vengeance mechanism is in full swing; it will reverberate from the heavens to earth, and those who inhabit the latter will pick up the tune and make it their own.[8] Although Hércules deserves to be punished for his arrogant challenge of the divinely ordered state of human life, *Fieras's* ironic view will also reveal the dual nature of love, at one time tender and caring while at another fierce, brutal, and monstruous, the result of Cupido's being a "monstruosa fiera."

The plot moves forward on a dual track that emphasizes traditional views of men and women. Hércules, the *alcaide* of Parnaso, relies on his physical strength and power to dominate others. Yole, the princess of Libia, will become Hércules's victim as he subjugates her to his will. The motif of woman as object and victim is quite a familiar one by now. But Yole's victimization, at Hércules's and her father's hands, is made more pathetic in view of the requited love she feels for Anteo. *Fieras* eventually reverses this traditional power scheme as the play ends. Yole becomes the dominant character, avenging the wrongs done to her and to all other women. Hércules, then, appears as "victim," subjected to the whims of feminine caprice and exposed to the scorn of all. A victim of his own lust, he stands clearly revealed as Amor celebrates his victory over the once crude Hércules. In both Yole's and Amor's vengeance on the now contrite Hércules, the two also stand revealed: Amor as a "monstruosa fiera..." and Yole as a savage woman who has assimilated the values of vengeance.

What brought Hércules to this low ebb was his antagonistic view of the relationship between love and fame. The play opens with his defeat of the Nemean Lion. The hero is set on a course of action that recognizes only fame and the values that support it. He is boastful; he represents an exclusivistic view of life that underscores his lack of personal harmony. He sees the world in opposing terms, but rather than attempt to harmonize the dual poles, he chooses one and ignores the other. For instance, though he recognizes the physical beauty of women such as Hesperia, he declares "que para mí las hermosas / son solamente las fieras" (2028a). This interior disharmony is not due to faulty knowledge on his part, but to a deliberate choice to live a particular life style that ignores the basic realities of nature. With echoes from *Prodigios*, Hércules speaks of *"suprema / opinión"* as the highest value to be pursued. The lessons of the heroes' lives speak to him:

> de altos héroes que afearon
> la grata faz de suprema
> opinión, con el lunar
> de que el amor los divierta,
> el de Aquiles me bastara
> no más, para que aborrezca
> amor y mujer, cuando oigo
> cuán vil, por Deidamia bella,
> vistió femeniles ropas,
> peinando el cabello a trenzas.
>
> (2030b)

Dressing himself in the lion's skin, he declares his clothing's symbolic value:

> porque vea
> el mundo que si hubo héroe
> que en dama el amor convierta,
> hubo héroe que contra amor
> el odio convirtió en fiera....
>
> (2030b)

As the hero who rejects love and champions the advocacy of hatred, Hércules not only wears the beast's skin, but assumes a symbolic stance in which what makes us human is rejected for the beastly view of life.

His conscious recognition of the quality of his life does not mark, however, a new departure as much as an acceptance of the significance of past deeds. In what first appeared a traditional *fineza*, Hércules killed the Nemean Lion, thus saving the Hespérides' and others' lives. In her flight from the beast, Hesperia falls into a deep cavern from which Hércules rescues her: another *fineza*. But when in gratitude she prefers not to disclose to him who she is nor the nature of the palace he beholds before him, Hércules resorts to physical violence:

> No fíes
> tú que por mujer te tenga
> respeto, porque no hay
> cosa que más aborrezca.

(2028b)

He is truly a man/beast who lacks basic civilizing qualities, extolling instead physical force, the recourse of the brute. This duality of *amar-aborrecer*, the love of his fame to the exclusion of all else, translates into a hatred of all women, the embodiments of the love principle. Hespero left his daughters in Atlante's charge in order to "hacer su fama eterna" (2029a). He proceeded to lock them up until his return, which never occurred. Since Hércules has a similar view of women as obstacles to fame's pursuits, Hespero's story is significant for our appreciation of Hércules's.

The hero has come to Libia at Euristio's request to save his kingdom from Aristeo's invasion. When the King offers Yole to Hércules as recompense for his efforts, the hero declares:

> yo tengo, señor,
> pocas lecciones de amor.
> Sé vencer y no sé amar;
> y puesto que me hallo aquí
> empeñado a parecer
> descortés a bruto, ser
> bruto elijo, pues nací
> tan sin uso de razón,
> que opuesto a quien me dio el ser,
> tengo a cualquiera mujer
> natural oposición.

(2034b)

He then goes on to mention that only one woman, and at that a phantasm, has managed to please him. This scene recalls Segismundo's having been moved by Rosaura's veiled femininity, for both are in need of feminine complementarity. Hércules chooses to disdain Yole without first seeing her and to reject the King's offer of marriage. Though he believes that his passions are under control, he has not yet been tested nor achieved victory over himself. Explaining his antirational opposition to all women, he proudly accepts his brutish nature.

Yole will be the woman who avenges this distortion of life's values as Hércules ultimately abandons his fame for the delights of passion. Although he espies what is in the offing for him, in his pride, which remains in spite of his having killed the Nemean Lion, its symbol, he cannot take seriously the difficulties to be faced. He can only ridicule what he does not sufficiently understand nor adequately respect.

Hércules's discovery of the amatory powers contained in the magic apples of the Hesperides anticipates the havoc he will personally wreak upon male-female relations. He theoretically rejects violence in matters of love, though it is acceptable in pursuing other objectives. To acquire information about the mysterious garden, he threatens Hesperia with physical force. He clearly reasons that the use of enchantments to further love is basically offensive and asseverates:

> ¡Qué bajo espíritu debe
> de tener quien se contenta
> con que lo que es voluntad
> lo haya de adquirir por fuera!
> Una mujer violentada,
> ¿es más, si se considera,
> que una estatua algo más viva,
> con alma algo memos muerta?
>
> (2030a)

Hércules's initial rejection of the use of force in matters of the heart condemns his subsequent forcing of Yole to yield to his lust and revenge.

Political Expediency Vs. Personal Happiness

The first hint that there is much more wrong with the world of *Fieras* than Hércules's aberration comes with the disclosure of Euristio's political machinations. The King of Libia requested Hércules's assistance to repulse Aristeo, who first sought Yole's hand in marriage and, once his proposal was rejected, subsequently attempted to impose his will by force on the kingdom and Yole. Machiavellian-like, Euristio feigns his reaction to Hércules's refusal of Yole and plans on avenging his "tan necia respuesta" (2035a), but only after using him for his own designs. It is easy to overlook the fact that Yole's life is at the service of Libia's political and dynastic necessities. The raising of such an issue could not but reverberate through the Hapsburg court where marriage was a matter of state interest. Yole is a pawn in an international game that demands personal sacrifice as the price of royalty. Euristio's determination to punish the rude warrior sets in motion a cycle of vengeance that will not end with the King's own death. When Hércules returns victorious from the field, having delivered Libia from Aristeo's attack, Euristio is celebrating the marriage of Yole to Anteo. The King's rationalization of his duplicity ("la fama, / si allá premia al que lidia, aquí al que ama" [2040a]) only masks his revenge of Hércules's crass refusal of his daughter. Euristio does not marry his daughter to Anteo because that is her wish, but because through it he can avenge the insult he suffered at Hércules's hands, thus humiliating the proud warrior: "Y ofreciéndole a Yole, no se alabe / de que sabe vencer y amar no sabe" (2040a). For the proud King his daughter is another pawn in the politics of state. Euristio will be punished in battle, dying when an arrow strikes him in the face.

This deception of Hércules sheds light on a matter that directly affects the hero's own confused web of personal and political motivations. After Hércules conquers Libia's forces, the latter acclaim him king. But before he secures his place as their new ruler, he plans on forcing Yole to become his slave. Aristeo, who by this time has become the hero's ally, strongly advises against Hércules's misguided priorities. He suggests that triumph and victory depend not so much on their acquisition on the field of battle, but on their maintainance in the political arena:

> ¿no es mejor acudir
> a establecer esta voz,
> que dejarlo, por venir
> tras un afecto que puedes
> lograr después?

> (2046a)

Here is a confused world in which personal ambition and desire replace political wisdom. Euristio's attempt to punish Hércules's affront to his regal dignity, while yet using him to save the kingdom, unwittingly throws that kingdom into political chaos that results in his own death. And Hércules, by placing personal vengeance before political necessity, satisfies his vengeance and lust before securing his place as king. Both men view Yole as an object in their personal confrontation.

The "Feminist" Perspective of "Fieras afemina Amor"

King Euristio highlights what is at loggerheads in *Fieras*. Before entering battle, he exclaims to Yole:

> Nada me digas
> (¡ay, belleza desdichada!)
> cuando a perder por ti voy
> honor, vida, reino y patria.

> (2042a)

Undercurrents of fate, reinforced by allusions to feminine beauty, form an ominous background to the action, but the foreground clarifies the real issues for the males. As Euristio first found himself obligated to defend Yole from Aristeo's onslaughts, he now must defend her from Hércules's. The real battleground of male pride and ambition consists in the possession and defense of women.

Towards the end of Act I, as Yole is caught up in the offense-vengeance mechanism that Amor has set in motion, she exclaims:

> ¡Oh nunca naciera antes
> que el arbitrio el rendimiento,
> y entre respeto y temor
> pusiera el honor en medio!
>
> (2036b)

Her pitiable lament for her lost freedom, bartered away on the table of state, underscores once more the victimization of women. She cannot choose her husband, and she should never be forced to pay honor's homage in the conflict between respect of her father and fear of Hércules's brutishness. She is trapped in the larger issues that put enmity between men. When Hércules becomes aware of Euristio's betrayal of his word and the marriage of Anteo and Yole, he discovers *celos* ("¡A mi amor celosas ansias!" [2039b]). In his lack of moderation produced by jealousy, Hércules claims a warped universal right:

> con más noble venganza
> y a menos costa que ser
> esposo de Yole ingrata,
> llego a coronarme en Libia;
> y aun ella puesta a mis plantas
> he de ver, no solo que es
> mi esposa, sino mi esclava,
> mostrando que no hay tan soberana
> mujer que del hombre a serlo no nazca.
>
> (2040a)

Hércules's desire for vengeance moves from personal satisfaction to universal claim. He will humiliate Euristio and all of Libia by subjecting Yole to his will; they will not be able to defend her, and their claim to manliness will thereby be annulled. The brutish man who denied love its rightful place in his life now believes that he is justified in humiliating Euristio through the dehumanization of Yole.

Although Euristio's claim that love is superior to martial exploits smacks of expediency, Yole's spirited defense of her rights resounds with sincerity. First, she asserts that her freedom to choose a husband should be respected:

> Hércules, mi padre
> ofreció a tus esperanzas
> mi libertad, suponiendo
> mi gusto; pues cosa es clara
> que mi padre no querría
> que me casase forzada.
>
> (2041a)

Second, she reminds Hércules that his professed hatred of women caused her to become horrified at his sight. Thus, she deliberately chose to marry Anteo, ultimately preferring death to a marriage with Hércules (2041b). Hércules will hear none of this impassioned defense of personal dignity and sets out to avenge the wrongs done to him by Euristio, Yole, and Anteo. As all the characters rush off to prepare for battle, Yole too is swept up in the violent emotions unleashed by the events now out of her control. She explains:

> pues es de Hércules la ira,
> ser de Yole la venganza. . . .
>
> (2042a)

Once more the cyclical nature of vengeance is manifest. Amor will assist Yole who, learning of her father's death, throws herself into battle:

> Yo, humana víbora hecha,
> desesperada, a morir
> en su venganza me entré
> en la batalla.
>
> (2043b)

The beastial imagery underscores how Yole voluntarily accepts her dehumanization as she adopts the characteristics that make Hércules a brutish man. Although Hércules was a brute right from the start, the desire for vengeance brings out the beastly character of the once innocent *infanta*.

While these events lead to Hércules's physical triumph over the forces opposing him, they also lead to his subsequent surrender to passion. And this surrender is, in symbolic and emblematic terms, a victory for all women over those who seek to oppress them. Yole states this interpretation clearly:

> No dirá sino que Yole,
> vengando en él sus ofensas,
> vengó también las de todas
> las mujeres.
>
> (2061a)

Hércules, dressed in woman's attire, confounds all onlookers. Once more Yole stresses the exemplary nature of Hércules's punishment and concomitant shame:

> ¿Qué ha de ser, sino que vea,
> no tan solo Libia, pero
> el mundo, cuán vil, cuán ciega
> fue, deponiéndome a mí,
> y obligándome a que sea
> forzada esposa de un bruto,
> la infame aclamación vuestra?
>
> (2061b)

Libia deposed the rightful heir to the throne, forcing Yole to become the wife of a brute. Since they proclaimed Hércules King, let them appropriately acclaim their now effeminate ruler. Calíope the Muse emphasizes this interplay of the various motives that lead to Hércules's shame:

> vea el teatro del mundo
> tu triunfo, para que vea
> quien quiso que las mujeres
> esclavas del hombre sean,
> que él es su esclavo, pues es
> esclavo de amor por ellas.
>
> (2062a)

Amor takes revenge on the heedless and crass conqueror of brutes and beasts through Yole's vengeance of the wrongs done to women by those, like Hércules, who seek to subjugate them to their will. But *Fieras's* supremely ironic stance also shows that there is a price to be paid for this vengeance, for it brings out the beastly characters of both Yole and Amor.

Hércules as Hero and the Question of Self-Domination

From the beginning Hércules was not so much hostile to women as indifferent. He fought the urges of nature that he saw as deflecting him from his expressed goal of seeking fame. What wrought the sudden change in the hero's attitude and behavior was the intrusion of jealousy into his life, disrupting his emotional control. Jealousy obliges him to confront those aspects of his nature he would prefer to ignore. First and foremost he must deal with *celos'* contradictory fury:

> (Mas, ¡ay!, que no es esto solo
> lo que me hiela y me abrasa
> tan a un tiempo, que no sé
> qué fiera en el pecho inflama

> tal ira, que excede a todas,
> con haber lidiado a tantas. . . .)
>
> (2038b)

The hero laments not so much Euristio's broken promises as the image of his phantom lady in another's arms. Jealousy's ability to provoke passion is described in detail, for previously Hércules was not profoundly moved by Yole's beauty. After a carefully reasoned description of the progress of jealousy from an imagined "brasa / . . . envuelta en cenizas" to an "ascua," Hércules realizes that he is in love:

> Pero ¿qué digo? ¡Yo amor!
> ¡Yo celos! No es sino rabia
> de la desestimación,
> y así, he de intentar vengarla.
>
> (2039a)

In this rationalization, Hércules attempts to flee the truth that his nature is forcing upon his consciousness.

Hércules defeats Euristio and kills Anteo in a wrestling match. But he really wants to punish Yole and, through her, his own love:

> Para mí
> ni el triunfo ni el reino importan
> tanto como destruir
> encantos de amor, llevando
> esclava a Yole, a asistir
> a mi coronación. . . .
>
> (2046a)

As consciousness of his passion for Yole grows, he is obliged to deny the real nature of the interior struggle against which he finds himself more and more helpless. The Muses appear with a song that addresses the hero's emotional turmoil. Calling Yole an "hermosa fiera" (2048a), he begs their assistance not to love her, but to despise her. They respond:

> ¡Ay de ti!
> Que vencer a las fieras
> no es vencerse a si!
>
> (2048b)

The Muses openly doubt that Hércules is capable of victory over his passions, and Calíope advises him not to take vengeance (2048b). She reveals to Hércules that it is his hurt feelings that cry out for vengeance. The main battlelines are not drawn between Yole and Hércules, but between the unsuspecting hero and the wily god of love. She stresses Hércules's only route of escape:

> No te vengues, si te quieres
> vengar de Yole; que vi
> muchas veces que el dejar
> alcanza más que el seguir.
>
> (2048b)

Hércules does not take seriously this enigmatic statement and proceeds to invade the garden, kill the monster, and satisfy his desire for vengeance. At this point Amor pierces both Hércules and Yole with the opposing passions of love and disdain. Referring to his campaign duties as general of Libia's troops, Hércules asks himself: "¿Cómo es posible que venza / el que va a vencer huyendo?" (2036b). He flees from Yole's attractiveness to the field of battle whose din is his music. He trusts that time, coupled with absence, will cure his newly discovered *devaneo*. Amor is only apparently defeated, for the "flecha de celos" (2036b) remains in his quiver.

The Muses' warning is correctly interpreted by Hércules as referring to his own situation:

> *Riuseñor, que volando vas,*
> *cantando finezas, cantando favores,*
> *¡oh cuánta pena y envidia me das!*
> *Pero no, que si hoy cantas amores,*
> *tú tendrás celos y tú llorarás.*
>
> (2048a)

The warnings that follow, from Caliope's concern about vengefulness (2048b) to the Hespérides' concerns about self-control and learning from one's experiences, are ignored. He can not understand how avenging oneself may result from not taking vengeance. The action advances toward the question of self-knowledge and its role in a world of perilous attractions.

Verusa, one of the Hespérides, brings a mirror to Hércules. He has no idea of his own appearance and the reaction it produces in others. His life up to this point has been one of blissful ignorance. First, he is shocked by his unkempt appearance. Second, on beholding his image, he begins to comprehend the inappropriateness of the union of his "fealdad," "fiereza," and "monstruosidad" with Yole's beauty. He even excuses, or at least understands, Yole's desire to be free of him. But as he learns more about himself and others, the truths thus discovered become unpalatable and are rejected out of hand (2055b). The interplay of the rejection of self-knowledge and the seeking of vengeance is clear.

Venus and Amor's vengeance swiftly advances due to Hércules's ignorance. The gods advise Yole:

Fingir halago traidor;
que con flechas más severas
que él domestica las fieras,
fieras afemina Amor.

(2052b)

Yole will defeat the hero through deceit; feigning love for Hércules, she laments her fate. Hércules weakens in his resolve not to love. At Amor's counsel, she cunningly manipulates Hércules for her own purpose. Once Yole is given freedom to choose a husband, she selects the champion who has not desisted from taking vengeance—Hércules's vengeance has only provoked Yole's. And as avenging wrongs done to oneself brought out Hércules's brutish nature, so too Yole's beastly potential is released when she takes revenge on her oppressor.

In characteristically dual fashion, two choruses begin to acclaim or regret the "love" of Hércules and Yole. As Hércules is about to return to Parnaso as its *alcaide*, he is informed of Cibele's revenge for the death of her son Anteo. But Yole prevents his departure. Calíope advises him: "Volved a acordar su fama." Yole implores him: "Mi amor a acordar volved" (2058b). Cibele's vengeance is violent and public; Yole's is subtle and secretive. Hércules tells Calíope:

Calíope, dile a Apolo
que si me oyó alguna vez
que sé vencer y no amar,
ya sé amar y no vencer.

(2059a)

Incredulously, the Muse departs wondering how it is possible for Hércules to abandon fame for love. The hero is like a child manipulated by the now more powerful Yole. Her vengeance is possible because Hércules does not recognize what is happening to him. His effeminate attire is the exteriorization of what passion has wreaked on his soul.

Yole's Brutalization

One amazing aspect of *Fieras* is how Yole subtly acquires the values associated with the masculine world of Hércules, Euristio, and Anteo. When Yole goes off to battle, her runaway horse plunges her from the heights of the mountain to the valley below. She is not hurt because Amor cradles her in his arms in order to use her in his revenge of Hércules's insults. The symbolic value of the runaway horse, the passions ruling over reason (the rider), applies here. Yole has been used by her father, pursued by Aristeo, and scorned by Hércules. Rather than represent love and its values, Yole becomes an avenging presence threatening Hércules's very being. The change in her character is not surprising in light of what she has had to endure at the hands of men. Yole's assumption of vengeance's prerogatives signals a brutalization of her character that relates her more intimately to Hércules's world and its masculine values. Though still a victim, Yole accepts with relish the new role as victimizer.

Yole's vengeance must be examined in light of the advice given to Hércules not to avenge wrongs. The theme of forswearing vengeance permeates the story of Hércules and invades Yole's own personal world; but, like Hércules, she will not be able to restrain her own base desires. Though Amor master-minds Hércules's shame, Yole is more than a mere instrument in that process, for her sight is set on personal revenge.

Yole's vengeance covers three separate but related wrongs she has suffered at Hércules's hands: first, the death of her father; second, the death of Anteo; third, Hércules's deposing of her as Queen, proclaiming himself King of Libia. Her revenge is simple: to kill him. But Hesperia, mindful of the fact that Hércules twice saved her life, dissuades Yole from committing murder, recommending instead Hércules's debasement. Removing Hércules's club, Yole replaces it with the distaff. Calling for the Hespérides' assistance, she sets out to give Hércules a new coiffure:

> la nunca peinada greña
> de su cabello, de cintas
> en desaliñadas trenzas
> prended.
>
> (2060b)

Standing righteously tall, she claims:

> si hay hombres que las agravian,
> que hay mujeres que se vengan.
>
> (2060b)

Calling the guard to witness Hércules's shame, she urges them to insult and mock the captivated hero. Awakened by the call to arms, Hércules discovers the distaff and is immobilized by this sudden change in his appearance. He does not recognize himself and even utters "¿... que yo / no soy yo?" (2061a). Verusa then thrusts a mirror in his face, revealing his womanly attire. Recall-ing Aquiles's shame, the Hespérides allude to love as the cause of Hércules' fall. But Yole rejects this suggestion, asserting the nature of her vengeance on the now effeminate hero:

> No dirá sino que Yole,
> vengando en él sus ofensas,
> vengó también las de todas
> las mujeres.
>
> (2061a)

Remembering that the three warnings given to him by the Hespérides were not sufficient to move him, only Yole's tears could do that, Hércules laments not so much his dishonor (*desdoro*) as the fact that Yole has deceived him (2061a). He tearfully pleads for Yole's pity, not for his honor, but for his love. With all the cohort present, she reveals to Libia a "Hércules afeminado," the vengeance of a "forzada esposa" (2061b). Confronted with this sight, a soldier exclaims:

> Pues es Yole vuestra reina,
> y Hércules afeminado,
> ni oye, ni mira, ni alienta,
> no forcéis su libertad.
>
> (2061b)

Yole escapes a forced marriage at the same time as Hércules, his valor eclipsed, seeks to flee the scene. The hero pathetically confesses "que contra el Amor no hay fuerza" (2062a).

As the play approaches the denouement, Calíope calls on Venus and Amor to reveal themselves and confirm Hércules's punishment:

> vea el teatro del mundo
> tu triunfo, para que vea
> quien quiso que las mujeres
> esclavas del hombre sean,
> que él es su esclavo, pues es
> esclavo de amor por ellas.
>
> (2062a)

Amor's vengeance is fundamentally the revelation of Hércules's lust, by which he became enslaved to passion. The hero who wished to exclude from his nature what contributes to defining us as human finds himself reduced to that passion, to the exclusion of his heroic deeds and their fame. As the gods phrase it in song:

> Para que suenen mejor
> sus cláusulas lisonjeras,
> de Hércules en deshonor;
> que si él domestica fieras,
> fieras afemina Amor.
>
> (2062a)

Though Yole triumphs over the rude hero at the play's close, the price she pays demonstrates the effects of vengeance on the avenger. As Hércules flees from the wrathful Lybians, they cry out for his death. Calíope intervenes preventing any further violence. Yole asks the Muse: "¿Cómo en su defensa? ¿No es / también mi venganza vuestra?" (2061b). Yole has become a frenzied, pitiless woman; she pays a terrible price for her vengeance.

The play ends with celebration of Amor's triumph. Chained to Amor's chariot, Hércules laments that he has been betrayed: "traidora Yole, / sin amor al Amor venga" (2062b). But there is one bright spot in this otherwise contradictory world of passion. Aristeo, who originally attempted to marry Yole by force, finds his love of Verusa rewarded with her hand in marriage. The world is not entirely pessimistic, for there is hope for those who nobly pursue their obligations and their passions.

Conclusion

Hércules assiduously avoided any female influence on his life which he exclusively dedicated to fame and its values. His meeting with Yole is indeed a type of initiation. Yole as a figure of death does not represent the death of any infantile nature in Hércules's passage to a higher state of being, as Andrómeda did for Perseo, but rather signifies the hero's failure to transcend his immature and incomplete form of being-in-the-world. As a death figure Yole ultimately symbolizes the death of Hércules's fame, the "desdoro de sus triunfos," as well as his regression to the more beastly forms of existence. Hércules's ontic suffering, though, is not as total as was Narciso's, which led to actual death. Perhaps his suffering is more acute because he has glimpsed, though briefly and incompletely, the true happiness that awaits those who love nobly and well. At the play's conclusion Hércules becomes a more integrated person who elicits our compassion. Aristeo's and Verusa's happiness is not just tidying up the last act, but a glimpse of a better and truer world of requited love that the hero has come to recognize. Yole, on the other hand, becomes a negative presence in the play. Though victimized and dehumanized by men, she becomes a brutal and vengeful person who assumes the values of a corrupt masculine society. If there is growth and insight on Hércules's part, on Yole's there is only regression to a brutish life signalling her deliberately accepted dehumanization.

In Calderón's two plays dealing with the Heracles myth, the hero is shamed and brought low by his unruly passions. In *Prodigios* Hércules's shame results from his exaggerated sense of honor that sees accusing glances in everyone's face. In *Fieras* his exaggerated sense of honor leads him to neglect the full range of his humanity, which violently rebels against this unnatural and unhealthy form of being-in-the-world. Hércules may indeed be the greatest hero of Greece, but in Calderonian theater he is a boaster, a brute, and a fool who allows his life to be ruled either by others' opinions or by his desperate need of their acclaim. The three plays that comprise this chapter demonstrate that masculine power rests on a very loose and sandy foundation. Much of what induces men to seek fame and power derives from a faulty system of values. Men are given to physical violence, and through it they confront the world. What ultimately brings about their undoing is their failure to conquer the unruly world writhing within themselves. Be they gods or be they men like Hércules, they cannot dominate the world and those who live in it for any extended period of time, for the very violence they use to assert themselves is the same violence that denies them victory. They live lives out of harmony with what creates true happiness. For in the end happiness is not won through violence, but by the flowering of one's inner being. Apolo, though god of reason and light, surrenders himself to blind passion. Hércules, though valiant and brave, commits the very acts that tarnish his life's goal, to gain fame and worldly recognition. Masculine pride creates an illusion as to who we are and why we are in-the-world. The power these characters thought was theirs proved illusory.

Notes

1 The text of *Fieras afemina Amor* referred to is that found in the Valbuena Briones edition, pp. 2023-63, with reference to the *loa* from the *Quinta Parte* (Madrid, 1677). In the title of the play *Amor* should be capitalized since it refers to Cupid. After having completed the study of *Fieras*, I came across Edward M. Wilson's edition of the play (Kassel: Edition Reichenberger, 1984).

2 For pertinent details on the texts of *Fieras*, see E. M. Wilson, "The First Edition of Calderón's *Fieras afemina Amor*," in *The Textual Criticism of Calderón's "Comedias"*, ed. Don W. Cruickshank (London: Gregg and Tamesis, 1973), pp. 183-200.

3 See Sebastian Neumeister, "La fiesta mitológica de Calderón en su contexto histórico (*Fieras afemina amor*)," *Hacia Calderón: Tercer Coloquio Anglogermano: Londres 1973* (Berlin: Walter de Gruyter, 1976), pp. 156-70, for a different perspective that grants deterministic properties to the context of the first performance. Wilson's introduction to the play, "Calderón's Ignoble Hercules," found in his edition of *Fieras*, provides a well-reasoned overview, but oftentimes raises issues that are then not adequately addressed, such as Yole's role in the play. See pp. 39, 44, and 46.

4 Text cited, the *Quinta Parte* of Calderón's works, dated 1677; text modernized.

5 For a study of the *loa*, see Jorge Aguilar Mora, "Notas sobre la loa a *Fieras afemina amor*," *NRFH*, 23, no. 1 (1974), 111-15.

6 My own contribution to criticism on the play, "Hércules y el mito masculino: La posición 'feminista' de *Fieras afemina Amor*," *Estudios sobre el Siglo de Oro: en homenaje a Raymond R. MacCurdy* (Madrid: Cátedra y Universidad de New Mexico at Albuquerque, 1983), pp. 171-80, while focusing on an important aspect of the play, does not address the text's extremely complex nature.

7 "La comedia mitológica calderoniana: soberbia y castigo," *RFE*, 56 (1973), 76.

8 Hércules's dream reminds us of Perseo's in the grotto of Morfeo in *Fortunas*.

VII   The Myth of the Prudent Male

A. El mayor encanto, amor

Circe.	Venceréle mi hermosura,	*Ap*.
	pues mi ciencia no ha podido.	
Ulises.	Libraré de aquella fiera	*Ap*
	a Trinacria, si amor finjo.	

(1520b)[1]

Tradition has transformed Ulysses, that crafty warrior who originally feigned madness to avoid sailing for Troy, into a symbolic representation of prudence. In his introduction to *Encanto*, Valbuena Briones stresses this traditional interpretation of Ulysses's wanderings as the allegorization of an interior journey. Citing Seneca's 87th *Epistle*, he states that "las tempestades y aventuras sufridas por el héroe griego bien pudieran explicarse como figuras de las pasiones y peligros que acechan al espíritu humano" (p. 1508a). To approach Calderón's dramatization of Ulysses's dalliance with Circe in this fashion may provide us with the "approved" traditional view of this mythic figure, but it will not deal with, nor account for, the ambiguity that defines and gives human shape to his character and actions.

The Renaissance approached Ulysses's adventures as a psychomachy, an interior battle of the soul with the body, that rebellious element in the uneasy union of flesh and spirit. Pérez de Moya emphasized that the myth of Ulysses represents the entire life of man (II, 214), and I stress "man" in this context. Ulysses symbolizes Reason, the master and lord of appetite and desire. Placed in a male-female context, Ulysses becomes a masculine paragon dominating dangerous and deadly female monsters: "Pasar Ulises por Escila, y Circe, y Sirenas sin daño alguno, denota que la sabiduría, ententida por Ulises, menosprecia la lujuria" (Pérez de Moya, II, 216). Circe is, therefore, "amor deshonesto" (II, 219), and Ulysses's stay with her may be interpreted as follows: "Por Ulises se entiende la parte de nuestra ánima que participa de la razón. Circe es la naturaleza. Los compañeros de Ulises son las potencias del alma, que conspiran con los afectos del cuerpo y no obedecen a la razón" (II, 219). Such an allegorical approach fails to address first and foremost the blatant misogyny of the myth itself and secondly the particular dramatization that is *Encanto*.

Calderón's *El mayor encanto, amor* stands as a unique dramatic text in terms of its plot, characterization, and action. Allegorical interpretation tends to form an overlay that reduces *Encanto*'s action to a symbolic formula, such as the one cited above from *Philosophia secreta*. Even a contemporary mythographer may view that same action in similar *symbolic* terms. For example, Hathorn states that "all the lands that Odysseus (Latin Ulysses) visits are lands of the dead" (p. 392). I shall approach *Encanto* as human drama with narrative rather than allegorical significance. According to Paul Ricoeur, narratives portray "the features of temporal experience."[2]

Encanto is Calderón's first dramatization of a Greco-Roman myth, and it reveals artistic tendencies and directions characteristic of the mature dramatist's inchoate courtly style. Though originally meant for St. John's Night of 1635 (23 June) in the Buen Retiro, the play was postponed and performed between 25 June and 29 July of the same year.[3] Whenever it was eventually performed, it was a great success.[4] *Encanto* is famous, however, for bringing to light a conflict of dramatic conception between the Italian engineer Cosme Lotti and Calderón.[5] Lotti had proposed an elaborate scheme in which the ingenious and spectacular effects would dominate the dramatic action. Calderón, expected to provide some text for this dramatization of Ulises's stay with Circe, firmly responded that drama is representation and that the stage machinery would have to serve it and not vice versa. Charles Aubrun opines that the *comedia-fiesta*, typified by *Encanto*, was a hybrid production that was not viable, at least until Calderón fixed the genre in 1661 with *Eco y Narciso*, *El monstruo de los jardines*, and *Faetonte* (p. 435). While the debate raged as to the form these productions were to take, I would emphasize that, for our purposes, thematic and ideological concerns are of equal, if not more, importance. As in the case of *Prodigios*, dramatic innovation may lull us into a critical stupor duplicating the effect of Circe's drugs on Ulises's companions, unless we remain alert to the dynamics of the text itself. Much more was at stake than the definition of courtly spectacle, for *Encanto* reveals a rift in the Baroque mindset that would become more pronounced and more explicit twenty-two years later in *El golfo de la Sirenas*. Accompanying this debate on the definition of a dramatic subgenre, there would be an equally interesting, if not more subtle and significant, tension or dialectic in operation regarding traditional views of men and women. *Encanto's* theatrical success may overshadow the fact that the plot and characterization portrayed an essential feature of temporal experience – the distorted nature of male-female relations.

"Encanto" and the Mode of Romance

Susan L. Fischer has demonstrated that *Encanto's* dramatic mode is that of romance.[6] We must also take into account other generic markers that place *Encanto* in what Haverbeck Ojeda has called "la comedia de enredo de tipo palaciego" (p. 76). In *Encanto* Ulises does not fight monsters like those that confronted Perseo, Teseo, and Jasón, but a more insidious and subtle form of danger, his own unruly nature. Therefore, in terms of a traditional psychomachy he must overcome his own concupiscence. This struggle is set in the feminized world of Circe's palace where love, jealousy, deceit, and betrayal underscore the basic conflicts between men and women.

Most of Act II is devoted to courtly intrigue. The preceding act ended with Circe's declaration that her beauty will conquer Ulises since her science failed. Ulises, discounting the danger of remaining with the witch, declares that by feigning love he will rid Trinacria of Circe's fatal presence. Thus is set the basic dichotomy between beauty (the female power) and heroism (the masculine power), a tension that *Fieras afemina Amor* would exploit thirty-five years later. Instead of a straightforward presentation of objectives, the characters employ subterfuge and deceit to further their ends. In the esoteric environment of Circe's palace we discover a mirror-like image of the intrigue that makes up courtly life.

As courtly intrigues accentuate and problematize economic and political reality, so too do they affect the emotional and affective well-being of courtiers. Circe's plans to captivate Ulises have backfired; instead she becomes enamoured of the Greek hero. She summarizes her interior conflict as follows:

> Quiero, digo; pero quiero
> tanto, a mi ambición atenta,
> que quiero a Ulises, y no
> quiero que Ulises lo entienda.
>
> (1521a)

To avoid her shame yet still indulge her passion, Circe orders Flérida, who truly loves Lisidas, to woo Ulises and invite him to a noctural meeting where Circe will await him. This charade reminds us of Dafne's request in *Laurel* that Silvio and Céfalo feign emotions opposite to those they really experience and anticipates a similar request Circe will make of Ulises and Arsidas. This deceit ostensively protects Circe from the ravages of *celos*, since Flérida does not love Ulises. Both Lisidas and Arsidas, however, become vehemently jealous of Ulises. Circe sacrifices Flérida's happiness to maintain a haughty but now false image of herself, for in actuality she has been brought down by her passion.

Ulises, too, finds himself compromised by his heroic but unwise pretensions. As he enters Circe's palace he says:

> Temeroso vengo, ¡ay triste!,
> a ver a Circe, si es fuerza
> que como sabia la admire,
> y la admire como bella.
> ¡Quién no se hubiera fiado
> tanto de sí!
>
> (1522b)

The action proceeds, then, to reveal true feelings and at the same time to conceal them. Ulises explains this contradiction in terms that differentiate "cortesana fineza" from "fineza amorosa" (1523a). Circe furthers this mode of deceit, in which illusion is maintained at the expense of truth, by fostering the "role-playing" potential of the action. In order to communicate her compromised position to Lisidas, Flérida proposes "una aguda cuestión" (1523b) for discussion: "¿cuál es más dificultoso? / ¿Fingir o disimular?" (1523b). As Ulises and Arsidas hotly debate the issue, they arrive at the point where argument yields to violence. What was a *duelo de ingenio*, or miniaturized *certamen poético*, now becomes an opportunity for Circe to indulge her passion at the same time as she upholds her haughty reputation. She proposes a trial of the two contenders: each one shall feign the opposite emotion of that which he has publically proclaimed. Ulises shall court Circe; Arsidas shall dissimulate his love. Thematically this *vivir al revés* anticipates and foreshadows Ulises's emasculation at Circe's hands, for the hero will assume the supine, feminine position in Trinacria as Circe assumes the erect and masculine role of warrior and defender of the realm. What is at stake is traditional gender-roles that *Encanto* problematizes through role-reversal.

To further our understanding of the mode of romance in Calderonian court theater, it would be illuminating to contrast the first two myth plays, *Encanto* and *Prodigios*, given in 1635 and 1636 respectively. Each work represents a different aspect of romance. In *Encanto's* case we shall discover a type of drama similar to *Devoción*, in which a tragic outcome is averted through supernatural intervention. In *Prodigios's* case the tragic issue is emphasized, and the dramatic movement is from the mode of romance to a more all-encompassing generic classification within Calderonian dramaturgy, tragedy. *Encanto's* dramatic movement, however, is from romance to a form of "divine" or "supernatural" comedy. On examining more closely the two structures we discover that Time plays a crucial role in differentiating the tragic from the "comedic" issue. In the tragic outcome Time is *Chronos*, or ordinary time, and it manifests itself as cyclical or reductional time entrapping men and women in passing events and everyday circumstances. In the comedic outcome Time is *Kairos*, or the opportune moment, and it manifests itself as progressive or teleological[7] time allowing men and women to escape from the pull of ordinary time and the confinement of everyday occurrences. The dramatic manifestations of these two distinct views of time are found in the notion of fate, accompanied by a singular emphasis on chance and fortune, and in the notion of providence, accompanied by a strong emphasis on human liberty, liberation, and freedom. The following chart summarizes these contrasting relations:

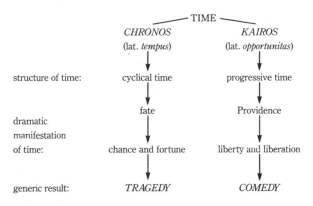

Like *Devoción*, *Encanto* proceeds as if it were to issue in tragedy. Ulises has been wandering throughout the Mediterranean for six years, unable to return to Greece and his long-suffering wife Penélope. In the conflict between love and duty, or between passion and honor, Ulises is trapped in a sequence of events that would prevent his return—adventures with Polyphemus, Circe, Charybdis, Scylla, the Sirens, and Calypso. In *Encanto* the Music sings prophetically: "¿Dónde vas, Ulises, si es / el mayor encanto amor?" (1537a). He would appear to be destined to wander endlessly through the Mediterranean, fated not to return to Greece. Only the direct intervention of Juno and Iris prevents the tragic flowering of Ulises's fate. In the world of myth, this divine intervention parallels that of providence in a play like *Devoción*. At the end of Act III, when Circe returns triumphant from battle, she finds that Ulises has fled her island. To avenge her shame, she sets the ocean ablaze to destroy her former lover. Galatea, however, arrives in "un carro triunfal" (1544a) to calm the sea and permit the Greeks to escape. This *dea ex machina* saves the hero who avenged Polifemo's murder of Acis. In both instances, Ulises receives divine assistance from goddesses: first, Juno and Iris protect Ulises from Circe's poison through the gift of the theriac; second, Galatea saves him from the "tormentas del mar" (1544a) conjured up by Circe. Pérez de Moya states that Circe-like pleasures may turn us into beasts, "si la divina clemencia no nos ayudare, no nos permitiendo resbalar, lo cual se entiende por el don que Mercurio dio a Ulises" (II, 220). Calderón's deliberate substitution of Iris for Mercurio as the provider of the theriac is significant and will be examined in more detail below. Without this supernatural aid Ulises would have fallen victim to Circe's magic, not once, but twice. Though supernatural intervention is conventional in romance, in terms of our outline of the overall generic conception of dramatic action, it is decisive. *Encanto* is a romance of comedic design, whereas *Prodigios* is one of tragic dimensions.

The Character of the Greek Hero

Calderón depicts Ulises as an ambiguous character, tossed about by fate and victimized by his unruly passions. A storm raised by the vengeful Neptuno has driven him to Trinacria, a land full of horror, fear, and enchantment. As he strikes a tree with his sword, the trunk cries out its human pain. After sending out a party to reconnoiter the island, a squadron of beasts urges Ulises to flee this horrible place. As he tries to regroup his men, Antistes returns with the news that the Greeks have been turned into brutes by Circe's magic potion. Calling on Juno to aid him in this time of need, Ulises receives the theriac with the warning:

> Toca con él sus hechizos,
> desvaneceránse luego,
> como al amor no te rindas.

> (1513b)

This divine aid makes Ulises overconfident, for he now underestimates Circe's powers and wiles (1514a). The overt motive for such confidence is Ulises's belief in his heroic stature; the underlying explanation, however, depends on different reasons, his pride and self-assurance.

Ulysses was never a simple, unidimensional character. As the Greeks prepared for war against Troy, he feigned madness in order to remain at home with Penelope. He acted as Achilles did when the latter hid himself among Deidamia's companions. Ulysses's dalliances with several women after the Trojan War undermine his representation as the champion of true love and fidelity. And it will be remembered that he was eventually killed by his son Telegonus, whom he sired with Circe (Pérez de Moya, II, 214). While Western mythographers such as Pérez de Moya viewed Ulysses as an apt figure for allegorization, there were contradictory aspects to his life and career that would detract from and problematize that process. The Greek hero would eventually become a symbol of the wise man as well as a symbol of human reason. While it is possible to depict him as the prudent and wise wayfarer through life, Calderón's dramatic vision explores the conflictive potentiality of his character, revealing not the allegorical straw man, but one defined by contradiction and ambiguity.

Heroism Vs. Eroticism: The Question of Identity

El mayor encanto, amor was originally scheduled to be presented on St. John's Night of 1635, but was postponed due to the outbreak of war with France. The thought of the French King on campaign, while his Spanish counterpart was enjoying himself in the Buen Retiro, was too much for the Spanish nation to bear, so political and military considerations dictated the delay.[8] With this political background in mind, the choice of Ulises's dalliance with Circe takes on new significance. The play's thematics reflect the conflict within Ulises himself: Is he to continue his heroic exploits, or is he to surrender himself to sensuality and sexual pleasure? Such a dilemma explicitly reflects the love/war conflict facing the Spanish nation: Should Spain continue to indulge herself to the neglect of vital national interests?

Frederick de Armas has established a critical framework for *Encanto* that views the play as yet another manifestation of the Mars-Venus struggle.[9] As Circe, the despiser of love and reverer of chastity, figuratively becomes the goddess Venus, so too Ulises, the representative of *sapientia*, eventually shuns erotic delights and becomes "the perfect hero," Mars, adding *fortitudo* to *sapientia* (p. 5). Whereas iconographic parallels are unmistakable, *Encanto*'s more subtle dynamics challenge this traditional view. What is at stake in the play is Ulises's identity and destiny.

Ulises has been buffeted by the winds of fate that propel him into one danger after another. Antistes summarizes the peril that Circe represents:

> ¿Y quién vio que, siendo hermosa
> una mujer con extremo,
> para hacer los hombres brutos
> usase de otros remedios,
> pues de estas transformaciones
> es la hermosura el veneno?
>
> (1513a)

Though Ulises will defeat Circe's magic through the use of the theriac, he will not be able to withstand her *hermosura*. As Act I closes, the basic issue of the play is emphasized through Circe's recourse to a more subtle plan of attack than that provided by her magic charms: "Vencerále mi hermosura, / pues mi ciencia no ha podido" (1520b). And Ulises, seeing himself as the perfect hero, will gain new fame by directly confronting the witch and her powers: "Libraré de aquesta fiera / a Trinacria, si amor finjo" (1520b). The lines are drawn. Both are attempting to uphold and further their self-images: the disdainful beauty and the heroic male. Both will employ love as a means to deceive and defeat the other. Instead of uniting man and woman, such love divides and destroys them.

Though Ulises is forewarned of the real danger Circe presents, he unwisely trusts in his powers to resist. Though he originally planned to kill her, he pardons her life. As events unfold Circe undergoes a subtle transformation, for she previously viewed herself in the following terms:

> yo fiera y monstruo
> tan dada soy a los vicios,
> solos delitos de amor
> fueron para mí delitos.
>
> (1518b)

Both, for different reasons, underestimate the power of love/lust as they become entrapped in circumstances they believed they controlled.

What is most curious in this situation is the role of woman, or the view taken of her as obstacle to, or destroyer of, men. A good example of the triumph of feminine wiles over masculine heroism occurs in *Fieras afemina Amor*, where Yole, through tender tears and hypocrisy, enthralls Hércules and causes him to forget his heroic nature and exploits. In a somewhat similar manner, Ulises and Circe set out to deceive and conquer each other, thereby avenging themselves and protecting their self-images. These two characters undergo subtle tranformations, or "metamorphoses," that they do not understand nor control.

As a foil to this process of metamorphosis, Clarín undergoes a comic change from man to *mona*. Though this punishment of the *gracioso's* abusive remarks about Circe supplies many hilarious scenes, it also serves a predictive function for Ulises's eventual recognition of his duty and honor. Clarín ceases to be a *mona*, a monkey, but not a drunkard, on contemplating his visage in a mirror. He only accidently escapes from his animal nature. Fischer has commented on the central image of descent narratives as that of metamorphosis (p. 104). The *gracioso* and the hero both change form: the one in a physical sense, and the other in a symbolic sense. While Clarín changes form a second time by chance or accident, Ulises will do so only through *rational* choice:

> yo fui de vuestros venenos
> triunfador, Teseo felice
> fui de vuestros laberintos,
> y Edipo de vuestra esfinge.
> *Del mayor encanto, amor*,
> la razón me sacó libre. . . .
>
> (1543b)

Calderón stresses here the role and power of reason in freeing Ulises from his lust. In the late myth plays, however, the will assumes a more significant role than reason in liberating both men and women from their entrapment in time and circumstance.

Since the play's dynamic tension depends on the mutual exclusion of sensual love and heroic fame, Ulises's emasculation results from his choice of love/lust. After all the conflict of Act I and role-playing of Act II, Ulises and Circe become lovers in Act III. Antistes underscores his leader's present plight when he comments: "solo de sus gustos trata, / siempre en los brazos de Circe" (1534a). Honor, fame, reputation, and home are all to be sacrificed to his "love." When Antistes's plan to remind him of his duty by sounding

"¡Guerra, guerra!" (1536b) fails, *Encanto* stresses the reason for such an outcome. Echoing the famous phrase "yo soy quien soy," Ulises voices its negative counterpart: "No soy sin duda el que fui" (1536b). The trumpet of fame is
incapable of overcoming the *gusto* of what Circe labels "dulce pasión" (1537b).
The options are clear and unmistakable: love/lust or war/honor. Ulises's
choice is unequivocal:

> Esclavo tuyo he de ser.
> No hay más fama para mí
> que adorarte. . . .
>
> (1537b)

When the Greek's two jealous competitors attack Circe, we find ourselves in
a world turned on its head. The one to face "la sangrienta venganza / de dos
celosos amantes" (1539a) is not Ulises, as should be the case, but Circe. Circe
has become the active member of this love duo, as the former hero lies "en
mudo letargo" (1539a).

   Two scenes occur which remind the hero of his depraved state, what we
could call the nadir of his heroic career. In the first, the armor of Aquiles
serves as a "talisman of recognition" (Fischer, p. 109), reminding Ulises of his
reputation as warrior. In the second, Aquiles himself appears to recover his
armor that is in the possession of the now "afeminado griego" (1542a). The
dead hero orders Ulises, in the name of the gods, to depart Trinacria. Ulises
then declares the symbolic significance of his decision to flee Trinacria as
reaffirmation of his identity:

> ¡Ay amigos!, tiempo es ya
> que a los engaños me usurpe
> del mayor encanto, y hoy
> el valor, del amor triunfe.
>
> (1542b)

From degenerate sensualist Ulises moves to rhetorical moralist:

> Huyamos de aquí; que hoy
> es huir acción ilustre,
> pues los encantos de amor
> los vence aquel que los huye.
>
> (1542b)

   In the meantime Circe has conquered the invading army led by Lisidas and
Arsidas, confirming the *mundo al revés* previously seen. The victorious
witch/lover returns expecting Ulises to greet her, much in the manner the
female population was expected to greet their male champions as they
returned victorious from battle. What has been so far a reversal of traditional
gender-roles now shifts to the allegorico-moral plane as Ulises emphasizes

the function of reason in his eventual liberation (1543b). Though he declares that "la razón me sacó libre," his victory is a reaffirmation of traditional roles and responsibilities, a dual victory of moral righteousness and manly virtue. The same conclusion was to be expected of the populace and court that viewed the production. More importantly, perhaps, such a conclusion reassures the faltering male ego that change is possible in spite of indulgence. But the ideal image of society depicted in *Encanto* would have to be called exclusivist and extreme. To stress manly valor violence has been done to the role and value of love, not lust, in human affairs. *Encanto* does not present us with the whole fabric of human relations, only a distorted sample.

"El mayor encanto, amor's" One-sided View

There is an inner contradiction in *Encanto* attributable to the allegorical impositions on the plot material. After stressing Ulises's role as that of reason, Circe's as that of Nature, and the companions' as that of "potencias del alma, que conspiran con los afectos del cuerpo y no obedecen a la razón," Pérez de Moya goes on to state: "Mas la razón, entendida por Ulises, permanece firme sin ser vencida, contra estos halagos del apetito" (II, 219). Ulises was defeated and overcome by his apetites and was only saved by outside intervention. This factual opposition to allegory's forced view of *Encanto*'s plot reveals an inner contradiction at the play's ideological core. Circe may represent lust, *lujuria* and *lascivia*, but her figure and its allegorization distort the role of woman and the nature of the relationship between men and women. Throughout the play Ulises has received divine assistance from Juno, Iris, and Galatea. In the divine background action, Juno avenged her affront at Paris's judgment through the Greek invasion of Troy. Venus, the goddess declared most beautiful by the son of Priam, sought to avenge the wrongs committed by the Greeks. Against this background filled with vengeance, we find a subtle change in the plot. The one who provides Ulises with the theriac is not Mercury, as Calderón well knew, but Iris, the messenger of Juno. She warns Ulises about Circe's magic and adds:

> Toca con él [ramo] sus hechizos,
> desvaneceránse luego,
> como al amor no te rindas.

> (1513b)

Love here is not true love, but lust, and thus viewed is a negative influence on the life of men. The feminine assistance of Juno, Iris, and Galatea reminds us of a more positive form of love. A trace of that true love asserts itself in the cases of Flérida and Lisidas's true affection and Acis and Galatea's true but tragic love. The substitution of Juno and Iris for Júpiter and Mercurio shifts our perspective from a masculine world view to a more integrated one, one that includes the feminine. *Encanto* may advise the rejection of love/lust, but the fuller view of male-female relations would have to await plays like *La fiera, el rayo y la piedra*, *Ni Amor se libra de amor*, or *La estatua de Prometeo*.

A significant dimension to the plot involves the movement of *Encanto's* internal conflict from the personal to the univeral plane. Ulises arouses the jealousy of Arsidas over Circe's affection (her lust) and also that of Lisidas over Flérida's love (feigned by her). In both instances the masculine view stresses the world as a place where status results from competition for females. But *Encanto* claims a more important insight concerning the nature of male-female relations. What undermines the traditionally accepted view of the Ulises-Circe episode as depicted in *Encanto* is the misogynous view of women portrayed therein. Not only are women viewed as dangerous to the male enterprise, that of heroic action, but the inherent goodness of the natural order is seriously questioned. Feminine beauty plays a significant role in the divinely ordained natural order, and plays like *Encanto* distort that role by positing a negative value to what otherwise is good and wholesome. It is precisely the underlying misogyny of plays like *El mayor encanto, amor* and *El golfo de las Sirenas* that produces their one-sided, and hence false, view of the natural order.

While the first performance of the play in the Buen Retiro during wartime may help explain the political message implicit in this dramatized myth, it is not sufficient to overcome this distortion of human relations. The Greeks may be viewed as Spanish males neglectful of duty; Ulises as their King, diverted from true honor and glory; and Circe and her palace as the Buen Retiro and its many pleasures, captivating these otherwise valiant and heroic males. But *Encanto's* momentary convenience betrays nature's divinely ordained goodness, for its misogynous view of woman reveals ideological conflicts within the Calderonian corpus, conflicts that would not be resolved but renewed in *El golfo de las Sirenas*.

Conclusion

What allows us to perceive and explicate this conflictive strain in Calderón's depiction of Ulises as the prudent male is the nature and value of the comic scenes in both *Encanto* and *Golfo*. In the former play we have dual *graciosos*, Clarín and Lebrel. Clarín is an excessive misogynist in the comic manner required of his type, whereas Lebrel is a more "normal" comic figure, the dupe of Clarín's more wily intelligence. The comic scenes become significant with Clarín's mordant criticism of Circe (1522a). The latter tricks him into believing that he will receive a treasure from the monster Brutamonte, but what he obtains is a *dueña* and a midget whose purpose is to spy on him. Similar scenes will occur in *Golfo*, where instead of *una dueña* the *gracioso* must confront his wife. In *Encanto* the trickster is tricked. Lebrel, the other *gracioso*, receives jewels and riches beyond measure whereas Clarín finds only disillusionment, a *dueña* and an *enano*.

The comic scenes are hilarious and very pronounced in *Encanto*. They undermine the play's misogyny, or, if this be too strong a description, they establish a countervailing dramatic movement that problematizes the main plot's exclusivist claims. Astrea, the female counterpart to Clarín, comments on her situation in Trinacria:

> Holgaréme de salir
> de religión tan estrecha
> como es el honor. Vestales
> vírgines Diana celebra
> entre gentes, mas nosotras
> entre animales y fieras
> somos vírgines bestiales.
>
> (1520)

Though comically expressed, honor as a substitute for, or an alternative form of, religion is nonetheless criticized. What Spanish honor does is to falsify the real world of men and women, and in this regard it defies the goodness and sacramental quality of the natural order, divinely ordained and blessed in *Genesis*. As men have set up substitutes for religion, such as the honor code, so too have they substituted their own narrow codes and views for the divinely ordained wholeness found in the relationships, sexual and otherwise, of men and women.

Twenty-two years later Calderón would return to the theme of Ulises as he attempts what could only be labelled the secularization of the *auto sacramental*. The implicit misogyny of the material in *El golfo de las Sirenas* would once more resist facile compartmentalization. While the *zarzuela* was born, Calderón's attempts to harness the figure of Ulises to his dramatic purpose would again fail. Prudence may indeed dictate flight as the only course of action open to the embattled hero. But as *Encanto* made clear in 1635, Ulises only negatively symbolizes what men must do to obtain a secular and temporal counterpart to divine and eternal salvation. Ulises cannot symbolize how males are to realize their human potential. Because *Encanto* and *Golfo* fail to show us the inner sacredness of human love, their allegorizations remain partial and incomplete. As a symbol, Ulises is incapable of shaking off his misogynous partrimony and representing reality.

Notes

1 The text cited is from the Valbuena Briones edition, I, 1507-45.

2 See *Time and Narrative*, p. 3.

3 For details on this question, see N.D. Shergold, "The First Performance of Calderón's *El mayor encanto amor*," *BHS*, 35 (1958), 24-27.

4 See N.D. Shergold, *A History of the Spanish Stage*, pp. 280-84.

5 Besides Shergold, see also Charles V. Aubrun, "Les Débuts du drame lyrique en Espagne," in *Le Lieu Théâtral à la Renaissance* (Paris, 1964), pp. 423-44.

6 See "Calderón's *El mayor encanto, amor* and the Mode of Romance," in *Studies in Honor of Everett W. Hesse* (Lincoln, Nebraska: Society of Spanish and Spanish-American Studies, 1981), pp. 99-112.

7 I am grateful to James A. Parr for having suggested the use of this term during a session at the AIH held in Berlin, Germany in 1986.

8 See Jonathan Brown and J.H. Elliot, *A Palace for a King: The Buen Retiro and the Court of Philip IV* (New Haven and London: Yale UP, 1980), p. 196. de Armas, though he gives a positive depiction of Ulises, integrates the social criticism of the Buen Retiro Palace into his astral-political interpretation of the play (*The Return of Astraea*, pp. 139-49).

9 "Metamorphosis in Calderón's *El mayor encanto, amor*," *RN*, 22 (1981), 1-5.

B. El golfo de las Sirenas

> Ulises.   entre Caribdis y Escila
>   atado y vendado escapa
>   de vuestros riesgos, porque
>   le quede al mundo *enseñanza*
>   que así huyen los extremos
>   de la hermosura y la gracia.
>   (1737b; emphasis added)[1]

Golfo continues the dramatic account of the wanderings of Ulises through the Mediterranean, begun in 1635 with the Circe adventure and resumed in 1657 with the hero's exploits with Escila, Caribdis, and the Sirens. This experimental play inaugurated on 17 January what was to be known as the *zarzuela*, a short dramatic piece in which singing, in freely structured recitatif,[2] was combined with the ordinary declamation of verse. What makes this dramatic work so unique is its one-act format, strongly resembling that found in the *auto sacramental*. In addition to this structural distinctiveness, the play emphasizes the comic element to a significant degree. *Golfo* is a short text, approximating in length what would normally be one act of an ordinary *comedia*, and it is the only mythological work published in the *Cuarta Parte* of Calderón's works with its *loa* and *mojiganga*. Perhaps its shortness dictated that these "minor" pieces be added to the main text in order to flesh out the play's length. A more probable explanation, however, lies in the centrality of the comic dimension, so accentuated in the *loa* and *mojiganga*, to the play's overall design. The work would lack coherence if these book-end forms were omitted. What in *Golfo* is an obvious contrast between the comic emphasis of the minor forms and the serious nature of the main play, becomes in *Laurel* a more integrated effort. In this latter case the *zarzuela* would, in addition to stressing the more lighthearted nature of the genre, assume its distinctive two-act format.

While these structural and generic concerns are significant for our understanding of the evolution of the myth play in Calderonian theater, especially in the late 1650s, we should not lose sight of the thematic links *Golfo* has with prior dramatizations of classical material. *Golfo* is a negative image of the rite of passage dramatized in plays such as *Fortunas* and *Eco y Narciso*. Since Ulises cannot but be destroyed by his encounter with these two women, such an adventure holds only *negative* potentiality for the hero. There can be no growth, no passage to a higher, more mature state. As a married man, Ulises faces not so much a rite of passage as the negative version of a former stage in his life. This negative dimension, which proceeds from the presentation of Escila and Caribdis, condemns the play to inner contradiction and ultimate failure, revealed by the ironic nature of the framing pieces that serve as ideological markers for our reading. The Woman-As-Death motif, characteristic of rites of passage, becomes not a symbol of future growth but rather a terrible reality of the threatening present.

"El golfo de las Sirenas" as Dramatic Experiment

As Calderón had experimented in such plays as *Encanto* and *Prodigios* with the *comedia's* adaptability to the more technologically sophisticated environment of the Buen Retiro, so too would he adapt its structural elements to the less courtly, more rustic setting of the Casa de la Zarzuela, "a small hunting lodge in the grounds of the Pardo" (Brown and Elliot, p. 220). The 1650s became the decade of musical plays, and *Golfo* was Calderón's first attempt to harmonize the *comedia's* structure with the court's desire for more refined and, at the same time, less formal theater. Music had always played a significant role in court productions, and *Golfo* sought to harmonize the rustic setting with a musical experiment that combined singing and acting into a unified whole. While the form thus achieved assumed the locale's name as its own, we should not overlook the contradiction this implied. The *zarzuela* was a most refined genre that attempted to appear simple, rustic, and uncomplicated. The illusion of rusticity only added to the pleasure of discovering such cultivated elegance.

This inner tension between appearance and reality is highlighted by the play's title, given in the *Cuarta Parte* of 1672 as "Comedia famosa. El golfo de las Sirenas, égloga piscatoria."[3] Though the elegant verses more than justify the use of "*égloga*" on this account, for *égloga* may be defined "como versos escogidos y bien compuestos,"[4] the primary meaning, "Razonamiento à manera de diálogo entre pastores," contradicts the subtitle's claim. *Eglogas* take place in Arcadia and not in Trinacria, that place of danger and foreboding, and their characters are shepherds and shepherdesses, not coarse fishermen and monsters. The "égloga piscatoria" designation advises us that this new genre is indeed a hybrid.

More than the unique combination of free recitatif and declaimed verse, *Golfo* attempts to transfer to the secular theater those allegorical characteristics that define the *auto sacramental*. Escila and Caribdis are threats to all mariners who land on Trinacria's shores. In Ulises's case their destructive desires translate into a symbolic battle, a psychomachy for the spectators' instruction. These female monsters are in competition with each other to prove which is the stronger sense and resultant passion, hearing or sight. Caribdis, for instance, states her position in these clearly symbolic terms: "Por ver si consigo así / probar que es pasion más fuerte / el oír que el ver" (1730a). When Ulises flees from the allurements of the two women, he states unequivocally the play's message:

atado y vendado escapa

> de vuestros riesgos, porque
> le quede al mundo *enseñanza*
> que así huyen los extremos
> de la hermosura y la gracia.
>
> (1737b; emphasis added)

Ulises thus becomes a dramatic symbol of Prudence that dictates that one must guard one's eyes and ears from temptation, for earlier he had directed Anteo and Dante to blindfold his eyes and stop up his ears. The passage of Ulises through the Sirens' song, as narrated in the original myth, yields to allegory's lesson. Ulises's docent function urges the application of foresight to human affairs at the same time as it dictates the interpretation of the tale itself.

Ulises's story teaches flight from temptation. Confronted by the charms of the two women, the hero is strongly tempted to follow both (1731a). Although his senses are inevitably captivated by beauty and grace, his reason recognizes the danger, acknowledges the apparent good, and concludes that his senses only react to physical stimuli without judging their moral value. In allegorical terms Ulises is the man buffeted by sensuality, trapped in the alluring charms of the physical world, rudderless in a tumultuous sea of delightful sensations. Dante, Ulises's trusted companion, symbolizes Reason's clear vision and proper ordering of human and worldly "goods." When Ulises becomes confused and indecisive regarding which course of action to undertake, Dante provides the only correct one: "Huir de aquí, que estos contrarios / huyendo se vencen" (1733a).

Golfo is yet another example of the mode of romance in Calderonian theater. In *Encanto* Ulises was liberated by Juno and Iris from the emasculating influence of Circe's love, and so too in *Golfo* he will have to rely on some outside force to free him from the dangers that characterize the Gulf of the Sirens. *Golfo's* dramatic movement is from romance to a type of "supernatural" comedy. Once Ulises decides to flee, he suddenly becomes enthralled by the song of the Sirens, the sight of Escila, and the delightful notes of Caribdis, and again becomes indecisive. His solution is to throw himself into the sea, ending his confusion and trial. Countering the "embates de la fortuna" (1737a), *el aura*, a soft and gentle breeze, moves Ulises and Dante out of harm's way. The latter comments:

> Que, pues, que ya en la vela
> sopla favorable el aura,
> y della el barco impelido
> no le hacen los remos falta,
> cerrados ojos y oídos
> correr nos dejemos hasta
> que dé del hado el arbitro

con nosotros a otra playa.

(1737)

Hado here is akin to providence that counters the malevolent influence of malign fate. Even with this outside assistance, Ulises finds himself incapable of resisting the temptations to commit suicide or to yield to sensual delights, because his memory now betrays him. At this point Anteo and Dante bind him to the mast, blindfold his eyes, and stop up his ears. Thus the Greek hero escapes danger and becomes an emblematic *enseñanza* of how to overcome temptation.

The Comic Dimension of "El golfo de las Sirenas"

Comedy is accentuated in *Golfo*. Alfeo, the Juan Rana of the piece, was thrown overboard and swallowed by a huge fish during Ulises's flight from danger. After the defeat of Escila and Caribdis and their metamorphoses into two reefs, Alfeo reappears on the scene, regurgitated by the "coche pez" (1738b). This scene is a burlesque treatment of Ulises's having been delivered by providence and helps us better to understand the nature of this light operetta or musical comedy.[5] Through the entire work there is a comical, but significant, tension between Alfeo and his wife Celfa. While this comic conflict between the *graciosos* is a foil to the serious oppositions between Ulises and Escila and Caribdis, we should not overlook a more revealing dramatic irony contained in what may appear to be conventional and expected humor. The text of *Golfo* struggles for both dramatic and ideological coherence as unassimilable elements of the dramatic design "refuse" to be taken into the serious pretentions, the moral lesson, of the *fiesta* as a whole. This tension emanates from the basic misogyny of the myth, and the Alfeo-Celfa comic relief enhances its unhealthy and negative impact.

From *loa* to *mojiganga Golfo* depicts women only as threatening presences to masculine valor and heroism. In the *loa*, Alfeo expresses his antagonism towards Celfa, principally due to her *malas costumbres*. As Alfeo expresses dejection on returning empty-handed from fishing, he cannot pass up the opportunity to comment on Celfa's *aviesas costumbres*:

pues que mucho quedar sienta,
viendo contra mi a las dos
en sus efectos opuestas,
con la mala pesca allà,
y aqui con la buena pesca?

(493b)

Moreover, Alfeo is constantly afraid that Escila or Caribdis will turn into Mari Brava, his nemesis. Such will indeed transpire in the *mojiganga*. Alfeo moves from hints and insinuations to accuse Celfa openly of infidelity, the very betrayal of one's spouse that Ulises is about to contemplate. In the former case, Alfeo accuses Celfa of making up for his absences and infirmities (498a), and she herself confesses the deceitful nature of all women: "¿ahora sabe su merced / que el engañar con halagos / lo hace cualquiera mujer?" (1733a), becoming a spokesperson for this type of humor. Alfeo also voices the traditional charge that his wife is a liar (1736a). The negative and comic portrayal of Celfa reflects the broader misogyny at the heart of this dramatic narrative.

The comic dimension assists us in putting into perspective the characterizations of Escila and Caribdis. Though not portrayed comically, their background stories flesh out a view of the world in which women are inevitably victimized by men and the society ruled by masculine values. Escila is a *semidea* who, on land, avenges past wrongs done to her by Anfitrite and Neptuno. The *loa* emphasizes how Anfitrite was scorned by Neptuno, who found Escila's charms more to his liking. Once this infatuation was discovered, Escila was made to pay the price. She now lives removed from society; her beauty is now perverse: "cuya nociua belleza, / es veneno de los ojos" (497a). Victimized by Neptuno's lust and Anfitrite's jealousy, Escila avenges her past wrongs on any hapless seafarer who falls into her clutches. The victim has turned victimizer.[6] Caribdis, the daughter of Aglauco and the Siren Caribdis, avenges, on the sea, her father's scorn of her mother. She too now lives removed from society; her voice is now perverse:

> cuya regalada voz,
> traydoramente alhagueña,
> es veneno del oido.

> (497b)

These two former victims are brigands who entice unwary men to their deaths. Without the fuller account of their lives supplied by the *loa*, the simple statement found in the play itself, "vengando ambas las afrentas / de Aglauco y Neptuno" (1725b), lacks perspective and significance. What ties their histories to the comic portrayal of Alfeo and Celfa's relationship is the misogynous attitude of males and the status of females as victims. Escila and Caribdis have not passively accepted their societally given roles, and neither will Celfa, though she is to be liberated in a different melodic key.

Metamorphosis and the Question of Identity

At the conclusion of *Golfo*, Escila and Caribdis are metamorphosed into two "mountains" that threaten mariners. These metamorphoses are the negative image of those tragic deaths depicted by Ovid where unending love defies annihilation. In *Encanto* Circe committed suicide in a frenzy of passion because Ulises spurned her love. In *Golfo*, Escila and Caribdis, likewise fren-

zied by Ulises's escape from the death they planned for him, kill themselves
in spiteful anger. Therefore, metamorphosis is not that positive recognition
Ovid sometimes paid to love, but rather a negative symbol resulting from
hatred and betrayal. The metamorphoses suggest that we examine the characters' natures, their motivations, and their values. The character of Ulises,
like those of Escila and Caribdis, is not a given, but something forged upon
the anvil of circumstances. The emasculation of Ulises—the act of his being
deprived of vigor and strength—is brought about by his surrender to concupiscence. *Golfo* dramatizes the interior struggle between essence, the heroic
view of Ulises, and those existential aspects of character that make up and
ultimately tarnish his self-image.

Ulises becomes aware of the dangers that Escila and Caribdis represent
through Alfeo's comic narration. But this present danger causes him little
concern because the hero fears more the revelation that he "evilecía / el anti-
guo honor de Grecia" (1727b) during his dalliance with Circe. He is primarily
concerned with his public image, his *fama*. He then goes on to define what
was at risk in the Circe affair and what will be at risk in the Escila-Caribdis
affair:

> La voz más armonïosa,
> ya suene sutil, ya cuerda,
> ¿es más, di, que una asonancia?
> La hermosura más perfecta,
> ya afable mire, ya esquiva,
> ¿es, di, más que una apariencia,
> tan hija aquella del viento,
> tan hija del tiempo esta,
> que cualquier aura la gasta,
> cualquier hora se la lleva?
> Pues ¿por qué se ha de pensar
> que en heroico pecho pueda
> perfección que es accidente
> postrar valor que es esencia?
> Mi vista y mi oído, es justo
> que a ajeno dueño me vendan?
> no, ni es posible.

(1727b)

After this moralistic tirade, Ulises exhibits the arrogance that led to his prior
fall and will presently entangle him in greater dangers. Part and parcel of the
hero's *hamartia* is the belief that he controls the events that are only now
beginning to unfold. He believes in the heroic image he projects to the world,
what he calls his essence. In characteristic fashion, Ulises declares:

Siempre los sentidos fueron
vasallos de la prudencia,
y no tienen contra mí
ni vista, ni oído fuerza,
más que aquella que yo quiero
que livianamente tengan.

(1728a; text altered.)

Ulises does not understand that his recognition of the problem at hand does not necessarily translate into its immediate solution. As a believer in his own heroic essence, he underestimates the power of sensual attractions.

The Greek hero expresses the psychomachy he is about to undergo in terms of a battle between essence and accident. Can his senses betray him? Can his hearing, which is attuned to the melodious beauty of the human voice that is as insubstantial as the assonances it produces, betray his heroic valor for that which may be dissipated by the wind? Can his sight, which is captivated by the alluring image of physical beauty that is as insubstantial as the appearance it projects, also betray his heroic valor for that which is destroyed by time? Can these sensual perfections, these accidental properties of the physical world, overcome Ulises's manly valor, his essence as hero? His pride cannot contemplate such an eventuality. Therefore, the impending conflict is set first in terms of a symbolic battle between prudence and the rebellious tendencies of the senses of hearing and sight and second in terms of an abstract battle between Ulises's "essential" characterization as manly valor and the "accidental" factors of environment that detract him from living up to that Greek ideal. We realize that Ulises's essence is not a given, but is in the process of being formed by the difficulties he faces. The desire to commit suicide to escape from those difficulties attests to the severity of his trial. But such an escape is cowardly, unworthy of the hero.

The theme of ontological instability is subtly introduced by the poetical description of the royal family. In terms of astral imagery, Mariana de Austria is depicted as Alba, Felipe IV is Sol, and Margarita is Aurora. The ladies are just as easily portrayed as goddesses who in the rustic *loa* become rivals for beauty and grace's accolades. They too have dual possibilities: Mariana is "Mari-Diana," Margarita, "Mari-Tersa." There is even a Mari-Brava awaiting Alfeo (497b). In terms of the gods, Felipe represents a mounted Adonis, a radiant presence in the Zarzuela. The changling quality of this world is more forcefully highlighted in the comic relief of the *mojiganga*, the concluding piece of the *fiesta de zarzuela*. We are all subject to mutability, and Alfeo drives home this point in his burlesque defeat of the savage monster Gasparilis de Aravaca. When the latter is not allowed to fulfill his destiny as the narrator of tales, he dies, for "el grande cuento de cuentos" (516b) depends on narration for his existence. He has guarded the enchanted victims of Trinacria through his recounting of old tales that Alfeo finds tedious: "Tenía una dueña una enana" and "A cuatro o cinco chiquillos." Though the cowardly Alfeo could not stomach direct battle with the monster, his aesthetic rejection of hackneyed tales proves too much for Gasparilis. How does Alfeo defeat this monster without powerful arms? Gasparilis de Aravaca informs us: "Cõ no oirme, que a vn salvaje, / quien no le escucha le mata" (516b).

With the defeat of Gasparilis, Alfeo reverses the beastly metamorphoses of Escila's victim and disenchants Celfa, who appeared at first to be a "Grande Infanta," but in reality was Mari Brava y Zarzuela. The comic de-metamorphoses that occur as the *mojiganga* concludes underscore the question of identity. The frightening beasts of Trinacria, though they revert to their original natures, continue to exhibit their predatory qualities. A harpy becomes a "tía," as her male companion sheds his wolf-like appearance. A dark green serpent becomes the proverbial mother-in-law, as the lion reverts to the status of coward. The tiger assumes her role as go-between, as her male companion sheds his wildcat image. And finally the magpie becomes a "dueña," as her male counterpart ceases to be a great pig only to assume his role as a wild boar. One wonders whether the original metamorphoses, which comically revealed the actual characters of these personages, were more beneficial to humankind by alerting us to the dangers they pose. Regardless, through this burlesque treatment of the duality of human character, its penchant for good and evil, the theme of Ulises's exploit is highlighted. Metamorphosis, the work appears to suggest, is not so much the transformation of nature as the revelation of character.

The Intertextuality of "El golfo de las Sirenas"

Golfo is replete with comical allusions to the dramatic nature of the illusion that is theater. Alfeo believes the day has finally arrived in which he will deliver "una relación," only to realize that "no puedo ser largo" (1726b). Celfa alludes to the *loa* in which "forasteras deidades" (1732b) from the Hapsburg court were entertained in Escila's rustic domain. There are allusions to Calderón's *Peor está que estaba* (1727a) as well as to *El mayor encanto, amor* (1733b). And one of Gasparilis's stories, "A cuatro o cinco chiquillos," brings to mind Juanete's repeated attempts to narrate the same story in *El pintor de su deshonra*. But *Golfo's* fundamental relation to the allegorized Eucharistic play, the *auto sacramental*, so much so that one may call this work a secularized *auto*,[7] leads us to the realization that allegory's clarity demands the sacrifice of narrative's insight. While *Golfo* is perfectly comprehensible in terms of the symbolic framework Calderón established for the work's elucidation, the play does not satisfy us. The *loa* and *mojiganga* reveal a discordant note in the dramatization of the myth. Though Ulises represents Prudence, his actions betray a misogyny that has crept into the myth and its traditional allegorization. The graciosos put a different light on matters that we have been accustomed to viewing in exclusivist terms. *Golfo*, therefore, chronicles the failure of Calderón's attempts to apply his *auto-sacramental* formulae to the secular stage. Allegory's one-sidedness was not capable of capturing dramatic narrative's ambiguity and timelessness.[8]

The *loa* dramatizes two principal themes. First, it establishes the antagonism of Alfeo towards Celfa, revealing thereby a latent misogyny in male-female relationships. Though we laugh at their stupidities, we recognize in ourselves similar attitudes and beliefs. Second, Alfeo sets out to demystify the poeticized view of nature. In spite of poetry's beauty and power, its ability to transform reality into a more suitable creation is temporary at best and figurative in fact. The *loa's* attempt to create an imaginative spring in the heart of winter cannot change the cold outside the hall. Poetry cannot make Felipe IV a great and wise ruler, nor can it transform Ulises into a model of masculine prudence. Something at the core of reality refuses compromise as Calderonian art remains faithful to its representational commitment in the face of political and ideological pressures.

The *mojiganga* emphasizes in its comic humor the themes of the main work. Alfeo, once deposited on the beach by the Marinatarasca, confesses he does not know who he is: "Que sè yo quien soy" (515a). In the world of honor, one is ultimately defined by what others say one is, and Alfeo's disorientation burlesques the fundamental dependence of the man of honor on opinion. The music finally informs Alfeo that he is Juan Rana and that he is in la Zarzuela, or la Zarzuela de Trinacria. When Alfeo fails to find his wife Celfa, he experiences a certain relief. The enchanted Celfa, on the other hand, underscores the burlesque treatment afforded the world of romance and the motif of the White Knight who liberates the captive heroine from horrible dangers. She shall remain imprisoned until a knight free her from Escila's vengeful enchantment. Alfeo unwittingly faces and defeats two monsters, a savage beast on entering and a dragon on leaving the enchanted precinct. These obstacles suggest to Alfeo the high social rank of the captive personage:

> Grande Infanta
> sin duda es, que estos primores
> las de la Villa no gastan.
>
> (515b)

But fear finally overcomes his curiosity and valor. According to Mari Brava y Zarzuela, Juan Rana undertakes the adventure "por mi amor" (516a). The *desencantadorcito del alma*, Alfeo, refuses to free the *encantadorcitos del cuerpo*, including Celfa, for good reason, as he previously explained:

> Lleuara Bercebù el alma
> que tal sacara, que fuera

> muy heroyca patarata,
> que la que me prendiò antaño,
> desprendiera ogaño.
>
> (516a)

Since Juan Rana does not want to free Mari Brava at the cost of personal risk, he refuses battle; but Gasparilis forces the issue.

Although Alfeo frees the enchanted from Escila's spells by not listening to what makes men little better than savages, he must still face the dragon. In the meanwhile Mari Brava descends in a *nube* or *banasta*, the "nube de moji-ganga" (517a), only to discover that her knight is Alfeo. Alfeo's great princess is none other than his wife, and under no circumstance would he have willingly freed her from imprisonment. To avoid reunion with her, Alfeo accepts his incarceration and Celfa's liberation. As Juan Rana is hoisted aloft in the *nube-banasta*, the ropes of the winch become entangled, dumping him to the ground. The *mojiganga* smashes more than Juan Rana to pieces, for in the process of caricaturing the world of romance both male and female illusions are exposed and dashed on the boards of reality. All men are not White Knights ready at hand for any adventure; neither are all women great princesses won by dream and daring. For Celfa, the future without Alfeo is bright:

> Sin marido, y desencantada,
> q̃ dos venturas, venturas tan raras.
>
> (517b)

But Alfeo recovers and returns to his accustomed role. Celfa then sings:

> Que con marido, y desencantada,
> q̃ dos venturas, venturas tan raras.

Though peace is eventually made between them, Celfa repeats the former declaration. As the *mojiganga* closes, the gender-illusions we tend to live by stand comically, ridiculously revealed.

Conclusion

The dividing line between comic relief and serious action is more clearly drawn in *Golfo* than in *Laurel*, due to the prominent roles of the graciosos in the former's *loa* and *mojiganga*. The *fiesta* was intended to be more light-hearted, less serious than such works as *Fortunas* or *Fieras*. But in spite of its chaotic mix of frivolity and *enseñanza*, ideological concerns could not be easily dismissed. Ulises's wandering fancy and *Golfo's* underlying misogynous tendencies that envision women as detractors from male heroism could not be overlooked. What is obviously an inner structural tension between allegorical imperialism and representational fidelity problematizes the text. Allegory's one-sidedness, its exclusivist view, could not capture the ambiguity inherent in the human condition. *Golfo's* comic relief lays bare the ideological rifts in the allegorized view of the quality of Ulises's life and wanderings.

Golfo's significance depends on two factors. First, it is an experiment in dramatic form that attempts to adapt to the secular theater the structure and formulae of the *auto sacramental.* Second, it reveals a certain evolution within Calderonian theater that warrants an immediate dramaturgic caveat. The biological analogy implied in the term "evolution" suggests growth and maturation. While the dramatic form is "evolving" to meet the demands placed on traditional structures by advanced stage machinery and heightened musical accompaniment, the content of this particular play represents a throwback to ideological positions, such as those found in *La vida es sueño,* which are no longer acceptable nor relevant. Denial is a fact of life and at times a moral imperative. But this negative view is no longer adequate in addressing the broader concern of how one can become more fully human, more in tune with the goodness inherent in creation, or how one denies one's humanity, tragically rejecting the divine plan for human "perfection." Because "love" is viewed only in terms of lust, *Golfo* fails to capture the salvific potential of male-female relationships. *Golfo's* contradiction of a particularly Calderonian view of these relationships, especially characteristic of the 1650s, leads to the problematization of the text as a whole. The uniqueness of *Golfo* consists in its attesting to its own problematization, but only when the *fiesta* is viewed as a whole.

Classical texts use every available strategy of repression to conceal the heterogeneity of their signifying operation.[9] *Golfo* attempts a one-sided view of male-female relationships, but its *loa* and *mojiganga* alert us to this fact and point out its inadequacy. Once attuned to this text's inner contradictions and differences, we are privy to an ideological struggle and reaction characteristic of *Golfo* and the creative process that produced it. *El golfo de las Sirenas* is not great drama, though it is an interesting work with some very amusing moments. Its ultimate significance lies in the chronicling of a conflictive strain in Calderonian theater that tempers its Baroque brilliance and problematizes its apparently ideological orthodoxy.

Notes

1 The text cited is the same edition, I, 1723-38.
2 I owe this term to Louise K. Stein.
3 Quoted from the facsimile edition (London, 1973), p. 493.
4 *Diccionario de las autoridades,* s.v. *égloga.*
5 See Shergold, *A History,* p. 317.

6 For a full background account of Escila, see Pérez de Moya, I, 119-20.

7 Ciriaco Morón Arroyo has stated that "las comedias mitológicas no son sino autos sacramentales laicos," for both genres are composed "de pura historia y plasticidad sin intriga." See *Calderón: pensamiento y teatro* (Santander: Sociedad Menéndez Pelayo, 1982), p. 20. What Morón fails to address is the structural dynamics of such plays as *Golfo* that transcend "la edificación religiosa" or "la belleza clásica."

8 See my article, "Formula Thinking/Formula Writing in Calderón's *El golfo de las sirenas*," *BCom*, 38 (1986), 25-38. For an analysis of Astrea's symbolic role in the play, see *The Return of Astraea*, pp. 181-85.

9 I am grateful to Betty McGraw for bringing this fact to my attention.

VIII   The Myth of Love as a Salvific Force

A. La fiera, el rayo y la piedra

> Quien ama a lograr amando,
> porque es interés su fin,
> no puede decir que ama
> a su dama, sino a sí.
> Mas quien ama por amar,
> bien merece conseguir
> que el correspondido amor
> haga su vida feliz.
>
> (1622b-1623a)[1]

La fiera, el rayo y la piedra was performed in May of 1652 in the Coliseo of the Buen Retiro on the occasion of Queen Mariana de Austria's birthday.[2] Calderón wrote the text, and Baccio del Bianco, the Italian designer and engineer who succeeded the famous Cosme Lotti, designed the set. The royal feast celebrated the young Queen's youth and potential fecundity as Spain anxiously awaited a male heir to the throne. The concluding *máscara* states that official and popular hope:

> felices viváis y sea
> para ver en vuestros reinos
> la dichosa sucesión,
> que aguardan nuestros afectos.
>
> (1637a)

How appropriate it was to celebrate the nation's longing for an heir, and the resultant political stability he would bring, by depicting the duality of Amor's powers represented by Cupido (unrequited love) and Anteros (requited love)! Pérez de Moya had explained the contradictory influences of Cupid as follows: "oro es el mejor de los metales; plomo es el de poco valor, para denotar ser el amor mejor que el desamor, como el amor convenga a la conservación de la naturaleza, y el desamor, estorbador desta conservación" (I, 249). Calderón dramatizes these conflictive tensions and potentialities of nature by counterpoising two famous tales from mythology: first, the tragic love of Iphis for Anaxarete; and second, the transcending love of Pygmalion for his simulacrum of woman. In both stories life and love are viewed as one, and Ovid even includes this truism in Iphis's bitter denunciation of Anaxerete (*The Metamorphoses*, Book XIV). Though *La fiera* depicts the destinies of love and disdain, it is the former that gives purpose and meaning to the play.

We need but recall Hércules of *Fieras afemina Amor* to understand that both the hero and Anajarte infringe, in Haverbeck's words, on the "principio

de concordancia, de armonía" (p. 81). Their rejection of love, which stems
from their excessive pride, denies the goodness of the natural order and one's
procreational duty within society.[3] The dramatization of these myths, which
includes an intrigue centering on the right of succession, is not portrayed in
black and white, but in more subtle hues that give life to what could have
been mere dynastic allegory.

For years the importance of *La fiera* in *comedia* studies rested on the evidence the play supplied concerning staging techniques employed in the seventeenth century. Angel Valbuena Prat's "La escenografía de una comedia de
Calderón" brought to light the set designs used in a 1690 production that celebrated the marriage of Carlos II to Mariana de Baviera y Neoburg.[4] In his history of the Spanish stage, Shergold explains how three distinct versions of
the text assist us in better understanding the evolution of staging practices in
the second half of the century (pp. 305-10.) The first of these was, of course,
the May 1652 production with rubrics by Calderón. This version was published in the *Tercera Parte* of 1664. The second version was published by Vera
Tassis in 1687 and contained expanded rubrics that most likely correspond to
a later production. And the third version refers to the 1690 production in
Valencia. While this kind of evidence referring to the *mise-en-scène* is of ines-
timable value, we should not, in consequence, overlook the dramatic world
that the work creates.

La fiera dramatizes the thematics of love manifested in their dual and contradictory potentiality. Towards the end of the play, the Music clearly proclaims the work's message:

> ¡Muera, muera el amor vendado y ciego!
> ¡Viva el correspondido amor perfecto!
>
> (1636a)

There are but two paths open to humankind: the first, represented by
Cupido, is unrequited love, whose ultimate motivation is self-interest and
whose destiny is spiritual and physical death; the second, represented by
Anteros, is requited love, whose ultimate motivation is the pure and perfect
love of the other and whose destiny is spiritual fulfillment and physical regeneration. Love is the mainspring of all life. Valbuena Briones stated the moral
lesson of the play as follows: "El amor generoso es el camino de la felicidad.
La ingratitud conduce al fracaso y a la muerte espiritual" (1592a). Yet the play
is more than these statements would lead us to believe.

Before analyzing the plot, it would be helpful to review some of the alterations and additions Calderón made in melding the story of Iphis and Anaxarete with that of Pygmalion and his Statue. First, in his introduction to the
play, Valbuena Briones states that Pigmalión hated women. In Calderón's version the character is not the misogynist who disapproves of wanton female
behavior on the isle of Cyprus.[5] Though Calderón minimizes this aspect of

Pigmalión's character, he nonetheless emphasizes a more traditional form of misogyny in the *gracioso* Lebrón, Pigmalión's companion.[6] Second, contrary to the original myth, Pigmalión does not fabricate the Statue he eventually comes to love passionately. Calderón creates a supernatural origin for both the Statue and Pigmalión's irrational devotion to it (1633a). Third, while Calderón's understanding of dramatic decorum may be adduced for Ifis's not committing suicide on being rejected by Anajarte, there is a more sound explanation for this twist in the plot. Each of the three *galanes* is rewarded by Anteros for delivering him from Cupido's murderous designs. Though Ifis loses Anajarte, he gains his life through Anteros's intervention. Fourth, Anajarte is such a consummate hater of men that she plans to kill Ifis, her persistent suitor, in spite of the obligations she has incurred due to his many *finezas*, not the least of which was to restore her to her putative status as Queen of Trinacria. Fifth and finally, *La fiera* adds a third love intrigue involving Céfiro, the Prince of Trinacria, and Irífile, an "humano monstruo," who proves to be the rightful queen of Trinacria.[7] Such a succession intrigue would naturally fascinate the Hapsburg court, and the theme would be amplified in *En la vida todo es verdad y todo mentira*, written during the acting year 1658-59.[8]

The Divine Background to the Human Action

La fiera, el rayo y la piedra functions on two planes: the divine, in which Cupido and Anteros are at loggerheads over who will control the affective direction of the world; the human, where the supernatural conflict is finally played out. Cupido is an ambiguous god whose fickleness is described by Pérez de Moya as "poder de mover a amar y de desamar" (I, 249). Depending on the source consulted, one finds contradictory statements concerning Anteros, who in Edith Hamilton's *Mythology* is "said sometimes to be the avenger of slighted love, sometimes the one who opposes love."[9] The former characteristic is dramatized in the Ifis Anajarte plot of *La fiera*. But originally Anteros represented, in Hathorn's words, "the return of love, the requital of love." Through a misunderstanding of the etymology of the name of "*Anteros*," some employed him as a personification of "disdain for a lover" (p. 240). In our play Cupido is a totally capricious god whose only purpose is to sow seeds of discontent, while Anteros is the positive erotic force bringing together lovers so that the world may be renewed. In Neoplatonic terms, Cupido represents discord and opposition, whereas Anteros, harmony and correspondence.[10] Once again the disharmony of the earth is directly attributable to that which obtains in the heavens.

La fiera begins amidst terrible lightening and thunder that greet Céfiro, Pigmalión, and Ifis. Disoriented by these natural manifestations of fire, sea, air, and earth's lament, the three seek refuge in the mountains, that place of primitive mystery. They encounter Irífile, the "humano monstruo," whose astrological studies reveal the meaning of these natural phenomena:

> es cumplir una amenaza
> que tienen los dioses hecha,
> de que ha de nacer al mundo
> una deidad tan opuesta
> a todos, tan desigual,
> tan sañuda, tan violenta,
> que ha de ser común discordia
> de cuanto. . . .

(1595b)

Though part of the prophecy has just been fulfilled by Cupido's birth, there was no indication or suggestion in that prophecy of Anteros's countervailing presence and force. Once again prophecy and astrological prediction in Calderonian theater are incomplete, either telling only one part of what is to occur or leading to poor understanding of *how* the prophecy will be worked out.

When the three wayfarers attempt to inform themselves of the significance of the eclipse that announced Cupido's birth, Irífile flees, advising them to consult the Fates concerning "quién nace a ser ruina vuestra" (1596b). As Céfiro directs himself to Laquesis, Ifis to Cloto, and Pigmalión to Atropos, they are each in turn informed that a beast (*una fiera*), a thunderbolt (*un rayo*), and a stone (*una piedra*) have been born for their common ruin. As the three ponder how such a deformed monster could be created, Anteros's "chance" cry of fear, "Cupido" (1598a), answers their question Who could this be? Thus the stage is set for the unfolding of these three men's fates, somehow tied to *una fiera, un rayo,* and *una piedra.*

Though the prophecy announces that each character will be affected by Cupido's fickle and capricious intervention in human affairs, in no case does the eventual resolution of the plot conform to Irífile's prediction of ruin. The statement of one's fate appears vastly different from how that fate is worked out. We are reminded of this discrepancy in another way. In Act III Cupido and Anteros present their cases to Venus. Anteros requests his mother to avenge Anajarte's tyrannous disdain of Ifis, whereas Cupido begs vengeance on Irífile. In addition, Anteros requests pity and mercy for Pigmalión's *irracional amor.* Amid cries of "¡Piedad, piedad!" "¡Rigor, rigor!" and "¡Venganza!" Venus asks each to summarize in one request what is desired. They respond:

> Ant. Que quien no sabe querer,
>   sea mármol, no mujer.
> Cup. Que quien en amar se emplea,
>   mujer y no mármol sea.

(1631b)

The tripartite structure of the play is reduced to this bimember request that announces the eventual denouement. Curiously enough, both obtain literally what they request: a) Anajarte, who does not know how to love, is transformed into marble; b) the Statue, the object of Pigmalión's great love, is transformed into flesh and blood. As the prophecy regarding the three men does not accurately predict their outcomes, so too the gods' requests eventuate in something different from what was expected, at least in Cupido's case. Once again, certainty and control are outside of the ken and power of both humans and gods.

The Question of Identity

The ¿quién es? theme repeats itself throughout the play. In almost each case the main characters' identities correspond at first to their social status, but not to their inner qualities and traits. The fullness of personhood results from the reciprocal giving of one's soul to another. La fiera suggests that ordinary identity is but a veneer of social reality, a mere convention. The profound reality of love transcends social identity by fusing it with the personhood of the other, providing thereby not only another means of social identification, but a telos toward which the entire person, body and soul, may be positively directed. Pigmalión addresses the Statue as follows:

> Y pues mi afecto te dio
> el alma, ¡oh estatua bella!,
> vive, vive al poseella. . . .

(1617a)

Céfiro expresses his love of Irífile in like manner:

> que pueda adorar aquella
> hermosa fiera, a quien
> di toda el alma.

(1617b)

What this Neoplatonic imagery conveys is that the outer sign of personhood, social identity, is but convention; the inner reality of the soul, its other-centeredness, is its destiny. The full life of the soul is to love another, and only in this love does one's personhood become maturely established.

Throughout the play we are constantly asking: Who is this person? We grasp only fleeting impressions reflective of current social position and not of actual personality. Irífile is a good example. Dressed in animal skins, she appears to be an "Humano monstruo" (1595a). Inevitably Pigmalión, Céfiro, and Ifis ask who she is as well as where they are. Subtly the answer to who she is becomes linked with the announcement of the birth of a deity opposed to all, Cupido, who will sow discord and disharmony in Trinacria. The three wayfarers are then informed that the birth of that god signals their ruin. After visiting the grotto of the Fates, they come upon Cupido and Anteros. The three galants save Anteros from the arrogant and proud youth, only to become objects of Cupido's violent anger, a Cupido who declares himself to be beast, lightening, and stone. These three men cannot take seriously the pretentions of the arrogant youth, and immediately following their departure the capricious god begins to demonstrate his vengeful power through Anajarte.

Though the conflict between Anteros, requited love, and Cupido, unrequited love, defines for us the nature of the opposition between the gods and of the vengeance they will exact, it is only with Anajarte's appearance that we begin to understand how each god symbolizes traits of personality already existent. Anajarte will become proof of Cupido's power on earth. She is an orphan who has been victimized by her Uncle Argante, who usurped her throne for himself and his son Céfiro. Since she suffers under the tyranny of her uncle, Anajarte's thirst for vengeance on Argante and Céfiro is understandable, but her hatred of all men and her uncontrollable thirst for blood are not. So often past injustices mold a life in their image, establishing a basic orientation towards the world and others. Anajarte is not so much chosen by Cupido, due to a chance mention of her name, as she is fundamentally linked to the vengeful god by hatred and by her violent desire for vengeance.

Anajarte is the negative counterpart of Segismundo of *Vida*. Though both are unjustly imprisoned, Segismundo opens himself to love, generous, self-sacrificing, and heroic love, and thus frees himself from the bonds of his past upbringing and fate. Anajarte does not and thus falls victim to them.

Anajarte's victimization forces us to sympathize with her initial situation, that of the "legitimate" heir to the throne who finds her rightful place in society usurped by powerful men. But throughout the play her actions are haughty and disdainful of others. Though Cupido has chosen Anajarte as the recipient of his leaden arrow, its baneful influence only confirms an already existing disposition on her part. Anteros attempts to counteract the deadly influence of Cupido by advising her to open herself to love. After having expelled the Statue and any trace of love from her garden, including the three galants, Anajarte asks rhetorically:

> ¿habrá quien me hable de amor?
> ¿habrá quien pueda decir
> que corresponda ya más
> yo a ningún afecto?

> (1622b)

Anteros answers simply, straightforwardly, and mysteriously "Sí." The ¿quién es? theme reappears as she asks: "¿Quién es quien así me habla / de quien solo percibí / el eco?" (1622b). Anteros advises in song that the disdainful woman open herself to love:

> Ama al que ama, Anajarte
> hermosa y gentil;
> que el amor no es defecto, no,
> y el olvido sí.
>
> (1622b)

She repeats her question, "¿Quién eres?" and receives in return a detailed explanation of her plight as Cupido's victim. Anteros advises Anajarte with the words cited in the introduction to this play, clarifying the conflict between "el correspondido amor" and self-interested love. Tragically, forcefully, she rebuffs Anteros's pleas that she become other-directed, holding firmly to her hatred and fate. Her choice is fully conscious for she recognizes Anteros as a god. He pities the misguided woman, admonishing her that "De quien sentir no sabe, / merece. . . . No sentir" (1623). The inevitable issue of this decision to hate and to reject love is stated unequivocally; Anajarte first declares:

> Por más que me persüadas,
> no he de amar, ni he de admitir
> tu correspondido amor.
> Para ser rayo nací.
>
> (1623b)

Anteros responds:

> Pues mira que el rayo es piedra,
> después que llega a morir.

Anajarte's blindness leads her to retort: "¿Qué me importa ser piedra yo?" (1623b). Love of others leads to life; love of self, the love that "es interés su fin" (1622b), leads to death. These themes are powerfully presented and will receive maximum expression in the dramatic masterpiece *Eco y Narciso*, to be staged in July of 1661.

Ifis, though expelled from Trinacria by Anajarte, returns with an armada to liberate his beloved from her captors. But Anajarte believes his return is motivated by the desire to avenge her *ingratitud*. Ifis rejects "*venganza infame*," declaring his purpose as follows: "A lo que vuelvo es a que / sepas quién soy" (1626a). Though his social status as Prince of Epiro is what is superficially communicated, his more basic role as lover is the key to his identity and Anajarte's salvation. Ifis fears not his fate announced as death from a *rayo*, and, motivated only by love, he sets out to free Anajarte from her gilded prison. Though his act is a mighty *fineza*, he underscores that the love that spurs him on is "no / grosero ni interesable" (1627a). Like the adventurers of old he "sirve a merced de otros gajes" (1627a). Anajarte, nevertheless, cannot appreciate the quality of his heroism, and she reaffirms her life's commitment to hate all men and to reject any hint of love. Ifis's love, though great and pure, cannot move the hardhearted Anajarte.

To demonstrate the degeneration of Anajarte's humanity, *La fiera* exposes the quality of her life and its motivating principles. Put in astrological terms, she accepts her ill-fated star:

> pues no tienen
> esos orbes celestiales
> estrella que a mí, no digo
> que me incline para que ame,
> más para que no aborrezca,
> por más que del cielo baje
> el correspondido amor
> a persuadirme süave
> yugo suyo, contra quien
> mi pecho armó de diamante
> Cupido, absoluto amor,
> interesado y mudable.

> (1629a)

Hatred over love, a diamond-hard breast over a tender and feeling heart: these deliberately chosen positions summarize the quality of Anajarte's life. Even more damning is her ready disposition to kill Ifis. If she cannot *buy* him off with a queen's generosity nor dissuade him with disdain and rigor, she suggests more forceful and deadly measures:

> ¿faltará
> un veneno que le acabe,
> una cuerda que le ahogue,
> o un acero que le mate,
> aunque venganza después
> pida Anteros a su madre?

> (1629a)

Anajarte is not a feeling person, but an automaton-like replica of Cupido's antivital presence. Her sign is death.

Irífile is all that Anajarte is not. Dressed in animal skins, she is forcefully attracted by the harmonious music whose timbre reverberates in her very soul. Though not yet in harmony with her world, such a natural affinity indicates the orientation of her life, its disposition to unity and harmony. When we try to find out who she is, the surface appearance reveals an "Humano monstruo," but there are inner harmonies that indicate a greatness of soul. In Anajarte's palace, Irífile becomes another person, one who immediately loses any trace of her beastly upbringing. She naively remarks: "me parece que entre pompas / reales estoy en mi centro" (1612a). She confesses not knowing who has changed her attitude or what has affected so drastically her view of reality. Somehow she knows that she belongs in a palace in spite of her animal garb. Céfiro, the heir apparent of Trinacria, has recognized something special in the human beast, for he loves her ardently. This mysterious woman lived a sheltered life in the mountains due to some *agüeros* that her "father" Anteo read in his occult studies. She will become the positive counterpart to Anajarte's negative role in the play, and the two of them constitute the dual possibilities of existence for a woman and a queen. In spite of the fact that Cupido will manifest his power and rule in the world as *fiera*, *rayo*, and *piedra*, the concrete representations of that power, Irífile, Anajarte, and the Statue, will not be mere agents of that god, but independent participants with the ability to choose their own courses.

The key to Irífile's identity is found in her reactions to the new experiences she undergoes in Anajarte's palace. Outwardly, the answer to "¿quién es?" is *una fiera*. But once again this response only deals with appearances. Her amazement and wonder quickly pass to something more active and more significant. Instead of just feeling that she is in her rightful environment, she begins to experience definite envy of Anajarte's privileges (1619a). The Music that celebrates love further demonstrates the differences between Anajarte and Irífile. In Anajarate's opinion the song would be harmonious were it not for its theme, love, whereas any music forcefully moves Irífile (1619b). When Anteo appears on the scene and attempts to get Irífile back to the mountains, she states:

> que quiero más servir
> en palacios, que reinar
> en montañas.
>
> (1620b)

When the three gallants appear from hiding places in the garden, a typical palace-play scene results. Ifis defends Anajarte, Céfiro, Irífile, and Pigmalión plays the mediator. Anajarte finally decides the issue: 1) by banning Ifis, having asked him first to carry out a *fineza* on her behalf; 2) by sending Irífile back to her mountain; and 3) by having the Statue removed from the garden. During Irífile's departure Céfiro attempts to follow his beloved but is confronted by Anteo. Céfiro is bewildered by a subject's effrontery to his royal person, because Anteo refuses to acknowledge him as King, declaring that he does not have a King, but a Queen. When asked that famous question, "¿Quién lo es?," Anteo replies: "Yo diré quién es / cuando lo pueda decir" (1621b).

As the fates of the characters draw them together, so too does Pigmalión's passion bind him ever more closely to his cherished Statue. His love of an inanimate object quickly becomes the butt of Lebrón's jokes, for his affection is labelled "mal amor" (1608b). Pigmalión's past is clouded in mystery: in Lidia he killed Alfeo over the question of the *amor propio*, the personal worth, of the artist. Now that he desires to live incognito, he finds himself irretrievably attracted to a marbel Statue. Though his love is impossible and mad, it becomes the symbol of the transforming property of pure love. As the artist is not an artisan, a mere laborer, but a creator, a fruitful imitator of nature, so too the artist's love will not be futile, a mere outpouring of affection with no hope of reciprocity, but the sign of nature's fecundity. Public estimation may be determined by social status, but that is a limited and superficial view of the whole person. Personal value and worth is linked to other-centeredness, and the flowering of personality is intimately connected to dedication to the other. This is the active principle of personality formation, one much more meaningful than the inherent passivity of recognition by others or of worldly fame.

La fiera demonstrates that who one is indicates what one will become. Social status determines the public regard due to each individual as a member of society. The quality of one's life, however, determines the personal worth of each individual as a member of that society. The action makes clear that these two are not opposing modes of existence. Céfiro's love of Irífile manifests that love can heal the body politic rent asunder by ambition and tyranny. Their mutual love heals their fractured society at the same time as it fulfills each of them individually. Irífile suffered from a malign fate that prophesied her doom. Although Anteo attempted to shield her from society and her destiny, it was only in society that she could realize both her proper social status and her personal worth. Anajarte and Irífile, like Segismundo, are potential victims of fate. Segismundo's options in *La vida es sueño* become Irífile's and Anajarte's modes of existence in *La fiera, el rayo y la piedra*.

Vengeance: The Stumbling Block for a Full View of Life

In a fallible world pardon of transgression is the restorative element that brings society back into harmony. *La fiera's* world is disharmonious as the opposition of Cupido to Anteros both symbolizes and demonstrates. Cupido is a vengeful god who punishes the three wayfarers' disregard of his powers and position. The hateful Anajarte is linked to Cupido by their common trait of being vengeful. She hunts to give vent to a thirst for blood that she cannot execute on Céfiro and Argante. The companion of hatred is invariably a strong desire for vengeance. As Cupido was prevented from killing Anteros, so too will Anajarte be prevented from murdering Irífile whom she captured during a hunt: Ifis embraces the former as Céfiro does the latter, thus saving Irífile's life, but causing rivalry and opposition between the two gallants.

Although Anajarte and Cupido prove to be capricious and hateful, Cupido has a more drastic effect on society. His shafts of lead and gold teach all to fear his power. The decisive proof of Cupido's disharmony is his threat to take vengeance on his own mother. This brutal passion reminds us of Hércules's threat against Hesperia in *Fieras afemina Amor* (2028b). Cupido fulminates against Venus who tried to protect Anteros:

> Calla, calla;
> que si lloras por su ausencia,
> al ver que del mundo falta
> el correspondido amor,
> tomaré de ti venganza
> también; y quizá algún día. . . .
>
> (1606b)

Cupido's contradictory shafts are fired at random producing varied results: Irífile recognizes her obligation to Céfiro at the same time as her soul is set ablaze by the gilded arrow. Céfiro is hit by a similar shaft. Anajarte, though she recognizes her debt to Ifis, finds herself incapable of gratitude. Ifis, however, burns with passion for the disdainful maiden. And Pigmalión discovers an *ignorado fuego* (1607b) in his soul that will fundamentally change his life. Even the *graciosos* prove not to be immune to Cupido's influence, as Lebrón ponders how love could affect his life:

> ¿Cuánto va que me enamoro,
> según suelto el amor anda,
> que es peor que el diablo suelto?
>
> (1607b)

Could not Isbella become disdainful like her mistress? While Cupido glories in his mischief, Anteros appears promising to oppose Cupido now that he has Diana's javelin, a mightier weapon than Cupido's arrows. If Cupido can cause the beastly Irífile to fall in love, Anteros can make the beast human. If Cupido can cause the beautiful Anajarte to hate the one who loves her, Anteros will make her love him, or he will *avenge* her rejection. If Cupido can cause one to adore a stone statue, Anteros can infuse a soul in that stone. It is, however, Anteros's recourse to vengeance in Anajarte's case that clouds the dramatic picture. Anteros's power is by and large positive, but when he fails to move Anajarte, he destroys her. The mediating principle of pardon and forgiveness has no place, or cannot operate in this starkly defined world, at least until Irífile accepts love and Céfiro and forgets the past. But for Anajarte pardon is not allowed to resolve her anti-vital stance, and this is her tragedy.

La fiera's symbolic message is quite clear: love leads to a fullness of life and a healing of society; hatred and disdain produce death and the fracture of the body politic. Anteros explains this duality in terms of the denouement of the plot. In gratitude for their having sided with him against Cupido, Anteros favors each of the gallants as follows:

A Pigmalión, pues puede
una piedra enternecer;
a Céfiro, pues que una
fiera le asegura rey;
a Ifis, dándole *venganza*
de un rayo, que había de ser
muerte suya: con que vienen
a convertirse en placer
piedra, rayo y fiera, siendo
cadáver, reina y mujer.

(1636b; emphasis added)

Vengeance is an action whose valence is death. Though Anajarte's disposition towards the murder of Ifis helps explain Anteros's action, it also underscores the limits of love. Anteros and love are not omnipotent, and Anajarte's death represents the frustration and failure of love. Anajarte, as stone-cold statue, symbolizes the unredeemable portion of humankind.

Pigmalión's Impossible Love

Anajarte's death is counterbalanced by the Statue's coming to life. The motivating principle of this miracle of life is Pigmalión's love, labeled previously "mal amor" (1608b). In conversations with Lebrón the master's passion for that marble creation is designated a *desvarío* (1615a) and *locura* (1616b) by Pigmalión himself. The attraction for this perfection of creativity contains within it a potentiality that is monstruous, a regard for the inanimate that could lead to all manner of unnatural behavior. Anajarte calls Pigmalión's passion a *frenesí*, *delito*, or *locura*. She rejects the Statue, considering it now a lamia or Flora. A lamia is composed of a woman's head and breasts with a serpent's or beast's body; it is a man-devouring creature that lures children to their deaths. Flora, of course, is a vegetative deity. Anajarte's rejection of all that suggests love links her with the lamia since she will represent death for Ifis. Though ejected from the garden, the Statue now becomes the exclusive focus of Pigmalión's art and love as he goes off to prepare a suitable temple to house it.

Pigmalión's love is now sterile, but through it he has become other-centered. Because of Pigmalión's faithfulness and love, Anteros will be able to change stone to sentient material. The artist willingly marries the Statue even though it is still only stone. Its inverse relationship to Anajarte is made patent as the Statue, now animated, explains how love requited is superior to disdain and hatred:

se vea que en una fe
firme, en un amor constante,

tierno llanto, afecto fiel,
si una mujer y una piedra
porfían a aborrecer,
se deja vencer primero
la piedra que la mujer.

(1635a)

Pigmalión's marriage to the Statue/Woman is a triumph of love and a celebration of love's life-giving properties. What began as an irrational and impossible passion is transformed into a mature love that will be fruitful with Paphos's birth. Love transforms all that it touches and can make even marble bear fruit, an important lesson for society and Philip IV's young wife.

The Metamorphoses as Dramatic Symbols

Golfo's metamorphoses are negative in terms of the conversion of women of flesh and blood into lifeless stone barriers to navigation. In *La fiera* the metamorphoses are both positive and negative. Anajarte is turned into a stone statue principally due to her refusal to open herself to love and to recognize her obligations as a member of society, but also morally due to her cruel plan to kill Ifis. It is significant that Ifis does not commit suicide, as in the original myth, but rather becomes the beneficiary of Anteros's protective care. And Pigmalión's great love leads to the transformation of marble to flesh and blood as his stone wife becomes a living person. Therefore, the duality of the concluding metamorphoses, celebrating love and life and lamenting hate and death, reminds us of the ambiguity of living in time.

During Ifis's attack and pursuit of Céfiro, Anajarte actively participates as warrior. A traditional dramatic symbol found in Calderonian theater alerts us to what is about to occur, for Anajarte cannot control her horse and is thrown from it down the mountainside. As Pigmalión goes off to rescue her, Lebrón jokes with the stone Statue, calling her doña Mármol, by asking first of all whether Pigmalión's helping of Anajarte is a knightly duty. To his surprise she answers "Sí." Then he asks whether she is jealous of this action. She responds "No" (1633b). Pigmalión then enters carrying Anajarte in his arms, and the servant, who was previously speaking with the Statue, now requests not to be given yet another statue who for him is "Ana Juárez." In this case the comic scene anticipates the *desenlace* by contrasting the living Statue to the death-like, unfeeling Anajarte.

The *caballo desbocado* image dramatically conveys the quality of Anajarte's life, for as an example of her uncontrollable passions she wishes she could pay off Ifis as easily as she has Lebrón, her putative rescuer. Lebrón is easily satisfied with a jewel, and Anajarte is thus relieved of any further obligation:

que ¡así pudiera pagar

> a precio de otro interés
> otra fineza!

(1634a)

That is, of course, Ifis's championing of Anajarte's cause. On seeing the Statue Anajarte wonders how the marble creation escaped the lesson of her haughtiness by allowing itself to be loved. She then resolves:

> Pero si al correspondido
> amor sigues, yo veré
> si de un mármol lo apacible
> desagravia lo crüel
> de otro mármol: en tu pecho
> admite tú un amor fiel,
> mientras yo otro fiel amor
> altiva desprecio, a quien
> después de haberme servido
> muerte le he de dar. . . .

(1634a)

Shortly afterwards, the music warns her:

> La que no sabe querer,
> sea mármol, no mujer.

(1634a)

Anajarte comprehends the significance of these prophetic words, but chooses to disregard them. Ifis returns victorious, offering all to his beloved Anajarte, who feigns appreciation as she is slowly transformed into marble. She declares the symbolic significance of her metamorphosis as follows:

> si ya no es que sea venganza
> de Venus, dando a entender
> que la que querer no sabe,
> más es mármol que mujer.

(1635a)

The Statue's metamorphosis into flesh and blood is a positive transformation that occurs immediately afterwards, balancing the negative and punitive transformation of Anajarte. While life and death are thus brought back into harmony, the full vision of a healthy society is realized only with Anteo's revelation that Irífile is the rightful heir to Trinacria's throne. Now that she is Céfiro's equal, they too can marry, healing the body politic by reconciling the opposing factions. Irífile expresses succinctly what has been accomplished:

> ¡Dichosa quien llega a ver
> logrado reino y amor!

(1636a)

Personal happiness is the route, and not the obstacle, to societal stability and growth. In this manner Céfiro and Irífile's marriage is the necessary complement to Anajarte's tragedy and Pigmalión's triumph, bringing love's message out of the private sphere and into the public domain. Love indeed makes the individual's life fuller and richer. It is also a civic imperative.

Conclusion

As love was able to metamorphose stone to flesh, and hate, flesh to stone, so too love can metamorphose the rent society of Trinacria into a conduit of human happiness. *La fiera, el rayo y la piedra* is a good example of what Alonso and Bousoño call *trimembración* in Calderonian theater. Stylistically this is so, but thematically the play depends on a complex *bimembración*. These authors speak of the contrast between Anajarte's and the Statue's fates as establishing a fundamental contrast that becomes a *correlación bimembre*.[11] The play's structure is based on a bipartite theme, similar to that found in *Eco y Narciso*, that is stylistically realized in a tripartite fashion.

The theme of *La fiera* is filtered through a prism that appears to be tripartite, but in fact reveals two bipartite members. The first contrasts the love/life, hate/death duality, while the second moves from individual happiness to the societal harmony that love eventuates. How much more original is this interpretation of the myths of Iphis and Anaxarete and Pygmalion and the Statue than those given by Pérez de Moya: 1. "Por la fábula de la muerte de Isis [sic] por causa de Anaxarete, nos amonestan cuán vehementes son las llamas de amor y la bondad de algunas mujeres, que con ninguna cosa se encienden sus corazones, por guardar castidad, más que si fuesen una piedra" (II, 238). 2. The two lessons he cites for Pigmalión concern excessive love of material things and the following: "Amonéstanos esta hestoria en decir que aborreciendo Pymaleón las mujeres, criase mujer para casarse con ella, que muchos, aunque aborrecen el pecado, le aman y se están en él" (II, 239). Calderón's creative and innovative dramatization of these myths, while involving radical alterations, nevertheless far surpasses the catechistic readings of Pérez de Moya. Calderón, the dramatist of love, was able to write an interesting script that was very suited to the Hapsburg court and Mariana's birthday. Pérez de Moya's limited moralizing yielded to effective drama with a broad symbolic reach.[12]

Though *La fiera, el rayo y la piedra* is an intellectually challenging and dramatically effective play, the full tragic and pathetic vision of love unrequited would have to await *Eco y Narciso*. *La fiera* is optimistic about the opportunity for both individual happiness and societal harmony. It celebrates love's triumph more than it laments hate's failure. Anajarte was never a sympathetic character, and we accept her death as her just deserts in spite of her mysterious origin and troubled life. Fate shaped her life because she cooperated with it. There is only one sin that is not pardonable for the Christian, and that is the sin against the Holy Spirit. In a gloss to Matthew 12:31-2, the Confraternity version notes: "The sin against the Holy Spirit is to ascribe to the devil the works of the Holy Spirit. One who thus attacks directly this source of all grace, rejects the source of salvation."[13] Anajarte, on the human plane, attacks and rejects a secular counterpart to divine grace, human love, and thus cannot be "saved," live happily, on this earth. Those who do accept human love, Pigmalión, Céfiro, Irífile, are saved and triumph. The Statue dramatizes love's transforming properties just as Ifis does its protective drives. Only Anajarte stands outside the pale of love's amazing "grace."

Notes

1 The text of *La fiera* cited is the Valbuena Briones edition, pp. 1591-1638.

2 Valbuena Briones supplies the date and the occasion of the first performance in his introduction to the play, citing León Pinelo's *Anales de Madrid* (p. 1592). The *Tercera Parte* (of 1664) of Calderón's works simply states that *La fiera* was a "Fiesta Real, que se hizo a sus Magestades en el Palacio del Buen Retiro." Vera Tassis's *Tercera Parte* (p. 687) specifies that it was performed "en el Coliseo de Buen Retiro." Though Queen Mariana de Austria's birthday was 22 December, I do not recall any explanation of the May celebration of her *años*.

3 See Haverbeck, p. 83.

4 *Archivo español de arte y arqueología*, XVI, 1 (1930), 1-16.

5 See Ovid, *Metamorphoses*, Book XIV, and Hathorn, pp. 81-82.

6 See p. 1596 for normal *comedia* fare directed at women.

7 Dámaso Alonso and Carlos Bousoño analyzed *La fiera* as a good example of the trimember structure in Calderonian theater. See *Seis calas en la expresión literaria española*, 2ed. (Madrid: Gredos, 1956), pp. 137-45. The play totters between the bimember and trimember structure reflecting the divine and human planes dramatized therein, as explained below.

8 See Don W. Cruickshank's edition of the play (London: Tamesis, 1971), p. xxxvii.

9 (New York: Mentor Book, 1942), p. 36.

10 See Valbuena Briones, p. 1591a.

11 See pp. 145-46, *n* 28.

12 While Haverbeck's criticism of the play is accurate ("El desenlace significa que todos deben someterse a las leyes del amor. Si alguien ama bien—puede pensarse en Ifis—, lo que merece es ser amado; sus sentimientos deben ser correspondidos. La mujer que no sabe querer, debe ser castigada por no acatar las leyes de la naturaleza y del amor" [p. 81]), it does not adequately address the societal dimension of the work.

13 *The New Testament* (New York: Catholic Book Pub. Co., 1957-52), p. 47.

B. 1. *Amado y aborrecido*

> De amado y aborrecido
> las dos pasiones padezco.
> Aborrecido de muchas
> puedo ser, ¿quién duda? Pero
> pocas hallaré que me amen:
> y así, al amor me resuelvo
> a coronar, no el desdén.

(1720b)[1]

The two plays studied in this section deal with victories of love and celebrations of life. The first of these, *Amado y aborrecido*, is not a real myth play but rather a *comedia palaciega de enredo* that is set in some mythic time during which the gods were still active in human affairs. Therefore, we do not have the dramatization of a known myth, such as the Cupid-Psyche myth found in *Ni Amor se libra de amor*, but the evocation of a mythic past that serves as backdrop for Calderón's dramatic narrative about the warring states of Cyprus and Cnidus.[2] The play itself begins sluggishly, Act I having three distinct narrative *relaciones* that tend to retard the dramatic action. But Act III reveals Calderón at his best, for it is suspense-packed and quick-paced, riveting our attention on the rapid development and denouement of the action. That action concerns for the most part a divine "experiment" to be carried out in the human laboratory with regard to the conflicting powers of love and disdain. *Amado's* optimistic view of human affairs discloses how hope must infuse and direct our actions and lives.

While the optimistic perspective eventually prevails, the play underscores, especially through the repeated use of the word *riesgo*, that life is a risk. To love is to risk all for the sake of the loved one. Pure, unselfish love commits everything, even one's life, to the other. The play emphasizes that self-sacrifice for the other's sake is the greatest *fineza* the lover can make. The risks willingly assumed are proportional to the rewards finally achieved.

The Divine Background to the Human Action

The play is structured on a duality between the goddesses of love and disdain. Both kingdoms and subjects align themselves with either passion, and this orientation of one's life accounts for the hostilities between the peoples of Chipre and Gnido. Irene, the *infanta* of Gnido, neatly summarizes the result of this commitment to either *amor* or *olvido*:

> de cuyo opuesto rito ha procedido
> entre las dos la enemistad tirana
> que las mantiene en iras y rencores,
> hija de olvidos una, otra de amores.

(1687a)

Chipre has defeated its archrival Gnido and holds its Princess captive. As Lidoro, the Princess Irene's cousin, approaches the coast, his boat is destroyed. When he cries out for Diana's assistance, she acknowledges Venus's defense of her beloved isle Chipre. The goddess of love then expresses why she is particularly protective at this moment and refuses Lidoro's pleas for mercy:

> No hay piedad
> con quien estos puertos busca,
> en sus entrañas trayendo
> tan grande traición oculta.
>
> (1688b)

While in Act I it is suggested that these two goddesses and their opposition are at the root of the dramatic conflict, both personal and international, Act II clearly states that Diana and Venus create the situations in which the human participants serve as guinea pigs for an experiment concerning which is the greater passion, love or disdain (1702a). When Dante earlier asked what end his sufferings served, he received the following reply from two distinct choruses:

> Coro 1.O   A fin de que venza amor.
> Coro 2.O   A fin de que el desdén venza.
>
> (1700b)

The goddesses' experiment creates a tangle of human relations that are at first confusing. Dante and Aurelio passionately love Irene, the captive Princess of Gnido. Aminta, the sister of Chipre's King, passionately and profoundly loves Dante. Irene loves nobody, and later Lidoro will fall in love with Aminta. Aminta is an admirable character whose love rings true whenever it is sounded. She even provides Dante with half of her jewelry when he is exiled, knowing full well that he continues to love Irene. This most generous woman runs the risk of jealousy's ravages, for in Act II the famous *caballo desbocado* image symbolizes her plight: a generous lover who finds her love scorned. In spite of this dramatic warning signal, she withstands jealousy's urgings, but not before she slips into a deep melancholy that reveals her inner sufferings. Irene, on the other hand, manifests all the haughty traits of the social rebel who rejects nature by denying the rightful place of love in building society. From general disinclination her disdain/hatred has become specifically directed at men:

> Si yo en los ejercicios de Dïana,
> por ser a su deidad más parecida,
> tan altiva nací, viví tan vana,

> que siendo de las fieras homicida,
> quise llegar con ambición ufana,
> quise pasar con fama esclarecida
> a serlo de los hombres, porque vieras
> cuánto son para mí los hombres fieras. . . .
>
> (1687b)

A feminine counterpart to Hércules, Irene participated in the war against Chipre, where Dante conquered her and made her his prisoner. For this reason she hates him and is incapable of ever looking upon him with favor. She would prefer prison or the civil death of exile in a remote mountain before becoming his consort, even if he were to make her queen of the world. She summarizes her feelings thus: "te aborrecí con tan suma / adversión. . ." (1690b).

Dante is the plain-spoken, straight-shooter type who leads Chipre's armed forces. His competitor for Irene's hand is the smooth-tongued flatterer Aurelio who is the chief politician of the island kingdom. While the competition for a woman normally depends on the qualities of the masculine rivals, in this case Dante becomes the object of the goddesses' competition between love and hate as Aurelio all but disappears from the scene. At the end of Act II Dante recognizes and declares the nature of the divine experiment whose object he has become:

> ¡Oh nunca, y oh siempre yo
> viva, mezclando en mis ansias
> de amado y aborrecido,
> las dos pasiones contrarias,
> hasta que declare el cielo
> quién mayor victoria alcanza,
> quien ama a quien le aborrece,
> o aborrece a quien le ama!
>
> (1707b)

Whereas Dante is the recipient of Aminta's love and Irene's hate, he is also the one who disdains the former and loves the latter. Since the two women will remain firm in their passions, only the goddesses are able to resolve the impasse that they have created.

As is to be expected in a play of palace intrigue, the basic emotional issue is debated through a *duelo de ingenio*, or miniaturized *certamen poético*:

> *¿Cuál más infeliz estado*
> *de amor y desdén ha sido?*
> *¿Amar siendo aborrecido,*
> *o aborrecer siendo amado?*
>
> (1710a)

As the Musicians alternate *feliz* with *infeliz*, we come to realize how appropriate these questions are for all the characters. The mystery of love/disdain is inexplicable, in spite of the courtly reasons adduced for the opposing positions. Aminta puts an end to this poetical excursion by blaming the disharmony on fate's designs (1711a), which is yet another attempt to explain a mystery by reference to another power whose workings are still mysterious. Neither the poetical discourse nor the plot of *Amado* explains anything; what we realize is that, while these emotions are actual and significant in human affairs, they are not axiologically equal. Aminta's love will prove to be more powerful and positive than Irene's hatred and Dante's disdain. The reason for this victory will be found in love's ability to carry out Nature's plan for establishing harmony and concord between the sexes. Love heals the rift between male and female by making those of two flesh one body.

The only character who loves and hates in sexual terms is Dante. Irene's valence is negative, hatred/disdain; Aminta's is positive, love. While the others suffer the disharmony of this contradiction, only Dante realizes the universal significance of his plight:

> Sin duda que convino
> a la gran providencia
> de los dioses hacer en mí experiencia
> de cuánto el alto Júpiter previno
> extender los imperios del destino. . . .
>
> (1714b)

Why? That is the question that suffuses the play with the imponderable and the inexplicable, because it places the human being in a passive state, the receiver of destiny's dictates rather than a participator in determining them. Dante exemplifies this passivity when he ponders the inaction of his free will:

> ¡Qué digan que mi albedrío
> es mío, y usar de él puedo,
> cuando no puedo pagar
> este amor ni aquel desprecio!
>
> (1716a)

This human befuddlement is understandable, but not accurate. The mystery of love and free will depends ultimately on self-determination, as Aminta's heroic self-sacrifice will prove in Act III. Therefore, all the mysterious action and inaction are not attributable to chance or to fate or to fortune or to destiny. The narrative significance of *Amado* rests on a complex depiction of the interaction of human and divine planes, in which the human beings must become agents of their freedom, if they are to escape fate, or remain passive in the face of what appears to be already determined.

The Role of Prophecy

Though Chipre vanquished rebellious Gnido, the victory was threatened by *vaticinios* that accompanied Irene's imprisonment. The King, Basilio-like both in his studies of the stars and in his attempt to prevent the prophecy's fulfilment, decides that by marrying Irene to a Cyprian he may avoid utter ruin. But what was this prophecy?

> vaticinios que amenazan
> riunas, tragedias e injurias,
> con bellezas, que aun después
> de verse vencidas triunfan. . . .

(1689b)

The King's attempts to conceal Irene in the mountains, as Segismundo was imprisoned in the tower, prove to be inadequate, since the two supports of the Cyprian monarchy are now battling over this foreign *infanta*. From confident ruler the King quickly changes to pessimistic determinist:

> Y pues infatigable el hado,
> ni se estorba ni se excusa,
> pues antes busca su efecto
> quien su impedimento busca. . .

(1689b)

At this point he proposes Irene's marriage as a perpetual imprisonment and check on Gnido's rebellious tendencies. The King interprets the prophecy to refer exclusively to Irene. He takes his judgment to be infallible since the prophecy appears to conform to his appreciation of the current state of the nation.

But the prophecy was ambiguous and the King's interpretation of it incomplete. In Act II he once again insists that the prophecy refers to Irene, and that the ruin of Chipre will be due to his freeing her from prison. Aurelio, perceiving the King's excited *imaginación* and insecurity, reminds him of life's ambiguity:

> No siempre lo que adivina
> humana ciencia es verdad,
> y no siempre una deidad
> lo infalible vaticina.

(1702b)

While the prophecy may refer to Irene, it might just as well be applicable to Aminta's triumph after threatened ruin, tragedy, and injury in the sea. The prophecy mentions threatened horrors, but predicts triumph. The only *belleza* that triumphs is Aminta, and such a possibility never formed part of the King's considerations.

The Role of Women and the Question of Freedom

Irene is a very unlikeable personage, and through her predicament *Amado* examines the question of personal freedom versus state security. Her presence on Chipre assures the safety of the state, and freeing her would apparently set in motion a dreaded fate. Thus the King's political decision to have Irene marry sentences her to perpetual imprisonment, for her husband will be her warden (1690a). This utilitarian view of marriage contains within it a view of woman as subservient to both men and the state. Marriage is, in consequence, the surrender of one's freedom through bondage to another. Irene's negative view of marriage is counterbalanced by Aminta's positive appreciation of it as love requited, personhood fulfilled.

Irene's impassioned pleas for self-determination are based on her freedom as a human being. She reminds the King that, though master of her life, he cannot be master of her soul and free will (1693a). Even the gods lack that power. Aurelio has not won her favor; she vehemently hates Dante. Aminta relieves the situation by requesting that Irene form part of her entourage, thus becoming neither free nor imprisoned. Aminta serves two distinct ends by this stratagem: her brother appears to be less the tyrant as she satisfies her jealousy by having Irene under "guard." And in Act III Aminta promises Irene that the King will not marry her against her will. Declaring that jealousy is not her motive, she assures Dante that her regard for him is at the root of her actions. In what appears to be self-serving posturing, Aminta reveals her purpose:

> que es mi voluntad tan fina,
> tan hidalgo mi dolor,
> tan noble la pena mía,
> que porque ella no os desprecie
> tan cara a cara a mi vista,
> quiero yo que de mejor
> aire su desdén se vista,
> y no obligue una violencia
> a lo que un amor no obliga.
>
> (1714)

The purity of Aminta's motives will be proven in the trial by sea, where she willingly offers her life for Dante's. She also prevents violence to Irene's freedom. Only after Irene has plotted with Lidoro does she eventually have to marry Aurelio. Both Lidoro and Irene have betrayed their nobility, and in this light their punishments are just retribution for their actions: the first for his deceit and traitorous plan to murder Dante; the second for her relentless adherence to disdain. Aminta's triumph is the reward of her noble love as well as the triumph referred to in the prophecy. Irene's marriage represents a

punishment that guarantees the safety of the state. While the picture of
human freedom, love, and marriage is thus not uniformly positive, the various outcomes represent a powerful statement about the quality of one's life
and the nobility of one's soul.

The Nature of Nobility

A significant theme of *Amado y aborrecido* concerns the nature and obligations of being noble, the implications of the famous phrase "yo soy quien soy."
From the honor plays we have become inured to the obligation of vengeance,
and Lidoro, Irene's cousin, typifies this drive. Lidoro has come to Chipre to
free Irene and kill Dante. Reminding us of Don Rodrigo of Lope's *El caballero
de Olmedo*,[3] Lidoro expresses his purpose as follows:

> Empiece pues
> mi venganza, sin que sea
> infamia sobre seguro
> matarle; que no es bajeza
> en quien no viene a reñir,
> sino a matar, que lo emprenda
> como pudiere.
>
> (1699a)

The nobleman's claim to preference rests on the purity of his blood and his
adherence to a higher code of conduct. Lidoro denies this code by his rationalization of honor's demands. Expediency rules his life. Once Lidoro discovers that Dante has saved him, he must put aside his plans until that debt is
paid in full. *Amado's* world is one defined by a strict code of conduct that
spells out one's duties and obligations. In Lidoro's case they bind and con-
strain him, but in Dante's they will liberate him from the shackles of social
existence.

The one who transcends the call of vengeance by adhering to a higher
sense of nobility is Aminta. Instead of wreaking vengeance on Dante for his
scorn of her love, she gives him half of her jewelry so that he might survive
exile. She manifests her generous and noble soul in terms that relate to the
formulaic expression of traditional nobility:

> no me he de vengar celosa
> de ti ni de tus desvelos;
> que *soy quien soy*, para que
> mi sentimiento se dé
> al partido de los celos.
>
> (1693b; emphasis added)

Jealousy tarnishes the noble soul just as generosity reveals its luster. Since Aminta cannot hand over Irene to Dante, she can provide him with material support:

> tan noble se halla
> mi voluntad, que ofendida,
> aun sabrá volver por sí.

(1693b)

While this issue of nobility and vengeance is clouded by the fact that Lidoro is male and Aminta, female, the dynamics of the play are moving us toward a better understanding of what true nobility implies and, indeed, demands.

The key words and concepts for an understanding of nobility are *fineza* and *hidalguía*. *Fineza*, according to the *Autoridades*, is an "accion ù dicho con que uno dá à entender el amor y benevolencia que tiene à otro." In a courtly context, *fineza* summarizes the multitude of obligations nobility incurs, such as that of giving freely and performing heroic and magnanimous deeds. *Hidalguía* is a rare term, and Irene (1704b) and Dante (1706a) employ it. It signifies "generosidad, magnanimidád y nobleza de ánimo." All relationships are governed by these concepts that seek to establish the ideal as the normal mode of human conduct. And a distinction made in *El mayor encanto, amor* between *cortesana fineza* and *amorosa fineza* (1523a) should be kept clearly in mind.

A good example of a *fineza* to be performed by a man in favor of a woman occurs at the beginning of Act II. Lidoro risks his life to save Aminta from a runaway horse by hamstringing it with his sword and catching her in his arms. Aminta responds appropriately: "A tanta fineza / deudora soy de la vida" (1694b). Later Dante hears the cries of Irene and Aminta as a lion threatens their lives. Over and above Dante's doubt about which to save, we find the goddesses' *experiencia* concerning love and disdain. Instead of choosing between Irene and Aminta, Dante saves both by attacking the beast and driving it off. Aminta's noble self-sacrifice refuses such a price: "Que yo a riesgo de tu vida, / te perdono la fineza;" whereas Irene's egotism demands it: "Yo no: que solo tu muerte / será lo que te agradezca" (1701b). Life is a risk, and the obligations of nobility force one to spurn personal safety in order to save the other. There is no higher expression of what is meant by *fineza* than this assumption of risk, this willingness to sacrifice oneself for another. Dante further risks his life when a fire strikes the palace. Paralleling closely the former exploit, this situation demands that Dante choose between Aminta and Irene, between *amor* and *desdén*. True to form, Dante refuses to choose, again saving both of them. Irene's disdain remains: "¡Oh, nunca yo te debiera / fineza, Dante, tan rara!" Aminta's love is confirmed: "¡Oh, siempre estuviera yo / debiéndote acción tan alta!" (1707b). While Irene affirms that she will never repay such a deed, Aminta declares that she will repay it with her life and soul. These declarations of intent, and of character, prepare us for the dramatic and final test of Dante by sea, where love ultimately wills out over disdain (1720).

For each *fineza* performed the beneficiary incurs a debt to the one executing it. Dante manifests his chaotic state by using the jewelry Aminta has given him for his sustenance in exile to perform a *fineza* for Irene. Instead of seeking to repay the debt he owes to the Princess, he plans to honor his beloved Irene:

> si yo pudiese con ellas,
> sin que sepa que yo soy
> el dueño de la fineza,
> socorrer a Irene que,
> fuera de su patria, es fuerza
> no tener, yendo a la corte,
> con qué lucirse.
>
> (1700a)

His servant Malandrín reminds him that such a plan substitutes an insult for gratitude and repays a favor with an offense. Dante's disordered life is a reflection of how unable he is to control his will as he becomes the object of Diana and Venus's experiment.

Another example of distorted nobility arises when Lidoro requests that the King lift Dante's banishment for his having saved Aminta from the runaway horse. His purpose is ostensibly to repay Dante's *fineza* of having saved him from drowning after his shipwreck. But what he really intends is to be free of any obligation to his enemy so that he might, with a clear conscience, kill his benefactor. While the debt may be paid, he creates further trouble for himself by assuring the return to court of Aminta's loved one. The bizarre outcome of this tangle of human relations is expressed thus by Lidoro:

> ¿Quién creerá que me haga mi tristeza
> hoy del agravio cargo de fineza,
> y que cuando de amor rendido muero,
> de mi enemigo venga a ser tercero?
>
> (1705a)

Lidoro and Dante are at the mercy of social norms that dictate one or another course of action. But what distinguishes the one from the other is the traitorous conduct of Lidoro. Dante never forgets his obligations, or seldom does he forget them. He tries to bridge the chasm of honor and love. But Lidoro has come to avenge Gnido, and this demands Dante's death. What characterizes both Lidoro and Irene is their traitorous conduct in Chipre, and only by contrasting Lidoro's conduct to that of Dante do we begin to see how qualitatively different these two men are. Dante repays Lidoro's intercession with the King by awarding him the post of governor of the port. Lidoro uses this position of trust to betray Dante and to free Irene. While Dante's nobility of heart is never in doubt, Lidoro's meanness and baseness are everywhere evident. Dante can never be outdone in generosity by Lidoro, and thus the latter never really frees himself from some obligation to his benefactor. Only Aminta's willingness to sacrifice all for Dante's sake will outdo the general's own nobility of spirit.

The values the characters live by receive comic treatment from Malandrín, that acute observer of both life and the theater. When Dante debates whether to save Irene or Aminta from the lion, the *gracioso* remarks:

> Si a propósito se hubiera
> buscado un león que diese
> lugar a la competencia,
> ¿se hubiera en el mundo hallado
> otro de tanta paciencia?

> (1701b)

As Dante charges off to attack the beast, it heads straight for Malandrín, who invokes the assistance of Baco, his special deity. After witnessing Dante's heroic rescue of the two ladies from the fire, Malandrín, if he were but a poet, would write a play titled "el Leonicida de amor / y el Eneas de su dama" (1707a). In this light we need to judge Malandrín's earlier remarks concerning the King's decision that he who marries Irene will lose his favor:

> ¿Vale tanto una hermosura,
> señor, como una privanza?

> (1691a)

Dante's interior struggle characteristically sets the formal obligations of *nobleza* against the desires of the heart, honor against love. In all the trials he undergoes never once does he betray either, and thus both goddesses find themselves at impasse with regard to their experiment. But Malandrín's early statement of the matter for Dante, *privanza* or *belleza*, is not an accurate formulation of the problem, for Dante's interior struggle revolves around the basic direction of his life. Irene's disdain is barren; Aminta's love is fruitful. The former will be punished for rejecting life's goodness; the latter will be rewarded with her heart's desire, Dante.

The final trial of the three main characters takes place in a stormy sea where Irene and Aminta are found adrift. Disregarding his personal safety, Dante undertakes yet another *fineza*. He leaves Lidoro saying: "No huyo de tu riesgo, pues / voy buscando mayor riesgo" (1717b). It is precisely this desire to risk all for the other that ultimately directs his life to a safe harbor. The overarching presence of Diana and Venus moves the trial of Dante from earth and fire to water and wind. The King, who sees Irene as the scandal of his kingdom, believes the beast, the fire, and the storm are in league to destroy Aminta. The astrologer King hears echoes in the air of the goddesses' words, but confesses that he does not understand them.

Dante's great *fineza* receives predictable responses from Irene and Aminta. The former states flatly that Dante's sacrifice (*fineza*) will not obligate her, in spite of her betrayals. She accepts death because it also translates into Dante's death. Her valences are hatred and disdain, the antivital proclivities of her personality. Aminta, however, would accept any risk, even death, to ensure Dante's life. Her spirit is that of self-sacrifice:

> ¡Pluguiera al cielo que en mí
> quebrara la suerte el ceño,
> y vivieras tú, por quien
> gustosa mi vida ofrezco
> en humano sacrificio
> a la gran deidad de Venus!
>
> (1718b)

Irene invokes Diana to assure Dante's and her own death. At this point Dante is severely tried; he must, to save his life and that of another, sacrifice one of the ladies. Though he willingly offers his own for both, he must choose between them:

> ¡Ay infelice de mí!
> ¡En qué confusión me veo,
> entre aquel desdén que adoro
> y aquel amor que aborrezco!
>
> (1719a)

Irene and Aminta both ask for death, the one to cause him greater suffering than death, and the other to remove the cause of his hatred. For Dante to sacrifice Irene would be a tyrannous harshness, to sacrifice Aminta, a gross slight. His honor and love are at risk. Dante's trial proceeds without resolution, for "Perder a Irene es venganza; / perder a Aminta es desprecio" (1720a).

Urged to act swiftly, he first chooses honor by deciding to sacrifice Irene. She chides Dante saying she never really meant for him to take her advice. Her tears save her. Dante then prepares to throw Aminta overboard; she does not retract her advice:

> échame al mar; que más quiero
> morir alegre que ver
> a Irene triste, supuesto
> que tú has de sentir su llanto.
>
> (1720b)

Such self-sacrifice was foreshadowed at the end of Act II when Aminta said that she would someday repay Dante's great *fineza*:

> yo porque sé que la tengo
> de pagar con vida y alma.
>
> (1707b)

Irene proves to be false and deceitful. With these two revelations Dante learns to value correctly what his choice signifies:

> De amado y aborrecido
> las dos pasiones padezco.
> Aborrecido de muchas
> puedo ser, ¿quién duda? Pero
> pocas hallaré que me amen:
> y así, al amor me resuelvo
> a coronar, no el desdén.
>
> (1720b)

Dante chooses the positive, the loving Aminta as he rejects the negative, the hateful Irene. He chooses to live! Once the issue is decided by Dante, the chorus declares "¡Victoria por el amor! / ¡Viva la deidad de Venus!" (1720b). Diana and Venus were testing whether the most noble affection of a beautiful woman was love, and Aminta proved it to be so.

Dante's subsequent marriage to Aminta signifies that his chaotic emotions are now tranquil and serene as positive direction is given to his noble soul. The *máscara* that celebrates Aminta and Dante's love reveals that love is the object of the noble soul. Aminta declares: "Logró mi fineza el cielo." Dante replies: "¡Dichoso yo!" (1721b). Malandrín cannot understand how Dante can be happy with one he loves less than Irene. The answer is simple:

> Sí, que para dama es buena,
> Malandrín, la que yo quiero;
> para esposa, la que a mí
> me quiere.
>
> (1721b)

Irene's ingratitude and disdain are punished, curiously enough, by marriage to Aurelio, who always placed his fortune as the King's confidant before Irene's favor as lover. Her marriage is the opposite of Aminta's for she now remains a virtual prisoner in Chipre, the guarantor of peace with Gnido. Lidoro loses Aminta and fails in his mission. The patent nobility of Aminta and Dante exemplifies the import of *finezas*, and their happy marriage directs their worthy souls to their true object, the love of the other. Lidoro and Irene's baseness led to their traitorous behavior and punishment, for they were not able to live up to the obligations of *nobleza*.

Conclusion

Amado y aborrecido has been ignored by contemporary Calderonian criticism, primarily because it has been labeled a mythological play. It is not a great work, though Act III is one of the most suspenseful and melodramatic Calderón ever wrote. Through the characters' experiences we learn a great deal about love and hate/disdain, nobility and baseness, fidelity and betrayal, and *finezas*. There is a social nobility that is determined by birth; Aminta and Irene, Dante and Lidoro, all share it. But nobility of soul cannot be acquired save by deeds, as suggested by the incessant references to *finezas* throughout the dramatic narrative. Social nobility may be marred by betrayal of those principles that direct proper conduct. In all these considerations risk defines the limits of one's nobility, for just as one risks death to perform a *fineza*, the noble soul risks hurt and rejection in loving another. Dante performs daring deeds, proving his nobility of character. But Aminta's love proves to be greater than his daring deeds, for her love sacrifices all, even her personal happiness and life, for the one she loves. Aminta's example prods Dante's conscience and helps him to recognize that love leads to life, whereas hatred produces barrenness and death. Aminta's great *fineza*, her love of Dante above even her own life, confirms that love is the life of the soul, and only when Dante is able to orient his love positively, and only when it is reciprocated, does he begin to control and direct his life. *Amado* celebrates a marvellous victory of love, revealing that one's will is truly one's own only when it is directed at the other's good, when it serves the other. Self-direction demands mutuality. This enigmatic truth motivates *Amado's* action and informs its theme. This traditional view of a woman's love and its power is transformed by Calderón's great artistry into a dramatic experience that transcends the bonds of time and space. Aminta's love may appear to be remarkable, even unbelievable; but love is a miracle worker.

Notes

1 The text employed is found in the Valbuena Briones edition, pp. 1681-1722.
2 See Peter Dunn, "Garcilaso's *A la flor de Gnido*," *ZRP* 81 (1965), 288-309.
3 Don Rodrigo's famous phrase is "yo vengo a matar, no vengo / a desafíos."

B. 2. Ni Amor se libra de amor

Tus lástimas han podido
obligar, no solamente
a mí, que te adoro, pero
a Venus que las atiende,
y al verte dar muerte, y que,
yo había de llorar tu muerte,
convencida de mi llanto,
en mi casamiento viene:
con que diosa de Amor Siquis
vivirá adorada siempre.

(1980b-1981a).[1]

La fiera portrays love as a salvific force through its duality of vision that dramatizes disdain's barren result and love's fruition that eventually secures personal happiness and civic harmony. *Amado's* optimism confirms love's victory, and it goes farther in scope by transforming unrequited love into mature, sexual love that once again assures both personal and state harmony. *Ni Amor se libra de amor*, staged 19 January 1662, dramatizes a different dimension of love as a salvific force, encompassing pardon's curative powers for distressed personal relationships. As *Ni Amor* celebrates love's and pardon's defeat of malign fate and vengeance, it provides us with a redemptive view of human experience.

The play takes place in Gnido, an island consecrated to Venus.[2] *Ni Amor's* optimism is not inveterately naive, for all the characters must first traverse a sea of anguish and sorrow before arriving at love's safe port, where all will be set aright by Cupido's love of Siquis. The naughty and violent Cupido experiences a "metamorphosis" brought about by his sudden and unexpected love of the beautiful Siquis. She, demonstrating a penchant for violence in her wounding of Cupido and her attempted suicide, will find happiness assured only after great suffering and loss. While the play is unabashedly optimistic about love, it is at the same time realistic about the nature of human experience. Love is not a saccharine state that avoids pain and suffering, but that hard won victory whose price is precisely pain and suffering.[3]

The Role of the Gods

Ni Amor se libra de amor, Even Love Cannot Avoid Love, depicts how that mischievous god Cupido becomes unsuspectedly and inadvertently entangled in the affairs of gods and of humans. The god who toys with human passion by letting fly either the gilded shaft of love or the leaden one of disdain finds himself engrossed in a love that transforms him from childish prankster and avenger to serious and mature lover. Cupido's encounter with Siquis becomes the god's rite of passage to a higher state of being, one that demands that he lay aside the things of a child as he assumes the responsibilities of man and lover. Siquis too will undergo a "metamorphosis" as she becomes Cupido's wife. Love's power is universal, for it can unite a god and a mortal woman, transforming the latter into "diosa de Amor" (1981a).

The play begins with Venus's vengeance on a mere mortal who is declared by her subjects to be more beautiful than the goddess of love herself. In order to placate an angry Venus, Atamas the King consults Júpiter's oracle, discovering that Siquis must be sacrificed or abandoned on Mt. Oeta. In the meanwhile, Cupido falls in love with Siquis, and, instead of becoming the victim of wild beasts, she receives his loving devotion and attention. In Act II we learn that Júpiter's oracle has deceived Venus as it indulges Cupido. While Júpiter satisfies Venus's desire for vengeance, he provides Cupido with the opportunity to pursue covertly his passion. Cupido, who originally wished to be the instrument of his mother's vengeance, discovers that, while vengeance satisfies one's anger and outrage, only love orients his life toward the good. Therefore, the play focuses on Cupido's discovery of the life-giving quality of love, for only love can vanquish fate by developing the rich and positive potentiality of personhood both in human beings and in gods.

Siquis's Fate

Siquis's fate is a function of her great beauty. During a religious ceremony in which young maidens supplicate Venus to make them happy in their marriages, the misguided people commit an unthinkable sacrilege: they deny Venus her proper homage and sovereignty by proclaiming Siquis the second goddess of beauty. Envious of the young Princess's beauty as well as offended by the people's outrageous claim, Venus prophetically declares:

> "Infelice tu hermosura,
> Siquis, será, pues tu dueño
> un monstruo ha de ser". . . .
>
> (1948b)

Venus avenges her affront on the innocent Siquis instead of on the offending people. Though Siquis has refused the people's acclamation, she nevertheless becomes the scapegoat who will pay for the offense, thus saving Gnido from destruction. After the pronouncement of Siquis's fate, Cupido churlishly appears swearing to make his mother's cause his own. When the people interpret Venus's pronouncement to be provoked by envy and the desire for vengeance, they rebel, destroying the temple and declaring Venus not to be a deity. The offense-vengeance mechanism is now in full operation;[4] the stage is set for what appears to be Gnido's destruction.

While Venus's call for revenge occupies the play's foreground, we should not overlook the background circumstances which advance the plot. The young maidens were imploring Venus to make them happy in their marriages, for these young girls had no voice in the choice of their husbands. As Astrea and Selenisa, Siquis's elder sisters, discuss their future husbands, their companion Flora remarks:

> ¿No es rigor que una mujer,
> porque principal nació,
> case con quien nunca vio?

> (1951a)

For us in the twentieth century the logic of such a declaration is obvious, but it contradicted the business-like nature of marriages of state. This theme of arranged marriage may appear to be characteristic of eighteenth-century drama, but it was already a serious preoccupation of Golden-Age dramatists.

Arsidas and Lidoro, the prospective husbands of Selenisa and Astrea, fall in love with Siquis at first sight. The two *infantas*, in turn, fall in love with Cupido. Thus is raised the question of mutual attraction, compatibility, and love. Lidoro pinpoints the issue by referring to the word *agrado*:

> No siempre el agrado está
> vinculado a lo perfecto;
> agrado hay voluntarioso
> que se contenta con menos,
> porque tiene ciertos casos
> reservados el afecto
> para sí, que nadie puede
> ni alcanzarlos ni entenderlos.

> (1946a)

He then comments on the phenomenon of the unhappy beauty and happy woman of ordinary appearance, concluding:

> es cierto
> que aunque amor todo es cuestión,
> es cuestión sin argumento,
> y así nadie le concluye
> a razones. . . .

> (1946a)

The arranged marriages of the *infantas* Astrea and Selenisa deny a fundamental human truth and point out the cause of much marital unhappiness. It is not that men and women are inevitably antagonistic to one another as the fact that arranged marriages exacerbate the natural tension between the sexes. At the conclusion to the play, only Cupido's magical power as god of love is able to reconcile Astrea and Selenisa to Lidoro and Arsidas. Cupido, however, will earn Siquis's affection by his mighty *finezas* and not by force or deceit. The reality of "arranged" *agrado* stands as silent testimony to the impossibility of forcing the capricious love instinct to bend to human and state needs. Calderón's resolution of the two couples' happiness will be conventional and disingenuous. Although the final reconciliation ties up loose ends in the plot, it contradicts the play's comment on the independence, importance, and effect of love on personal relationships. Siquis's sacrifice by Atamas on Mt. Oeta is linked to her sisters' sacrifice during the epithalamia of state. The three sisters pay the price dictated by men, serving Gnido's needs.

Cupido does not accept Siquis's abandonment, claiming instead that only his vengeance as Venus's son will suffice. However, Siquis's beauty startles the young god who has come to execute her. When he finally stirs himself to take out the shaft, Siquis awakes, calling him a monster. Cupido drops the arrow and confesses that, though he came to avenge and to kill, he has "died" in the attempt. Then the crucial lines of Act I are declaimed:

> Siquis.   Toda soy prodigios hoy,
> pues cuando el monstruo soñé,
> a ti en su lugar hallé.
> Cupido.   Quizá yo, Siquis, lo soy.
>
> (1957a)

Cupido confesses his traitorous intent, and, when Siquis cries for help, he seizes her hand. Picking up the abandoned arrow, she smites him with it, avenging her offense. Immediately regretting her rash action, she flees in horror. Cupido suddenly discovers the power of love, a passion that he believed under his control.

Act I deals at length with the offense-vengeance mechanism that dominates both human and divine relations. The cyclical pattern of offense and vengeance was only broken once when Cupido was overcome by love. There is one force, *Ni Amor* suggests, capable of counterbalancing this deadly passion for vengeance, and that is love.

In Act II, Siquis is abandoned on a deserted island. Hearing beautiful music, she asks from whence it comes. A nymph declares:

> De quien en tanta tragedia
> compadecido de ti,
> vencer tus hados intenta. . . .
>
> (1964b)

Though Cupido is the one who has arranged this unexpected reception, secrecy is required to prevent Venus from finding out about Siquis's new found fortune and hidden location. Love, particularly Cupido's love of Siquis, may counterbalance her fate, but that love also requires trust on her part. She does not know her benefactor's identity and thus is sorely tested by this experience. Siquis is like a character in an *auto sacramental* who cannot rely on her sight since she can never see his face. She must trust her protector and have confidence in his good will. One indication of that good will is the storm that brought her to the island. Siquis is informed that she is in a safe haven where "no será mucho / que de los hados triunfes" (1966a). But safe though she be, her human nature is put to the test. Human beings rely on sight to confirm many things, and only those with strong faith in another are able to trust in words alone. Siquis's release from the grip of malign fate is not guaranteed by Cupido's presence nor by his assistance, for she must do her part to ensure that love triumph over fate.

Siquis may not ask nor may she be informed of the identity of her lover. He assures her, however, that he is not beastly and that it is imperative that he conceal himself, for a greater deity may be wronged by his attentiveness. The least shaft of light, moreover, will reduce the enchanted palace to dust. Siquis responds to these explanations with mistrust, stating that the enigmas she now faces are not reasonable, for only the traitor conceals his face. Siquis cannot accept Cupido's conditions and requests to be released to confront her fate in the light of day. As Siquis flees, Cupido declares the quality of his love:

> Bien pudiera forzarte
> mi gusto, al ver que huyes;
> pero mis vanidades
> tan baja acción no sufren:
> que es baldón de lo noble,
> bajeza de lo ilustre,
> juzgar que con violencias
> los méritos se suplen.
> Oblíguete mi ruego,
> mi llanto te asegure,
> muévate mi fineza.
>
> (1967)

There is no more eloquent condemnation of rape in Calderonian theater than this tender plea of Cupido's. When Anteo's cries for Siquis are suddenly heard, Cupido experiences jealousy, the sure sign of his love. At this point Siquis cannot trust in Cupido, for she still believes that somehow this situation forms part of Venus's revenge. Siquis's battle with reason's demands allows us to comprehend better what is at stake in her case. She believes that the monster foretold by Venus is now her pursuer, her lover. In one way Cupido is a monster, as we learned at the conclusion of Act I. But at the conclusion of Act II it becomes clear that Siquis's "monster" may also be an interior one, her inability to trust in Cupido's love, her lack of confidence in his *finezas*, and her excessive reliance on visual confirmation of verbal declarations of love. Siquis's belief in the monster exteriorizes and makes palpable the condition of her troubled soul.

Vengeance As Reflexive Reaction

At the conclusion of Act I, Cupido, in an attempt to calm and quiet Siquis, takes her hand and kisses it. Profoundly offended, Siquis declares:

> Suelta, atrevido, villano,
> y ella y este acero fuerte
> en quien mi *ofensa* se advierte,
> los instrumentos serán
> que *venganza* me darán.
>
> (1957b; emphasis added)

Taking Cupido's shaft, she wounds him with it. Siquis reacts automatically as did Cupido at the affront to his mother. Though offended by the mistreatment of his mother, Cupido experiences the assuaging power of love, a passion he is supposed to control and direct. In fact he discovers that love is the greatest and most powerful force in human/divine affairs, for only it is capable of challenging the drive for vengeance, the most powerful negative force operative in them. Cupido's discovery is the key to the play's eventual resolution.

As Act II begins Siquis laments her victimization at Venus's hands:

> Divina, enojada Venus,
> si fue de un vulgo *la ofensa*,
> y no mía, ¿por qué en mí
> tiranamente *te vengas?*
>
> (1958b; emphasis added)

Being a decisive person, Siquis rejects the role of scapegoat. Yet she expects an offense to be avenged in the form of some concrete punishment. The world view in the play is a harsh one that allows no room for pardon and forgiveness, at least until Cupido exemplifies how this vicious cycle may and should be broken.

Siquis believes that she has come to Mt. Oeta to offer special sacrifices to Júpiter so that he might serve as mediator between her and Venus. But Atamas knows that Siquis has come to pay for the sins of others: "pues delincuentes de Amor / todos, en Siquis se vengan" (1960b). For the King the gods are vengeful beings, so spiteful that they even take vengeance on the soul in addition to the body. When Anteo asks whether he has more to lose than life and honor in attempting to rescue Siquis, Atamas responds:

> Sí, si a ver llegas
> que tienes alma, y los dioses

> hasta en el alma se vengan,
> que es la útlima desdicha.

(1961a)

This world is bleak, blighted by the unforgiving nature of human and divine societies.

Once Siquis realizes that she has been abandoned by her father, the pattern or cycle of vengeance resumes its course. Siquis is no submissive female as she calls for a horrible vengeance on those who have just abandoned her. Struck by her frenzied demand for her father's death, she suddenly repents her rash words and asks for pity for them all, even wishing them safe harbor. But on recognizing that she is being sacrificed by others, she cries out once more for vengeance, only to desist and to wish all safe home again. Confused, troubled, full of rancor and pity, Siquis finally comprehends the full extent of her plight.

Cupido had previously discovered the power of love, a power great enough to overcome his desire for vengeance. But the offense to be avenged at that time was another's. In Act II Cupido is rejected by Siquis, and his first impulse is to force himself upon her, to take her by violence, to rape her. Rape is a vengeful act, and on realizing it Cupido repudiates both its ignoble dimension and its retributive function. He is further tested by the discovery of his jealousy of Anteo, and in Act III he experiences its full fury. His first impulse is to kill him, but he controls himself and tries to warn Anteo. He informs Siquis's cousin that she already has a *dueño*, as the prophecy foretold, and that a monster protects her. He departs admonishing Anteo:

> el que la ama
> sabrá vengarse de vos
> en ser, honor, vida y alma.

(1973a)

Although Cupido threatens Anteo, ultimately attempting to conceal Siquis's location from Venus, he manages to control his desire to strike at the one who offends him. As love overcame vengeance before, so too in this trial Cupido demonstrates that his love for Siquis is greater than his jealousy of Anteo, placing her interest before his impulses. Cupido proves that fate can be overcome by love, and at the end of Act III he demonstrates love's greatest *fineza*, the pardon of the erring Siquis.

The Theme of Identity

At the end of Act I Siquis dreams of the monster who will become her master, suddenly awakening to discover Cupido. The god of love even admits to her that he may be that monster. Whereas Siquis's preoccupation concerning the identity of the monster is understandable, what she fails to comprehend is how her present experiences are turning her into something monstruous. After wounding Cupido, the young maiden describes herself thus:

> Porque
> de piedad e ira se mira
> en mí un compuesto.

(1957b)

This composite nature defines one aspect of monstrosity, and Siquis, justifiably worried about her fate, is slowly becoming the monster she fears awaits her.

In Act II Siquis is bewildered by the sumptuousness of the enchanted palace and surprised by the attentiveness of its master. Naturally she asks: Who is he? only to hear Cupido declare "Yo" as he puts out the torch. To remain in the palace's secure confines, the only conditions he places on her are that she cannot see his face nor inquire about his identity. While this may be expecting a great deal of the young woman, she is not without clues as to his purpose in loving her. He courts her gently, solicitously, indulging her with one *fineza* after another. He even brings her family to the island to mitigate her loneliness. *Ni Amor* stresses that social status is not an adequate clue to one's identity, only acts, such as Cupido's mighty *finezas*, reveal the real person, the self beneath the conventional name tag.

Anteo is a totally admirable character who is willing to sacrifice all to save Siquis. He typifies in a most positive manner what he himself calls "la más noble hidalguía de los celos" (1975a). His motives are pure and good; he is willing to perform any *fineza*, even to sacrifice his own life, in order to save Siquis from the monster. But Siquis's monster is one of *finezas* and not of horrors. After arranging for Siquis's family to visit her, Cupido proudly approaches her:

> ¡Qué airoso llega un amante
> a los ojos de su dama,
> día en que un obsequio la hace!

(1977b)

Cupido even describes his act as a *fineza*. When Siquis asks who goes there, Cupido responds "Yo soy." Siquis asks again: "¿Es mi amor?" to which he responds:

> No sé qué respuesta darte,
> pues no solo tu amor hoy,
> que soy diré, mas de modo
> te amo, que entiendo que todo
> el amor de todos soy.

(1977b)

In a profoundly subtle sense the nature and quality of one's experiences contribute to the formation of personality, thus defining the self. Cupido discovers that as Siquis's lover he is a generous and gentle person, not the mean-spirited and vengeful god we found in Act I. Siquis will discover to her dismay that being with her lover is more important to her than knowledge of his identity. On viewing the god of love in the light, on discovering his identity, she loses that master of the palace who has been called a monster. The real monster who destroys their fragile happiness turned out not to be Cupido, but Siquis's lack of faith in his love.

Suffering and Pardon: Vengeance Thwarted and Fate Overcome

Ni Amor stresses that love and reason pertain to distinct categories. What satisfies the one may not necessarily satisfy the other. Anteo underscores their independence when he refuses to acquiesce in Atamas's plan to abandon Siquis:

> La vida
> es vasalla: ella obedezca;
> el amor no, que es muy libre.

(1961a)

These reminders of knowledge's limits and passion's independence help us to understand Siquis's dilemma in the enchanted palace. Though she has experienced the depth of Cupido's love, she has not yet been reassured by the revelation of his social identity. This trial leads to her betrayal of his love.

At the beginning of Act III Siquis is convinced that her lover is a god who descends every night to be with her. She is also in love with him. Yet she is dissatisfied with her situation, and that dissatisfaction compels her to seek reassurance through knowledge about her family. Conscious of her torment, Cupido magically reveals the weddings of her sisters. In asides we learn of the unhappiness of the couples. In spite of Cupido's *fineza*, Siquis continues to be concerned with her family, now wanting to share with them her newly found happiness. When Cupido proves his love for Siquis by bringing her sisters to the island, he unwittingly introduces envy into his domain. Because of the sisters' unhappiness, they envy Siquis and advise her to betray her lover. They demand proof of his identity, rekindling Siquis's prior doubts. "See his face, and if he is a monster kill him," they advise their doubting sister. Like the man of honor who is finely tuned to opinion, she begins to question her lover's goodness: "Todos lo dicen. Sin duda / mis desdichas son verdades..." (1976b). Siquis ignores the *finezas* performed on her behalf because others believe her lover to be a monster. Their unfounded suspicions cause her to doubt her real knowledge of him and to deny the intimate experience of his nature. In fact, in denying her experience of Cupido, she betrays the loving self (her mature womanhood) that blossomed only in and through his love.

Siquis requests that her servants prepare the light necessary for the revelation of her lover's identity. Her doubts are revealed in the additional request of a dagger. Though Siquis knows Cupido through his actions (1978a), she in fact knows neither him nor herself. As Cupido sleeps, Siquis calls for light and dagger, stating her resolve as follows: "el desengaño toquemos" (1978b). She hesitates. Although she needs to see him, to know whether she has mistakenly loved a monster, she fears that she will have to kill the one whom she has come to love. What she discovers far surpasses her wildest imaginings:

> El que dijo que este es
> un monstruo, dijo bien, pues
> es un monstruo de hermosura.
>
> (1979a)

She immediately recognizes him as the one who sought her death in Act I. Then the famous "¿Quién eres?" phrase underscores the purpose of her scrutiny. Duplicating Cupido's *turbación* when he was about to wound Siquis, she too becomes *turbada*, claiming that the beautiful youth has already avenged himself on her. All the major concerns of the play (the role of knowledge and the place of love, the theme of identity, and the question of vengeance) converge in this powerful scene. At the end of Act I, Cupido discovered that love is more powerful than vengeance, and Siquis discovers it to her dismay at the end of Act III.

When a drop of hot oil falls and burns Cupido's hand, he wakes from his slumber to discover Siquis armed and threatening his life. Though the god fears the light more than the dagger, the real damage has been Siquis's breaking of faith with her lover. Twice now Cupido has been wounded by Siquis, first with his own shaft and now with hot oil. The god's reflexive reaction is to avenge this wrong, just as Siquis did previously, but he forswears vengeance. Informing her of his role in her life, Cupido states that, since Venus is now aware of their love, it is doomed. With knowledge there comes a great loss for Siquis.

The offense-vengeance cycle resumes its deadly trajectory in the play. Cupido's departure is quickly followed by Siquis's frantic and pitiful laments over her loss. She accuses everyone of conspiring to convince her that her lover was an evil monster. Admitting her own part in this betrayal, she concludes: "verle quise, / y le he perdido por verle" (1980b). Since she is deeply offended by what has occurred, she wants some form of vengeance:

> y supuesto que yo en todos
> no es posible que me vengue,
> en mí sola podré hacerlo. . . .
>
> (1980b)

She attempts to kill herself with the very dagger she would have used to kill her monster/lover. It is significant that Eco and Narciso committed suicide on realizing their loss, but *Ni Amor* is to end differently. Cupido announces that Siquis's *lástimas* have moved the gods (1980b-1981a). Siquis's suffering has moved Cupido to pardon her, and Venus, on considering the effect of the young woman's death on Cupido, also pardons her and further agrees to her marriage to the god of love. To pardon is truly to be god-like, and this truth will configure the denouement of *La estatua de Prometeo*. Pardon puts an end to the vicious cycle of offense followed by vengeance that has characterized the plot.

Though Cupido's pardon is important, Venus's is crucial if harmony is to be restored to both heaven and earth. This essential pardon, which reunites the lovers, comes from outside of the pair themselves and is granted only after Siquis's great suffering (her expiation). A similar situation obtains in *La estatua de Prometeo* because Apolo must pardon Prometeo's theft of his sunray before harmony can be restored to a fractured Cáucaso. Both Siquis and Prometeo suffer greatly, and through their expiation of guilt, happiness becomes possible for them. Human suffering is the only redemptive option for sinful humans.

The Offense-Vengeance Mechanism and Fate

This pattern of offense and guilt duplicates the situation of humankind's first sin against God as recorded in the Bible. Adam and Eve lived happily in Eden until, through disobedience, they offended the almighty God. This original sin destroyed not only their terrestrial happiness but also caused the loss of their innocence. Their guilt could only be divinely repaired by redemption through Jesus Christ. *Ni Amor*'s Edenic state occurs in Cupido's enchanted palace, far removed from the tumult of Gnido's court. Siquis's disobedience parallels Adam and Eve's sin, revealing a lack of faith in her lover. Her offense brings about the loss of both palace and lover and the acquisition of guilt, a sin whose reparation is beyond her powers. Only Venus's and Cupido's pardons, ultimately motivated by Cupido's great love, can restore Siquis to her former happiness. In addition, she is apotheosized by that love into a goddess so that she might live with Cupido forever and ever.

The view that happiness and transcendence may result from insuperable guilt, great pain, and profound sorrow is typically Christian and forms the deep structure of *Ni Amor se libra de amor*. In fact the play transfers and translates that redemptive process into mythic and humanistic terms. Lest we lose sight of the daring scope of this play, we need to emphasize the optimistic vision it entails. First and foremost *Ni Amor* is a victory of love, *Omnia vincit amor*, brought about by Cupido's great love of Siquis. Implicit in Cupido's victory over fate is a second victory over the reflex reaction that governs human and divine affairs that I have labelled the offense-vengeance mechanism. Part and parcel of human fate is the automatic functioning of vengeance in personal relationships, and by conquering it one has an opportunity to defeat hostile fate itself. Siquis, a feminine version of the man of honor, is able to escape the terrible consequences of her mistrust of Cupido's love only because more powerful forces, Venus's pardon and Cupido's love, intervene to restore harmony.

Conclusion

In the original myth Cupid avenged the wrongs done to him by Psyche's sisters by causing their deaths. But in Calderón's version they live happily ever after with their husbands. This alteration demonstrates that the vengeance motive is to be definitively suppressed at the play's conclusion. In the myth Psyche's flaw was her curiosity; in *Ni Amor* it is her lack of trust and faith. Both of these changes reinforce Calderón's original interpretation and dramatization of the myth. It is a beautiful account of love triumphant; but, by overcoming vengeance through love and emphasizing Siquis's need to trust in her lover, Calderón neatly balances Cupido's and Siquis's active participation in the play's action. Cupid and Psyche would eventually have a daughter, Joy, the symbol of *their* redeemed state. For, as Siquis is liberated from guilt by Cupido's love to live happily ever after, so too the god of love finds happiness by leaving aside his childish swagger and assuming his mature role as husband and lover. Cupido's love works miracles on his personality too!

Hathorn states that this myth depicts the "redemptive experiences in miniature" (p. 244) of the larger tale of Lucius, the main character of *The Golden Ass*. Pandora and Psyche are pagan versions of the Judaic Eve, for in *Ni Amor se libra de amor* and *La estatua de Prometeo* we find magnificent dramatizations of "the soul's damnation and salvation" (Hathorn, p. 245). As readers of these plays we are exposed to that redemptive experience they were intended to dramatize.

Notes

1 The text consulted is found in the Valbuena Briones edition, pp. 1941-81.

2 In *Amado* Gnido was dedicated to Diana.

3 See Shergold, pp. 340-41, for an account of *Siquis y Cupido* staged 13 December 1679 in the Buen Retiro.

4 See my study, "El 'optimismo' de *Ni Amor se libra de amor*," in *Calderón: Actas del "Congreso Internacional sobre Calderón y el Teatro Español del Siglo de Oro"* (Madrid: C.S.I.C., 1983), I, 533-40. See also de Armas, *The Return of Astraea*, pp. 185-6.

C. El monstruo de los jardines

> pues desdicha no hay, no hay desconsuelo
> que no enmiende el vivir.

(1985b)[1]

> ¡Desdichado
> del que no vive engañado!

(1991a)

El monstruo de los jardines narrates the amorous adventures of the youthful and beardless Aquiles with the beautiful Deidamia. Antiquity's "Achilles at Scyros" becomes Calderón's dramatization of the hero's rite of passage set in the kingdom of Gnido. The boy who was hidden among the ladies of court by his goddess-mother Tetis sheds his effeminate garb to assume the obligations of honor as he enters the masculine world. Summarizing Aquiles's psychological problem in typically Calderonian terms, Valbuena Briones states: "trata de oponerse a su destino sin saber vencerse a sí mismo" (1984a). The moral lesson of the play is, therefore, that "el hado solo se vence al triunfar de sí mismo" (1984b). A native Spanish source for such critical approaches to the myth is found in Pérez de Moya's commentary "De las bodas de Peleo y Tetis, y juicio de Paris sobre la manzana de oro" (II, 202-8). In his view Aquiles is the perfect man undone in the last analysis by his lust (p. 206). Tracing backwards Aquiles's death from his involvement with Polyxena, this mythographer finds King Licomedes's house to have been "el reino de la lujuria," where the hero first experienced the allure of the flesh. While this approach satisfies the moralist's and churchman's desire to see attractive pagan stories translated into edifying Christian material, it does not adequately address the play's dynamics.

Everett W. Hesse approaches the play as a manifestation of gender-identity problems in Aquiles's inchoate personality:

The most important sexual problem to be raised in both plays [*El Aquiles* of Tirso is also considered] deals with Aquiles's gender identity in which he must overcome the *anima* side of his psyche by asserting the masculine and accepting the responsibilities and duties that go with it. Thus by the integration of his personality and the fulfillment of his mission in life (to be the leading Greek warrior against Troy) will he finally find happiness.[2]

I believe that both the moral and psychological approaches produce important results that address some of the contradictions in the plot, but not our experience, dramatic or otherwise, of those contradictions. The Valbuena Briones/Pérez de Moya approach suggests that Aquiles's life is a failure due to his victimization at the hands of fate and lust. Hesse opines that, since the gender-identity crisis is resolved, the Greek warrior finds happiness by taking the full burden of fate upon his shoulders. These positions are mutually exclusive. Alexander A. Parker, emphasizing the role of fate in the working out of Aquiles's destiny, finds that, because an announced fate infallibly predicts one's destiny, there is a tension between the horoscope which warns of the young man's death and Marte's oracle which foresees victory for him. This adolescent is forced to choose between happiness (life with Deidamia) and duty (the Trojan War). When he sacrifices love, he sacrifices happiness and ultimately his life.[3]

Monstruo dramatizes the conflictive claims of love and honor on the young man Aquiles. The denouement appears to reconcile them: first, Aquiles accepts his foreordained role in the Trojan War; second, when Tetis rescues her son from the vengeful wrath of Lidoro and the King, Aquiles is able to marry Deidamia. Aquiles's last words in the play, "Feliz soy" (2022b), appear to support Hesse's view.[4] But what we have is a dramatic irony of significant proportions. Though Aquiles wins Deidamia and experiences temporary happiness (the Hesse view), his rite of passage now includes a direct confrontation with malign fate leading to his eventual death on the fields of Ilium (the Valbuena/Pérez/Parker views).[5] Exploration of this dramatic tension will reveal the play's fundamental ambiguity, one so pronounced that it is indeed hard to say whether the work is disingenuous in its apparent reconciliation of love's and honor's claims, and hence is a dramatic failure, or whether it is a subtle exploration of the implications of their distinct claims and ultimate irreconcilability. In this latter case we have before us a complex work that problematizes *our* experience of honor's and love's claims upon Aquiles.

The Human/Divine Background to the Play's Action

While the action fluctuates between an apparently deserted island and the court of Gnido, the backdrop to the play is one of antiquity's most monumental events, the Trojan War. At the heart of Calderón's depiction of this action there lies the Greek attempt to avenge Paris's abduction of the beautiful Helen. Paris's betrayal of Menelaus's trust, the offense, provoked the Greek nation's desire for vengeance. As the chief organizer of the expedition against Troy, Ulises visits Gnido to enlist the King's support, claiming that "presto de Troya ha de vengarse Grecia" (1986b). When Polemio consults Marte's long-neglected oracle on the adjacent island, he is informed that the Greek cause will succeed only if Aquiles joins the expedition. Since Polemio will not join the Greek armada unless and until Aquiles is found, Ulises now faces a new challenge, the discovery and enlistment of this young man.

Marte's oracle prophesies the future conquest of Greece's enemies:

> "Troya será destruida
> y abrasada por los griegos,
> si va a su conquista Aquiles,

> a ser homicida de Héctor.
> Aquiles, humano monstruo
> de aquestos montes, en ellos
> un risco. . . ."

(1989b)

The oracle's deciphering of the prognostication is interrupted by Venus, ever protective of her cherished Troy. It is evident that a traditional Mars-Venus struggle forms a significant part of the action. Not only did the goddess of love reward Paris for having granted her the golden apple of beauty over Juno and Palas Athena, but in addition she continues to guard Trojan interests. In this particular case she muffles the declaration of Aquiles's whereabouts.

The gods of love and war represent distinct values, and their corresponding axiological systems become part of the play's dynamics. At one point Aquiles forsakes Deidamia because she is scheduled to marry Lidoro, and his renunciation of her becomes ironically predictive:

> y pues me guardan los cielos
> para tragedias de Marte,
> no empiece por las de Venus.

(2020b)

The dangers he faces in Gnido are truly life-threatening. Yet this young man willingly accepts equal, if not greater, dangers in Marte's cause, rejecting that of Venus. When Deidamia offers herself to the warrior, both body and soul, he responds:

> Pues ¿cómo he de ir con esto?
> Piérdase vida y honor,
> fama y gloria. Mas ¿qué es esto?   *Clarín.*
> La voz de Marte me llama.

(2020b)

Though attracted by Deidamia, Aquiles heeds the greater call of war. He has made his decision to forsake love for honor's laurels on the fields of Ilium. The Mars-Venus struggle represents two distinct modes of "being-in-the-world" at loggerheads in the character of Aquiles. While Aquiles may experience a momentary reconciliation of these disparate claims, *Monstruo* highlights their fundamental incompatibility. Aquiles's marriage to Deidamia will be but a brief respite en route to honor's ultimate claim, Aquiles's life.

Another significant dimension of the background action concerns Aquiles's origin. The marriage of Peleus and Thetis prevented Jupiter's siring of a son who would become greater than himself. In spite of being attracted to the marine goddess Thetis, the ruler of Olympus felt obliged to marry her off to a mortal. Pérez de Moya expressed the goddess's reaction to this marriage thus: "Hacíasele de mal a Tetis, siendo deesa marina, haber de ser mujer de hombre mortal" (II, 202). Although Peleus forced himself on Thetis, he did not technically rape her. Pérez de Moya described this ambiguous situation as follows: "trabajaba tener acción con ella" (II, 202). Thetis, recognizing the futility of resisting Jupiter's will, begrudgingly accepted her marriage to Peleus: "hubo de consentir en el casamiento" (II, 203).

Calderón configured this ambivalent situation, in which force is applied to Tetis, according to a well-know pattern in his dramaturgy: Peleo rapes Tetis. Deeply offended, the goddess then murders her attacker, a novel situation in Calderonian theater. As in *Golfo*, this particular account of the Peleo-Tetis relationship is a key for our understanding the play. The rape of Tetis and the murder of Peleo condition our responses to the play's eventual resolution: We expect the worst. In the original myth the alienation of the couple occurs when Peleus curses Thetis on discovering her roasting the infant Achilles.[6] Calderón depicts the subsequent action in dark and lugubrious hues filled with ominous forebodings, for Aquiles is an "embrión de una violencia" (1998b). Due to the providential guidance of Mercurio and Palas, Perseo was able to avoid the inheritance of violent, premature death, whereas Liríope's ineffectualness compounds Narciso's fortune, assuring his death. The rape of Aquiles's mother Tetis alerts us to a potentially tragic issue, for her intervention in her son's life more closely resembles Liríope's failure than Mercurio and Palas's success.

The Cyclical Nature of Vengeance

At this point it would be advisable for us to review the prominent role of revenge in *Monstruo* and, in particular, the functioning of the offense-vengeance mechanism.

1. Paris's abduction of Helen provoked the greatest event in Greek myth, the Trojan War, a punitive expedition formed by Greece's leading heroes.

2. Ulises, the jealous guardian of Greek honor, sails about the Aegean mustering support for the war effort, for "presto de Troya ha de vengarse Grecia" (1986b). Paris's abduction of Helen imbues all the Greek males of the play with an indomitable desire for vengeance. Both Danteo (1988b) and Lidoro (1994a) make explicit references to the Greek need for revenge on their Trojan enemies.

3. There are two instances in Act II in which Ulises, at a loss as to where Aquiles is to be found, rhetorically asks: "¿dónde está Aquiles?" only to hear "Aquí" (2004a); and to "¿Dónde, fortuna, hallaré a Aquiles?" he hears Deidamia respond "Conmigo..." (2006). Even the *acasos* of the play appear to collaborate in revealing Aquiles's location so that the war may proceed.

4. The act that establishes the play's tone, however, is Peleo's rape of the

goddess Tetis. Deeply offended by this violation, Tetis takes vengeance by killing Peleo. But her revenge does not stop there, as Danteo explains:

> Ella, ofendida
> del injusto atrevimiento,
> el tálamo destruyó,
> inundando a nieve y fuego
> los edificios, los troncos
> y los vecinos, que fueron,
> sin cuidar de su defensa,
> cómplices de su desprecio. . . .

(1989a)

The goddess attempts to protect her honor, reputation, and *decoro* by destroying any potential witness to her shame. This readiness to take a life to protect or advance one's interests is further underscored when Tetis drowns Astrea in a storm so that Aquiles might assume her identity.[7]

5. Peleo's rape of Tetis contributes to Aquiles's unnatural upbringing. The young goddess attempts to raise her son in seclusion so that he might ostensibly escape the predicted violence that threatens his life. But Aquiles's suffocating upbringing and lack of knowledge of the world place him in the very dangers his mother seeks to avoid.

The Trojan War and the Peleo-Tetis affair remind us of the cyclical nature of vengeance that eventually overtakes all the characters of the play. We have before us a desolate portrayal of vengeance's reach into both the human and the divine realms. Ulises represents the unrelenting nature, the ingrained human drive for vengeance, whereas Tetis demonstrates the range and fury of an offended god. No one is exempt from the consequences of revenge. We become witnesses to a bleakness both human and divine.

As a character in myth Achilles's life forms part of a larger mosaic. Prometheus held a secret that was of vital importance to Jupiter, and, when he eventually became reconciled to the lord of the heavens, he revealed that "any son of Thetis would be greater than his father" (Hathorn, p. 345). Once a child is born to Tetis, she attempts to read his fate in the stars:

> y hallé que al tercero lustro
> te amenaza la más fiera
> lid, la más dura batalla,
> la campaña más sangrienta
> de cuantas en sus teatros
> la fortuna representa. . . .

(1998b)

Tetis interprets this declaration of Aquiles's fate to refer to the upcoming war with Troy. While it has obvious reference to the Trojan War, Tetis learns that it also alludes to his passage from boyhood to manhood in the palace of King Polemio. Tetis wished to break fate's eyes (1999a) by raising her child of violence in complete seclusion. While her purpose was good, the nature of his upbringing creates the very situation Tetis hoped to avoid. Once again the attempt to confront her son's fate forms the counterpart of that fate. All Greek males are implicated in the upcoming war, and Aquiles will enter it ill-prepared for what faces him.

The Education of Children and Human Freedom

Monstruo raises the question of human freedom from both masculine and feminine perspectives, though each is not necessarily gender specific. Aquiles's strange and unnatural upbringing addresses the issue of the proper education to prepare the young man maturely to assume his responsibilities in society. Hesse's article illuminates this point from a distinctly psychological perspective. When we first meet Aquiles he emerges from his obscure cave, drawn by the sweet and alluring sound of music. He wonders whether it proceeds from some new bird, but has no way of knowing since he has been brought up in ignorance: "Todo mi vida lo ignora" (1991b). While from Aquiles's perspective the sudden appearance of musical harmony brings to the fore the sterility of his present life, from that of Deidamia her arranged marriage to Prince Lidoro of Epiro epitomizes the sacrificial nature of her life. Her human dignity and freedom serve the state of Gnido, and Deidamia rebels at becoming an object, a pawn, in those affairs. Thus the experiences of Aquiles and Deidamia raise different aspects of fundamental human questions: How are children to be educated to live well in the world? and To what degree should their human freedom be respected?

When we first meet Aquiles he breaks out of his prison/house, disobeying the goddess who has raised him there. Beastly in appearance, the beautiful youth is drawn away from his hiding place by strange and wonderful music. On discovering the sleeping Deidamia, he falls in love with her. Alhough he does not know who he is, he does know that he is the son of a deity (1993a). His knowledge of self is limited to a name, Aquiles. The meeting of Aquiles and Deidamia is similar to Eco and Narciso's encounter. They both feel a spontaneous outpouring of emotion. Aquiles is ill-prepared for this moment, due to his lack of knowledge, and Deidamia is unable to respond to it, due to her lack of freedom.

Once Aquiles's identity is revealed, the other characters seek to detain him in order to proceed with the Greek vengeance on Troy. At the very moment he emerges from his prison (1994a), others seek to reduce him to a new bondage. Even Lidoro puts aside his desire for personal revenge in view of the greater claim of the Greek nation:

> porque siendo, como eres,
> a quien destinan las sacras
> deidades para que Grecia
> logre de Troya venganaza,
> quiero ser tu amigo.

(1994a)

At the very time Aquiles discovers new and conflicting emotions, love and jealousy, he also hears what destiny has in store for him. Ulises informs him that:

> quiere el cielo que yo sea
> quien te dedique a las aras
> de Marte, para blasón
> de Grecia.

(1996a)

Even Deidamia attempts to influence him:

> No huyas,
> sabiendo que no te agravia
> quien para tu honor te busca

(1996a)

Rejecting their pleas, he prepares to fight "en demanda / de mi libertad" (1996b). In this impasse Tetis saves him, dea ex machina, "para librarte de que / cumpla el hado su amenaza" (1996b). As Aquiles returns to his dark grotto, he laments, like Segismundo, the loss of a woman.

As Act II begins Aquiles is terribly frustrated by his reincarceration after exposure to the world and to love. He wants to kill himself, to exchange one tomb for another. According to Aquiles, Tetis has employed a "tirana fuerza" (1997a) in raising him, converting his rustic, rocky abode into a veritable prison. With these new experiences of the world, he cannot accept his former way of life. Calling Tetis "piadosa crüel" (1997b) and detailing oxymoronically her ambivalent attitude toward him, Aquiles states that, though his will seeks to obey her, his passion refuses to comply. The emerging man cannot revert to the simple and trusting child he once was. Whether his life is ruled by fate or cruelty, he can no longer accept his mother's direction because the very safety she seeks has already become a living form of death. He demands the freedom to decide his own course of action, to determine his life:

> deja
> que la pierda a gusto mío,
> si es preciso que la pierda.

(1997b)

Having been raised in total ignorance of his past and of his fate, Aquiles seeks to discover who he is and who is his mother. Indirectly he wants some justification for the strange mode of existence he has been forced to assume for almost fifteen years. Though the precipitating cause of this crisis is Deidamia, the issue surpasses mere passion and encompasses the question of human freedom. Tetis continues to see her son's rebelliousness only in terms of Aquiles's burgeoning sexuality, the very cause of her tragic rape and shame. Exercising continued control over her son, she informs him of the danger threatening his life at the same time as she assures his safety by introducing him into the court of Gnido.

Tetis provides her son with a full account of his origin and fate. Informing him that she is the goddess Tetis, she recounts how Peleo raped her, and thus Aquiles was an "embrión de una violencia" (1998b). Fighting back her shame, she clarifies for Aquiles that, though all were born in love, "naciste tú de una fuerza" (1998b). Deeply offended, she killed his father and attempted to hide from the world the proof of her "shame." Aquiles's birth produced ambivalent feelings in his mother, rancor and tenderness, and thus she attempted to read in the stars what the future would bring. She informs Aquiles of the three events that now appear to conspire against him. First, there is the announced fate that Tetis is hoping to avoid by concealing Aquiles until the "tercero lustro" passes. Second, there is Marte's oracle by which Aquiles's participation in the Trojan War is declared to be essential for eventual success. And third, this new found love arises as the fulcrum upon which Aquiles's fate and destiny are balanced. Since satisfying the sexual drives of the young man appears to Tetis to be the immediate issue, she disguises her son as Astrea and places him among Deidamia's ladies in waiting. But Tetis is seeking a control and direction of her son's life that is impossible to both humans and gods:

> deja
> que averigüemos al cielo
> si tiene el ingenio fuerzas
> contra el poder de sus hados
> e influjo de sus estrellas.
>
> (1999b)

This mother is compensating in her son's life for the lack of control she had in her own. For Aquiles all is reduced to being with Deidamia. As nymphs arrive to transport Aquiles to court, they sing:

> Veamos si sus hados
> vence, cuando sea
> monstruo en los jardines
> quien lo fue en las selvas.
>
> (2000b)

Abandoning his rustic environment, Aquiles enters an unfamiliar world.

In Deidamia's espousal to a man she does not know, the play explores the obligations of royalty. Her personal happiness must be subjugated to the larger issue of Gnido's welfare. In less acerbic terms than Aquiles's denunciation of Tetis, Deidamia, calling her father "tirano de mis deseos" (1990b), asks how can she be married to the Prince of Epiro since she detests men. Cintia, her companion, reminds her of her duty:

> Las soberanas deidades,
> antes de nacer, tuvieron
> sabido para quién nacen.

(1991a)

Diedamia responds: "Aun eso es lo que yo siento" (1991a). In Act II Diadamia complains bitterly that her freedom and free will are being sacrificed for extrapersonal reasons. Since she has never met Lidoro, her marriage is doubly offensive to her. At this point her lack of knowledge of her future husband echoes Aquiles's lack of knowledge of himself and his world. The theme of identity, ¿quién es Lidoro?, raises yet again the question of the education of youth and the extent of their human freedom. Though Aquiles knows who his parents are, he is aware of himself only in a superficial way. For the rest of the characters, Aquiles's identity is not an issue, only his location is a problem, for they have already determined what the young man will become. Both Aquiles and Deidamia suffer from a subtle form of human enslavement, the one to the interests of the Greek nation and the other to those of the kingdom of Gnido. Neither is given a choice concerning who or what he or she will become.

In Act III the amorous entanglements come to a head when Polemio decides to marry Deidamia on the morrow. When Deidamia discusses her plight with Aquiles, she insists that she is suffering greatly because "es en mí mi obligación primero / que mi pasión" (2018b). Deidamia has internalized the norms of conduct expected of a princess, just as Aquiles will assume at the play's conclusion both the attitudes and values expected of a male member of society.

At the denouement Aquiles marries Deidamia, and personal happiness appears to carry the day. But Aquiles's personal happiness is ironically made possible only by acceptance of his duty as the leader of the Grecian expedition. Deidamia is allowed to marry him only because he will depart for Troy. For both these young people service to the state claims priority over personal happiness; only in serving the state can their personal happiness be realized. Aquiles, however, will pay the price of his honor and fame, and Deidamia will be left a widow. The marriage of these two young people is a brief, but happy, respite in their lives defined and controlled by the code of honor and *razón de estado* of the Greek states.

Aquiles's and Deidamia's Rites of Passage

In Act III love begins to transform Aquiles. Lidoro describes the specter he encounters in the garden as:

> galán y airoso en el talle,
> valeroso en el denuedo,
> recatado en el lenguaje,
> prevenido en la cautela
> y en la ejecución constante. . . .

(2013a)

This is not the rustic beauty Deidamia discovered in Act I. His transformation is not due to any physical intercourse, but to his spiritual development under love's guidance. Hesse believes that "the two are enjoying a pre-marital heterosexual relationship" (p. 184). I do not believe this to be the case, especially in view of the words Deidamia uses to prevent Aquiles's premature departure for Troy:

> No te ausentes, no me dejes
> conmigo a mí, y yo te ofrezco
> ser tuya, aunque se aventuren
> padre, esposo, honor y reino.
> Tuya he de ser: no te vayas.

(2020b)

Although her offer to be his is clearly sexual in intent, Deidamia has risked, but not lost, her honor. Perhaps this delay in the sexual union of the two lovers accounts for the change of the King's name from Licomedes to Polemio. According to Hathorn, "Lycomedes means 'He Who Takes Care of the Wolves (i.e. the Boys Undergoing Initiation),'" and this personage "plays a part in the symbolic initiation of Achilles" (p. 320). Calderón eliminates this secretive initiation into full sexuality for both characters and places it squarely under the orthodox banner of marriage. The rites of passage of the two characters involve more than the commencement of sexual relations. While Aquiles's rite of passage is from the state of boy to that of man in the full sexual sense, it also includes the acceptance of the masculine world of honor and obligation. While Deidamia's rite of passage is from the state of girl to that of woman in the full sexual sense, it too includes the acceptance of the feminine world of duty and obligation, defined, in the last analysis, by masculine interests.

Tetis has transferred Aquiles from the deserted island to Polemio's court in the hope that proximity to Deidamia will satisfy his burgeoning erotic feelings. As Astrea during the day and as *el monstruo de los jardines* during the night, Aquiles has not failed to arouse suspicion: first, because Astrea has been reported lost at sea in a violent storm; second, because the mysterious nightly visitor greatly concerns both Lidoro and Ulises. The former is jealous while the latter is suspicious of the mysterious personage, and thus they plan to trap him. Ulises enters Deidamia's room with rich presents, including "espadines y plumajes, / bandas, escudos" (2013b). When Deidmia's ladies choose rich jewelry, Aquiles/Astrea elects arms. When asked why "she" has chosen arms instead of jewels, Astrea responds: "Sí, pues hay entre mujeres / mujeres que no lo son" (2016a). When "she" maintains this bold stance before Ulises, Deidamia remarks "Necia estás" (2016a). At this point we recall Tetis's warning to Aquiles who became *turbado* on entering the palace:

> Pues vuelve en ti, y con prudencia
> recóbrate y disimula.
>
> (2004a)

This first probe by Ulises demonstrates how ill prepared Aquiles is to carry out such a subtle and ingenious ruse.

Ulises's second probe involves the interruption of the nuptial celebration by martial music. Aquiles becomes caught up in the excitement of these foreign sounds and declares:

> Vuestro discurso yerra;
> que aqueste es el idioma de la guerra
> que grandes cosas llama,
> pues su concento grave,
> mezclando lo horroroso y lo süave,
> el pecho anima, el corazón inflama,
> y la muerte apellida
> en glorioso desprecio de la vida.
> . . . .
> ¡Viva el imperio griego,
> y Troya se destruya a sangre y fuego!
> No quede a vida bárbaro enemigo. . .
> Mas loca estoy: no sé lo que me digo.
>
> (2017b)

Ulises now has solid reasons to support his suspicions. In the third probe of Astrea's indentity Ulises says unsuspectedly: "'Guárdate, Aquiles; que te dan la muerte'" (2019a). Aquiles immediately reacts, revealing his identity. When he tries to dissimulate, Ulises begins to insult Aquiles's sense of manhood by intimating that a person dressed in such feminine garb could never be the future leader of Greek warriors. Simply and decisively Aquiles asks Ulises to ready a horse for him. The young man who sought love over war now attempts "Poner en slavo mi honor" (2019b). With his acceptance of the obligations of honor, Aquiles passes into the world of masculine values and the fated war with Troy.

Hathorn has written that Achilles "is a strange kind of archetypal hero. He undergoes initiation three times, twice as an infant, in the fire and in the waters of death, and again as a youth when he leaves the world of women to become a warrior.... Yet his initiation somehow miscarries" (p. 354). It is precisely this miscarriage that *Monstruo* explores in a subtly ironic manner. As Aquiles enters the world of men, he inevitably begins a journey that will lead to his death. His present crisis only highlights the conflict at the heart of the play between love (life) and honor and fame (eventual death). The two motivating factors in his decision to accept his fate as leader of the Greek expedition are: 1) the realization that tomorrow Deidamia will be married to Lidoro, and the consequent jealousy he experiences; and 2) the fact that his hiding in Polemio's court exposes him to insults and the resultant loss of honor.

As Aquiles sheds the feminine dress of his assumed personality, that of Astrea, he exposes his manly clothing and reveals his masculine nature. In the ensuing scene Deidamia begs him to remain with her and to forgo the war. Venus and Mars, symbolic of the values of love and war, are struggling for ascendancy in his personality and life. Aquiles responds to Deidamia: "La voz de Marte me llama" (2020b), "el honor me está llamando" (2021a), and "fama y honor pretendo" (2021a). When Lidoro and Polemio arrive, the hero now declares:

> Aquiles soy, que a tu casa
> y a ti tal traición he hecho,
> de Deidamia enamorado,
> a quien por esposa tengo.
> Vengan, pues, y llegad todos.

> (2021b)

Aquiles expects his offense to produce swift and brutal vengeance—he is fully a member of male society.

When Tetis appears peace is restored to the kingdom. In her attempts to shelter her son from the dangers that awaited him in war, she delivered him to the full fury of his fate during his rite of passage. When the King and Lidoro pardon the hero, Aquiles's marriage to Deidamia is ratified by male society. What the conclusion apparently states is that love and war are not mutually exclusive. The denouement resolves the conflict of love and honor, life and death, but that solution is momentary and unsatisfactory. Both Tetis and Aquiles sought to fathom whether by *ingenio* they could conquer fate and ignorance (1999b and 2000b). Only through authorial ingenuity do they appear vanquished, for we recall that Marte's oracle omitted the fact that Aquiles's glorious participation in the war would also spell his death. Tetis says of her son's future:

> y pues hoy trasciende el punto,
> siendo desde aquí trofeos,
> victorias, triunfos y aplausos.

(2022a)

Aquiles's ambiguous fate included two possibilities: the dangers encountered in the palace episode and those yet awaiting him in the Trojan War, a fact that problematizes this conventional denouement.

Conclusion

El monstruo de los jardines juxtaposes two distinct and ultimately disharmonious sets of values: those associated with honor, vengeance, and war, and those associated with love, life, and peace. While the action of the play appears to reconcile them, the Trojan War and its inevitable progression of events problematize what was conventional and ultimately contradictory in the plot. Moreover, neither the option symbolized by Venus nor that symbolized by Marte recognizes Aquiles's human freedom. The former sidesteps Aquiles's need to assume his rightful place in adult society, while the latter slavishly chains him to a duty to warped honor and demeaning vengeance. The youth's ultimate tragedy proceeds from this real limitation of his options for living. The drama's lack of synthesis reveals the fracture in the Baroque mindset, a fracture of the Renaissance ideal of the harmony of opposites. Aquiles's espousal to Deidamia comes, ironically, only after his espousal of honor, war, and death. At the surface his encounter with Deidamia represents his espousal of love, an encounter with "Woman As Death," the symbolic death of his puerile nature as his manly personality emerges. But a more fundamental rite of passage occurs at the same time. Aquiles's acceptance of the obligations of honor brings him to an encounter with "Destiny As Death," a predictive event that reminds us of what awaits him at Troy. In spite of its "optimistic" ending, *Monstruo* is unable to reconcile the claims of honor and love.

Since Aquiles's rite of passage is a composite, composed of his espousal of Deidamia and war, it is a monstrosity. Rather than resolve the basic problem that contributed to Aquiles's being called Astrea, to his monstrous androgyny in the garden, it repeats his hybridization: love/honor, glory/death. The *discordia concors* of the denouement, the harmonizing of the conflictive values represented by Mars and Venus, stands as a sham solution to Aquiles's cry for freedom (his need for love) and the call of war. The young man's tragedy translates the play's title from the purely personal into the broadly historical as Aquiles becomes a monster of Greek revenge.

The Trojan War would upset Greek society, creating a topsy-turvy situation in which war and death would rule over peace and life. Aquiles's induction into that society is not his liberation from falsity and deceit, but his enslavement to a society fundamentally doomed to destruction in spite of its predicted victory over Troy.

Valbuena cites Antonio Minturno's comments on the concept of *admiratio*:

> Debe admirarse aquellas cosas que conducen
> a la piedad o que producen el terror, y
> todavía mayormente aquellas cosas que
> siguiendo como consecuencia, suceden
> contrariamente a lo que se esperaba o deseaba.

(1984b)

This is precisely what occurs in Aquiles's life after his momentary happiness in the court of Gnido. Although he marries Deidamia, soon he will have to depart for Troy to meet Héctor and his own death. Tetis predicts "trofeos, / victorias, triunfos y aplausos" for her son and the Greeks, but in the midst of this celebration we perceive Death's gloomy specter. We began this section with the following quotation:

> pues desicha no hay, no hay desconsuelo
> que no enmiende el vivir.

(1985b)

Aquiles's predicted premature death reminds us that his initiation into sexuality and manhood is at the same time his monstrous initiation into honor and death. As the second quotation of the introduction suggests that to be happy one must live a life of illusion, only in delusion can Aquiles be truly happy. We are not, however, deceived, and this is the source of our pity for Aquiles. What begins for him on a happy note will inevitably end in disaster. This knowledge produces our *admiración*.

Notes

1 Text cited is the Valbuena Briones edition, pp. 1983-2022.

2 "Sexual Problems in the Achilles Plays of Tirso and Calderón," *KRQ*, 28 (1981), 187. See also his "Calderón's *El monstruo de los jardines*: Sex, Sexuality, and Sexual Fulfillment," *Revista Canadiense de Estudios Hispánicos*, 5 (1981), 311-19. Frederick A. de Armas's view of *Monstruo* is in accord, though for different reasons, with Hesse's analysis. See "Achilles as Astraea" in *The Return of Astraea*, pp. 197-211.

3 See "*El monstruo de los jardines* y el concepto calderoniano del destino," in *Hacia Calderón: Cuarto coloquio anglogermano. Wolfenbüttel 1975.* (Berlin and New York: Walter de Gruyter, 1979), pp. 92-101). I discovered Parker's article after writing this section, and I believe his appreciation of the ironic nature of the play to be accurate.

4 de Armas writes that "Aquiles as Astraea-Venus is thus an icon for the reconciliation of the coldness of justice with the warmth of charity" (p. 205).

5 In his book on imagery, Blue sees Aquiles's acceptance of his fate in positive terms; the Trojan War is a positive heroic exploit (p. 179).

6 See Hathorn, p. 353.

7 Blue states that Astrea "perished at sea" (p. 173). The murder of Astrea is a key element that forces us to examine with care the relation of Aquiles to the fate of the Greek nation.

D. *Fineza contra fineza*

> pues vencer y perdonar
> es ser vencedor dos veces.
>
> (2102a)[1]
>
> ya es triunfo de amor vencerme
> yo a mí mismo. . . .
>
> (2137a)

On 22 December 1671, *Fineza contra fineza* was performed in Vienna to celebrate the birthday of Mariana de Austria, the Queen of Spain.[2] While the work is not a representative mythological play, one that dramatizes a pagan myth for a contemporary audience, it is, nonetheless, set in mythic times during which the gods and goddesses were active in human affairs. It is similar in conception and execution to *Amado y aborrecido*. The plot narrates events that reflect the influences of Venus (love) and Diana (disdain) on humankind. As the mythic dimension is downplayed, the emphasis on palace life and intrigue is accentuated. *Fineza* abounds with questions of honor and soundings of the obligations of nobility. Valbuena has observed that "El conflicto de la obra es propio de las comedias de enredo" (p. 2099b), and I would add that the typical urban environment is replaced by an antiquarian setting in Tesalia where court life and obligations receive prominent billing.

Fineza's action provides us with the mature Calderonian view that summarizes the thematic directions of his theater. As the introductory quotations suggest, mature love assists a character to "vencerse a sí mismo," to put aside self-interest in favor of the other. In addition, the play demonstrates that love's crowning achievement is the ability to pardon, as already seen in *Ni Amor se libra de amor*, and the disposition to perform mighty *finezas*, as attested to by *Amado y aborrecido*. Moreover, the plot evinces how only love is capable of overcoming the desire for vengeance, leading to a fullness of life symbolized by the concluding marriages. Hatred, vengeance, and death are rejected by both gods and humans who yield themselves to the miraculous workings of love.

The World of Vengeance

Fineza's imaginary world is one in which vengeance rules the lives of gods and humans. Anfión, the King of Cyprus, unwittingly reveals how internalized the norm of vengeance is in all the characters when he explains how "natural" it was for Diana to avenge herself on Acteón, his father (2103b). Diana, venerated in Tesalia, and Venus, the patroness of Chipre, represent the opposing axiological poles that define this dramatic world. Anfión, the son of Acteón, has come to Tesalia to wipe out every temple dedicated to

Diana, effectively eliminating her cult. Though Anfión was disposed to accept his father's violent death as a just punishment for his intrusion upon the goddess's bath, Diana's involvement with Endimión shattered his simple view of the matter:

> Deidad que en sus estatutos,
> contra naturales leyes
> manda al aborrecimiento
> que a pesar del amor reine;
> deidad que por el melindre
> de un fácil acaso leve
> mata a un noble Acteón, y admite
> a un vil Endimión, o miente
> aquel honor o este amor
> o entrambos; que no convienen
> bien un amor que se abata
> con un honor que se ostente.
>
> (2103b-2104a)

Once Diana yielded to Endimión's love, Anfión believes that her apparently chaste revenge was not due to *honestidad*, but to *ojeriza* against the Cyprians who revere Venus (2104a). The revenge that Anfión eventually exacts, the conversion of Diana's temple into a center for Venus's cult, demonstrates the generational reach of this automaton-like passion. Acteón's affront induced Diana's revenge, which in turn motivates Anfión's retribution. What is novel in this case is the role switching by which a human being seeks vengeance on a goddess, reminiscent of Eróstrato's setting fire to Diana's temple in Lidia (see *Celos, aun del aire, matan*).

The Diana-Venus conflict produces repercussions on the inhabitants of Tesalia. Amongst the priestesses of Diana's temple is one woman who, though apparently sincere in her dedication to Diana, inwardly contradicts what she outwardly professes. Doris, the secret love of Tesalia's general Celauro, despises Diana, whom she nevertheless publically worships, and privately reveres Venus. When Anfión captures Diana's temple, he intends to burn it to the ground. The idea is then proposed to covert the temple to Venus's cult, and the conqueror spares both it and its priestesses. Doris feels betrayed by Venus because, when the opportunity arises to yield herself to love, she is mistakenly informed of Celauro's death. This situation reminds us of Doña Serafina's dilemma in *El pintor de su deshonra*, but in *Fineza* there will be a happy resolution due to providence's intervention. Doris's life story typifies the place of women in this society. At an early age she was consecrated by her father to the goddess Diana. Celauro supplies us with the motive for this dedication:

¿Ves la prisión
y destierro, en cuya ausencia,
a este templo de Dïana
tu padre quiso que vengas?

(2119b)

Like the Hespérides of *Fieras afemina Amor*, Doris was to be entombed alive, a living sacrifice to her father's honor.[3] She stands as a victim of the masculine preoccupation with honor, and her love for Celauro, though natural and good, contradicts her life of enforced virginity.

As spokesperson for the priestesses, Ismenia accepts the new cult of Venus while secretly longing for Diana's restoration. Though she awaits King Aristeo's counterattack, she is ready to take matters into her own hands (2113b). She is a woman of strong passions, and throughout the play she seeks vengeance on Venus and Celauro. Her passionate words (2121b) are translated into action when she secrctly removes Venus's statue and throws it into an abyss. Her promise of vengeance occurs toward the conclusion of Act I, and her defilement of Venus's simulacrum closes Act II. The discovery of who is responsible for this outrage will occupy all of Act III, testing the character and nobility of each of the principal personages.

Doris and Ismenia represent two distinct modes of being-in-the-world. Although the former publicly laments the affront to Diana's cult, she privately rejoices in love's restoration to its rightful place in human society. The latter, though she is the chief priestess of the new cult to Venus, inwardly personifies Diana's deathlike influence on those who adore her. The love-hate antagonism that typifies so many Calderonian plays receives dramatic expression in the opposing personalities of Doris and Ismenia. What is at stake, however, is not merely the destiny of private citizens, but the direction of a society toward its natural *telos* or its unnatural dissolution.

There is another offense-vengeance intrigue that involves Ismenia and Celauro. At some unspecified point in the past Tesalia's general killed Ismenia's brother Fabio in a duel. Since that time she vehemently hates Celauro and thirsts for revenge. All we know is that Celauro felt justified in slaying him ("dio muerte a su hermano / más mi razón que mi diestra" [2117a]), and that no suspicion fell on Doris as a consequence (2119b). We may speculate on a love triangle or Fabio's discovery of Doris and Celauro's love affair, but in any case Fabio's death influences Ismenia's antivital proclivities toward vengeance. As Doris's life is ruled by love and directed toward society's betterment, Ismenia's is ruled by hatred and revenge and dedicated to dividing and ultimately destroying the social fabric. Disdain and love, the states produced by adhering to Diana's or Venus's cults, have pernicious or beneficial effects on the lives of individuals who compose human society as well as deadly or life-giving effects on that society itself.

Ismenia's removal of Venus's statue from her new temple produces the offense that will lead to the *finezas* of the play's title. Anfión, with dagger in hand, opens Act III by pursuing the nymphs of the new cult and swearing death to all if the perpetrator is not found. Doris appears to be guilty, but Celauro knows that Ismenia committed the sacrilege. We wait to see whether he will break his promise to guard Ismenia's secret in order to save Doris's life. Attempting to soften Anfión's desire for revenge, Celauro suggests the drawing of lots to discover the criminal. The stage is now set for the trial of the characters. Who shall die to pay for the offense to Venus? What will shock our sensibilities, however, is the disregard of truth and justice in the search for the culprit, for it does not matter whether the guilty party dies or not as long as someone dies.

Love and Jealousy

Once Anfión conquers Tesalia, he fully intends to burn Diana's temple and put all to the sword. Celauro's heroic defense of the city and temple, however, moves him to pity. Attempting to disregard this noble impulse, he seeks further violence and bloodshed only to be interrupted by the pleas of Diana's nymphs for mercy. Moved deeply by the sight of Ismenia, the conqueror allows these women to choose death and fidelity to Diana's cult or life and rededication to Venus's. The nymphs' response is significant: "La vida / es amable" (2104b). Venus's cult celebrates life, love, and fruitfulness, whereas Diana's honors death, disdain, and barrenness. Venus's cult celebrates love, and Anfión, try though he may, cannot deny this life-celebrating orientation to his life. Although he entered Tesalia like an avenging angel, sword in hand, he has been smitten by love (2109b). On seeing Ismenia, Anfión undergoes a sudden change of heart, and the consequences of this transformation are notable:

> No solo, pues, como dije,
> (fuerza es repetirme en esto),
> de mi *venganza* la fiera
> indignación venció, pero
> hizo que todas viniesen
> en la adoración de Venus,
> y yo en la adoración suya.
>
> (2110a; emphasis added)

By reorienting Anfión's life to the other, love smothers or mitigates his desire for vengeance. This redirection of his energies allows the pro-life dimension of his personality, symbolized by his dedication to Venus, to reassert itself. At the play's conclusion, Anfión's love will prove itself to be more powerful than Ismenia's desire for vengeance.

IN THE THEATER OF CALDERÓN

There is, nevertheless, a contradictory aspect to love, and it is revealed through Celauro's jealousy of Anfión. Based on a case of mistaken identity, the former believes that the Cypriot leader has fallen in love with Doris. Lelio, Celauro's servant, reminds him that jealousy forms part of the experience of love:

> tener amor sin celos
> es lo mismo que querer
> tener coche sin cochero;
> *Conditio sine qua non*
> se da amor.
>
> (2111a)

Though jealousy is a proof of love, it must be controlled and conquered if love is to blossom. The power of love to orient a life towards the good is dramatized by Anfión's experience, while Celauro's trial dramatizes the purifying of his love for Doris, a higher and more noble experience of this passion.

Guarding Appearances and the Question of Truth

Along with the obligations of nobility, *Fineza* probes the nature of truth as it is filtered through society's demands and honor's requirements. The key words in this regard are *deshecha* and *engaño*. Early in Act I we hear Anfión's criticism of flattery:

> ¡Oh lisonja, cuántas veces
> juzgas que a tu dueño halagas,
> y es tu dueño a quien ofendes!
>
> (2103b)

While this remark was prompted by Anfión's recounting of Acteón's death by his "traidoramente leales" hounds, adherence to truth demands a price many are unable or unwilling to pay. Anfión believes that Ismenia is the new champion of Venus's cause, and his passion creates a vision of reality that serves Ismenia's interests and flatters his self interest. On the other hand, Anfión incorrectly judges Doris to be the recidivous nymph opposed to Venus's cult. Appearances mask truth and distort both reality and judgment, leading Doris to exclaim:

> Enigma parecerá
> verme defender a quien
> aborrecí, y ver también
> que a quien amé, no me da
> gozo el mirarla aplaudida.
> Pero si enigma no fuera
> mi vida, ¿cómo pudiera

atormentarme mi vida?

(2106b)

The nymph's existential plea introduces us to a world where truth and reality are not neat and tidy categories, but the elusive goals of misguided and mistaken men and women.

A case of mistaken identity has led Celauro to believe that Anfión loves Doris. This error results from Anfión's attempt to identify ("quién es" [2116a]) the nymph he loves without revealing his passion, for she must first be worthy of his love. Anfión loves the nymph holding a basket of turtledoves to be sacrificed to Venus, and he requests that Celauro tell him her name. As Ismenia hands Doris the basket, Celauro turns to look at her, discovering his beloved. When Celauro discusses his resultant jealousy with Lelio, the latter advises him to be constant and to ignore his fear until Doris responds positively to Anfión. But for Celauro it is a matter of fear or anticipation of the worst (2117a). Lelio rejects this irrational argument based on fear, but fails to convince his master. Truth is not what is wanted, for Celauro prefers his perceptions and fears.

As a political leader Anfión is aware of the difference between truth and reality and falsity and appearance. Accepting Celauro's suggestion that lots be drawn to select the guilty party, he proceeds to avenge the removal of Venus's statue from Diana's erstwhile temple. As a conqueror from another land, he asks Celauro to supervise the drawing of lots to prevent the least suspicion of "maña, fraude o dolo" and to assure the populace "que hay quien justicia las guarda" (2127a). But this appearance of probity is a sham, as he directs Celauro in an aside:

> Si pudieres,
> sea dolo, fraude o maña,
> hacer la suerte precisa
> para que en Doris no caiga,
> hazlo así: mira que en Doris
> me van amor, vida y alma.

(2127a)

The illusion of justice is for public consumption, as every effort is made to uphold the appearance of fairness in the drawing. Ismenia, Anfión's love, goes free, as Doris, his enemy, is selected. However, Doris is not destined to die since Celauro previously suggested to Anfión that, in case the lot fell to Doris, he should pardon her after allowing himself to be importuned by her for mercy. Vengeance and pardon are but tools at the service of the victorious general.

Even in the private sphere falsehood rules. When Doris and Celauro meet after the lot has fallen on her, she expresses how she does not fear death now that Celauro no longer cares for her. The proof of this assertion is his failure to meet her in the garden the night before. Since he has pledged his word to Ismenia not to disclose her sacrilege, he cannot be forthright with Doris. Reminding her that as a prisoner he is not free, Celauro blames Anfión for detaining him so that he missed the tryst. Admittedly this is a small white lie, a falsehood accepted to spare Ismenia's life and Doris's feelings. But the chance encounter with Ismenia the night before leads to the protection of the guilty Ismenia and the exposure of the innocent Doris to the fickleness of Fortune. Celauro's previous declaration on the sacredness of truth was grandiloquent:

> (¡Oh ley severa   *ap.*
> de sacra verdad, que aun no
> permites que el noble mienta
> tal vez en su favor!)
>
> (2118a)

Although he felt obliged to reveal Doris's identity to Anfión, Celauro cannot denounce Ismenia because 1) he has sworn to protect her and 2) as he later expresses it:

> ¿Qué hombre de bien
> dijo nunca criminal
> dicho contra una mujer?
>
> (2133a)

This is a grey world ruled at one time by the obligations of honor incurred to a man and at another time by different obligations owed to a woman. The victim of this convoluted social code of conduct is truth. The lives of the characters are not so much governed by the grand principles encased in words such as honor, truth, and justice as they are by the code of honor that must interpret and apply those principles in oftentimes ambiguous circumstances. Honor is not the best guide for these errant mortals; only self sacrificing love is capable of extricating them from the morass of social codes and from the pitfalls of human weakness. We do not have before us a batch of evil characters who deserve punishment, but a group of basically good people caught in emotional turmoil and circumstantial peripety.

The Obligations of Nobility: Honor and "Finezas"[4]

As was pointed out in the section "The Nature of Nobility" in the analysis of *Amado y aborrecido*, honor establishes the ideal as the norm for conduct. This norm is then codified in various ways so that honor may be the beacon for individual action. Celauro epitomizes the true nobility one is capable of attaining by adhering to its directives. When Anfión attempts to enlist him in his army, Celauro refuses the Cypriot's generous offer alleging that, since Aristeo is still his King, he may not raise arms against him. Anfión, the pragmatist, reminds him "Que el que viva quien vence / es político proverbio" (2110b). Though Tesalia's general can neither join Anfión nor Aristeo, he remains loyal to both by adhering to honor's dictates (2110b).

A typical *comedia de capa y espada* episode occurs at the end of Act I. Like the protagonist of *El galán fantasma*, Celauro appears in the garden to Doris and Libia who believe him to be dead. When the former, as on cue, faints, the latter sounds the alarm. What is Celauro to do with his unconscious lady when the priestesses of Diana are about to discover them?

> ¿Quién se vio en igual aprieto?
> Dejarla así, es villanía;
> hallarme aquí, grave empeño;
> cargar con ella es hacer
> público escándalo el nuestro;
> llevarla donde no sepan
> ni de mí ni de ella, es yerro
> infame, pues es faltar
> al homenaje.
>
> (2113a)

Since his careful reasoning only produces indecision, he resolves to hide among the branches, because that course allows him neither to leave nor to remain. When Doris is carried to her room, we once more become privy to his thoughts. To prevent her departure is to forestall her recovery; to remain is to risk much and gain little. Therefore he departs, leaving the impression that the two priestesses saw an illusion.

The other dimension to nobility concerns the obligation to perform *finezas*. In our analysis of *El mayor encanto, amor* we categorized two principal classes of *fineza*: *cortesana fineza* and *amorosa fineza* (1523a). In *Fineza* the distinction remains valid though the terminology slightly shifts. Cupido characterizes Celauro's actions on Ismenia's behalf as follows: "pues su fineza no fue / de amor, sino de nobleza" (2136b). Consequently, those actions undertaken for Ismenia's benefit are *finezas de noble*, or *cortesanas finezas*, whereas those undertaken on Doris's behalf are *finezas de amor*. In either case, Celauro epitomizes both aspects of this fundamental obligation of the nobleman to expose himself to risk for the sake of others. We shall see how Celauro's willing self-sacrifice, through both *finezas de nobleza* and *finezas de amor*, inspires Doris, Ismenia, and Anfión to perform the noblest actions, self-sacrifice on the part of the women and Anfión's conquering of self through a magnanimous pardon.

When Celauro discovers that Ismenia has removed the statue of Venus, he proposes a simple solution: its return to the altar. Ismenia cannot do it and begs Celauro not to expose her (2125b). Celauro nobly accedes to her pleas, alleging that his duty is to protect her. Employing the traditional phrase that indicates the obligations of honor, "Yo soy quien soy" (2125b), he swears to guard her secret. He returns good for the evil received from Ismenia, rejecting this opportunity to avenge the wrongs done to him.

Celauro's nobility of heart and character is severely tested when he learns that Doris is to die for Ismenia's crime. His interior struggle is between the love he owes to Doris and the honor he has sworn to Ismenia. How can he stand by and allow Doris to die, whom he knows to be innocent, as he protects Ismenia, whom he knows to be guilty (2133a)? Each course of action betrays one aspect of his nobility and contradicts the *finezas* he has performed for others. He balances ever so delicately Doris's life against his *opinión* and decides that, while he must save her, he cannot denounce Ismenia. Therefore, he surrenders himself for judgment and execution by the first word, "Yo" (2133b), of that phrase that acknowledges honor's obligations, "Yo soy quien soy." He admits to stealing the statue to avenge his defeat in battle and subsequent imprisonment, echoing the familiar offense-vengeance mechanism:

> mejor se diga la fama
> que murió por una dama,
> que no una dama por él.
>
> (2133b)

Ismenia recognizes Celauro's nobility of soul and comments in an aside:

> ¡Qué generosa hidalguía!
> ¡Por no romper mi secreto
> condenarse a sí!
>
> (2133b)

Previously, Ismenia witnessed Anfión's apparent rejection of Doris's pleas for mercy. He feigned severity in order eventually to pardon Doris, whom he believed to be Ismenia. Ismenia could not stand idly by and allow Doris to perish for her crime. Risking the incurrence of an obligation to her enemy, Anfión, she was determined to help the pair by begging the conqueror for mercy (2131b). As the noble general has risked much on her behalf, so she too now risks possible love for his sake.

Celauro has just denounced himself to save Doris, and she, motivated by his example, intends to imitate it: "haya pues en mi nobleza / *fineza contra fineza*" (2134a). Anfión consequently condemns Celauro and pardons Doris. But she then denounces herself with the now familiar "Yo" (2134a). Since both claim to be the guilty party, Anfión states that the one who hands over the statue will accomplish the *fineza* and die. Since neither can do it, he condemns both to death. At this point Ismenia intervenes, declaring that both are innocent. When Afión asks who is responsible for the statue's disappearance, she responds with the third fatal "Yo" (2134b). Ismenia then narrates the events that led up to the statue's disappearance, emphasizing Celauro's nobility and protection of her, even at his own and Doris's risk. She categorizes Celauro's and Doris's actions as a "noble competencia" (2135a) that calls forth from each admirable *finezas* that she must now match by declaring her guilt and performing "fineza contra fineza" (2135a). When the statue appears from the abyss where Ismenia threw it, her death seems inevitable.

Pardon: The Great "Fineza" and Love's Fruition

Though *Fineza* is moving toward an emotional climax where pardon will become the crowning jewel in a tiara of *finezas*, it should be pointed out how we structurally anticipate such an outcome. First, Anfión was so impressed by Celauro's valiant defense of Diana's temple that he spared his life. When asked by his troops how he could pardon his enemy, the Cypriot leader responded: "que es bueno para amigo / enemigo tan valiente" (2101a). Second, when Anfión was about to destroy Diana's temple, Ismenia appeared importuning him: "pues vencer y perdonar / es ser vencedor dos veces" (2102a). Furthermore, Ismenia and the nymphs appealed to Anfión's nobility by exclaiming: "Que quien vence sin contrario, / no puede decir que vence" (2102a). Third, in Act III, when Anfión vehemently pursued the nymphs to avenge the disappearance of Venus's effigy, Celauro reminded his lord of the mercy that law demands. If two are charged with a crime, but it is known that only one is guilty:

> que se perdonen entrambos,
> teniendo por más fundada
> razón que el culpado viva,
> que no que al suplicio vaya
> el no culpado.
>
> (2126b)

Anfión ignores these examples of magnanimity when he discovers that the real Doris, condemned by chance or Fortune, is not his beloved. In spite of Ismenia's pleas, he orders Doris's death, emphasizing that the lot that fell to her is not due to chance, but to justice. Turning to Ismenia, he says:

> Tú perdona no otorgarte
> lo que me pides; yo haré
> otras finezas por ti.
>
> (2132a)

The serial self-denunciations of Celauro, Doris, and Ismenia then occur.
When Ismenia shows Anfión where Venus's statue may be located, all the

major themes of *Fineza* converge on this crucial aspect of vengeance. Pointing to the abyss, Ismenia exclaims that she deserves to die more for the outrage than for the robbery. Anfión pathetically remarks:

> ¿Quién pudiera
> hacer que no hubiese sido
> tú de tan *pública ofensa*
> la agresora?
>
> (2136a; emphasis added)

The man who lives in the public limelight recognizes that his hands are now tied by public disclosure of the truth, for Anfión can find no maneuverability. When he asks for a volunteer to descend into the dangerous cavern, Celauro responds with his expected magnanimity:

> Yo; mas será a no sacarla,
> porque contra mí se vuelva
> a quedar la presunción,
> y vivan Doris e Ismenia.
>
> (2136a)

Displeased by this ingenuous declaration, Anfión orders:

> Detente; que es tarde ya
> para andar fino con ellas.
>
> (2136a)

As Lelio the *gracioso* is about to be forced to descend into the abyss, the Music sings out:

> Finezas contra finezas,
> mas la madre del Amor,
> que las castiga, las premia.
>
> (2136b)

Cupido ascends from the trap door bearing the statue of Venus in his arms. Informing all present that Venus has forgiven her *offense* on witnessing "tan amante competencia" (2136b) between Celauro and Doris, Cupido hands over to Anfión the statue. However, since Ismenia's *fineza* was one *de nobleza* and not *de amor*, Cupido further informs them that Venus's offense is remitted provided Ismenia become the victim Celauro and Doris were to be.

Anfión realizes that he, as Venus's champion in Tesalia, has a unique opportunity to further her cause in that hostile land formerly dedicated to Diana. Declaring the import of what has just transpired before them, he turns to Ismenia:

> que si en finezas de amor
> Venus sus enojos templa,
> finezas de amor te alcanzan
> que de la muerte te absuelvan.

(2136b)

When Cupido asks "¿Qué finezas?" (2136b), Anfión responds: "Perdonarla / yo" (2137a). Emphasizing that he too suffers because of the sacrilege against Venus, Anfión demonstrates that Venus's cult, rather than avenge wrongs, celebrates pardon:

> ya es triunfo de amor vencerme
> yo a mí mismo.

(2137a)

Cupido is convinced by Anfión's argument, and he pardons Anfión in Venus's name for not carrying out the execution of the guilty nymph, provided that Ismenia become Anfión's bride. Ismenia immediately becomes a fervent devotee of Venus, as the betrothals of Doris to Celauro and Libia to Lelio close the play.

Venus's triumph in Tesalia began with Anfión's invasion and subjugation of Diana's followers to Venus's rites. The proof of the correctness and rightness of this substitution is found in Celauro's and Doris's *finezas de amor*, better and more perfect acts than *finezas de nobleza*, Ismenia's principal motivation. But Venus's real triumph occurs when the conquerer, Anfión, is conquered by the power of love that he only dimly understood and less perfectly practiced. When he pardons Ismenia he follows a higher set of values than those dictated by vengeance, for he then epitomizes the values symbolized by *finezas de amor*: love, pardon, life, regard for others. Anfión's passion for Ismenia does not alter this truth. The confirmation of Anfión's conversion to the correct veneration of Venus occurs when she pardons these erring mortals. Venus herself is brought to affirm her life-giving presence by the example of Anfión, whose *fineza de amor*, just as those of Celauro and Doris, can move the heavens.

Conclusion

Fineza contra fineza is structured on a series of protracted dualities, symbolized by the cults of Diana and Venus and typified in minor areas such as Anfión's recognition of Celauro's inherent virtue: "que es bueno para amigo / enemigo tan valiente" (2101a). As an extended conceit, *Fineza* celebrates Ismenia's plea to Anfión, "pues vencer y perdonar / es ser vencedor dos veces" (2102a). While the offense-vengeance mechanism advances the plot along familiar lines, the bankruptcy of this antivital motivation stands revealed in the face of love's triumph.

Calderón's artistic genius was able to dramatize love in action so well that we see and hear what ordinarily we only perceive by intuition. Love is the vital force that gives meaning to life. As we ponder the action of *Fineza* we realize that there is a pronounced social dimension to what is normally taken to be a private concern.

Fineza contra fineza is not a masterpiece, but a well-written play that contains the mature Calderonian view on life, death, pardon, vengeance, love, and hatred. It is a positive and optimistic play that expresses great hope: love is not only a wildly disruptive passion, but also that force upon which we depend to live, to move, and to express our being. The *finezas* performed under love's influence and the miraculous transformations of Anfión and Ismenia into mature, loving people attest to its superiority over Diana's barren cult.

Notes

1 The text of the play is found in the Valbuena edition, pp. 2099-2137.

2 See Valbuena's introduction, p. 2099a.

3 See p. 2029.

4 Robert ter Horst describes *fineza* as moral refinement, an ennobling process that leads to "civilized self-sacrifice" that occurs within a love competition in a courtly setting (*Calderón.* p. 180). He despairs of rendering the concept into English. For some observations on the problem of translating *fineza* into acceptable English, see my review of David M. Gitlitz's translation of *La gran comedia Gvárdate de la agva mansa. Beware of Still Waters* (San Antonio: Trinity UP, 1984), which appeared in *BCom* 38 (1986): 151-53.

IX Myths of Suffering and Destruction: The Formation and Disintegration of the Family

This chapter will examine myths of suffering and destruction from two distinct perspectives. The first part will consider how the family is established and eventually destroyed in a hostile society fundamentally at odds with this basic unit of human organization and development. The second part will explore the destruction of individuals. The two plays in the first part supply a long view of these matters. In the first Calderón has dramatized in an imaginative manner the love affair of Apolo and Climene, one about which myth has little to say. The second narrates what occurs to the offspring of this union of the human and the divine. The uniqueness of these two dramatic narratives rests upon the particular perspective they afford us on the cyclical nature of time as one of the principal structural supports of what may be called malign fate and Calderón's tragic vision. In these two plays we witness the dramatic narrative of two generations, whereas previously in our study we were able to examine only the consequences of prior events on the second generation. For example, in *Eco y Narciso*, Liríope's cruel rape served only as background for these young people's tragic love. *Apolo y Climene* dramatizes the rite of passage of the young woman Climene, priestess of Diana, who has been compelled to accept a life of virginity by her violent and fatalistic father Admeto, who seeks to avoid the prophecy that her son will bring about the destruction of Etiopía. *El hijo del Sol, Faetón* narrates the youth's failed rite of passage, a negative version of Perseo's in *Fortunas de Andrómeda y Perseo*, but one similar to Narciso's.

Calderón has taken a great deal of poetic license regarding the plot of *Apolo*. The offense that precipitates Apolo's fall from Olympus is his killing of the Cyclopses who produce Júpiter's thunderbolts, an act labelled "un noble delito" (1820b) and "un heroico yerro" (1835a) by Apolo himself.[1] Whereas in mythology "Apolo mató a los Cíclopes por venganza contra Júpiter por la muerte de Faetón" (Pérez de Moya, I, 201), Calderón utilizes this episode to account for Apolo's presence in Etiopía as shepherd of Admeto's flocks. Act I deals with Climene's liberation from a forced confinement in a temple dedicated to Diana. Act II, which is very long and reflective of many Calderonian *comedias de capa y espada*, narrates the imbroglios in the temple's garden that lead up to Apolo's abduction of Climene to save her from Admeto's wrath. And Act III dramatizes the tricking of Apolo and Climene into yielding to

their love as Fitón assures them that they will overcome their son's prophesized destruction of Etiopía. In *Apolo* Climene's father is Admeto, whereas in
Faetón he is Eridano, the priest of Diana. Such liberties shocked the realist
and neo-positivist sensitivities of critics like Pierre Paris who wrote in 1925:
"Nous en avons assez, peut-ëtre trop dit, pour mettre en évidence les pro-
cédés de Calderón et la désinvolture avec laquelle il triture la Mythologie."[2]

Paris, following Hartzenbusch in *Comedias de Calderón de la Barca*, volume
IV, 673, states that *Apolo* and *Faetón* were staged in 1638 and 1639.[3] Valbuena Briones notes in his edition that "*El Faetonte* se estrenó el 1 de marzo
de 1661, ante los Reyes, en el Buen Retiro" (1862b). Shergold provides an
interesting account of the production for Carnival of 1662 in which the
Marqués de Heliche attempted to blow up the scenery due to his envy of the
Duque de Medina de las Torres. The latter had replaced the former as governor of the Buen Retiro and would be credited with the luxurious sets upon
which Heliche had expended considerable sums of money (pp. 325-27).
Because of the narrative and thematic links of the two works, Paris considers
that they form "une véritable dilogie" (p. 558). Gómez Mingorance, stating
that they were given in the Salón del Palacio Real, adds that "Ambas se com-
plementan y podrían considerarse una sola obra" (p. 467). While Paris is accurate in his assessment, Gómez overstates the case when she calls *Apolo* "una
obra-preludio" (p. 467). Failure to consider *Apolo* as a distinct dramatic work
worthy of close examination in its own right has led critics to overlook a play
of significant insight, especially with regards to Calderón's handling of questions of freedom, the education of children, and the significance and influence
of fate. Gómez sees the characters not as "personajes sino ideas, símbolos" (p.
472). Parker considers *Apolo* within the emblematic and philosophic traditions of the time. According to him, Calderón's symbolism demonstrates that
"el hombre ansía alcanzar el Sol, en el amor es donde más siente el calor de
sus rayos, pero el Sol se va, dejando la Noche. Al irse Apolo, Climene se
esconde en la oscuridad de su cueva, prisionera, es decir víctima de la imper-
fección de la vida."[4]

The question of sources that preoccupied critics of Paris's generation has
little meaning or value for us today. When Gómez Mingorance, following this
tradition, states that "A nuestro parecer, casi todo el pensamiento, en estas
dos obras mitológicas de Calderón parte del de Pérez de Moya y no hace falta
acudir a otros tópicos, ni a otras fuentes" (p. 473), she grandly dismisses
Calderón's unique poetic genius in this dramatic work. I prefer the suggestion
that Parker made, but then failed to follow himself: "aunque existía una tradi-
ción de interpretación simbólica de los mitos, Calderón no tiene que atenerse
a ella; tiene completa libertad no sólo para interpretar las historias, sino para
cambiarlas y elaborarlas de nuevo" (p. 143 *n* 6). When Paris found himself
most likely not understanding, or not sympathizing with, *Apolo* and *Faetón*,
he felt compelled to reject the plays as trivial. In words reminiscent of

Menéndez Pelayo's critical prejudice against Calderón, Paris states: "Il est plus que probable que Calderón n'attachait pas grande importance à ces compositions rapides où il s'agissait de plaire aux yeux plutôt qu'à l'espirit" (p. 557). Gómez dutifully echoes these remarks: "Calderón componía esta clase de obras, sin mucho empeño" (p. 476). A close scrutiny of the plots of these plays will give the lie to these mistaken critical positions.[5]

A. 1. *Apolo y Climene*

> ¡Qué ajenos de mis motivos
> su seguridad presumen,
> sin saber que van a fin
> solo de que se consume
> lo que dije una vez!
> Pues si la [Climene] hallaran, no dude
> que con su muerte mintiera
> mi estudio; y así, que dure
> quise en mi encanto con dueño,
> y dueño de quien se arguye,
> siendo el sol, que nazca el rayo
> que abrase, encienda y supure
> toda Etiopía. . . .

Fitón (1855b)

Although Apolo is a significant character in Calderonian myth plays, the physiognomy he presents to us in *Apolo* is very distinct from that already seen in *El laurel de Apolo* or to be seen in *La estatua de Prometeo*. Calderón has shuffled various episodes from mythology to create a narrative that is eminently meaningful within the Calderonian corpus. Having Apolo serve Admeto as shepherd of his flocks and making Admeto Climene's father allow Calderón to mold his dramatic narrative in such a way that major themes in his work become the motivational structures behind this theatrical experience, themes such as the problem of fate, father-daughter relations, questions of freedom, and human participation in the workings of destiny.

When *Apolo* ends with Fitón's announcement of a second part that will dramatize "el infausto nacimiento / de Faetón, hijo de Apolo" (1860b), we tend to look forward to the events yet to unfold rather than reflect on those that have just transpired. And when the gracioso asks for our indulgence, he ironically adds that the play is a theatrical novelty:

> dama y galán dividiendo,
> de acabar ella en divorcio,
> cuando otras en casamiento.

(1860b)

In view of the intrigue characteristic of the *comedia de capa y espada* and the *comedia palaciega*, it is easy to let this claim pass unexamined in favor of relishing the irony for its own sake. Both Apolo and Climene are very sympathetic characters who are separated at the play's conclusion by forces, both human and divine, that seek their own ends.

Apolo y Climene is a play principally about the dehumanization, victimization, and destruction of an innocent girl by those members of society most closely related to her. Seeking to avoid the prophesized destruction of Etiopía by her future son, Admeto has condemned his daughter to a life of virginity and servitude to the state's interests. And Climene is cruelly betrayed by her fellow devotees to Diana, as they seek to escape guilt and to blame her. For Fitón Climene becomes a pawn to be manipulated in his attempts to guarantee the accuracy of his prophecy and of his occult sciences. Her life appears to have no inherent importance; Fitón's vainglory demands that her life, and that of her son, be sacrificed on the altar of his ego. And finally, Apolo himself, though a sympathetic character throughout the play, finds himself compelled to abandon Climene to resume his role as Sun God. She is left a virtual prisoner of Fitón and returns to a state of servitude from which she sought to escape from the beginning of the play. Coming full circle,[6] Climene stands as a dramatic figure of the suffering women so often encountered in Calderonian plays. And her suffering is but the generational impetus that will produce additional suffering for her son Faetón.

The Corruption of Human and Divine Societies

Apolo opens with a garden scene in which Céfiro profanes the temple of Diana in his attempt to court Cintia. Suddenly Apolo falls from the heavens, expelled by Júpiter. This *fall* of the god of light into the human realm of darkness and error is followed by a second fall into the secret passage that Céfiro uses to gain entry to the garden. These dramatic actions, both human and divine, become symbols for the corruption of the two societies. In both reigns a disharmony brought about by passion and the desire for vengeance. Though Júpiter at first wanted to kill Apolo, the most he could do was to deprive him of his light (reason), converting him into a groping, erring god (1820b). When Apolo falls into the "boca de la mina" (1821a) that carries water pipes to the garden, our expectations of the worst are fully aroused.[7] Not only is there disharmony amongst the immortals that inhabit Olympus, Júpiter-Apolo, Diana-Venus, but the fallen god who abruptly enters human society becomes just like the mortals who live in it, except for the fact that he remains immortal. Moreover, he cannot "see" and quickly becomes entangled in the disharmony that characterizes this earthly garden.

In Act II Apolo further elaborates Júpiter's despoliation of his divine gifts: "de dotes y de ciencias despojado" (1835a). Apolo pays dearly for what he now calls "un heroico yerro." Erring mortals find themselves affected by gods who themselves err in judgment and action:

> con que a nadie hacer puede repugnancia
> que dios que tuvo error, tenga ignorancia.
>
> (1835a)

Apolo decides to serve as shepherd of Admeto's flocks in order to be near Climene, who is now his light. His new-found love of the King's daughter places him in a position where he must save her life by seizing her and crossing the Eridano river. Act III finds an indecisive god caught between the threats of Admeto and the "favor" of Fitón. This prophetic god cannot divine Fitón's motives and therefore surrenders Climene to him as he flees from Admeto and his pursuers. It is not that Apolo is an amoral god but rather one so debased in his divine nature that he has become subject to what may be termed "human" failings.

Toward the middle of Act III we become apprised of the reasons for Apolo's exile from Olympus and also of the workings of divine society ruled by an all-powerful, jealous god. In the distribution of the universe, Apolo was granted responsibility for the sun along with its rays and light. In time the cult of Apolo grew in popularity while that of Júpiter declined. This latter god became jealous of Apolo's Delphic veneration and eventually decided to take vengeance on his younger rival. Apolo emphasizes the flaws of his fellow gods:

> que no es mucho en dioses dados
> a amorosas inquietudes,
> si hay lascivia que los aje,
> que hay envidia que los frustre. . . .

> (1853)

Having ordered the cyclopses Estérope and Brontes to prepare special thunderbolts, Júpiter razed Delfos to avenge the neglect of and affront to his godhead. Although Apolo recognized that he could not directly avenge this insult, he nonetheless killed the two cyclopes by collapsing their grotto upon them. Deeply offended by this new outrage, Júpiter cast Apolo out of Olympus. The offense-vengeance mechanism rules heavenly relations just as it does human affairs. What should be the pristine world of truth, beauty, and goodness is but a reflection of our world as lust, envy, and vengeance prove to be the ruling tempers of the gods.

Etiopía is ruled by King Admeto, a figure reminiscent of Basilio of *La vida es sueño*. Because of the prophecy concerning Climene's future son, Admeto determined to save his realm by doing violence to his daughter. She was brought up in a temple/castle where, though royal *infanta*, she had no opportunity to exercise her freedom. Then she was dedicated to an enforced virginity, as priestess of Diana, in order not to procreate and thus contribute to the prophecy's fulfillment. Admeto is another of the seemingly endless line of rigorous fathers depicted by Calderón. Valbuena speaks of his "intransigencia y crueldad egotista" (1815b), traits that describe his rule as both King and father. Climene's companions in Diana's cult are not willing virgins joyfully serving the chaste goddess, but enslaved women yielding to the will of

Admeto. Céfiro, Flora's *galán*, has followed her to the temple where she, an expert in floral decoration, has been obliged to serve Climene. Céfiro states explicitly that she was forced, "violenta" (1832b), to serve. Clicie, a former lover of Apolo, was also brought to serve Climene at Admeto's insistence (1834b). Thus three priestesses of Diana have been subjected to a life of virginity. Admeto's violence to these young women creates the sexual tension that underlies the play's action. As Júpiter is a corrupt and brutal ruler in Olympus, so too is Admeto a violent and egotistical ruler of Etiopía.

Once fear directs his life, Admeto becomes a violent ruler who significantly contributes to the prophecy's fulfillment. Toward the end of Act II he readily believes the false witness brought against Climene by Flora, Céfiro, and Clicie. His predisposition toward fatalism leads him quickly to condemn her, throwing her into Apolo's arms and ensuring the continual unfolding of the prophecy.

A further sign of social corruption is epitomized by Fitón's egotistical and self-serving intervention in the action. Since he prophesized what Climene's offspring would do to Etiopía, he does all in his power to create the circumstances in which the prophecy may be realized.

To round out this picture of human and divine corruption, we need to examine the immorality of Flora, Céfiro, and Clicie. Although they are victims of Admeto's cruel reign, they also actively participate in condemning the innocent Climene, a young woman who has endeavored to live up to her responsibilities as priestess of Diana. These three lie, condemning Climene to save themselves. Just as Admeto betrays reason and justice, and all the values we associate with family, so too will Climene violate her vow of chastity. The former believes he is justified by reason of state, whereas the latter is tricked into yielding herself to Apolo's love by the malevolent Fitón. Moreover, the "virgins" of Diana's cult are sexually promiscuous. While Flora arranges trysts with Céfiro, Clicie seeks to rekindle her love affair with Apolo. Apolo even lies to Climene regarding his knowledge of that nymph.

Cyclical Time and the Offense-Vengeance Mechanism

Apolo y Climene deals with betrayal, guilt, and eventual punishment. The opening scene, where Céfiro has profaned Diana's sacred precinct, reminds us that betrayal of Diana's cult (an offense) will bring future reprisal (vengeance). This scene is *predictive* for Climene. Her love of Apolo, though natural, good, and understandable in an untrammelled context, is, nevertheless, a violation of her vows of chastity and a profanation of Diana's cult. In the opening scene of Act I Climene recognizes that the penetration of the temple's garden demands immediate punishment of the aggressor and his accomplice (1818b). Following this scene we see Apolo fall from the heavens, expelled by a jealous and violent Júpiter. Once on earth, Apolo falls a second time, and this particular fall into earthly circumstance will be *predictive* of his future *delito* against Diana, his virgin sister, and the future fall of his offspring, the result of his union with Climene. The latter even prophetically imagines the scene of the chariot's errant course across the heavens, the result of a "traición de amor" (1821a):

> ¿No veis, no veis que su carro
> de la continua tarea
> errando el curso, y cayendo
> precipitado a la tierra,
> abrasa montes y mares,
> de cuya encendida hoguera
> son las espumas cenizas
> y las montañas pavesas?
> ¡Que me quemo! ¡Que me abraso!
> Pero ¿qué digo? ¡Qué idea
> tan vana! ¡Qué fantasía
> tan loca! ¡Qué ansia tan necia!
> arrebatóme el dolor
> vida y voz.

(1821a)

These violent allusions are continued by Flora and Clicie, in their accounts of what has just transpired in the garden (1826a-1827a), and by Climene (1827) when Admeto arrives on the scene. In Climene's vision the errant sun is a symbol for Faetón's eventual fall from heaven, as well as for her proximate fall from virginity to sexual experience. We should not overlook in its transparency that the events that shall precipitate Faetón's fall are *now* occurring. Beneath the obvious offense-vengeance structure that is the mainspring of much Calderonian drama, we find in addition the cyclical notion of time that reminds us that the sins of one generation will be visited upon the next one.

The offense-vengeance mechanism operates efficiently both in the heavens and on the earth. When Céfiro hears the earthquake that announces Apolo's fall from heaven, he naturally assumes that his violation of the temple precinct has produced such a mighty reaction (1820a). And Climene, as Diana's priestess, believes likewise. She suspects Flora as the culprit of the disturbances, and in Act II, when Céfiro returns, the gallant unwittingly betrays his mistress. Climene has the right and obligation to punish Flora for her profanation of the temple, but underlying her righteous indignation there is a pent-up sexuality seeking expression. Her participation in the events that unfold in the garden scenes reminds us of the roles of the jealous husbands in the honor plays. She even employs a formulaic expression of their designing patience in the expectation of discovering concrete proof of her companion's guilt: "calle, disimule y pene" (1839b). She repeats the resolve of a feminine version of the man of honor: "calle, sufra y disimule" (1840a). As the man of honor feels wounded in his reputation and his manhood, so too Climene is affronted in her *decoro* and her feminine vanity. Her frustrated sexuality seeks revenge on her companions for her own inability to express actively and openly her burgeoning eroticism.

Fitón's Prophecy

When Climene was born there occurred a solar eclipse, where the moon comes between the earth and the sun. The symbolic meaning of Diana's virginity interposing itself between the sun, life and sexuality, and the earth, Climene, does not need to be belabored. When she was born, her mother died. Applying the astrological sciences he learned from Fitón, Admeto read in the stars Climene's fate, which promised "infortunious y desgracias" (1830b). Not satisfied with his efforts, Admeto consulted Fitón, who employed "otras ciencias más altas" (1830b) to confirm the original prediction. This magician then specified what "Las desgracias e infortunios" were to be:

> de ella nacerá
> un joven, de altivez tanta,
> tan idómita soberbia
> y tan feroz arrogancia,
> que en el siríaco idioma
> le dé renombre la fama
> de *Faetón*, que significa
> *rayo*, cuya ardiente saña
> ha de atravesar Etiopía
> con tal fuego, que no haya
> desde donde el Nilo empieza
> hasta donde el Nilo acaba,
> siendo en Egipto sus bocas
> hidra de siete gargantas,
> distrito que no sea hoguera. . . .

> (1830b-1831a)

To prevent his country's ruin, Admeto dedicated the young Climene to the cult of Diana, where chastity would prevent any possible succession. But as the young Climene grows, she yearns for freedom. Her father then changes his mind in view of her developing maturity, her loyalty to his original plan, and the strange melancholy that profoundly affects her. She may leave the temple to view the outside world, but she must rigorously guard her vow of chastity to Diana. If she fails in this regard, Admeto himself, following the law to the letter, will sacrifice his daughter on the virgin goddess's altar. When the populace celebrates her newly found freedom, Climene realizes how the former physical restraint now becomes an inner check on her person and actions (1834a).

When the King attempts to exculpate himself from the charge of tyrant, he states that Climene's case is easily resolved through understanding. As a scholarly individual, Admeto views Climene's problems only in terms of knowledge (1830a). Once again Calderón demonstrates that, though knowledge is essential for prudent living, the human will is a rebellious subject who conquers the "absoluto monarca" of understanding. Moreover, Admeto could never envision how his own actions would contribute to the prophecy's eventual fulfillment. And Fitón's part in its fulfillment, a case of pure willfulness, is beyond his ken.

One of the most interesting scenes in *Apolo* depicts how both Apolo and Climene are tricked by Fitón into believing that her fate may be conquered by his magical arts. Here Júpiter's despoliation of Apolo's divine gifts is absolutely necessary for Fitón's purpose, the prophecy's fulfillment. As Climene enters Fitón's grotto, a new prison, she fears that she is entering one appointed by fate. The old magician solicitously assures her:

> No es sino nuevo sagrado
> que venza su indignación.
> En tu libertad estás....
>
> (1852b)

This is one of the most ironic statements made in the play, for it convinces Climene to believe in Fitón's powers and to accept Apolo's love. Toward the end of the scene Fitón pronounces the fatal words that introduced this play. And at the play's conclusion we hear him declare what has transpired during the three acts:

> Esto es salirse los hados
> con sus influjos severos,
> y yo con mis ciencias, pues
> a pesar de humanos medios,
> habemos ellos y yo
> de salirnos verdaderos
> en sus amenazas.
>
> (1860)

Climene's fate is a multi-levelled or complex series of actions that unfold with the cooperation of many participants. But the ruling force behind the announced fate is the haughtiness and willfulness of Fitón, and the poor couple, Apolo and Climene, as well as the deluded Admeto, are all caught up in the magic, and demonic, illusion created by this perverse character. What makes *Apolo* unique in the Calderonian corpus is precisely Fitón's demonic presence and decisive force in the development of the plot.

Climene as Victim

Whereas Fitón is perhaps the most interesting character in the play, Climene remains the most complex. As a priestess of Diana, she is responsible for the decorum of the temple. When someone suddenly enters the garden, she becomes an avenging fury, a woman whose "rencor" (1818a) will immediately punish this transgression. We come to understand that zeal for Diana's cult may be the overt motivation for her actions, but covertly she is intensely jealous of "tan fiera / traición de amor" (1821a). She lives as a prisoner of the temple, and as such is imprisoned in a virginity imposed upon her by Admeto. Her strange "melancolías" (1821b and 1836b) result from both her lack of freedom and her inability to channel the erotic impulse that grows within her. In her persistent attempts to discover and punish the culprit, Climene exteriorizes and punishes her own erotic feelings.

When she discovers the beautiful Apolo in the garden, she seeks to find out who he is. She even attempts to shoot him with Diana's bow and arrow, but they refuse to cooperate in the wounding of the goddess's brother. As the guards are about to enter and search the grounds, Climene urges the mysterious man to flee, ostensibly because she wishes to kill him herself. But she confesses to herself the truth:

> (Mejor dijera a un afecto
> con que sintiendo el que viva,
> también el que muera siento.)
>
> (1826a)

Like the women of the honor plays who unwittingly invite their former lovers to return and visit them, so Climene addresses Apolo. Referring to Apolo's life, she states:

> Pues mira que es dada a precio
> de que aquí no has de volver,
> porque en este mismo puesto
> he de estar a ver si cumples
> mi mandato.
>
> (1826a)

Since Climene's personality cannot develop naturally and openly, it does so surreptitiously. Signs of erotic pressure seeking escape are seen in various ways. When Clicie sings of Diana's punishment of Acteón, Climene excuses his behavior and then asks her companion to celebrate Endimión's having been loved by the goddess:

> Sepa Diana que amó,
> por lo que me sucediere;
> que al delincuente aseguran

> yerros de juez delincuente.
>
> (1836a)

Toward the end of Act II Climene meets Apolo during a hunting scene. In an aside she fears what is happening to her: "(Mucho temo que mi pena / me ha de despeñar)" (1843b). She fears, in fact, loss of control of her passion. As Climene converses with Apolo, Flora and Clicie overhear her speak of prior meetings with this putative shepherd. Since they are informed of all that has occurred between Apolo and Climene, she unwittingly provides them with the evidence they will shortly use against her. When she discovers Clicie and Flora in hiding, she swears vengeance on them:

> ¡Oh ciegas,
> traidoras a mí y Dïana,
> a tan vil amor sujetas,
> que estáis celosas y amigas!
> Yo vengaré ambas ofensas.
>
> (1844b)

This desire for vengeance will lead to her condemnation by her father, as she seeks to exculpate Apolo and to blame Flora and Clicie. Climene's ambivalent attitude betrays her. Though innocent, the appearance of guilt condemns her. Climene has not been able to handle the conflicting emotions that define her situation. Her silence, her inability to denounce Flora and Clicie's betrayal of their vows of chastity, stands as mute witness to her own subconscious desires and guilt.

In several ways Climene is undergoing a rite of passage from young girl, who obediently followed her father's will, to young woman, who experiences all the emotions and passions associated with burgeoning sexuality. Parker has correctly noted that in *Apolo* the sun serves as a symbol of love (p. 156). The handsome young god incarnates and concretizes the vague yet still powerful impulses that characterize Climene's emerging sexuality. In other circumstances this encounter would be a good and healthy outlet for the young woman's desire to love and to be loved in return. But she is committed to a life of virginity, and a malign fate overshadows any love she may feel. Parker takes a truly jaundiced view of this situation in which Climene is inclined to the love of Apolo: "La compulsión al amor que siente Climene es, por lo tanto, la compulsión del mal; sin embargo, ama a un dios, es decir, el bien. El objeto es bueno, la fuerza que la inclina a él es mala" (p. 156). What Climene's crisis makes clear to us is that she does not have a true "vocation" to a life of chastity and that her adherence to it is not based on a truly personal commitment. To describe her inclination to love, which is natural, as an evil compulsion is to misread her situation: what is evil in it is the sacrifice of this young woman for fear of the results of any expression of her sexuality. Parker's Manichean view of these sexual matters overlooks what this play is saying about Climene's experience of love. Parker states: "Los amores de Apolo y Climene, como los presenta Calderón, no podrían ser más castos; pero la sensualidad inherente al amor humano es lo que hace que Climene sea prisionera de Fitón y, en la segunda comedia, una fiera temida" (p. 157). Neither Climene's sensuality nor her inclination to love is evil; in point of fact they develop her as a person and bring her to a fuller maturity. Climene's naturally good impulses are suppressed by a fearful and fatalistic father and later used by Fitón as means for his own ends.

Like Segismundo of *Vida*, Climene complains of her unnatural upbringing, opening the question of the education of children. Besides *Vida*, *Eco y Narciso* and *El monstruo de los jardines* raise this fundamental issue for Calderonian theater. Towards the end of Act I, Climene pointedly asks by what right has she been brought up a virtual prisoner (1827b). She goes on to detail the treatment she has received from the hands of her father. How can he deny her the very freedom nature offers to all its creatures, rational and instinctual? If she is threatened by fate, could it possibly be worse than what she now suffers? What is poignant, of course, is how reasonable Climene's arguments are. Concerning astrological prediction, she notes:

> Dejo aparte si es cordura
> creer los fatales agüeros
> . . . . .
> los futuros contingentes
> tal vez prognostican. . . .
>
> (1828a)

Then she states what her father's decision has done to her:

> y voy sólo a si es cordura
> remediar un daño, a riesgo
> de que antes que venga el daño,
> me dé la muerte el remedio.
>
> (1828b)

If there is no recourse for her, suicide is preferable to her living death. Those familiar with Calderonian theater will immediately recognize the pattern presented to us. Admeto's attempts to avoid Climene's fate create the circumstances that contribute to its fulfillment. By denying her a natural upbringing, in which she would have married a neighboring prince, Admeto exposes Climene to the full impact of not what fate designed, but what fate saw as inevitable, the consequence of his conscious plan to avoid disaster.

Parker notes that at no moment is Climene free (p. 155). From her father's cruel and unnatural upbringing she passes to Fitón's equally cruel and deceptively evil guidance. For Admeto the issue consists in whether the good and freedom of one individual, Climene, can be weighed against the good of the society and its security. The people's voice clamors for the *infanta's* freedom. Yielding to this pressure, he declares:

> ¡Ay cielos!
> ¡Cuán en vano solicita
> el corto discurso nuestro
> enmendar de las estrellas
> los influjos, pues los medios
> que pone para impedirlos
> le sirven para atraerlos!

(1829a)

Thus ends Act I. Act II will reveal how Admeto delivers Climene into Fitón's clutches. Toward the end of this act Climene stands accused of violating her vows to Diana, of secretly fornicating with the mysterious nightly visitor. Once again Admeto surrenders himself to fatalism and quickly condemns his daughter in order to protect Etiopía. The evidence appears to be conclusive: 1) there are witnesses to her violation of her vows; 2) there remains the cruel fate that now is confirmed; 3) "y pues cesa / de todo el reino la ruina / con su muerte" (1846b), Admeto condemns her to death for political reasons; and, moreover, 4) the law of Diana already calls for her execution. These four confirmations of guilt are, however, all wrong: 1) the witnesses lie to protect themselves; 2) the fate is not yet confirmed, and Admeto's condemnation of Climene is the next step necessary for its fulfillment; 3) Admeto's desire to free Etiopía from danger motivates his participation in the fate of his country; and 4) Climene has not been unfaithful to Diana, rather she has protected and fostered the decorum of the cult. Admeto subconsciously wants to murder his daughter and to rid himself of this burden of guilt and fear. When Eridano returns reason to the deliberations, Climene is condemned for the moment "a más estecha / prisión" (1846b), for being a prisoner apparently is her birthright. When Apolo defends her and carries her across the river, the god unwittingly delivers her to Fitón. Like Don Juan Roca of *El pintor de su deshonra*, Admeto explodes in igneous imagery as all hurry to the boats:

> Mejor al fuego dijeran
> pues ya del amenazado
> previsto incendio revienta
> el volcán en mis entrañas,
> y en mi corazón el Etna.

(1846b)

Climene, the scapegoat of Etiopía's fate, now passes on to the next stage of her victimization at the hands of men.

Apolo and Climene's Self-Sacrifice

After various peripeties, Apolo declares his love for Climene. But she continues to fear her fate and therefore plans on rejecting his overtures. She vividly remembers that her first encounter with Apolo took place the night she dreamt "del despeño del Sol" (1854b). Just as her fiery and prophetic dream warned her then of danger, so too does the fire that now burns in her at the sight of Apolo. Fitón assures her that he can prevent this fate just as he was able to read it in the stars. With Apolo for lover and husband, Climene will conquer her fate and Fitón will be considered god-like in his wisdom and power. He substitutes "al alcázar de Dïana / el de Venus" (1855a) as the two unsuspecting lovers marry. Climene's "sin," if it can be considered such, pales in the face of the source of real evil, the egotistical will of this haughty and vain magician. Evil, presumptuous, proud, and deceitful, he craftily leads them to the hymeneal couch.

Their "idyllic" love is interrupted by the arrival of Iris and Mercurio who announce Apolo's forgiveness. However, Apolo's pardon at Venus's insistence spells Climene's punishment at Diana's hands. Apolo may return to his rightful place as charioteer of the sun, but Climene must pay the price of her crimes. Though he wishes to return to heaven with her, he cannot; therefore, the heroic god pleads to exchange fates with his lover:

> y así os ruego que troquéis
> los dos contrarios extremos.
> ¿Traes tú el perdón? Sea a Climene.
> ¿Traes tú el riesgo? Sea a mí el riesgo.
>
> (1857b)

Caught between his desire to return to heaven and his love of Climene, Apolo decides to forego his glory and splendor to remain faithful to her (1858a). When Apolo reveals to Climene what has transpired, the latter sacrifices herself for the good of her lover:

> En fe de que tú gozoso
> ilustres campos de cielos,
> páramos de montes, yo
> alegre viviré, viendo
> al amanecer tus rayos.
>
> (1858)

At this crucial moment, when Apolo refuses to leave without Climene, and she insists that he do so, Admeto and the others return to Fitón's palace. The three conspirators spot the pair. Climene declares that their only hope is for Apolo to depart without her and to assume his divine powers and role, for only in that way can he intercede with Diana on her behalf and favor her on earth. Can Apolo leave Climene in such danger? At this moment Fitón promises to hide her, as Apolo declares that he will punish the three liars by transforming them through his newly recovered divine power. As Apolo ascends to heaven, Climene returns ("descends") to the prison that has been her inheritance:

> Yo, Fitón, en confianza
> tuya, a tu encanto me vuelvo.
>
> (1859a)

A family, a union of the human and the divine, such as we saw in *Ni Amor se libra de amor*, is separated at the very moment it is needed to support love's fruition. Thus, the fruit of this love, Faetón, will not grow up in the healthy and loving environment that a home provides, but in the anonymity and frustration necessary for the continuing evolution of his fate.

We should not let pass without further comment the heroic love, and self-sacrificing nature of that love, displayed by both Apolo and Climene. These are not selfish individuals seeking their own ends, but noble persons disposed to sacrifice themselves for the good of the other. In the tragic resolution of their brief but true love, there is revealed a noblility of heart and soul.

The Significance of the Concluding Metamorphoses

When Admeto consults Fitón about the identity of the shepherd who abducted Climene, Clicie, jealous of her mistress's favor with Apolo, attempts to disclose that he was Apolo in disguise, but she finds that she cannot pronounce his name. Then Céfiro tries to reveal his identity, but is unable to say "Apolo." Then Flora endeavors to voice Apolo's name, with the same result. At this moment Sátiro, who was previously transformed into a satyr, appears, but, instead of informing them, frightens them away. Clicie's jealousy has transformed her into "pajiza flor de sol, / que va sus rayos siguiendo" (1860a). Céfiro, the lover of Flora, vanishes into the wind; Flora, Céfiro's beloved, is metamorphosed into the flowers that wave in his breezes. The metamorphoses stand clearly as Apolo's punishment of the jealousy and deceit of these three liars. The great irony, however, is that this punishment by the restored god allows the fate of his future son to proceed apace. Sátiro, who was previously punished, now cannot fulfill his role:

> pues al falso testimonio
> testigo fuiste, testigo
> también al más fino abono
> de amor, de lealtad y fe.
>
> (1851a)

Thus, Sátiro remains mute as to Apolo's love for Climene, and the fate alluded to by Fitón triumphs over both gods and humans. What appears to be Apolo's triumph, the metamorphoses of the false witnesses, is but a confirmation of his continuing blindness to what actually is happening. The god of light has now removed himself from the earth, and it will remain to be seen how effective he will be in favoring and protecting Climene.

Conclusion

Apolo y Climene is not merely the beginning of a two-part exploration of Faetón's fate, but a clearly demarcated exploration in dramatic action of the confluence of various factors on Faetón's mother, Climene. Her father's failure to educate and prepare Climene for life is a significant factor in the play. Apolo's blindness and ignorance allow the malign Fitón to guide fate's passage through these early but difficult stages. In many ways, Apolo's lack of knowledge and insight forms part of the fate, or at least makes it possible. Fitón's malevolent presence serves as an embodiment of fate's evil designs. He is the most demonic force we have found in the myth plays. There is no relief, no hope in this stark depiction of what constitutes the workings of fate. It is not a thing, but a process in which many must do their parts for its eventual fulfillment. The victimization of this young woman at Fitón's hands stands as brutal testimony to the evil we all carry in our proud nature. The sexual "crime" of the young Climene pales into insignificance in the light of his evil and demonic genius.[8]

Notes

1 The version of *Apolo y Climene* consulted is found in the Valbuena edition, pp. 1815-60.

2 See "La Mythologie de Calderón: *Apolo y Climene - El hijo del Sol, Faetón*," in *Homenaje ofrecido a Menéndez Pidal* (Madrid, 1925), 1, 568.

3 Margarita Gómez Mingorance, in "*Apolo y Climene. El hijo del Sol, Faetón* (Análisis de dos comedias calderonianas)," *Calderón: Actas*, I, 461, slavishly follows Paris and adds that these plays were *published* then.

4 See "Metáfora y símbolo en la interpretación de Calderón," in *Actas del Primer Congreso Internacional de Hispanistas* (Oxford, 1964), p. 158. A recent study by Susana Hernández-Araico, "Mitos, simbolismo y estructura en *Apolo y Climene* y *El hijo del sol, Faetón*," *BHS*, 64 (1987), 77-85, approaches these plays as political admonitions addressed to Felipe IV.

5 Parker wrote in 1962 that "Hace treinta años escribió Pierre Paris un artículo sobre ambos que convendría sepultar en respectuoso olvido" (p. 153). Gómez Mingorance's article sheds little critical light on the plays.

6 There is a close relation between my concept of cyclical time and Ruiz Ramón's notion of circularity of action in *Calderón y la tragedia*. Our appreciation of Calderonian tragedy, though coming from different critical frameworks, is remarkably similar,

as this chapter evinces.

7 See A. Valbuena Briones, "El simbolismo en el teatro de Calderón: La caída del caballo," *Romanische Forschungen*, 74 (1962), 60-76.

8 I read in proof Frederick A. de Armas's recent study of the play, "The Betrayal of a Mystery: Botticelli and Calderón's *Apolo y Climene*," *Romanische Forschungen*. He examines the influences of Neoplatonism and astral mythology in both. I appreciate his kindness in allowing me access to this interesting approach.

A. 2. El hijo del Sol, Faetón

Batillo.   ¿dónde vamos, penetrando
           las más intricadas breñas?
Faetón.   A dar principio a una vida
           que toda ha der ser tragedias.
           A buscar la fiera voy.

(1883a)[1]

When Faetón pronounces these prophetic words in Act II, we become aware of the dramatic irony about to unfold, for the creature that he seeks is his unfortunate mother, who has lived a beastly life since entering Fitón's "protective" care. In this pursuit of the beast, Faetón advances to his appointment with fate. For Pérez de Moya "Faetón fué vanaglorioso y arrogante, y presumiendo de sapientísimo sin serlo" (I, 192). Apolo y Climene had depicted a corrupt society that destroys the innocent. The fallen god Apolo is the only positive force of love and concern we meet in an otherwise bleak landscape. In El hijo del Sol, Faetón, Galatea will be the positive force, but she too will prove to be weak and ineffectual in her attempts to succor Climene's son Faetón. Once more an innocent person, Faetón, will suffer greatly, far beyond what the most severe morality could judge appropriate for Faetón's hybris. His tragic death will confirm the hostile nature of the world lacking true providential direction.

It would be illuminating to review some of the changes in the plot from Apolo to Faetón. First, Climene's father is now Eridano, the priest of Diana, and not Admeto, the King of Tesalia. Second, the history of Apolo and Climene's love affair and its consequences have been altered, almost beyond recognition. Third, Fitón is not the satanic magician we previously saw, but the more traditional and objective astrologer who simply "reads" the stars. Fourth, though the vengeful Diana continues implacable in her punishment of Climene and her child, the evil force in Faetón will be Amaltea, a dríade. These changes make Faetón a very distinct work from Apolo, and each play needs to be considered as a unique narration, related due to the plot line, but significantly different from its companion.

Apolo was based upon a love intrigue that disrupts the temple of Diana, and Faetón retains this structural framework by creating a traditional love triangle between Eridano/Faetón, his brother Epafo/Peleo, and the goddess Tetis. While the two young men compete for the goddess's affection, their ambitious natures belie their states as villanos. Each one is supported by naiads and dryads respectively. Eridano, or Faetón, receives special protection from Galatea and the nymphs of fountains and rivers:

en las hijas del Sol tienes
(la causa oculta no sé)

> tan ganados los afectos,
> que hemos de favorecer
> siempre tus hados.

(1864a)

As Admeto's long lost son, Epafo, the future heir to Tesalia, is favored by
Amaltea and the daughters of Aurora. Amaltea malevolently adds in an aside
the reasons for her protection:

> (Y más yo,
> que de Eridano crüel,
> contigo el amor de Tetis
> tengo de desvanecer.)

(1864a)

Amaltea advances Epafo's cause because she has a natural affection for him
as a daughter of Aurora, but also because she feels scorned by Eridano and is
jealous of his love for Tetis. Her jealousy will eventually lead to Eridano/
Faetón's destruction. The goddesses will come to the point where they draw
daggers and attempt to wound one another, as Amaltea expresses her contempt for Eridano, and Galatea, her favor. Faetón, "hating" the one and "loving" the other, tries to separate them. Asking for assistance, he receives an
enigmatic response from the Music:

> Sí,
> hasta que llegue el tiempo
> de saber si es tu fortuna
> amor o aborrecimiento.

(1876b)

The lives and actions of Eridano and Epafo are circumscribed by the influences of these goddesses, and in the last analysis Peleo's fortune will be propitious whereas Eridano's will be calamitous. Although Faetón truly loves
Tetis, Amaltea's hatred will prove to be so strong as to bring about his
destruction.

A tragic victim of Amaltea's scorn and jealousy, Faetón becomes more than
"a symbol of youthful foolhardiness" (Hathorn, p. 50) as he has traditionally
been depicted in Western literature. Faetón, 'shining' (p. 51), lives in a society
that configures his personality and shapes his life. Parker emphasizes that he
is ambitious, but also heroic, and that "No es un joven violento ni arrogante,
sino malaventurado sin culpa suya, un hombre a quien nada le sale bien"
("Metáfora y símbolo," p. 154). Valbuena stresses that Faetón is a proud but
heroic youth who squarely faces his destiny, a true tragic hero (p. 1861a).
These two aspects are clues to his character in *Faetón*. He is an unfortunate
young man who, in resolutely confronting his destiny, is brought low by it.

His heroic stature rests upon his determination to be recognized as the son of Apolo, to regain his rightful place in society.

Faetón is structured on a series of opposing dualities (Eridano-Epafo, Galatea-Amaltea) that even includes the identities of the two young men themselves, (Eridano/Faetón, Epafo/Peleo). There are many scenes that are lyrical celebrations, including music, singing, and dance, that do little to advance the dramatic action, but much to set the elegant tone of the play. For example, the first scene of Act I is a lyrical celebration of the goddess Tetis, and its structure closely parallels that of a traditional *loa* to a court production. A *batida* suddenly changes the tone of the scene as the beast that dwells in the mountain is pursued by King Admeto. And the *relaciones* that we are accustomed to hearing early in the first act curiously appear towards the ends of Acts I and II. The particular value of *Faetón* as a dramatic work will rest, however, upon its depiction of Eridano as an outcast of *próspera fortuna* and a victim of a malign fate that inevitably awaits him as he reaches what to him is the pinnacle of success.

The Remote World of the Gods

The major gods appear to be totally removed from human affairs, except where their lust or desire for vengeance is concerned. Galatea and Amaltea are minor goddesses who in all ways appear to be human. Tetis is the same. The one god whom we expect to be involved in the affairs of Climene and Faetón, Apolo, remains an aloof presence concerned only with his grandeur and privileges. Júpiter and Diana continue their spiteful and vengeful attitudes towards Apolo and Climene. When we ask, How has Climene fared since Apolo's departure? the answer shocks us. As the hunters seek the strange beast that inhabits Tesalia, we hear the broken woman exclaim:

> ¡Clemencia,
> Cielos! Doléos de una vida
> de tantas desdichas llena.

> (1883b)

The heavens appear not to hear her cries, for Apolo must be deaf or indifferent to her plight. He claims that Júpiter's anger and Diana's revenge curtail any intervention. The poor woman is denied even a drink of water by the irate gods opposed to her. Whereas Apolo remains deaf to his lover's pleas, Eridano is moved to pity for her plight (1884a). Finally, Climene is dragged off to Diana's temple to be sacrificed (1885b). Apparently the gods are operative in human affairs to punish and avenge, but not to assist and comfort. Apolo evinces no concern for his former lover. Providential concern does not exist. Humankind serves the lust of the gods and is then discarded as impertinent obstacles to a "higher" life, one of grandeur and glory.

Climene as Victim/Faetón as Victim

The innocent virgin of *Apolo*, who was tricked into loving the god and also into motherhood, appears in *Faetón* as a broken woman whose only purpose in life is the protection of her unknown son. When we first meet her dressed in animal skins, defiantly protecting herself from Tetis, her appearance evokes a familiar figure, the *fiera/mujer*. Her identity is a secret she jealously guards. Though she seems willing to accept death at Tetis's hands, if the goddess misses the mark with her weapon, Climene will not. Thus she will guard her secret (1869a). Climene, hated by Diana (1884a), protects her lost son by guarding his identity. This unfortunate woman could not foresee that her son's lack of identity would create the conditions that would replicate her suffering in his life.

After the lyrical welcome extended to the goddess Tetis, Admeto appears resolved to rid Tesalia of the beast that inhabits its forested mountain. The hunting scene quickly becomes predictive of the malign fate that awaits Climene and her son, for the King loses control of his horse and in his terror promises to offer the beast to Diana (1867a). What at first glance appears to be a chance occurrence is, upon closer inspection, part of a concatenation of events that lead to the disclosure of Climene's child. This mother's bad luck forms part of a larger pattern that will include Eridano's ill-starred life.

We are told that Eridano rescues Admeto from the runaway horse, and Amaltea labels the act "Tan noble acción" (1867a). Since Eridano had to abandon his courting of Tetis to assist Admeto, he believes that "Crüel fortuna" (1867a) is separating him from his love. However, Eridano's fortune is crueler than even he suspects, for his noble and valient rescue of Admeto is mistakenly attributed to Epafo, Eridano's brother and rival for Tetis's favor.

Since fate apparently is linking one event to another, forming a long chain that drags Climene back into society, we are not surprised to hear the elder Eridano lament in an aside the loss of his daughter Climene. She resolutely confronts the goddess Tetis, who tries to kill her. When Tetis is immobilized on discovering a human "beast," Eridano intervenes and saves his beloved from Climene's wrath. As Eridano reveals who he is, it is Climene's turn to be confused, startled, and *admirada*. She says to him that she now can:

> Ver
> a quien es todo mi mal
> y a quien es todo mi bien.

> (1869b)

Eridano wants to know who she is. She responds: "No sé," and adds later:

> Y pues por ti vivo y muero
> en aquesta desnudez,
> este pasmo, este terror,

> este ceño, este desdén
> del hado y de la fortuna,
> cansancio, afán, hambre y sed,
> no procures saber más;
> que harto sabes en saber
> que tú eres todo mi mal
> y tú eres todo mi bien.
>
> (1869b)

Eriando abandons Tetis, who had fainted, in the hope of discovering more about the enigma revealed by the strange woman. When Tetis regains consciousness, she finds Epafo and attributes her rescue to his bravery. Though Epafo denies he realized this *fineza*, Tetis is convinced that she owes her life to this young man. Underscoring how ill-fated Eridano is, Tetis reveals in an aside how much better it would have been if only Eridano had saved her.

When Admeto and Tetis meet shortly afterward, Epafo receives the public acclaim due his brother Eridano for the two noble *finezas*. When Admeto confers the honor of his rescue on Epafo, Eridano is humiliated because he had advanced to receive the King's appreciation. At the loss of this public esteem Eridano exclaims: "(¡Hay hado más impío!)" (1871a). Then Tetis relates how she was saved from the human beast. Eridano exclaims again in an aside: "Como esto no se pierda / piérdase lo demás" (1871a). Eridano advances to receive his lady's appreciation, saying:

> Si el hado
> movido de mi queja,
> ya que aquel bien me quita, este me deja,
> piadoso anda conmigo.
>
> (1871a)

But his fate is not merciful, and for a second time Eridano receives a public rebuke as Tetis attributes the *fineza* to Epafo. Eridano appears to be a vain, crazy man anxious to make his own what properly belongs to another, whereas Epafo stands as a modest and unassuming person who shuns the public reward due his noble deeds.

Amaltea is overjoyed at Eridano's humiliation, and Galatea celebrates Epafo's public acclamation. Though they publically favor one of the young men, each is secretly in love with his rival. Epafo seems destined to receive public acclaim, with no apparent regard for his actions or virtues, just as Eridano seems fated to receive only scorn and reproof. Epafo knows a good thing when he sees it:

> Si la suerte porfía,
> diciendo yo cúya es, que ha de ser mía,
> gócela; que traición no habiendo alguna,

no he de echar en la calle mi fortuna.

(1871b)

A realist, Epafo recognizes his self-interest and accepts his newfound fame. His attempt to disclaim these *finezas* could not be called vigorous. Epafo's *próspera fortuna* spells Eridano's *adversa fortuna*. The two brothers, formerly rivals for Tetis's hand, now become enemies as the irate Eridano challenges Epafo's cavalier acceptance of chance's dictates. Rejecting Epafo's *hidalguía*, Eridano invites his brother to enjoy "estos desperdicios míos" and advises him to stay close in order to acquire honor through his heroic deeds (1873a). This is ironically what will happen when Epafo, as Peleo, marries Tetis after Faetón's fiery plunge from the chariot of the Sun. Claiming modesty in his dealings with Eridano, Epafo refuses to put up with his brother's "siempre altivo fiero / espíritu" (1873a), which manifests itself in terms similar to those we heard from Climene when she addressed Tetis (1969a). Eridano threatens to kill Epafo. Ironically, his attempt to kill his brother leads to Epafo's recognition as Admeto's son Peleo.

The subplot involving the *graciosos* reflects the situation of Apolo and Climene in the main plot. Silvia and Batillo maintain a running battle throughout the play, with the latter expressing a violent attitude toward the former, oftentimes leading to slaps and punches. The gracioso plans on abandoning his wife in order to follow Eridano, as the unfortunate fellow assumes the life of an adventurer. This failure to live up to *la palabra de esposo* (1893a) reminds us that this phrase involves, besides pleasures, duties and obligations. As Apolo has neglected his obligations, so too does Batillo find it convenient to ignore his. The comic dimension of Silvia's plight makes Climene's more poignant.

The Social Context of Identity: The Question of Personal Vindication

The question of social identity and personal worth is significant in *Faetón*. The identity of the *fiera* who roams the mountains and scares the inhabitants is the first to come to mind. There are, moreover, the mysterious origins of Epafo and Eridano, two orphans taken in by Eridano senior in compensation for the loss of his daughter Climene. All three mysterious characters are, in one way or another, seeking personal vindication for what appears to be unjust treatment at the hands of fate.

1. *Epafo/Peleo.* Epafo's anagnorisis as Admeto's son is the only happy case of the three. When Epafo hears Admeto's cries for help, he becomes confused whether he should assist the old man or follow Tetis. Suddenly the voice of Admeto strikes some hidden register in Epafo's heart that draws him to the King's side (1868a). As the power of blood to recognize its own operates in the Admeto-Epafo action, so too will it make its presence felt in the

fiera/Climene-Eridano action. When Climene falls *despeñada*, Eridano feels pity for the miserable creature. In spite of his promise to Tetis to bring the beast to her, he finds his heart moved to defend it (1884b). *La fuerza de la sangre*, just as in Cervantes's famous work, functions mysteriously to bring together the lost children and their parents.

As Eridano seeks to kill his brother, he grabs his father's dagger. When Admeto arrives, he believes that Eridano's violent act was directed against his father. Once the King recognizes the dagger as his own, the past history is quickly narrated. Admeto, having been captured in battle by his enemy, fell in love with the King's daughter, Erífile. When Anfión planned to murder Admeto by poison, Erífile provided him a means of escape. In spite of promising to marry Erífile, Admeto was forced to abandon her and Lemnos to save his own life. Once Anfión became aware, through the infant's horoscope, that Erífile had delivered Admeto's child, he set them both adrift in a boat with a hole drilled in its hull. Before his departure, however, Admeto had given Erífile his father's daggar as a sign that he who would bear it would be his son. Before Eridano senior reveals who this lost son is, Admeto comments on the meaning of the events miraculously unfolding before his eyes:

> Y pues el cielo ha querido
> que a mis manos haya vuelto
> por tan no esperado acaso,
> ¿quién duda que quiere el cielo
> que no pague el inocente
> yerros del culpado, atento
> quizá a que los del amor
> son los más dorados yerros?
>
> (1875b)

This providential concern for Epafo's vindication may account for the remarkable success, luck, or fortune of the soon-to-be-announced Peleo. Where is this providential concern for Eridano? Malign fate seems to direct the course of his and Climene's lives. When Faetón is finally recognized, his death will quickly follow. Here we have clear representations of *próspera fortuna*, Epafo/Peleo, and *adversa fortuna*, Eridano/Faetón. Epafo's recognition as Admeto's son is his honor and glory; Faetón's recognition as Apolo's son will be his momentary honor, but also his eventual degradation.

Though Erífile paid a terrible price for her love of Admeto, at least her son survives to gain his rightful place in society. A victim of a vicious father who held tenaciously to his hereditary hatred of Tesalia, Erífile stands out as another self-sacrificing mother, but one whose sacrifice finally earns the salvation of her son.

2. *"La fiera"/Climene*. A significant change in the traditional tale of Faetón concerns Climene's removal from her son's upbringing. In this regard Cli-

mene is very different from Danae, who raised her son Perseo in human society, or from Liríope, who raised Narciso far removed from it. Climene can never socially vindicate her son due to the fact that Eridano's recognition as Apolo's son spells his death. She hides the facts from him, but reveals just enough to arouse his curiosity (1884). This admirable character accepts her fate as the human beast destined to roam the wilderness, as long as Faetón is safe. Even when she is caught and returned to Diana's temple, her death would be sweet if it preserved Faetón. Only when Eridano importunes her does she finally weaken and remit her dilemma to a higher power, Apolo himself. The moment she believes that her son's and her own vindication is at hand, she tragically delivers Faetón to his fate. As Apolo failed her after his departure from Tesalia, he will fail her yet again in this crucial hour. Her metamorphosis into a white poplar is a symbol of her suffering and deception.

3. *Eridano/Faetón*. Like Perseo, Eridano is convinced that he is more than a *villano*. After all his disappointments, the loss of the public honor due to him for having performed *finezas* on behalf of both King and lady, he remains steadfast in this belief in himself. Once again, those traits which exalt a man above his peers are the very ones that will bring him low. This *is* Faetón's fate. At the end of Act I he maintains an unflappable belief in his noble nature in spite of fortune's blows. When Amaltea believes that his refusal to accompany Peleo in his newfound fortune is due to envy, Eridano denies it and adds:

> Cuando entiendo que soy más,
> me valgo yo de mí mesmo.

> (1876a)

This is precisely the source of Eridano's *hybris*. Richmond Hathorn has remarked that "hybris is the fault by which man, aspiring to rise to a higher level of being and desirous of becoming godlike, attempts by force or fraud to leap the intervening stages and to behave in the here and now as he thinks a god behaves: above the level of other men, unbound by law or moral precept, swollen with pride of success" (p. 50). Eridano desires to have acknowledged by others the same opinion he has of himself; he is seeking a social vindication for an inner conviction. He will undertake the deliberate use of arms to further his cause, the force referred to by Hathorn. But what is lacking in Calderón's narration of his life is any hint of serious moral defect or outright moral error.

The one whose good opinion Eridano seeks above all others is Tetis's. Although she loves this unfortunate mortal, she reproves his presumptuous claim to the two *finezas* (1877b). It is primarily for this reason that Eridano intends to leave Tesalia to seek fame elsewhere. Calling himself "espurio aborto del hado" (1879a), he is determined to prove that his fortune will be at least as good as his former brother's. Accurately characterizing his and Epa-

fo's fates ("pues hijos de fortuna / fuimos próspera y adversa" [1879b]), Eridano promises not to return until Tetis learns that he who desires to win
"eterna fama" (1879b) could never appropriate that which pertains to another.
Later on when Amaltea promises to assist Peleo in winning Tetis, Galatea
prophetically swears to Eridano:

> que no he de ser del Sol hija,
> o he de verte en las estrellas.
>
> (1882b)

Once Eridano chooses to conquer the beast that inhabits Tesalia, he pronounces the words that introduce this study of *Fateón*. The young man plans
on beginning his life of adventure by first conquering his mother! Eridano
demonstrates that he is following an inner compulsion more powerful than
his will or reason, one that accepts and actively seeks risk (1883a). The *fineza*
he believes he "owes" to his homeland will bring him face to face with his
identity and his fate. Tesalia appears to be demanding this meeting of mother
and son, and after it both will believe that they have been vindicated. Both
need to seek their rightful places in Tesalia, and, when they finally achieve
them, their mutual tragedies occur.

Fitón's Prophecy/Faetón's Fate

Towards the end of Act II Climene narrates her love affair with the exiled
god Apolo, and it bears little resemblance to what occurred in *Apolo y Climene*. Simply stated, Climene fell in love with and entertained the god in
Diana's temple, and, once he returned to heaven, she bore him a son. This
"áspid del amor" (1888a) was turned over to the gardener to be spirited away.
Diana, however, discovered her betrayal. During a hunt, the virgin goddess
transformed Climene's dress to that of the beasts, the figure we encounter at
the beginning of the play. Apolo proves to be of no assistance to her, as she
complains bitterly:

> Apolo, que tenía a un tiempo
> indignados contra sí
> a Júpiter y a Dïana,
> o no me pudo asistir
> o no quiso, que sería
> lo más cierto, si advertís
> cuánto vive el olvidar
> vecino del consequir.
>
> (1888b)

This feminine Acteón was taken in by the magician Fitón, who in *Faetón* is
no longer the evil force encountered in *Apolo*. One day when Climene wished

to leave the magician's cave, Fitón told her what the consequences would be:

> ¡Triste de ti
> el día que de ese centro
> salgas, Climene, a vivir
> en oprobio de Dïana,
> pues ese se irá tras ti
> el cruel hado, que a su templo
> te ha de llevar a morir!

(1888b)

The old man then added that the reason for her punishment would be made known and her son would be discovered. Climene, knowing who picked up her baby, judiciously conceals this fact from her audience. Fitón then went on to prophesy the child's fate:

> el día que él sepa de sí
> y quién es, será del mundo
> la ruina, el estrago, el fin,
> tanto que *Faetón* por nombre
> tendrá, que es como decir
> *Fuego o lumbre, o llama o rayo.*

(1888b)

When Climene is forced by hunger and thirst to abandon the cave, the first of Fitón's prophecies proves to be true: Climene has been returned to Diana's temple to be sacrificed. She willingly accepts death as Diana's punishment of her fornication with Apolo and betrayal of her vows, knowing full well that her death seals the secret of her son's identity.

Hearing this remarkable tale, Eridano comprehends the meaning of the strange occurrences that previously had been enigmas. He will deliver Climene from death on Diana's altar and then declare himself to be Apolo's son. What should be Eridano's vindication as the son of Apolo turns out to be yet another occasion for public rebuke: Admeto declares him to be a madman who attributes everything to himself. Regretting her prior revelations, Climene denies all. So does Amaltea. As Eridano is chased from the temple with cries of "Vaya el loco, vaya el loco" (1889b), he declares:

> Loco no, he de presumir
> desde hoy de hijo del Sol.

(1889b)

As Act I concluded with Epafo's recognition as Peleo, Act II closes with a brutal denial that Eridano is Apolo's son.

In Act I Amaltea, in love with Eridano, chides him with the fact of his low birth. Referring to Eridano senior, she remarks:

> encontrándose sin más
> padres que la desnudez
> de hijo espúreo de los hados,
> piadosamente crüel
> te crió con tantas alas,
> como dicen la esquivez
> con que desdeñas deidad,
> a quien Júpiter después,
> del imperio de las flores
> dio la copia.
>
> (1866b)

Then Eridano, "hijo espúreo de los hados" like his foster father, refers to the circumstances of his birth and discovery: "pues de las flores fruto / somos los dos, yo al nacer / y tú al vivir" (1866b). Scorned by the man she loves, Amaltea curses Eridano:

> ¡Oh, plegue al Cielo, crüel,
> falso, fementido, aleve,
> sin lustre, honor, fama y ser,
> villano al fin, mal nacido,
> que esa soberbia altivez
> de tu presunción castigue
> tu mismo espíritu!, y que
> de ella despeñado, digas. . . .
>
> (1867a)

Suddenly Admeto cries "¡Ay de mí, infeliz!" (1867a), as his runaway horse endangers his life. Not only is Eridano's fate signalled by Climene's strange tale of abandonment and woe, it is also prefigured by Amaltea's bitter jealousy and wounded pride as she curses this proud orphan.

Faetón's Rite of Passage

This dramatic narrative may be profitably viewed as Faetón's failed rite of passage. It is a negative version of the initiation of the hero, such as that examined in *Fortunas de Andrómeda y Perseo*. This latter play evolves in the mode of romance, whereas *Faetón* reveals the hallmarks of tragedy. Climene too has undergone a rite of passage in which her infantile nature dies as she becomes a woman who assumes all the duties and responsibilities that word implies. Although Climene's encounter with Apolo signalled the death of her girlish nature, it also contained a transgressive dimension that would require her death, carried out in *Faetón* through her metamorphosis.[2] Faetón's meeting with his father will also translate into his death, but only after a by-proxy encounter with the Woman-as-Death symbol, Tetis, who is abducted by Peleo.

There are three specific stages that characterize the initiation of the hero, and Faetón goes through them all, although in some ways differently from Perseo. First, his birth is supernatural. Almost like Moses of the Old Testament, Eridano was placed in a wicker basket and left among the flowers. Second, the death of his infantile nature commences with his encounter of Tetis, the goddess. Especially after the peripeties of Act I, Eridano feels compelled to leave Tesalia to make his fortune, ultimately proving himself to himself and to others. Demonstrating his inner worth, he decides to assume great risk and to perform mighty *finezas*. This natural expression of his hidden nobility brings him to a confrontation with the beast, who is really his mother. As a result of this encounter both he and Climene are expelled from the community of Tesalia. Therefore, his encounter with Climene is a form of the duel with the Monster, but a phantom representation of the real thing.

Meeting on the deserted mountain, Climene reminds Eridano that his claim to be Apolo's son signifies his misfortune (1890b). Eridano accepts the risk because he already is paying the price demanded by this assertion (1890b-1891a). Galatea, who was listening to Climene and Eridano's conversation, advises them to submit their problem to a higher source, Apolo himself. Eridano, ambitious and bold, accepts his destiny. As they are transported to heaven, Tetis appears troubled by the events that have recently transpired. She has grave doubts concerning Eridano's claim to be Apolo's son. Suddenly she is attracted by the music emanating from the palace of the Sun and wants to know from whence it comes. Looking for someone who might inform her, she hears Silvia decry:

> ¡Mal haya
> ambición, diré mil veces,
> que a más de lo que es se ensalza!
>
> (1892b)

This voice that "suena / a oráculo" (1892b), though specifically referring to Batillo's intent to join Eridano in his adventures, alludes to Eridano's fate. Curiously enough, Eridano's need to be recognized as Faetón is not vaulting ambition, but an inner compulsion for personal and social justice. Though he will be elevated above his present station, that is his right and his fate. As Batillo responds to Silvia, his words also become prophetic:

> Quien no sabe lo que pide,
> ¿qué mucho, Silvia, que caiga
> o tarde o nunca en la cuenta?
>
> (1893a)

Now recognized by his father Apolo, Faetón drives the chariot of the Sun across the skies. From this elevated vantage point he spies Peleo's abduction of Tetis, and, driven to a frenzy by jealousy, a jealousy he can neither conquer nor dominate, he loses control of the chariot and, blasted by Júpiter's thunderbolt, plunges from the sky. This is the third stage of his rite of passage, a by-proxy Encounter with Woman as a figure of death. For Faetón, Tetis becomes the proximate cause of his physical death, as a violent passion overwhelms him.

The Social Context of Faetón's Tragedy

The providential concern expressed by Galatea for Eridano, based on some mysterious affection, proves ineffectual in the face of Amaltea's scorned love, a situation that incites her bitter jealousy. Amaltea's malevolent intervention on Peleo's behalf, motivated by jealousy of Tetis, creates the circumstances in which Faetón's jealousy overwhelms him, resulting in his tragic destruction. In addition to these obvious factors in Faetón's hapless life, there is Apolo's total ineffectualness in preventing Diana's vengeance. The providential factors in Faetón's life prove to be no match for the fate and vengeance that demand his death. Recalling how Perseo had the guidance and assistance of his brother and sister Mercurio and Palas, we are better able to comprehend Faetón's failure.

Tetis loves Eridano and disdains Epafo. The goddess explains to the latter that her affection is not something willed but dictated by the stars (1894a). Dejected, he seeks the solace and assistance of Amaltea, his protector and champion. Her advice to Peleo is blunt and brutal:

> Y pues del ruego se cansa,
> entre a alcanzar la violencia
> lo que el mérito no alcanza.
>
> (1894b)

This violence will lead to Tetis's abduction and Faetón's death. When Amaltea reiterates her advice to Peleo, "Hurta esta deidad al mar" (1894b), he accedes to his passion and her designing counsel: "hacer la deshecha quiero" (1895a). Rationalizing his villainy, Peleo repeats the excuses we have been wont to hear from such egotistical men:

> Ninguno
> esta acción acuse, hasta
> que sea tan desdichado,
> que adore sin esperanzas.
>
> (1895a)

Amaltea is a vengeful character who wants to punish Eridano for his disdain of her love. While he goes off to seek recognition as Apolo's son, she advances Peleo's cause by treachery and violence. Amaltea's vengeance, an unspoken portion of Faetón's fate, is more powerful than Galatea's solicitous regard for the unfortunate young man.

A cyclical sense of time underlies Faetón's malign fate, serving as a principal structural support for the developing plot. In *Apolo* we were witness to the actions of the parents of this boy, actions which now reverberate in his life. Climene, though guilty of breaking her vows to Diana, appears more innocent, more the victim in *Apolo* than in *Faetón*. In the latter play she is guilty of a *delito*. Whereas Admeto's *yerros* were "gilded" because both he and Erífile were free to marry, Climene's transgression of her vow of chastity brings retribution to her and to her offspring. This is not the case, of course, in Admeto's and Peleo's cases. As in *Devoción*, the innocent seem destined to pay for the crimes of the parents, and there is no saving grace in *Faetón* able or willing to interpose itself between this young man and this guilt.

We have already analyzed how Apolo's absence adversely affected Climene, and now we shall see how his recognition of Faetón turns out to be his son's and his former lover's undoing. Both are seeking vindication for lives of misery and despair, and Climene secretly hopes that Apolo's wisdom will be sufficient to check Faetón's fate. As mother and son stand before this god of reason and light, Apolo declares that Eridano shall hereafter be called Faetón, in recognition of his origin. He then begs Climene's understanding for his long delay in recognizing their son: since Júpiter and Diana were angry with him, Apolo dared not reveal his paternity:

> porque uno ni otro no juzgue
> que blasonando el delito,
> segunda vez los injurie.

> (1896b)

In her attempt to protect Eridano, Climene has denied that he is her son. She begs Apolo to provide Faetón with a sign of his parentage, otherwise he will continue to be scorned as the fool. When Apolo asks, What sign? Faetón responds with one that his *altivez, aliento,* and *soberbia* encourage. The god of reason, like Admeto who promised to sacrifice the beast, rashly replies:

> Nada habrá que tú me pidas
> que otorgarte no procure,
> en desagravio del tiempo
> que hizo el temor que te oculte.

> (1897a)

When Faetón asks him to swear to it, his father is miffed. Faetón has learned the lesson of his mother's sad experience with Apolo. Swearing by the river Styx, Apolo promises to fulfill whatever Faetón requests. This god who has ignored Climene, this god who feels guilt due to his abandonment of Faetón, and perhaps shame for his continuing fear of Júpiter and Diana, this god of prophecy must now comply with this youth's wish to drive the chariot of the Sun in order to be seen by the goddesses Galatea, Amaltea, and Tetis, who will then bear witness to his paternity. Apolo reminds Faetón that he is not prepared for such an arduous task. But no amount of reasoning can dissuade him.

At this point Climene intervenes on her son's behalf and pleads with Apolo:

> Y yo su intención ayude.
> Si es justo que en tu memoria
> aquella obligación dure,
> con que por tu amor a riesgo
> vida, alma, ser y honor puse,
> rija tu carro Faetón.
>
> (1897b)

The self-sacrificing mother, who has sought to avoid this moment, now pleads for it. Why? Both Faetón and Climene seek vindication for the suffering they have endured as Apolo's son and lover. Climene's visit to Apolo's palace is her last hope that he, the god of wisdom and light, the god of prophecy, will be able to frustrate the fate she has been unable to avoid. However, Apolo appears not to be aware of what is at stake, the life of his newly acknowledged son. This god who abandoned Climene has not concerned himself with his child. When at last mother and son are vindicated by Faetón's driving the chariot, his fate is tragically fulfilled. Though Calderón's text cites the traditional *ambición* as the motivation for Faetón's bold request, the underlying motives stand clearly before us. As Climene returns to earth to proclaim her son's *honor* (1900b), Apolo *fearfully* departs:

> Con temor voy de que tanto
> esplendor no le perturbe....
>
> (1897b)

The scene ends with a beautifully lyrical celebration of dawn as Apolo, slinking away, once more abandons his own to their fates.

Meanwhile, Amaltea and Peleo are planning Tetis's abduction. Peleo characterizes himself as follows:

> Y yo, que soy cauteloso
> áspid de amor hoy verás,
> pues en las flores me escondo.
>
> (1898b)

Climene formerly referred to her son as "áspid de amor" (1888a), as she hid the child away from Diana's eyes. Now this image reappears to describe Peleo's actions, motivated by "love," or lust, and jealousy. Amaltea's aim is to prevent the union of Eridano and Tetis. When Peleo finally abducts Tetis,

Admeto characterizes the act as "delito tan grande" (1901b). Apolo's *delito*, his forbidden love of Climene, and Peleo's *delito*, his violent abduction of Tetis, are the two events that frame Faetón's tragedy, the first setting his fate in motion and the second provoking his violently jealous response to his beloved Tetis's cries for help.

As Faetón drives his father's chariot, he discovers Tesalia below and rejoices on passing over his homeland, which now has reason to honor him (1900a). As Faetón satisfies his vanity by appearing before the three goddesses, Peleo awaits the propitious moment to abduct Tetis. Climene calls everyone's attention to her son's, and her own, vindication. Hearing Faetón's newfound fortune, Peleo decides that he must immediately abduct Tetis as he becomes fearful and jealous of his former brother. From his elevated position Faetón espies this violent act, this *traición*, and swerves from the appointed route. Since it is an indecorum for jealousy to dare rise to the heavens, Faetón begs their forgiveness as he alters his course:

> que he de seguirla,
> o morir en su socorro.
>
> (1901b)

At this point the horses drawing the chariot bolt, and he precipitates toward the sea as the earth begins to burn. Faetón pronounces his final words during a flaming descent:

> ¿Quién creerá que en tanto asombro
> yo abrase al mundo y a mí?
> Mas ¿qué mucho, si a mis ojos
> Tetis, ¡ay infelice!,
> llego a ver en brazos de otro?
> Y así perdido lo más,
> ni rienda que airado arrojo,
> ni curso que ciego pierdo,
> podrán hacer que sea estorbo
> de no despeñarme al mar:
> y pues ardo yo, arda todo.
>
> (1902a)

Faetón's death is a tragic spectacle of a man consumed by jealousy, a jealousy so violent that his death is willed, a form of "suicide" in the throes of passion. Climene comments in horror:

> Que sería su desdicha
> cumplió el hado riguroso,
> el saber Faetón quién era.
>
> (1902a)

The play quickly comes to a conclusion when Júpiter strikes Faetón from the sky and thus spares the earth.[3] Peleo and Tetis marry, for reasons of *decoro* (1902b), as Amaltea stands happily vindicated in her spite: "Y yo, pues venganza logro" (1902b). She appears here to be more an avenging fury than a goddess. As Fitón stood tall as the evil force behind the action of *Apolo*, Amaltea stands defiantly justified on realizing her hatred and obtaining vengeance on the innocent and hapless Faetón. Once again we are made aware that Faetón's *adversa fortuna* signals Peleo's apparently good fortune.[4]

"Faetón's" Metamorphoses

Apolo concluded with the transformations of Clicie, Céfiro, and Flora into sunflower, wind, and flower, Apolo's symbolic chastisement of these three characters' duplicity in wronging Climene. The metamorphoses that form the *desenlace* of *Faetón* are of a very different nature. Climene, standing awestruck by the sudden death of her son, exclaims pitifully as Admeto and Peleo celebrate their good fortune:

> Solo para mí no hay
> consuelo en mal tan penoso.
>
> (1902b)

Galatea, representing the naiads, echoes her grief:

> Ni para nosotras, puesto
> que apenas hermanas somos
> de Faetón, cuando obligadas
> a lágrimas y sollozos
> quedamos.
>
> (1902b)

Climene, Galatea, and the naiads are then converted into white poplars that will eternally lament the loss of their son or brother.[5] Batillo concludes the play with an ironic commentary on these metamorphoses:

> Con que los bobos
> lo creerán, y los discretos
> sacarán cuán peligroso
> es desvanecerse, dando
> fin *Faetón, hijo de Apolo.*
>
> (1902b)

Batillo's observation is a two-pronged commentary on both the play and its concluding metamorphoses. First, *desvanecerse* could refer to the traditional allegorical interpretation of Faetón's ambition and pride as the cause of his fall from the heavens. Indeed, during Faetón's ride through the skies he exhibits this vanity we expect from a newly vindicated outcast. But such a reading of these words overlooks the complex entanglement of motives behind and causes of this unfortunate young man's death. A second reading could refer to the metamorphoses themselves: only fools believe in such occurrences, whereas the discreet know how dangerous it is a) either to become swelled up with pride and ambition like Faetón, b) or to disappear due to excessive grief. Playing upon the dual possibilities of *desvanecerse* in the context of the denouement, the gracioso reminds us that Faetón's death also leads to the deaths of his mother and sisters. Fitón's prophecy concerning Climene could now be examined and declared erroneous, or we could revise our interpretation of the lines referring to her fate ("¡que a su templo / te ha de llevar a morir! [1888b]) to mean that her death would result from having been returned to Diana's temple, as the events that flow from that action inevitably demonstrate. At any rate, the spectacle of Faetón's death and the metamorphoses of his mother and sisters into white poplars are not shallow entertainment, but a significant dramatization of human experience. The fools clutch at the readily accessible, whereas the discreet will understand *why* these tragic events have occurred. The lives of Climene and Faetón were intertwined right from the start; little did we know, however, that his death would spell his sisters's deaths too.

Conclusion

Apolo's presence is conspicuously lacking from the conclusion of the play. The god who is remote from the needs of those whom he "loved" and generated once more abandons his family to their fate. His last words, "Con temor voy de que tanto / esplendor no le perturbe..." (1897b), characterize the timorous god, incapable of confronting Júpiter and Diana and unwilling to support his family. To realize how dastardly this Apolo is, we need but recall how providence guided the fates of the Curcio children in *Devoción*, or how Mercurio and Palas assured Perseo's success in *Fortunas*. These providential interventions lead to the partial integration of the Curcio children into the larger and more important family of God, on the one hand, and to Perseo's recognition as hero and integration into society, on the other. *Apolo* and *Faetón* dramatize the imperfect and casual formation of a "family" in the first instance, and the total disintegration of that "family" in the second. The crucial factor in *Faetón's* tragic issue, at the surface at least, is Amaltea's hatred and vengeance; as we probe deeper we discover a cowardly god who finds it convenient to shun his responsibility. The bleakness of human society in *Apolo* and shallowness of divine society in *Faetón* leave us in a state of despair. These two plays chronicle the hopeless state of humankind set adrift in a world bereft of providence. Peleo's good fortune reminds us only of the fickleness ruling such a world.

Notes

1 The text consulted is the Valbuena Briones edition, pp. 1861-1902.

2 While Blue rejects the allegorical interpretation of the play, he finds in it a cosmic rhythm from disorder to right order restored (pp. 153, 158-9). For him metamorphosis is regenerative (p. 159), a position I cannot accept.

3 Valbuena notes the following with regards to Faetón's death: "El simbolismo es cristiano. Faetón es un mancebo orgulloso, que desatiende los consejos de su padre cegado por la arrogancia. En el episodio de Tetis no es capaz de gobernar sus sentimientos y la agitada pasión le lleva a la catástrofe" ("Simbolismo," p. 75). Such an interpretation ignores the context in which Faetón's death occurs, underscoring only a moralistic punishment and ignoring a social commentary of significant proportions.

4 Though the plot of *El monstruo de los jardines* dramatizes the consequences of Tetis and Peleo's union, the birth and adventures of Aquiles, Calderón's unique account of the hero's procreation, a violent rape, is somewhat removed from *Faetón's* dramatic plot.

5 Blue finds not a tragic tone, but a transcendent melancholy in this play that promises a renewal of life (p.162).

Myths of Suffering and Destruction: The Death of the Individual

B. 1. La púrpura de la rosa

> soñé
> que el fiero jabalí
> que a ti te daba muerte,
> volviendo contra mí
> las aceradas corvas,
> navajas de marfil,
> con mi sangre manchaba
> las rosas, que hasta aquí
> de nieve fueron, para
> que fuesen de carmín.
>
> (1772a)[1]

Citing Cotarelo y Mori, Edward M. Wilson has observed that, though *Púrpura* was written in 1659, it had to wait until 5 December 1660 to be performed.[2] Intended for performance in the Palace of the Zarzuela, it was Calderón's first opera libretto. There is a natural evolution from *Golfo* and *Laurel* to *Púrpura*, from the *zarzuela* form to the operatic medium that this play reintroduced to Felipe IV's court theater. The exigencies of this totally sung text significantly affect the traditional structure Calderón had developed for his mythological dramas, causing *Púrpura* to appear at first glance more like a skeleton than a living body. Though the graciosos remain with their inverted image of the main plot line, gone are many of the traditional characteristics we associate with the *comedia*. We do not find almost entire acts closely resembling the traditional *comedia de intriga* or *comedia palaciega*. Gone also are the long *relaciones* and convoluted plot lines that flesh out myth's narrative simplicity into dramatic discourse. What we do have, however, is a dramatic flow that is direct and full of emotion. While Valbuena emphasizes *Púrpura*'s "perfección formal" (1765a), we should remember that the musical innovation demands a structural adaptation that must have been an artistic challenge to Calderón's Baroque sensibility. *Púrpura*'s brevity, conciseness, and directness reflect the formal response to opera's challenge. And Calderón did not fail to advert us to this fact in the *loa*:

> quien no se atreve à errar, no

se atreve à acertar.

(411b)[3]

There is an accentuated symbolic dimension to *Púrpura*, reminding us of Calderón's *auto* style that he attempted to adapt to the secular theater in *Golfo*. Though it is an impressive display of dramatic talent and symbolic thinking, the emphasis on the development of Marte's jealousy displaces our interest from the tragic Adonis and Venus to the vengeful god of war, Marte. Thus *Púrpura* becomes a play about jealousy, where the tender love of the pair is destroyed by a vicious Marte bent on vengeance, innocence destroyed by brute power.

The *loa* itself is a model of simplicity, if that adjective can ever be applied to Calderonian myth plays. Zarzuela, representing the palace where musical and rustic plays were performed, suffers from the conflicting emotions of Tristeza and Alegría. It appears that the royal couple has not visited the rustic *alquería* for more than a year; there were royal births, such as those of Próspero and Fernando, that delayed performances at that palace. Zarzuela's sense of loss is further aggravated when she learns that the Infanta María Teresa will, once she marries Louis XIV, become the Queen of France and leave Spain. This royal marriage of the houses of Spain and France seals the peace that dates from November of 1659, but it means that the Infanta will not witness another performance at la Zarzuela. Zarzuela, however, experiences joy once more when she is informed of the King's wish to have her perform in the Coliseo of the Buen Retiro, at which time she will again see María Teresa. This joy is short lived, for the writing and preparation for such a work as *Púrpura* demand talent and time. The *loa*, stating that "afectos no son fineza" (412b), nonetheless underscores that "afectos hacen milagros" (412a). This account of the play's first performance reveals that it was a hurried affair transferred from the Zarzuela to the Buen Retiro in celebration of the peace with France and the *boda* of María Teresa and Louis XIV. Such a major historical event also marks a milestone in the history of Spanish theater, for the "Representación música," as the *loa* labels the work, signals new dramatic directions that are making their presence felt in the Iberian Peninsula.

Vulgo observes that the novelty of the piece lies not in its plot, the fable of Venus and Adonis, but in its form. This cultural jingoist then states the motive behind such innovation:

> por señas de que ha de ser
> toda musica, que intenta
> introducir este estilo,
> porque otras Naciones vean
> competidos sus primores.

(411b)

Startled by such a bold departure from Spanish tradition, Tristeza warns
him:

> No mira quanto se arriesga
> en que colera Española
> sufra toda vna Comedia
> cantada?

(411b)

Vulgo tersely replies:

> No la será,
> sino solo vna pequeña
> representacion. . . .

(411b)

The qualification with regards to the operatic libretto reminds us of the evolving nature of Calderonian theater in the late 1650s and early 1660s. This is a
text that bears witness to its innovative role in Spanish theater. Although this
ópera will consist of a single act, the one to follow, *Celos, aun del aire, matan*,
will return to the three-act format, but in a significantly reduced fashion.
Broader European movements set the standard for Spanish theater, and,
while the *zarzuela* would appeal more to native taste, the exquisite experience of opera would continue as an aristocratic norm that would reach fruition in the century that follows.[4]

Adonis as Tragic Figure/Venus as Tragic Victim

After Adonis rescues Venus from a wild boar, he insults the god of love
before his mother (1767b). Explaining why he is opposed to "aquel escándalo
niño," Adonis narrates one of those horribly scandalous tales of mythology,
the incestuous love of Cinyas and Myrrha. The "aborrecido hijo" (1767b) of
this union, Adonis relates how he was raised without affection, another
young man, like Faetón, left to his own devices in a hostile world. Referring
to his procreation as an "amante traición," the beautiful youth narrates how
Mirra's father subsequently "abandoned" her, causing her death. This death
evoked the gods' pity, because they transformed her into a myrrh tree, from
which Adonis was born. The metamorphosis that accompanied Mirra's death
and Adonis's birth will become the prophetic sign under which Adonis lives.
A cruel father, an abandoned mother, a foundling child, and a cruel fate: these
are the elements of tragedy.

Once Adonis reveals his horoscope, we understand why he is opposed to
Cupid:

> nací bastardo embrión,
> maldecido de mis padres,

> y con tan gran maldición,
> como que de un amor muera.
>
> (1767b)

What Calderón's delicacy (?), or decorum, omitted was the precise circumstance of Adonis's birth. Myrrha fell in love with her father and eventually bore him a son. The "punishment" of the young woman resulted from her mother's boast that the girl was more beautiful than Venus herself. Once Cinyas learned of his monstrous love, he committed suicide, but only after striking Myrra with his sword. At that very moment Myrra metamorphosed into a tree.[5] This young woman, reminiscent in some ways of Andrómeda, pays for the sin of her proud and foolish mother; a sexual crime leads to the birth of an ill-starred son; and finally, a cyclical process of vengeance is set in motion in which the sins of one generation are to be visited upon another.[6] The young Adonis deliberately lives apart from human community in the attempt to flee his fate. His beastly attire is a symbol of the life he now leads: "huyo de las hermosuras / y de las fierezas no" (1768a). Sounding very much like Hércules, Adonis fails to recognize that the denial of love's proper place in society and in his personality creates the conditions in which his fate will be fulfilled. What Adonis never imagined was how love would not only spell his death, but also that of the one he loved, and would also affect the community as a whole.

There are other structural supports that further the sense of impending doom. First, Adonis saves Venus by driving off a wild boar. Afterwards, Venus literally *falls into* Adonis's arms, and this fall alerts us to the fact that something ominous is about to occur. Towards the end of the play this same boar, which indirectly brought Venus and Adonis together, will be used by a jealous Marte to divide them (1782b). Second, the metamorphosis of Mirra into a myrrh tree associates this transformational event with death. The play will end with the death of Adonis, a young man who attempted to flee his fate, but found himself, nevertheless, metamorphosed into a blood-dark rose. This symbolic death also includes one not foreseen, Venus's. And third, Marte's vengeance, the vehicle by which fate runs its course in *Púrpura*, evolves as a deadly passion that regards nothing but the need and desire to inflict pain and death on whoever offends.

Love as "Vengeance"

As Adonis sleeps, exhausted by his search for the wounded boar, Venus appears pondering the events that have recently occurred, particularly the stirrings of her heart for the young hunter. In a dream Adonis suddenly cries out: "¡Ay de mí! /Que me da muerte a quien la vida di" (1771a). A troubled Venus hesitantly approaches the sleeping figure, thankful for her rescue, but also offended by his mistreatment of Amor. She says:

> ¿Daréle muerte? No.
> ¿He de vengarme? Sí.
> ¡Oh si hubiera un matar
> que no fuera morir!
>
> (1771b)

Calculating what she can do, Venus advances toward Adonis, who once again cries out in his tormented sleep. Both are troubled: the one by the specter of his death at Venus's hands, and the other by her agitated state since meeting the wild but beautiful young man. Calling upon her son Amor to assist her, Venus informs the winged god that, though she is grateful to Adonis for her life, the young man disdains Amor's place in his life and thus requires chastisement. Amor immediately wounds him with a gilded shaft:

> que áspid de fuego
> muerde su pecho, a fin
> de que los dos vengados
> con tiro tan feliz,
> apuremos así
> si es el amar matar y no morir.
>
> (1772a)

This fateful image of the asp colors with tragic hues the burgeoning love of Venus and Adonis. Love as a means of vengeance duplicates in Adonis's life the situation his mother experienced, Mirra's passion for her father as Venus's vengeance. But here Venus's vengeance on Adonis will entail more than the "death" of the offending party, for her own death is implicated in Adonis's. In this instance love will actually produce death and not merely a figurative "matar y no morir." Love as a means of vengeance may right the imbalance in Adonis's life, but it also ironically advances his fate.

As Adonis relates his fateful dream to Venus (1772a), his death by the wild boar, he adds that a "sañudo áspid" has already wounded his heart. The suffering he first experienced in a dream continues in his wakened state. Forcefully affected by Venus's presence, the beautiful hunter forswears his brusque and discourteous manner to affirm a new self, one that is radically different. With passion stirring in his veins, Adonis promises to overcome his fate (1772b). He then explodes into a series of traditional praises of Venus's beauty, using the distribution-summary technique. Like a good literary critic, Venus responds: "¡Qué atrasadas lisonjas!" (1773a). Although Venus feigns surprise and indifference, Adonis persists in his protestations of love. The love of the two is eventually celebrated in a beautifully lyrical and concise style as Venus returns avenged to her garden:

> Corred, corred, cristales;
> plantas, vivid, vivid;

> aves, cantad, cantad;
> flores, lucid, lucid;
> pues que vuelve Venus
> hermosa y gentil,
> trayendo despojos
> del amor tras sí,
> porque nadie pueda
> exento decir
> que el vivir no amando
> se llama vivir.
> Corred, vivid, cantad, lucid.

(1773a)

The same technique of distribution and summary that Venus rejected as old-fashioned is employed to celebrate their love. Love, that force that destroyed Adonis's mother and father/grandfather, now rules his life. Adulterous love, that formerly brought Venus and Marte to shame before the other gods (1768b), now rules the goddess's life once again. We have the confluence of two fates, Adonis's and Venus's, where only the former's was perceived.

Marte's Deadly Jealousy

After Adonis saves Venus's life and departs, Marte appears on stage swearing to take vengeance on whoever has offended her. Confused and troubled, Venus dares not denounce Adonis to this brutal and bloodthirsty god. Her *turbación* reveals, as it had for the women of the honor dramas, her secret feelings and hidden guilt, her love of Adonis. (A similar *turbación* will later betray Amor.) Once Venus departs, Marte interrogates all her ladies in waiting, and only Libia the graciosa dares to say that Adonis saved Venus from the boar. This suspicious god immediately becomes jealous and wonders why Venus was not able to relate what had occurred. Like the husbands of the wife-murder dramas, he states:

> Aquí hay segunda intención.
> ¡Cuánto, cielos, se adelanta
> la amante imaginación!

(1769a)

When his sister Belona arrives to remind him of his martial duty, Marte, alluding to his "cobardes sospechas," decides, however, to return to the field of battle: "Pero mi fama es primero" (1769b). He holds in check for the moment his wrath: "si a verdades pasan / sospechas que ahora son" (1769b). The god of war is caught between conflicting emotions of love and jealousy.

In the comic subplot involving the graciosos, Chato expresses his jealousy of some mysterious visitor his wife Celfa entertains at night. Suspicious of

Marte's companion, he asks:

> ¿Qué soldadillo es aquel
> que suele venir con él?

Celfa responds:

> ¿Soldadillo? Es ilusión;
> porque no es sino dragón.

> (1770a)

Her lover is Dragón, Marte's aide, and her quick thinking, though it does not alleviate Chato's jealousy, contrasts comically with Venus's *turbación*.

A major portion of *Púrpura* is dedicated to the evolution and progression of Marte's *celos*. Using the allegorical means characteristic of the *auto sacramental*, Calderón traces the stages that closely approximate those found in the honor dramas. The love of Venus and Adonis serves as background for the unfolding jealousy that will dominate Marte's life. Though he returns victorious from battle, there is a more insidious war raging in this man, one provoked by fear and suspicion. Like the well-meaning servants of the wife-murder plays, Amor spies on Marte to forestall any news of Venus's betrayal of his love. Caught by Belona, Amor becomes *turbado* (1774a). This reaction elicits Marte's suspicion as he recalls Venus's confused stutterings. Marte confronts the young god, who flees. When he recognizes Amor, he pursues him in spite of Belona's warnings: "¡Ay de ti, si a Amor que huye / intentas seguir!" (1774b). Accepting this risk, Marte chases Amor into the Cave of Disillusionment, where he is warned once again:

> ¡Ay de aquel que en principio de celos,
> huyendo el Amor, no le deja que huya!

> (1775)

As Marte plunges into the nether reaches of his soul, Calderón represents the development of Marte's jealousy through allegorical figures that stand for psychic forces now at play. At first Marte meets Temor, Sospecha, Envidia, and Ira, and, though being frightened by what he sees, decides to push forward.

Marte's passions appear bearing symbols of how they affect the troubled and jealous soul. Temor bears a torch; Sospecha, field glasses or a spyglass; Envidia, an asp; and finally Ira, a dagger. These emotions conduct Marte to the prison of jealousy, where those who could not let Amor escape are held captive. Each allegorical figure appears, explaining the symbolism of the object borne and its effect on the soul. Temor may provide light, but he eventually leaves one in total darkness. He reveals the damage, but not how the pain is to be alleviated. Sospecha enlarges all that comes into its field of vision, converting a poplar into a mountain and a drop of rain into the entire rainfall. Envidia assures the good fortune of the other, entangling one asp with another and injecting all with poison. Ira converts the asps of Envidia into serpents of steel "que para venganzas afilen sus puntas" (1776a). Warning Marte again, a warning no one ever heeds, they declare that they guard Desengaño, the prisoner of jealousy. This figure then appears asking what Marte wants of him, this god who conquers all but himself, a god whose human passions belie his godhead. When Marte asks Desengaño why Amor spied on him and then fled, Disillusionment reveals in a mirror the love of Venus and Adonis. Even Dragón becomes jealous of Celfa's husband Chato. Though Marte wishes to destroy the mirror that reveals truth, in a flash everything vanishes from sight. As Marte flees from the terrible revelation, Dragón experiences "celos maridales" (1777b).

Amor interrupts an idyllic love scene between Venus and Adonis to announce that a vengeful Marte now threatens Adonis. Though he experiences jealousy, Adonis flees to the mountain, the place of his birth. Venus will defend herself with the waters of forgetfulness. The furious Marte is stopped cold in his tracks by these waters released by the Furies, as the god of war becomes himself *turbado*. Venus is immediately opposed by Belona's call to arms and vengeance (1779b). Venus and Belona here represent the contradictory emotions of Marte, a god who wishes to ignore and forget his affront, his loss of Venus's love, but cannot forswear the vengeance he believes it demands. Jealousy, demanding vengeance, and forgetfulness compete for Marte's attention, and the former wins out.

Adonis appears on the mountain hunting the boar in the attempt to conquer his fate at the same time as he takes out his frustration on the beast (1781a). When Marte espies Adonis, he realizes that the means of vengeance are at hand:

> y pues tras la fiera va,
> en que empezó la primera
> fineza suya el Amor,
> empiece de mi furor
> también la ira.

> (1781a)

Calling on Megera, the Fury, Marte asks that the boar avenge him (1781a). Jealousy unleashes the "all-powerful" force of vengeance and there is no providential concern, no mediating presence or force capable of deterring its march toward death.

In a comic interlude, Dragón avenges his jealousy of Chato not by beating him, but Celfa. His jealousy of Celfa's husband turns the jealousy motive topsy-turvy, inverting the normal state of affairs, but closely approximating the Marte-Venus situation. It is not the husband who takes vengeance, though Chato was previously jealous, but the wounded lover who punishes the errant wife with *coces*. Expressing his outrage, Dragón states that he could stomach a great deal, even Celfa's having accompanied another man on the beating for game, but not her husband! When Celfa complains of the *tunda*, Chato reminds her gleefully: "Hija, aquesas son las cargas / del matrimonio" (1781b). Receiving neither pity nor understanding from her husband, she attacks him to avenge Dragón's disdain. At this moment, Adonis cries out: "¡Valedme, cielos!" (1781b). What serves as comic relief in the subplot of the play turns deadly serious in the main plot line. As Venus appears on the scene with bloody hands, Adonis cries out twice more in his last agony "¡Piedad, cielos!" and "¡Favor, dioses!" (1782a), echoing Venus's terror.

Belona tries to prevent Venus's witnessing the "trágico asunto" (1782a) of Adonis's death. Informed that her lover's blood now produces living flowers, Venus cries out to the gods: How could this have happened? Marte comes on stage and explains how he employed the wild boar as the means of his vengeance (1782b). When Adonis is discovered amongst some flowers, Venus is overwhelmed by grief. Although Marte has taken bloody revenge on the hapless Adonis, he cannot take away, as Venus emphasizes, the great favor shown to him by Amor:

> porque tus celos
> su mayor triunfo no borren,
> vivirá a su ruego eterno,
> aunque ahora en él y en mí notes
> *las venas con poca sangre,*
> *los ojos con mucha noche.*

(1782b-1783a)

As Venus faints, she falls amongst the roses, whose thorns cause her to bleed. From the two lovers will be formed a flower on land and a star in the heavens.

Death as Transformation: Metamorphoses Revisited

As the conclusion of *Púrpura* celebrates the metamorphoses of Adonis into a flower and Venus into a star, Amor observes how the transformation from the human to the vegetative leaves something to be desired:

> Júpiter, pues, conmovido
> o indignado de que *goce*
> *sin los imperios de un alma*
> los de una vida tu nombre,
> de esa derramada sangre
> quiere que una flor se forme,
> y que de aquella se vistan
> roja púrpura las flores,

> para que en tierra y en cielo
> estrella y flor se coloquen. . . .
>
> (1783a; emphasis added)

The assembled crowd exclaims:

> El horror de la tragedia
> a vuestra vista se esconde,
> viendo que ya todo es dichas.
>
> (1783a)

Although Marte's jealousy returns at the sight of the two metamorphosed lovers, we remain unconvinced and troubled by this conventionalized ending that mitigates the tragic action, turning it into a pretext for happiness. All celebrate the event as follows:

> A pesar de los celos
> sus triunfos logre
> el Amor, colocados
> Venus y Adonis:
> y reciban ufanas
> y eternas gocen
> las estrellas su estrella,
> su flor las flores.
>
> (1783b)

This denouement, very appropriate for a celebration of the *boda* of María Teresa and Louis XIV, especially in view of the astral imagery used in the *loa* for the royal Hapsburgs and the fleur-de-lis for the French King, calls to mind Venus's criticism of Adonis's highly conventionalized praises of her beauty: "¡Qué atrasadas lisonjas!" (1773a). Adonis's and Venus's deaths represent a loss, the loss of their souls. Though metamorphosed into flower and star, each has descended in the great chain of being to vegetative or to mineral existence. This loss of life represents the unassimilable element in the myth that challenges poetry's and drama's transformational magic. Though Calderón ingeniously manipulates the myth to adapt it to the requirements of this state occasion, the "trágico asunto" refuses to yield its poignancy to pageantry's imperatives.

Conclusion

Púrpura dramatizes the destructive force of jealousy and the lethal power of vengeance upon both love and life. Whereas *Celos, aun del aire, matan* will explore how one's own jealousy leads to self-destruction, *Púrpura* depicts how jealousy of another may cause that person's death. Structurally, the play follows a pattern associated with the honor dramas, but one in which a jealous lover, not a husband, kills his rival. It resembles *A secreto agravio, secreta venganza*, though stealth has a very different role in *Púrpura*. As in the former play, the female's death quickly follows her lover's. In *Pintor* both lovers are killed, whereas only *Médico* spares Prince Enrique, respecting royal blood. Though Marte does not shed Venus's blood in vengeance, her death is nonetheless an indirect result of his vengeance on Adonis and corresponds to the larger pattern already adumbrated.

I have emphasized the cyclical nature of time and events underlying Calderonian tragedy. I would add here only the following observation. Mirra's *incestuous love* for her father led to Adonis's birth. Venus's *adulterous love* contributes to his death. But here Vulcano is not the avenging presence, Marte is. This son of an "amante traición" (1767b) is ultimately undone by a passionate and illegitimate love, just as his mother was destroyed by her love for her father. The horoscope predicted only that Adonis would die "de un amor" (1767b), problematizing his life through its lack of specificity. Adonis's fateful dream particularizes the horoscope by associating his death with Venus, the woman he rescued from the boar. Both the horoscope and dream failed to note, however, that Venus's death was implicated in Adonis's fate. Though we witness the metamorphic celebration that closes the play, the "trace" of Adonis's and Venus's blood reminds us that we have witnessed a tragic action. The symbols of flower and star, standing now for the royal houses of France and Spain, cannot erase the memory of that experience nor claim that there is "un matar / que no fuera morir" (1771b).[7]

Notes

1 See the Valbuena Briones edition of *Púrpura*, pp. 1765-83.

2 See "The Text of Calderón's 'La púrpura de la rosa,'" *MLR*, 54 (1959), 29-44.

3 See the text of the *loa* found in the *Tercera Parte* (Madrid, 1687).

4 The allure of this operatic form even "invaded" the colonies. Tomás de Torrejón y Velasco (1644-1728) provided a new musical score for Calderón's libretto in celebration of Felipe V's eighteenth birthday, a festival premiered on 19 October 1701 in Lima, Peru. See Robert Stevenson, "The First New-World Opera," *Américas*, 16 (1964), 33-35.

5 See Hathorn, pp. 230-31.

6 We need to ask, at least rhetorically, what resemblance this coition between father and daughter had to the actual state of Felipe IV and Mariana de Austria, uncle and niece?

7 We should also point out that the entire cyclical process began with Venus's vengeance on Mirra's mother, who foolishly praised her daughter's beauty as greater than the goddess's. Since Mirra's love of her father is monstrous and deadly, leading to both their deaths, so too the death/metamorphosis of Adonis entraps Venus herself. The irony of this conclusion, where the goddess of love who has used love as a means

of vengeance, not once but twice, dies as the cycle of offense-vengeance comes full circle, should not be overlooked.

B. 2. Celos, aun del aire, matan

> que aunque son nobles también las venganzas,
> tal vez blasonadas desdicen de nobles.
> Y así Venus a mi ruego,
> y a ruego de Venus Jove,
> mandan que del fino amor
> la tragedia se mejore
> sin el horror de tragedia
>
> (1813b)[1]

For Pérez de Moya the tragic death of the jealous Procris contains a clear moral lesson: "la poca prudencia nos guía las más veces a buscar lo que no querríamos hallar" (II, 238). This approach tends to reduce the literary, dramatic, and human value of *Celos* to a facile moral. Matthew Stroud summarizes the historicist approach to Calderón's myth plays, a critical perspective in conformity with Sebastian Neumeister's already stated position.[2] Historical determinism limits a play to what it most likely meant in its own time frame, and in this instance to the circumstances of its first performance. Stroud is explicit in this regard:

These court spectacles, however, are first and foremost pageants, spectacles in which the event itself takes precedence over considerations of the plot, character, or theme. A play such as *Celos* was not the result of an author trying to communicate a sense of the human condition to a people as a whole; rather it was a work commissioned by one man, viewed by only a few people whose attention was probably more focused on the King and the court than on the play, and subordinated, at least in its effect on its audience, to matters of music, dance, and spectacle. The plot in *Celos* has become a vehicle for extraliterary purposes, but that fact does not keep us from appreciating the play as literature nor from determining its archetypal structure. We should merely be aware that these plays pose special problems in our search for literary "truth" because they are, in fact, excellent examples of compromised poetry (*Celos*, pp. 34-35).

Although Stroud attempts to balance his historicist position against the demands of dramatic and literary criticism, his *privileging* of the historical moment of production circumscribes the interpretative endeavor. Recognizing the particular nature of *Celos* as a "masque-like opera," in Stroud's terminology (p. 21), I insist that its dramatic structure closely follows what is characteristically Calderonian in terms of the development of plot, character, and theme. *Celos* comments on the human condition, but its commentary is problematic. Is it possible to have tragedy without horror? While the text attests to such an attempt, tragedy's mark proves to be indelible. Calderón did not set aside his powers of observation nor did he put in abeyance his unique view of the human/divine condition on writing the libretto for *Celos, aun del aire, matan*. He extrapolated them, as he did previously in *Púrpura*, to a new medium, opera, that he would never again essay.

Celos, aun del aire, matan was Calderón's second opera libretto, and in this one he abandoned the one-act format of *Púrpura* to return to the more familiar and conventional three-act structure of the *comedia*. *Púrpura's* single act limited the dramatist to establishing only the skeleton of dramatic action. According to Stroud, *Púrpura* was staged 17 January 1660 to celebrate the marriage of the Infanta María Teresa to Louis XIV, whereas *Celos*, originally planned to celebrate the third birthday of the Infante Felipe Próspero, was delayed until 5 December 1660.[3]

The opera depends on a fundamental tension symbolized by the conflictive relationships of Venus and Diana, love and hate respectively. Diana represents fate and Venus, providence. But the presence of the two goddesses and their distinct axiological values accounts for only the surface tension in the work, for there is a more basic antagonism embodied in the very structure of the play itself. This structural tension, inherent in the conception of the action, proceeds from the question of whether it is possible to create tragedy "sin el horror de tragedia" (1813b), to produce simultaneously a tragic action as well as tragedy's transcendence. This conceptual tension manifests itself in the early metamorphoses of the play. Aura is rescued from Diana's vengeance on being metamorphosed by Venus into air. This change of substance is principally positive, the result of the positive force of love represented by Venus. But following it we witness another kind of metamorphosis produced by the negative force of hatred and vengeance represented by Diana, which transforms Rústico the gracioso into various beastly forms as seen through the eyes of several characters. Rústico's role in the play reveals the negative effect of metamorphosis and alerts us to its dual or problematic nature. Eróstrato's role demonstrates the negative effect of vengeance on the personality of the avenger. These two characters are key figures in our attempt to understand the uniqueness of *Celos* and to interpret the play as a tragedy "sin el horror de tragedia."

At the conclusion of *Celos* we see how jealousy, as demonstrated through Procris's life, and vengeance, as demonstrated by Diana's on the divine plane and Eróstrato's on the human plane, are destructive passions that rend the fabric of both human and divine societies. The offense-vengeance mechanism and its aftermath can only be confronted and defeated by the divine will for love, a will that reflects in essence the Christian concept of the world infused by redeeming love. *Celos* does not reflect the pagan world of antiquity, but a "christianized" world ripe for redemption. Only in this manner do we have tragedy without the horror of tragedy, for while tragedy is limited to the world of time and space, to human temporality, its horror and its impact are implicitly conditioned by the divine will that limits the tragic reach of the action to human time. In eternity all is set aright. Nevertheless, the memory of the tragic issue, the trace of human suffering, the frustration of human happiness remind us that the route to transcendence is through tragedy.

The Diana-Venus Rivalry: The Instability of Human Life

From the beginning of the play, Diana represents an ambivalent force in the world, one that exalts chastity but also denigrates the role of love, reducing it to what Procris labels *torpe amor*. Thus life for Diana is comprised of only two possible modes of being-in-the-world, based, according to Procris, "del puro amor que ensalzas, / del torpe que desprecias" (1786b). Despising human and sexual love, the goddess unnaturally exalts chastity and purity. This position indicates a lack of balance, a disruption of the divinely ordered state of human affairs and, in consequence, a bankrupt hierarchy of values that falsifies and dehumanizes human life. Diana does not represent merely one option for human living, but an active opposition to Venus. While at first this Diana-Venus opposition is expressed through the opposition of *olvido* to *amor* (1787a), later we learn that the realization of *olvido* is something more insidious and harmful than mere forgetfulness. Toward the end of Act II Céfalo reminds Procris that "no enmienda al amar / el aborrecer" (1799a). Diana and her followers deny the beauty and sacramentality of sexual love as a human expression and reflection of divine love. By their exclusive dedication to *olvido*, a good way of life in itself, they gradually lose the moderation required by prudence, becoming haters of others who do not practice their form of life. In the same scene Céfalo reminds Procris that "puede una ser constante / sin pasar a ser crüel" (1799a), or that one can remain committed to a life of chastity without the adoption of an antivital attitude toward human sexuality that distorts the human personality.

As a negative force in the play, Diana represents malign fate as well as that distortion of human destiny that provokes tragedy. Céfalo's passion for Procris reflects the "imperioso destino de mi estrella" (1801a) that Diana will manipulate to effect her vengeance on all the three principal human characters, Eróstrato, Céfalo, and Procris. When Céfalo sets out to hunt the wild beast that inhabits Lidia's mountains, Tesífone, a fury sent by Diana to avenge her, distorts Céfalo's sensory perception so that he will see Eróstrato as a beast rather than a man. Referring to his infallible javelin as "este de fresno / áspid" (1812a), a fateful image in Calderonian theater, Céfalo plans on killing the beast/man. In an aside Tesífone declares who the real target of the javelin will be, Procris. As the avenging goddess, Diana manipulates the human action to bring about a tragic outcome. She is very much like Fitón of *Apolo y Climene*, an evil force and presence whose egotistical impulse concretizes fate's abstract remoteness. When Procris dashes from cover to prevent her husband's pursuit of the wild beast, we realize that human fate in this case depends on the complex interaction of the human and divine planes, on Diana's desire for vengeance, Procris's jealousy of Aura, and Céfalo's pursuit of fame and glory. In seeking to save her husband's life, Procris is pierced by his infallible javelin.

To understand better Diana's exaggerated dedication to chastity, we must place it within the context of her rivalry with Venus for power and prominence in the world. The goddess's lack of moderation converts what should be a friendly and spirited rivalry into a bitter and destructive battle. Even when she accepts the offerings of those men and women who swear her fealty or pay her obeisance, she turns what should be a happy and joyous occasion into a bittersweet one by transforming the reverence shown to her into an opportunity to revel in the opprobrium of Venus (1796b). *Vencerse a sí mismo* is absolutely required for a dignified, prudent, and noble life. This key phrase in attaining mastery over one's base appetites and egotistical motivations is distorted in Diana's vision of the world into a destructive quality that can only deny and prevent the affirming of a positive orientation necessary for the good life. The chorus expresses this distortion thus:

> Pues la victoria mayor
> vencerse a sí mismo ha sido,
> ¡muera el amor y viva el olivido!
> ¡Viva el olvido y muera el amor!
>
> (1796b)

After the offering of gifts, Diana is about to say that their value depends upon their ability to affront Venus's godhead, when suddenly Aura declares offstage:

> ¡Viva el amor y muera el olvido!
> ¡Muera el olvido y viva el amor!
>
> (1797b)

When Aura declares the import of her message to be "que / no enmienda al amar / el aborrecer" (1798a), she criticizes Diana's lack of moderation:

> No, pues, de ingrata blasones;
> que bien puede una mujer
> mantenerse en ser constante,
> sin pasar a ser crüel;
> y es darle rienda al extremo,
> querer no haya medio. . . .
>
> (1798a)

Diana's disparagement of the golden mean proceeds from her intrinsic cruelty, her absolutist attitude towards life based on the negative and lifedenying proclivity of her personality. In seeking to unbalance the harmony of the world, based on these separate, yet complementary, modes of life, she will also become excessive in other areas, such as seeking vengeance on those who oppose or wrong her.

In Act III Diana sets out to avenge the wrongs done to her by Eróstrato, Procris, and Céfalo. Having already punished Aura, she rationalizes her vindictive actions by pardoning Rústico, restoring him to his human form. Diana's vengeance is thorough:

1. Eróstrato will become an "humana fiera" (1803b) who will flee from his fellow humans tormented by his loss of Aura.

2. Procris, the apostate of Diana's cult, will suffer from an excessive jealousy that will lead to her death. The poetic imagery employed by Diana is significant, since jealousy is compared to an asp: "de los celos el áspid, / que entre las flores del amor se oculta" (1803b).

3. And Céfalo, who now proudly employs Diana's infallible javelin, will find his senses so disturbed that he will rashly cast the weapon, bringing about the goddess's vengeance. The distortions evident in Diana's life will find their counterpart on the human plane in Eróstrato's.

These gods appear omnipotent, but there are limits placed on their fields of action, due as much to their natures as to the definition of the cosmos of which they form a part. While *Celos* concentrates on Diana's interventions in human affairs, there is another force, Venus, that at one time opposes Diana and at another balances her negative effects on human society. Though invisible throughout the play (we only hear her voice), Venus proves to be the positive principle informing human life. The goddess manifests her presence at that moment when Diana, defiantly proud of her power, is about to punish Aura with death. As the human calls on the gods to favor her, Diana boasts: "¿Cuál podrá contra mí?" (1788b). Without hesitation, Aura affirms the power of love (1788b-1789a). With a brief statement that responds to the chorus's "¿Cómo?" Venus declares: "De esta manera" (1789a), metamorphosing Aura into a nymph of the air. There are, however, even limits to Venus's power, attested to by Aura's metamorphosis.

Once frustrated in her vengeance on Aura, Diana then turns to Céfalo, who heard the nymph's pleas for mercy and hastened to her aid. Though she confronts him with a fierce and angry mien, Céfalo does not cower before her, for "heroicos pechos no / matan sin resistencia" (1789a). As Diana is about to hurl her unfailing javelin at this intrusive stranger, it mysteriously falls from her hand. Venus could not prevent Aura's death, perhaps due to the nymph's broken vow of chastity, but she is able to save the innocent, valiant, and noble Céfalo. In Act II, when Aura intervenes during the offering of gifts to Diana, proclaiming "¡Viva el amor y muera el olvido!" (1797b), the goddess believes that a devotee of Venus has profaned her temple. Eróstrato fears Diana's discovery of his plan for vengeance, the burning of her temple. Céfalo fears the revelation of his love for Procris. Even the servant Clarín is apprehensive about the discovery of his passion for Floreta. Not to be outdone, Rústico, though he appears as a dog, shudders at the thought of his unmasking, or "demetamorphosis." When Diana, using her divine power to probe each one's soul, finds that some sovereign presence opposes her, she explodes into a long discourse on her unique powers and prominence in the world, fearing in her heart that love's place in the cosmos is superior to her own.

When Diana drops the javelin and departs the scene, Céfalo picks up the weapon to honor Marte by placing it in his temple. When Procris informs him that the javelin is Diana's and disputes his right to possess it, Céfalo warns her that he will keep it by force if necessary. Angered by this boldness, she grabs the blade, cutting her hand. The sight of blood evokes a prophetic vision that now links the javelin with her future death, leading her to cry out in horror: "Detente, aguarda, espera: / no, no me mates" (1790a). Recovering her composure, she rejects the prophetic message contained in her sudden vision of death: "¿Yo a un acaso sujeta?" (1790a). The physical wounding of Procris precedes a figurative wounding of Céfalo, overcome by a sudden love for the nymph, provoked, curiously enough, by the sight of Procris's blood spilling out on her white flesh. This fateful encounter that predicts the death of the nymph presages not some chance event in the future, as Procris believes, but Diana's deliberate manipulation of events to bring about the deaths of both Céfalo and Procris.

The Causes and Consequences of Vengeance

Summarizing *Púrpura's* and *Celos's* themes, Stroud writes that "a victim of love's power is killed because of the jealousy of a god" ("Stylistic Considerations," p. 75). Whereas Marte's jealousy is based on his having been Venus's lover and not her husband, Diana's zeal for vengeance is based on a legitimate claim for retribution against Aura. As far as we know, Aura willingly vowed to remain faithful to Diana and the consequent "votada pureza" (1787a). By entertaining Eróstrato in the precinct consecrated to Diana, Aura and her lover committed a sacrilege worthy of punishment. This act provokes Diana's feelings of insecurity, and she demands the punishment corresponding to such an egregious crime:

> y pues es de mis ritos
> establecida pena,
> quien flechas del amor
> indignamente sienta,
> sienta no indignamente
> de mi rencor las flechas. ...
>
> (1787a)

While such a punishment appears harsh and cruel, Diana is demanding the price that Aura knew she would have to pay for her sexual surrender to Eróstrato. What indeed may shock us, however, is the statement Diana makes:

whoever unworthily feels the arrows of love is to be correspondingly shot by arrows. All are open to the influence of Venus, and if by "indignamente" Diana refers to those who elect to exercise their sexuality in spite of their vows, then the goddess is justified in her demand for the death penalty. But in her excessive zeal Diana subsequently seeks to deny Venus her rightful place in the world. Procris, a devoted follower of Diana, also demands that Aura, her close friend, be put to death. Not understanding how her "más amiga" could turn so violently against her, Aura curses Procris, hoping that she too may experience passion and its aftermath (1787b). Eventually Procris will suffer both the pangs of love and the threat of violent death. In this regard Aura's curse is a prophetic omen, just as the vision of Procris' violent death will prove to be.

Diana also punishes Rústico, the gracioso who served as Eróstrato's go-between. Milking his role for a good laugh, the servant comments on the consequences of his labors:

> ¡En qué cosas se mete
> el que se mete a...! Consonante, vete,
> pues nombre es más polido
> agente de negocios de Copido.
> Dígalo yo, testigo
> de tantos sustos, pues.

(1790b)

Diana metamorphoses him into various wild beasts, such as a lion, a bear, a wolf, and a tiger. This burlesque of metamorphosis undercuts the notion of it as an ennobling and dignifying act by revealing that it represents a loss, a descent in the great chain of being. While Rústico's comic metamorphoses will be only temporary, those of Aura, Céfalo, and Procris will be permanent.

Although Diana is justified in punishing both Aura and Rústico, *Celos'* finale reminds us that, as the gods have limits, so too does vengeance. Aura sings: "que aunque son nobles también las venganzas, / tal vez blasonadas desdicen de nobles" (1813b). Earlier she had commented on her own desire to take vengeance on Procris: "que más allá de la muerte / no llegan nobles venganzas" (1812a). One can avenge a wrong and yet remain noble provided one recognizes two clearly demarcated limits of noble vengeance: 1) it does not transcend death; and 2) it does not excessively gloat over vengeance taken. It is in both categories that Diana reveals herself to be an unworthy goddess, for earlier she had ordered:

> Que de tres venganzas mías
> publiquéis los tres *blasones*,
> una y mil veces conmigo
> diciendo en sonoras voces...

(1813a; emphasis added)

What Diana perceives as her honor and glory in fact results in her dishonor and shame. Because she seeks excessive vengeance, one that crosses over the boundary of death, her "noble" vengeances stand revealed in their ignoble reality.

Eróstrato is the human character who most closely represents on earth Diana's distorted hierarchy of values. Once he hears the account of Aura's metamorphosis, he silences Rústico, fearing that his lover's transformation is already effecting subtle, but profound, changes on his personality:

> Calla; que no quiero oír
> que con piadosas crueldades,
> a mí me convierta en estragos de fuego
> quien a ella convierte en halagos de aïre.
>
> (1791a)

Putting aside his pain and suffering, Eróstrato swears that the whole world, including Diana and her nymphs, will experience "los ultrajes / del abrasado despecho de un loco" (1791b). Alluding to fire as the means of his vengeance, he singles out Procris and Diana's temple as the objects of his anger. Underscoring the price this desperate man is willing to pay for revenge, he explains:

> Ea, Eróstrato, si grande
> tu fama no puede hacerte hoy eterno,
> veamos si eterno hoy tu infamia te hace.
>
> (1791b)

In Act II Eróstrato mixes with those who bring offerings to Diana's temple. Disguised as a rustic, he enters the temple outwardly singing Diana's praises, but inwardly promising revenge. After the disturbance caused by Aura's proclamation of Venus, he hides in the temple. Once alone, he sets fire to Diana's shrine, endangering the lives of all her nymphs. As he flees from the temple Céfalo asks, Who goes there? Eróstrato responds: "No lo sé" (1801b). Referring to the horrible sight of the burning temple, he then particularizes the effect of this deed on his personality:

> me ha dejado tan sin mí,
> de mí, ¡ay de mí!, tan ajeno,
> que de quien soy olvidado,
> de lo que fui no me acuerdo.
>
> (1801b)

Eróstrato, having lost the defining principle of his existence (*soy quien soy*), abandons human society and takes refuge in the wilds among the beasts and other untamed creatures of the forest. He is gradually losing his soul as the price of his dedication to revenge.

In Act III Eróstrato appears as the *humana fiera* who will play a decisive role in Diana's vengeance. Pursued and given no quarter, this wild man swears that, though Diana may punish him for his bold deed, she will not be able to take vengeance, for he will commit suicide first (1811b). When Céfalo spots the beast, Eróstrato, speaking in his human voice, begs him not to kill him, for he is about to shed human blood. Even Aura "turns against" her former lover, for he is no longer the same person she loved in Act I. At this point Eróstrato is converted into the means of Aura's and Diana's vengeance on Procris. Moreover, the dehumanizing process has not been imposed on him from without, for he willingly accepts it in exchange for revenge. That he becomes the means of Céfalo's and Procris's tragic deaths only compounds the tragic dimension to his life and to the dramatic world created in *Celos*.

Aura's role as avenger counterbalances the dehumanizing and "dedeifying" effects of vengeance we have witnessed in Eróstrato's and Diana's cases. Owing her favor to Céfalo for his assistance and her rancor to Procris for the harsh treatment at her trial, the air nymph satisfies both her desire for vengeance and her need to show gratitude by furthering Céfalo's love (1793b). While her favoring of Céfalo rewards his noble behavior, at the same time it undermines Procris's dedication to chastity. Aura's call to love becomes, therefore, an ambivalent and deceptive invocation.

Act I ends with Céfalo in love with Procris and the nymph profoundly moved by Aura's call to love. In Act II the two are visibly moved as Céfalo hands over to Procris his offering to Diana. As blood tinted the action of Act I with ominous warnings, its disquieting presence reappears in the image of a white and red iris that symbolizes Diana's purity and Venus's blood. Procris admonishes Céfalo:

> De azucena y rosa fuera
> acepto el don que me das,
> si la blancura no más
> sin la púrpura viniera.

> (1797a)

Though Céfalo responds by alluding to Procris's wounding by the javelin, both continue to experience the inspiration of love begun in Act I. The scene summarizes what has already occurred and predicts what is yet to come.

The confluence of Eróstrato's setting Diana's temple ablaze and Aura's support of Céfalo's love occurs as the nymph of the air fans her former lover's flames. Since all of Diana's nymphs are in imminent danger, the noble Céfalo boldly enters the temple and saves Procris. The flames carry out Eróstrato's vengeance on Diana and provide Céfalo with the opportunity to make off with his beloved. Those same flames symbolize the incipient passion that

Procris has been valiantly struggling against. The fire burning in Diana's temple reveals a deeper human truth that both Diana and Procris have thus far denied or repressed, the place of passion and love in human life. Once revealed to Procris's conscious mind, this passion or need to love will prove to be more powerful than her vow of chastity and dedication to Diana's cause. Only Eróstrato has been avenged by the fire. Though Aura has advanced Céfalo's love of Procris, her revenge on this nymph remains unsatisfied. When Céfalo makes off with Procris, Aura proceeds to the *rigor* and *rencor* owed to the latter, now that the former's *fineza* has been repaid. Procris will not only burn with desire and love, she will also be consumed by the fires of jealousy (1803b).

Whereas Diana's vengeance knows no bounds, Aura's will be moderate, recognizing "que más allá de la muerte / no llegan nobles venganzas" (1812a). Though both Aura and Diana are avenged at the conclusion of *Celos*, Aura stands for compassion and mercy that "transcend" the tragic potential of earthly existence.

Since there is a constant undermining of the serious nature of *Celos*, especially through the burlesque activity of the graciosos, it is not surprising to find Rústico's assumption of the role of avenger. Transformed into a dog, he has been accompanying Clarín. When the latter attempts to embrace Floreta, Rústico's wife, this jealous husband metamorphoses into a wild boar and charges his enemy. Clarín puns in mock terror:

> ¡Ay, que, Adonis del trapillo,
> sin por qué ni para qué,
> me da muerte un jabalí.
>
> (1801a)

The unflappable Floreta remarks that Clarín's hunting dog, actually Rústico, should help him. While vengeance may appear to be a noble obligation, this burlesque scene reminds us that it is also a base passion shared by all.

Noblesse Oblige

An important, yet subtle, theme reverberating through *Celos* concerns the nature and obligations of nobility. Céfalo embodies its true spirit which is always ready to sacrifice oneself for the other. When Aura cries for mercy, he is quick to come to her rescue, disregarding any potential harm to his person. The "míseras voces tiernas / de mujer" (1788a) act like an invisible magnet drawing him into a matter of little concern to him. Though born in Trinacria, he has come to Lidia to claim a legacy left to him by a deceased uncle. When he confronts Diana and her band of nymphs, his sense of obligation does not shrink before their threats, for:

> hidalgos procederes

> tienen tal encomienda
> en lo ilustre de un alma,
> que obligan, aunque ofendan.

(1788a)

With a typical flash of genius, Céfalo manages to defend Aura while not directly offending Diana and her nymphs, by placing himself between them and Aura, thus guarding the respect due to the one while still protecting the other. This noble disregard of safety characterizes Céfalo's comportment throughout the play.

In other works we saw how there were two basic kinds of *fineza*, that of the lover towards his lady and that of the noble towards others, especially those in need. But in *Celos* this division is expanded to include burlesque *finezas* and what Procris calls *fineza mayor*. The first is obvious. Once Diana leaves the scene, Rústico comes out of hiding to embrace his wife, who has guarded his complicity in the Aura-Eróstrato affair, although she in fact revealed his guilt to the goddess. Rústico is not aware of the transformation that has converted him into a lion in Floreta's eyes. As Floreta retreats in horror, Rústico expresses his bewilderment:

> ¡Yo león! ¿Estás borracha,
> mujer? ¡Cuando a que te pague
> mi amor la fineza de no haber contado
> que fui el agresor de culpa tan grande,
> vengo como un corderito,
> león te parezco!

(1792b)

And the *fineza mayor*, according to Procis, consists in "obedecer contra el gusto" (1793b). But the *fineza amorosa* still plays a major role in the lives of these nobles, for to incite Procris's jealousy Alecto whispers in her ear: "Que Céfalo ya / de tus finezas se cansa" (1806a).

While *finezas* characterize the life of the nobility, what defines and proves one's claim to position in society is the fame one acquires through noble deeds. Diana manipulates this mainspring of noble conduct to bring about her punishment of Céfalo and Procris. The former, recognizing that Diana's javelin contains divine properties, expects it to exalt him above his fellows (1805a). As he sets off to hunt the beast inhabiting the mountain, his destiny, controlled by Diana and directed toward the homicide of Procris, forms but one part of a duality whose other source is his real nobility of character. This ironic fact, that a man's real and admirable virtues become part of the motivation advancing the tragic issue, creates the dramatic tension that holds our attention.

The Tragic Deaths of Céfalo and Procris

As Act III begins Diana apportions to the three Furies the means of her vengeance, and in Procris's case the stirring up and provoking "de los celos el áspid" (1803b) falls to Alecto. Immediately following this scene we witness a tender and loving encounter between Céfalo and Procris, now happily married. Nevertheless, the javelin's fateful presence, as well as the circumstances of Procris's abandonment of Diana's service, undermines their idyllic love. Procris is concerned with Céfalo's excessive dedication to hunting, and she states her anxiety in an interesting manner: she is "envidiosa del monte" (1804b). Her husband leaves early in the morning and often does not return until late at night. The magical and infallible javelin, auguring great fame, pulls him from his recent legacy and newly wedded wife. In Céfalo's mind, the means of acquiring fame is somehow linked to the beast roaming the mountains. Clarín relates his master's strange retreat into the heart of the mountain, where he is serenaded by marvellous musical birds. There Clarín learns of a strange beast lamenting the loss of "Laura." The conditions are now ripe for Procris's growing uncertainty, her anxiety due to her guilt and foreboding due to her prophetic vision. At this point Alecto insinuates the worst, weaving together the separate strands of Céfalo's retreat into the mountain to form a fabric of betrayal. From uncertainty and doubt to fear and terror, Procris traverses Diana's well-laid path towards revenge. Disguised, she prepares to discover more about this strange retreat with its musical allure. As she mentions Laura's name, Alecto sings out "Aura," and Procris remembers Aura's request that Venus and Amor avenge her harsh treatment. Fearing that Aura has enchanted her husband, she pays no heed to Floreta's reminder that Aura now is but air, for: "que si el aire diere celos, / celos, aun del aire matan" (1806b).

Arriving on the mountain, Procris hears her husband's singing of "Procris por quien muero, / Aura por quien vivo" (1808b). When she hears her husband invoke Aura, Procris is convinced that the nymph of the air has avenged herself by disturbing their conjugal happiness. At this point Aura appears, but is not visible to the couple. Her purpose in not responding to Céfalo is to cause Procris greater pain and suffering. Procris, exercising great restraint, keeps her position, determined to see through what appears to be base betrayal by her husband (1811a). Eróstrato then appears on the stage. As Tesífone disturbs Céfalo's sense of perception, Procris rushes forth only to be greeted by the infallible javelin and Diana's revenge. Céfalo believes that he has achieved "la empresa más alta" (1812a), his desired fame, but his feat has only shed his beloved's blood. Aura, an accomplice in this vengeance, is moved to pity by the tragic scene before her.

Celos, aun del aire, matan is a play about tragic excess. Procris's excessive jealousy leads to her death, a tragic death in which all the major characters are implicated. Céfalo's inordinate dedication to hunting, motivated by a disproportionate regard for fame and honor, provokes Procris's jealousy and leads to her death. His infamy, the homicide of his loving wife, is so heavy a burden that he faints from the shock his deed produces. It is rare to have a *galán desmayado* in Golden-Age theater,[4] this reaction belonging more properly to females, but this unusual result of Céfalo's guilt underscores his pain. It is debatable whether Diana's vengeance, and Aura's participation in it, is excessive or not. What is not debatable is the reactions of the two to the tragic death of Procris, the nymph who offended them both. Diana calls on the choruses of nymphs and shepherds to broadcast her triumph over the three humans who have dared to offend her: "Que de tres venganzas mías / publiquéis los tres blasones" (1813a). Aura, who has been moved to pity by Procris's death and Céfalo's suffering, intervenes reminding all "que aunque son nobles también las venganzas, / tal vez blasonadas desdicen de nobles" (1813b). She explains her participation in the tragedy as follows:

> quise, ofendida de Procris,
> que ella me pagase en celos
> lo que él [Céfalo] me debió en favores.
>
> (1813b)

Since "más allá de la muerte / no llegan nobles venganzas" (1812a), Aura intervenes to mitigate the tragic consequences. Diana's vindictive excess is countermanded by Aura's merciful appeal to Venus, and the goddess of love's appeal to love. The only way to balance tragedy's suffering is by introducing mercy as a corrective for both human and divine excess.

The Metamorphoses as Dramatic Palliatives

Venus's role in *Celos* is the sign of a caring presence in the cosmos. She saved Aura from a violent punishment by transforming her into a nymph of the air. As she was about to be executed, Aura sang: "¡Ay infeliz de aquella / que hizo verdad haber quien de amor muera!" (1789a). Once transformed, she sings: "No ya infeliz de aquella, / que hizo verdad haber quien de amor muera" (1789a). The choice of words here is significant. Calderón did not write "feliz" but "No ya infeliz." Though Aura's metamorphosis expresses Venus's pity and mercy for one of her own, that transforming act cannot undo the loss of human happiness, Aura's love of Eróstrato, nor can it eliminate the price of her liberation, her new state of incorporality. Metamorphosis relieves a painful plight, but at a cost we can not overlook.

Rústico demonstrates in comic terms the negative effects of metamorphosis, creating thereby an inverted image of the transformational reality. The gracioso loses in ontological stature as he successively appears as a lion, a bear, a wolf, a tiger, and a greyhound. According to Rústico himself, there is a monstrous dimension to metamorphoses that his plight comically underscores. After his strange experiences in Act II, Rústico, still not aware of his canine state, comments in an aside:

> ¿Si se habrán cansado ya
> todos del pasado embuste
> de hacerme creer que soy
> monstruo?

(1796a)

The gracioso's dilemma exaggerates the deformational reality inherent in his metamorphosis, but in burlesque terms that are appropriate to his dramatic function. Once Rústico recovers his human form, he expresses surprise: "¿Luego yo soy yo mismo?" (1809b). This comic and ironic commentary on identity underscores once again the nature and reality of transformational events in which the loss of human personality, or one's identity, occurs.

In Céfalo's and Procris's cases, as well as in Aura's, we find the traditional elements that mitigate tragedy's sense of loss, one of which is the recourse to metamorphosis. This mitigation is so predominate that Matthew Stroud feels obliged to deny the classification of tragedy to *Celos*: "What keeps this play from being a tragedy is the added Neo-Platonic idea of love as redeemer" (*Celos*, p. 33). The apotheosis of love that concludes the play reinforces Venus's victory over Diana (ibid). But the issue is not that clear, as Diana's spiteful comment, the penultimate in the plot, proves:

> Una vez vengada yo,
> poco importa que blasones
> de estrella y aire.

(1814a)

Diana's vengeance is not noble and complete because she continues boasting about it even after the death of her victims. Neither is Venus's triumph total, for the traces of Diana's victories, air and star, continue to remind us of the loss tragedy exacts. The fact may be that "the love principle takes precedence over the violence principle" (*Celos*, p. 36), but love cannot definitively defeat violence nor can it eliminate vengeance. This tragic message emphasizes the limits of the human condition and the restraints mimetic art places on its faithful depiction.

Céfalo, now called Céfiro, is metamorphosed into wind, and Procris, into a star. The wording preceding the actual transformations is significant, for Venus and Jove:

> mandan que del fino amor
> la tragedia se mejore
> sin el horror de tragedia. . . .

(1813b)

Their lives remain, however, testimonials to their tragic past and to their tragic fates. The metamorphoses accomplish a figurative cleansing of spilt blood, the removal of the horror, but not the tragedy. When Aura orders that they rise to a higher state of being ("Subid, pues, restituidos / a mejor ser" [1813b]), they do not assume a god-like place in the cosmos nor do they resume their human natures. They rise from death to become symbols and signs, didactic markers for the living, of chaste love and fidelity in conjugal relationships. Their tragic past remains unaltered, and their happiness on seeing one another again is but a shadow of what they formerly enjoyed. The trace of tragedy is indelible. Only from the perspective of eternity, a perspective denied to mortals, can we claim any possible alleviation of the tragic potential to life.

The Comic Dimension of "Celos's" Dramatic Structure

The comic dimension of *Celos's* structure is accentuated, just as it was in *Golfo* and *Laurel*. While this comic vein runs from burlesque treatment of serious topics to slapstick-like routines, it functions as support for, and commentary upon, the serious action in the main plot. Floreta's dalliance with Clarín pokes fun at the serious themes of marital chastity in the absence of one's partner and of fidelity to the sacredness of the institution of marriage. Clarín's offering of Rústico, transformed into a greyhound, to the latter's wife Floreta reduces the idea of cuckolding to the bizarre. Clarín, far from being the perfect lover, is a surreptitious misogynist. When his master seeks to protect Aura from Diana's arrows, Clarín advises him:

> ¿Pues dime, hubiera fiesta
> como ver asaetear todas las hembras,
> cuanto más una?
>
> (1788b)

Clarín's treatment of Floreta pokes fun at the ill-conceived sense of masculine superiority. Floreta reveals to Diana her husband's complicity in the Aura-Eróstrato affair in spite of her declared purpose to protect him. And Rústico, who has witnessed this exchange, rushes out of hiding to reward his brave and faithful wife (1792). We laugh because we betray what we love most dearly in the attempt to protect it from harm. All the comic scenes of the play ridicule human pretentions. By paying close attention to the nature of the comic relief we become more sensitive to the world created by the dramatic text. By studying Rústico's metamorphoses we become sensitive to the negative quality of these transformations. By joining this insight to that provided by the analysis of the negative effect of vengeance on Eróstrato, we acquire key elements of a critical framework that allows us to interpret the significance of *Celos, aun del aire, matan*.

Conclusion

José Subirá writes about "la belleza literario-musical del producto nacido merced a la colaboración de tan esclarecidos artistas."[5] Indeed, *Celos* is a beautiful work. Some could charge, however, that the will to mitigate the horror of tragedy results in *Celos's* becoming an unconvincing text. While I believe that Calderón's dramatic world is basically comic, that does not obviate the tragic dimension in his dramatic production nor does it de facto do away with tragedies such as *Celos, aun del aire, matan*. Juan Hidalgo's music and Calderón's libretto form a challenging text that highlights the tragic dimension to life at the same time as it attempts a *partial* transcendence of tragedy's effects. The intertextual clues bring to mind episodes from Calderón's wife-murder tragedies. Procris's request to Céfalo, "Vete, pues, no vuelva yo / a hallarte aquí cuando vuelva" (1794b), reminds us of the women, such as Mencía, whose attempt to dismiss a former lover is interpreted by him as an invitation to return. And so does Céfalo interpret her request. Procris's foreboding over the javelin reminds us of King Pedro in *Médico*, and her prophetic vision calls to mind both this King's and Mencía's fateful visions. Procris's self-wounding is not mere chance, nor is her prophetic vision mere delirium. While the comedy relieves the tragic mood, as do the metamorphoses, neither is capable of eradicating the pity and fear aroused in us by *Celos, aun del aire, matan's* dramatic discourse. Though we marvel at the metamorphoses that conclude the play, the final words remind us that we have just witnessed cases of ignoble vengeance that only divine intervention is able *to limit to a just proportion*:

> que aunque son nobles también las venganzas,
> tal vez blasonadas desdicen de nobles.

> (1814b)

Venus, though triumphant at the end, is powerless to undo what Diana has brought about in the temporal order of men and women. The instability that characterizes temporality, in which we continue to live, remains unaffected.

Notes

1 The text cited is the Valbuena Briones edition, pp. 1785-1814. I have also consulted the text of *Celos* edited by Matthew D. Stroud (San Antonio: Trinity UP, 1981).

2 See *Mythos und Repräsentation: Die mythologischen Festspiele Calderón's* (Munich: Fink, 1978).

3 See "Stylistic Considerations of Calderón's Opera Librettos," *Crítica Hispánica*, 4 (1982), 75, and *Celos*, p. 21.

4 Perhaps the most famous case occurs in *Del rey abajo, ninguno*, when García faints as he attempts to kill his innocent wife Blanca.

5 "Calderón de la Barca, libretista de ópera: consideraciones literario-musicales," *Anuario Musical*, 20 (1965), 70.

X   The Myth of Human Origins

La estatua de Prometeo

> Pues si deidad te contemplo,
> te adoro; si hermosa, te amo;
> si discreta, te venero;
> si prodigiosa, te admiro,
> y si todo, te aborrezco;
> que hay otro yo que sin mí
> manda en mí más que yo mesmo.
>
> (2093a)[1]

Thus does Prometeo express the principle of contrariness that defines his being in Act III. His ardent love of Minerva and his unaccountable disdain of Pandora characterize the conflictive state of Prometeo's existence, directed by reason, but somehow undermined by a hatred he cannot comprehend. Calderón's *La estatua de Prometeo* is a dramatic representation of a creation myth through which we come to experience and to ponder that contrariness that defines our being. Death and suffering, pain and loss—these realities point out the negative condition of our common humanity. Richmond Y. Hathorn summarizes the interrogations the Prometheus myth puts to us:

More sophisticated myths such as those of the Garden of Eden or of Prometheus and Pandora attempt to give a figurative answer to the question: What is man's moral and spiritual position in the universe? Why does he go wrong? How does evil originate? What is this principle of contrariness that manifests itself internally in man's consciousness and seems to bring on him all his external sufferings (p. 39)?

Prometeo, the man of reason, has not been able to escape these limitations of his human existence, though he has mightily tried to scale the barriers to divinity. In a subtle manner Calderón depicts the enthusiasm of his desire as well as the pathos of his failure. Hathorn captures the inner workings of *Prometeo's* dramatic structure and reveals what lies at the heart of the Prometheus myth:

Prometheus and Pandora symbolize man's desire for progress and enlightenment, his yearning for divinity. Such aspirations are admirable, the source of man's glory. But such is man's desire that he tries to steal the heavenly gift, to make a violent assault on heaven. In so doing he allies himself with the forces of chaos; suffering comes into the world, and only suffering can right the balance of divine justice and raise man to the level of the heavenly cosmos (p. 39).

Calderón's dramatization of the human predicament is thorough and convincing principally due to the cosmological breadth of *Prometeo*. While focusing on the human plane, the play also includes a searching probe of the divine where a principle of contrariness is also found in operation. The Prometeo-Epimeteo opposition reflects a basic opposition of forces in the universe symbolized by Minerva-Palas. These dualities are not convenient means of representing dramatic tension, but reflections of the basic structures constituting the world.

The intellectual dimension of the play is so accentuated that Valbuena Briones feels justified in labeling it "una exaltación del intelectualismo" (p. 2065b). Chapman, caught up in the same enthusiasm, states that "la sabiduría trae la armonía al género humano."[2] Linking the thematics of *Prometeo* to those of *Vida*, he writes: "El orden se restaura y la armonía se restablece únicamente por sumisión a la razón. El Calderón de *La estatua de Prometeo* se de la mano con el Calderón de *La vida es sueño*" (p. 64). So prevalent is this view of *Prometeo's* intellectual character that Charles V. Aubrun affirms: "Subyacente en la obra es la aspiración de los 'intelectuales' a un nuevo reparto de las tareas, de las funciones en el gobierno del Reino, y, más inconscientemente aun, a una modificación de la jerarquía social."[3] While I can understand the emphasis on this intellectual dimension of *Prometeo's* structure, I believe such statements reflect a failure to grasp the problematic role of reason in the play.[4] *Prometeo* deconstructs the logocentric character of Western culture and much of Calderón's earlier theater. This critical position is based on a profoundly intellectual, philosophical, and theological understanding of the cosmos, and it includes an examination of the damage done to humankind and the cosmos by an exclusivist preoccupation with reason and wisdom. Any imbalance in the cosmos, in this particular case between the affective and the rational domains, is bound to produce disharmony. Prometeo's lack of balance and harmony reflects a more serious condition in the universe symbolized by Minerva/Palas and concretized by Discordia. The entire cosmos, human and divine, is precariously balanced on the harmony of opposites, and any disruption of this harmony is likely to produce tragedy.

Chapman's association of *Prometeo* with *Vida* is due to the similarity of these plays' thematics. Both deal with male-female antagonism, the role of reason in prudent living, the exceptional role of love in establishing or restoring harmony, pardon as the only exit from vital impasses, and finally the functioning of fate in the lives of the characters. Both plays deal with reason as humanity's greatest natural gift, but *Prometeo* finds reason to be limited in scope and problematic in nature. While not directly assuming the vantage point of faith, as in *Devoción* or *Mágico*, *Prometeo* exhibits a latent religious dimension in terms of Apolo's divine intervention to restore harmony. Thus, while *Vida* and *Prometeo* address similar thematic concerns, they do so from distinct vantage points. *Prometeo's* spirit is pessimistic in relation to man's ability to govern himself by reason alone. While *Vida's* is not necessarily optimistic, there remains a reservoir of hope from which it draws.

The symbolic dimension of *Prometeo* is obvious.[5] While it is not expressed in *auto*-like terms,[6] such as those of *Golfo*, one could establish an allegorical framework for the play. Minerva represents reason, wisdom, and love, whereas Palas stands for jealousy, vengeance, and hate. Discordia is a diabolic presence, whereas Apolo represents divine mercy. For some he is a Christ figure in the play. Prometeo is the man of reason, devoted to Minerva; Epimeteo is more the man of action, devoted to Palas. Pandora is woman, that disruptive force that turns these twin brothers into antagonists in a hostile world. Such a schema, though, oversimplifies the dramatic tension of the work, reducing the problematic actions of Prometeo and the ambivalent interventions of Minerva to logocentrism's excessive preoccupation with tidiness. In this regard the basis of the conflict, Minerva's reason (science) as opposed to Palas's force (*alto espíritu*), becomes imprecise. The opposition of the twin brothers, following the divine models they emulate, also becomes less clear. Though Prometeo is dedicated to study, he is prone to err and even takes up weapons to pursue a wild beast or to battle his brother. Epimeteo reasons clearly and well, though he is supposed to be a man of impulse and action, afterthought as opposed to his brother's forethought. Only Discordia, the advocate of unremitting violence, maintains a unidimensional character throughout the play. She sows dissension, especially jealousy, to divide the brothers who love one another. Her smoke blinds all, dulling their powers of reason. As a false messenger announcing the death of Pandora and the punishment of Prometeo, she can only be defeated by Apolo or Júpiter. While reason is humanity's surest guide to happiness, only divine mercy and pardon will be the curative for fallible mortals and erring gods. *Prometeo* becomes a profound dramatic depiction of, and commentary on, the social existence of humankind, the nature of men and women, and the cosmological conditions in which they evolve.

The Realities of Human and Divine Societies

Prometeo seeks to elevate his society from its primitive origins to a civilized state based on the rule of reason. Ironically, he will violate one of the most basic laws in his proud attempt to raise his society's consciousness. The simple understanding of justice held by his neighbors recognizes the antagonistic nature of human society, for "el pueblo. . . castiga / al que mata y al que hurta" (2070b). Such a conception of justice accepts conflict as inevitable and proposes means by which the society as a whole punishes violations of its code of conduct. While these laws address flagrant disruptions of social harmony, there are more basic antagonisms that characterize life. For instance, Prometeo's exclusive dedication to reason and study is not shared by his brother Epimeteo, who is the man of action, the hunter and warrior. These two brothers represent two basic lifestyles, the harmony of which contributes to a healthy and vibrant society. One finds, therefore, antagonism at the root of individuality itself. Prometeo's living in a obscure grotto symbolizes his need of light, of a more perfect form of being. His request of a ray of light from heaven is an implicit acknowledgment both of his imperfection and of the incomplete (selective) nature of his devotion to Minerva. Prometeo's disregard of the other gods in favor of exclusivity toward Minerva reflects his partial and imperfect grasp of the nature of the world in which he lives. C. Kerényi has summarized this relationship between the Titan Prometheus, light, and the nature of humankind:

The darkness of Prometheus signifies precisely the deficiency of one who needs fire in order to achieve a more perfect form of being. In obtaining this higher form of being for man, Prometheus shows himself to be man's double, an eternal image of man's basically imperfect form of being (*Prometheus*, p.78).

Since Prometeo is a *galán* in the play and not a Titan, his imperfect form of being is accentuated by the fact of his human nature.

Evidently Prometeo is an intelligent person, but his failure to discover the meaning of the harmony of the heavens ruled over by Júpiter ironically intimates his human limitation. His life, his wisdom, and his science are selective and partial. He has not found "le secret de l'Univers," in Aubrun's apt phrase, but only one part of its inner workings.[7] And his actions reflect this partial apprehension of the cosmos and its laws. Prometeo's discovery of Minerva proves to be a faithful duplication of his imperfect form of being, incapable of taking in the immenseness that the Olympians symbolize. Because Prometeo's cosmology is partial and distorted he ends up creating discord and disharmony where he sought only unity and harmony.

A deeper probing of the cosmos would have revealed a more conflictive and antagonistic universe than the one discovered by Prometeo. The division of the goddess into two separate entities, Minerva and Palas, is a felicitous way of representing the inner antagonism of divine society. The gods are not monads resplendent and distant, but representations of the inner forces that lay bare the antagonistic nature of the world of men and gods.

The births of the twins Prometeo and Epimeteo symbolize the conflictive nature of humankind, its lack of unity and harmony. They also reflect the divine reality represented by Minerva and Palas. In fact these two goddesses will use the human twins as a test of their separate axiologies and competing virtues (2074). An old commonplace, the conflict of arms and letters, is dressed up in the new clothes of arms and science, or wisdom. The human world becomes a vast laboratory where pain and suffering on the part of the human subjects become the means by which these egotistical goddesses obtain knowledge about the range of their powers. This picture of divine pettiness is neither flattering to them nor consoling to us.

Hope for progress and civilization motivates Prometeo's attempt to establish the cult of Minerva among the primitive inhabitants of Cáucaso. He calls them to worship her thus:

> Llegad, pues, llegad, veréis
> su efigie; y pues mi cordura
> ya no os da leyes, sino
> simulacros, substituyan
> a políticos consejos
> sagrados ritos.

(2070a)

Since Cáucaso's inhabitants are not capable of understanding the scope of Prometeo's hopes for them and their society, this man of study begins the transformation of his *pueblo* at a more elementary level. By introducing Minerva's statue as a focal point for new devotion, Prometeo prudently adapts his overall plans for advancement to his people's level of comprehension. It is indeed ironic that this man of eminent learning violates one of the primitive laws of Caucasian society, the prohibition against stealing, in his journey towards the more perfect society.

When Epimeteo, in the name of all the people, accepts this new rite, which implies "adoración a los dioses" (2070b), the event is to be marked by the erection of a larger and more luxurious temple than the one previously dedicated to Saturno. Therefore, Prometeo's introduction of Minerva's cult signals the transition from the old law, symbolized by Saturno, to a new law, epitomized by Minerva. Caucasian society advances from a more primitive fear-based cult to a more reasoned one grounded in the recognition of humanity's need to adore the gods.

The Offense-Vengeance Mechanism: Pardon as Curative for Personal/Societal Faults

Prometeo is an intellectual with the primary flaw of intellectuals, pride; he has not learned humility, his proper place in the cosmos. His exclusive dedication to Minerva represents, moreover, an egotistical exaltation of his own way of life. Prometeo disparages mortals because he does not respect them nor their way of life. The gods who favor and protect these different and valuable lifestyles are offended by this proud mortal's speech, and an envious Palas seeks retribution that will threaten all inhabitants of Cáucaso. Prometeo's exclusive dedication to Minerva will destroy the harmony and peace of the world. Declaring his total submission to the goddess, he adds: "(oféndanse o no se ofendan / las demás)" (2069b). Palas reveals why this attitude is offensive to the gods by exclaiming:

mayormente habiendo dicho
la sacrílega soberbia
de aqueste ignorante sabio
que en obsequio de Minerva
todas las demás deidades
se ofendan o no se ofendan. . . .

(2074b)

To emphasize that Prometeo's principles are not the lofty ones espoused in Act I, Calderón has him deliberately deceive his fellow citizens as to the origin of fire (2079a). To further Minerva's cult, Prometeo contends that the gift of fire came directly from the statue and not from Prometeo's theft of one of Apolo's rays. Nothing more definitively proves Prometeo's lack of harmony than his convenient and accommodating conscience.

Minerva, the goddess of reason, is profoundly grateful to Prometeo for all done on her behalf, and she seeks to reward his zeal with an appropriate gift. The ambitious mortal, urged on by the proud goddess, requests what is properly heaven's (2073a). The people of Cáucaso had rejected Prometeo's attempt to introduce *político gobierno*, perceptively grasping his underlying ambition: "notándome de ambicioso" (2069a). Prometeo is not a simple man of letters content to acquire knowledge through dedicated study; he is ambitious and seeks power. Like Apolo of *Faetón*, Minerva rashly promises to give Prometeo whatever he may request from the heavenly array (2076a). When Prometeo requests fire and Minerva assists him in stealing it, we grasp that what unites this mortal and this immortal is their pride and disregard of morality. Prometeo has no right to request what properly belongs to Apolo, so he must steal it. Minerva has no right to offer what is not hers, so she abets Prometeo's wrongdoing. The two act more as we would expect Epimeteo and Palas to act. The result is not, however, all evil. From this sin humankind will benefit, and like the Church at Easter Cáucaso will eventually be able to sing out: Oh Felix Culpa!

In a long rationalization of his request of fire, Prometeo reveals the state of his moral sensibility:

Si yo pudiese llevar
un rayo suyo, que fuera,
su actividad aplicada
a combustible materia,
encendida lumbre, que
desmintiendo las tinieblas
de la noche, en breve llama
supliese del sol la ausencia,
fuera buen don como tuyo,

> que quien da luz a las gentes
> es quien da a las gentes ciencia.

(2076)

Conscious of his crime, Prometeo robs a ray of light uttering: "Perdone Apolo esta ofensa" (2077a). This scene is doubly ironic. Prometeo's theft of Apolo's fire represents Minerva's usurpation of Apolo's domain as well as Prometeo's expropriation of forbidden knowledge.

The ambiguous nature of fire itself is revealed during the celebration of its distribution to mortals. As all acclaim that fire symbolizes knowledge, shouts of war and calls to arms interrupt the populace's joy. Pandora then prophetically reveals the benefits and disadvantages of this gift (2082a). Domesticated and wild, fire will be a boon and bane to human society, grace and knowledge as well as guilt and ignorance. When war erupts, this primitive society is shaken out of its innocence and ignorance by the sudden introduction of fire, or knowledge and strife.[8]

Palas, offended by Prometeo and envious of Minerva's spreading cult, calls for the punishment of Prometeo and the destruction of the statue, an act Epimeteo finds difficult to carry out. Calling on Discordia to assist her in her vengeance, Palas carefully plans her provocation of civil war. First, there must be *desavenencia*. Second, she calls on Discordia to multiply *corazones opuestos*, sowing in them "ojerizas, disensiones, / odios y aborrecimientos" (2083a). Discordia, an expert in this dirty business, plans on offering to Pandora an urn containing "los hados de la Discordia" (2083b) that, once opened, will poison the atmosphere of Cáucaso. Specifically, these evil fates will set at odds the two leaders of society, who are already rivals for social position and popular respect. Pandora will be the means of dividing the brothers and their society:

> pues su nueva
> deidad, a uno aborreciendo
> y favorcciendo a otro,
> es fuerza que entren los celos,
> última sedición mía

(2083b)

Discordia utilizes a natural division among individuals and within society to rend the social fabric. Jealousy is a very destructive passion, and in many ways it constitutes in Calderonian theater the greatest individual and societal threat. Once Epimeteo experiences jealousy of his brother, their natural bonding and fraternal affection crumble before the onslaught of a violent desire for vengeance.

Exaggerating the opposition found in the personalities of the two leaders, Discordia causes this natural variety to erupt into open hostility and antagonism. Pandora experiences a growing dislike for Epimeteo and a passionate regard for Prometeo. When she plans to share with all the rich gifts that she believes the mysterious urn contains, smoke escapes, poisoning the atmosphere. Discordia avenges the theft of fire by introducing smoke that blinds, chokes, and confuses the populace. Her revenge takes the following form: Epimeteo will love Pandora, but she will despise him; Prometeo will despise Pandora, though she will love him. The society will be divided into opposing camps that will blindly struggle for supremacy, hurtling Cáucaso toward destruction as jealousy and revenge rule the lives of the citizenry. Merlín summarizes what occurs in a pithy phrase: "El humo de la Discordia / a todos ciega" (2086a).[9]

This mayhem is inflicted and rationalized in Apolo's name. When the two goddesses appear before their brother to argue their cases, he is convinced first by the one and then by the other. Apolo becomes indecisive and in the end remains neutral in the dispute that began on earth but has now infected heaven. We could view Apolo as a pusillanimous god not daring to judge the opposing cases presented to him, but this position would not take into account Apolo's apparent stratagem. He allows his sisters's conflict to continue, thus surreptitiously testing their positions.

Like a jealous *caballero*, Epimeteo complains of the fire of jealousy that burns in his heart as he witnesses Pandora's disdain of his love and pursuit of Prometeo. His lot will be to suffer reproof and rejection, his fate will be to seeth with anger and to seek revenge on his brother (2090b and 2091b). When Epimeteo feels obligated to justify the cruel treatment of his twin, he rationalizes it in an aside in terms of love unrequited and jealousy (2096a). Epimeteo does not justify his cruel behavior as much as he ratifies, by expediency, his desire for vengeance.

By her very nature Discordia is given to excess, so, when she feigns her role as ambassador of the gods, she naturally lies and deceives the inhabitants of this mountain region. Her order that Prometeo be cruelly punished by the avenging eagle and that Pandora perish in flames reflects neither Apolo's vengeance nor Júpiter's judgment. Her melodious voice convinces all the mortals spellbound by its traitorous harmony.[10] What ultimately undermines her spite and vengeance, however, is the guilt she assumes on expropriating Júpiter's authority. Further compounding this abuse of authority and position is Discordia's revenge that seeks delight in the suffering of others. As an accomplice of Palas, Discordia's lying excess undermines this goddess's righteous anger and reveals the base motive of *personal* revenge that explains her "concern" for Apolo's honor.

Apolo's intervention prevents a great injustice, brings pardon to Prometeo and Pandora, and restores harmony to Caucasian society. Why has Apolo chosen to act at this time? Simply, he chooses to forgive the pair before Júpiter does so. Apolo's presence dispells the smoke that has blinded reason as he restores "razón y sentido, / sentido y razón" (2096b). Palas and Discordia flee the scene thwarted in their cruel revenge. The latter, moreover, now fears Júpiter's wrath. There is obviously a political statement made in these concluding verses to *Prometeo*. Apolo introduces himself to the populace by the word "Yo" (2096b), one used by the King to sign official documents: "Yo, el Rey." Those who usurped the royal authority would be held accountable, as Discordia fears she will be. But this political dimension should not diminish *Prometeo's* claim for the superiority of pardon over vengeance. Apolo was offended by Prometeo's theft of his fire and by Minerva's complicity in this robbery. But as the god of light and reason, he is not blinded by Discordia's smoke and thus affirms pardon as the reasonable course in confused and entangled human affairs. As a god he demonstrates his magnanimity: "porque nunca niega / piedades un dios" (2096b). Apolo's sudden appearance is justified in the plot, for he only temporarily suspended judgment between his two sisters' pleas. His decisive action does not so much adjudge their lawyerly arguments as affirm his divine essence, ratifying pardon as the reasonable solution to humanity's, and the gods', tendencies to offend. Only pardon cures the sick body politic by reconciling Epimeteo to his brother and by uniting Prometeo with Pandora. This deus-ex-machina resolution to the conflict contains a divine approbation of forgiveness for both personal and societal upheavals. While the erring mortals celebrate their rescue, terminating the cycle of offense-vengeance on the human plane, only the vengeful goddesses Palas and Discordia have anything to fear. But this pending punishment returns us to *Prometeo's* political message and suggests that the cycle of offense-vengeance may never be completely concluded.

Prometeo's Rule of Reason and the Reality of Passion and Ignorance

In the classical myth of Prometheus and Epimetheus, the former, the clever brother, stands for the forethinker, while the latter, the stupid brother, represents the afterthinker (Hathorn, p. 39). The twins manifest the two sides of man, constituting in their unity the traits we associate with the trickster (p. 40). Calderón's *Prometeo* does not follow this symbolic structure, and in fact these traditional formulations of character, to the extent that they are present in the play, become problematical as the action advances. What indeed characterizes the twin brothers are not so much distinct traits associated with individuality, but rather common elements constituting masculinity. Kerényi's description of the two equally applies to Calderón's characterization of them in *Prometeo*:

Hesiod repeatedly stresses his belief that the stern order of the Zeus world is based equally on the Epimethean, masculine desire for woman and upon a trait of man that we have seen to be at once Promethean and universally human: the impulse to modify the world by crafty inventiveness (p. 49).

Prometeo is, moreover, a forethinker who believes that his innate "lógica natural" has been sufficiently developed by his years of dedicated study. His "anhelo de saber" led him to philosophy, the queen of science, where the study of the cause-effect relationship opened the world of speculation to him (2068b). It is precisely this speculative trait in Prometeo's character, his penchant to conjecture without knowing all the facts, that induced him to abandon his homeland in order to study abroad. His desire for additional knowledge led him to the study of astrology, a science pursued by many "wise" men in Calderonian theater, like Basilio of *Vida*, who in spite of their good wishes and high motives end up wreaking havoc on their fellow citizens. Prometeo attempts to leap the gap or chasm between human knowledge, science, and philosophy and divine wisdom by delving into astrological *speculation*. Through this science he seeks to understand the causes of worldly phenomena and thus to manipulate, "to modify the world by crafty inventiveness." It is ironic that as an astrologer Prometeo fails to read in the stars the *effects*, the repercussions of his introduction of the statue into Cáucaso. Though he has reasoned out the distribution of the gods' spheres of influence, his lack of respect for and proper acknowledgement of all the gods upset the tenuous harmony of the world.

Epimeteo, while clearly the man of action, proves himself to be crafty and wise when confronted by Palas's order to destroy the statue. His love of the simulacrum of Woman, the concrete manifestation of his "masculine desire for woman," provokes Palas's jealousy and desire for revenge. In his attempt to balance Palas's demand against his new respect for, and love of, Minerva, Epimeteo demonstrates that he is more prudent, more rational, and more reasonable than his brother. In this case, at least, he is the forethinker who by means of an *industria* resolves an emotional impasse. In the realm of action Epimeteo is clearly superior to Prometeo. The latter is eminently wise in the study of abstract and speculative sciences, but once he enters the political realm, the world of action where knowledge of the possible proves to be decisive, Prometeo is ineffectual.

The supreme irony of the play is that Prometeo is responsible for all the problems that his lack of prudence and moderation causes. This man of reason seeks to mold the world anew according to his axiological system. By institutionalizing what is more properly individual preference, Prometeo seeks to impose his own private cosmology upon his fellow citizens.

To represent the fundamentally divisive nature of civil war, Discordia states the fates of the twin brothers in opposing terms. To Epimeteo: "amarás aborrecido;" to Prometeo: "aborrecerás amado" (2086a). The contrariness of their fates underscores the potentially conflictive position of humankind in the world, and, once moral error introduces evil into human society, that potentiality erupts into open hostility. Prometeo's failure as benefactor of civilization is attributable to his inability to recognize and accept his own limitations.

Though he avows Minerva, the goddess of wisdom, he is mysteriously compelled to reject Pandora, the woman of flesh and blood and her earthly image. Perhaps his aspirations toward the goddess dovetail with his own ambition to acquire knowledge characteristic of the gods, but forbidden to men and women. His rejection of Pandora reinforces his forswearing of his human limitations. Prometeo is a man at war with himself, a mortal seeking what is properly the gifts of immortality. In his pride and foolishness, in his grandeur and error, Prometeo, in Kerényi's phrase, "was no redeemer, but was himself in need of redemption" (p. 128).

The Question of Identity

Prometeo wishes to redefine human society, to modify human nature by bringing to his fellow citizens a "divinizing" gift that will radically alter their nature. Nowhere is the question of identity better underscored than in the Minerva-Pandora obfuscation. Prometeo molds the statue that the "divinizing" touch of fire will convert into a woman of flesh and blood. When Prometeo first sees Pandora he recognizes Minerva in form, but fails to appreciate Pandora in her humanity. Earlier Pandora did not recognize Prometeo, ["oh tú, quien quiera [sic] que seas" (2080b)], a fact that disconcerts her artificer. When he fails to hear Minerva's melodious voice, her recitative, he fears that he is being punished (2080b). Pandora, who had originally asked herself on emerging from the cave "¿quién soy yo. . .?" (2080a), cannot comprehend the questions put to her. When he asks his own creation "¿quién eres?," she responds truthfully:

> No lo sé;
> que solo sé que ilustrada
> de esta antorcha, por mí dijo,
> no sé si el euro o el aura. . .

Then the Music joins her to sing:

> Que quien da las ciencias, da
> voz al barro y luz al alma.
>
> (2081a)

The heavenly fire is a power that exceeds Prometeo's understanding, for it brings knowledge *and life*. He expects the effects of fire's power to alter men into more rational creatures, but he is not prepared to recognize nor understand how this gift also transforms clay, the base material of his statue's composition, into woman. The first one to realize this upgrading of nature is a symbolic representative of woman, Pandora, now Prometeo's equal.

When the people acclaim this new marvel, Pandora asks them:

> ¿Quién soy yo para que hagáis
> tantos festivos extremos
> en mi alabanza?

(2085a)

Timantes recognizes what she represents for humankind:

> que todos reconocemos
> la felicidad que en ti
> nos participan los cielos;
> pues de Minerva y Apolo,
> dando ella al retrato el cuerpo,
> y él la luz al alma, eres
> tan elevado concepto,
> que ya que no diosa, te hace
> semidiosa por lo menos.

(2085a)

Pandora signifies an amazing amalgam of physical or natural beauty and spiritual or mental achievement. Though she is a gift of the gods, Prometeo will find it difficult to understand and to accept her as she is. She is not Minerva, not a goddess, but her own human gifts are estimable. As Prometeo was not able to bridge the chasm between human and divine knowledge, so he will be incapable of managing the tension that exists between Minerva (godly perfection) and Pandora (human perfection).[11] In *Prometeo* Pandora etymologically signifies "la providencia del tiempo" (2083a), and, though she will provoke chaos in Cáucaso, she will not be responsible for it. Prometeo's inability to understand her, his refusal to accept her human voice in the light of Minerva's melodious song, and his failure to see her as a divine gift will be the principal elements in the unfolding of his fate and that of his society. Only when Discordia's smoke is dispelled will Prometeo come to realize the import of her presence and her function in human society: "la providencia del tiempo." Through her Prometeo will discover his humanity and become prepared for Apolo's mercy and pardon.

In Act III Prometeo mistakenly addresses Minerva as if she were Pandora, execrating her for all his woes. He blames her for everything, from his desire to reproduce Minerva's likeness in rude clay to his theft of fire that animated her statue. Poor perception later leads Prometeo to confuse Pandora with Minerva, symbolizing the ambivalent attitude of men towards women. Once he recognizes Pandora through her voice, he violently rejects her (2092b). He is unable to recognize his own voice in that of Pandora's.

As Prometeo before her, Pandora experiences extremes of love and hatred. The one whom she loves, Prometeo, flees from her, while the one whom she spurns,Epimeteo, pursues her. This contrariness, one of the mysteries of the cosmos, also characterizes Prometeo's estranged state (2093a).Vacillating between extremes of love and hatred, between Minerva and Pandora, Prometeo comes to experience the contradiction of his imperfect humanity. There is no reason that satisfactorily explains this disharmony, no cause sufficient to account for this effect. Prometeo must feel and suffer this inner reality, he must assume his humanity in its fullness, both its grandeur and its pathos. Only then does Prometeo realize on a human level a modicum of integration of his affective and sentient being with his rational soul. At this more primitive level Prometeo initiates a return to wholeness that only Apolo can fully effectuate.

Once Discordia announces Prometeo's punishment and Pandora's death in fire, the benefactor of civilization experiences the urge of his inherent nobility to defend the hapless Pandora. By placing the other's need before his suffering, Prometeo casts aside his own egotistical outlook and recognizes the other as a person in her own right. Going out of himself, he experiences first pity and then love for Pandora:

> No sé, ¡ay, infausta hermosura!,
> cómo ya en mi corazón
> se ha de cebar boreal fiera
> si al verte sin él estoy.
>
> (2096a)

Pandora tenderly laments both her own imminent suffering and death and Prometeo's cruel punishment. In their common suffering they reach a mutual understanding and harmony they did not previously experience. Merlín comments ironically: "Si ha de morir como una, / ¿para cuándo era el ser dos?" (2096b).

When Apolo arrives on the scene to announce pardon, he also announces a restoration of reason and feeling: "razón y sentido, / sentido y razón" (2096b). The resultant integration of the human personality is essential if happiness is to be a possibility. Therefore, the conventional concluding marriages symbolize the restoration of integrity and assumption of one's human identity. Epimeteo ceases to despise his brother Prometeo and is restored to unity with his twin. Prometeo ceases to hate Pandora and is united in the flesh to her, thus completing his imperfect being and integrating his personality into society. Prometeo, curiously enough, discovers who he is, his humanity, only on marrying Pandora. Personal integration and wholeness take place in a societal context presided over and blessed by Apolo.

Conclusion

Discordia, the goddess of sedition who creates "corazones opuestos" (2083a), pronounced Prometeo's and Epimeteo's fates, which were almost realized at the play's conclusion. When Apolo sings, announcing his arrival, the inhabitants are blinded and ask: "¿Quién causa este efecto?" (2096b). Apolo responds: "Yo" (2096b). The god of light restores reason by dispelling Discordia's enchantments contained in the smoke of ignorance and discord. The false Discordia, a magnification of Prometeo's attempts to alter human nature and society, cringes before Apolo's redemptive will. But Apolo's healing is dual, for it repairs the crumbling society at the same time as it unites the opposing and conflicting elements of human personality. Reason and sense should complement each other, and Apolo's pardon restores that complementarity, healing humanity's fractured being. Apolo's peace is a divine gift not earned in any way by men and women, but rather generously and divinely given to them. What Prometeo attempted through his theft of the heavenly fire becomes, by Apolo's grace, the abiding state of humanity. It is ironic how, through sin, Apolo becomes the benefactor of humanity.

While the play represents a deconstruction, on the one hand, of Prometeo's logocentric exclusivity, it celebrates, on the other, Apolo's integration of "razón y sentido / sentido y razón" (2096b), the wholeness of the human being. Prometeo's grand adventure to make humankind more like the gods failed not due to humanity's lack of regard for the divine element, reason, or of potential to be reasonable creatures, but due to Prometeo's failure to respect the integrity of the human being composed of body and soul, sense and reason. Although Prometeo brings knowledge to humanity, reason alone is not sufficient to overcome the destructive tendencies we all carry within us. When we least expect it, passion, jealousy, and vengeance ovewhelm us. The outside intervention of Apolo underscores humanity's need of a form of assistance greater than that which reason is capable of providing. *Prometeo's* deep structure reflects the Christian viewpoint that only divine pardon and love can restore peace to human beings torn asunder by contrariness and to a society rent by hostility. Calderón's *La estatua de Prometeo* is pessimistic about the effectiveness of reason alone as the guide for human affairs and finds the need of outside intervention to be crucial for any form of human happiness. In this regard *Prometeo* dramatizes on a more philosophical level the vital insight of *Ni Amor se libra de amor*.

Chapman has pointed out that *Prometeo's* thematics are similar to those of *La vida es sueño*, principally due to the characters' final submission to reason's dictates. I believe, however, that Prometeo's companion piece is more properly *La devoción de la Cruz*, where there is also an outside force, divine Providence, whose intervention into human affairs restores peace and harmony to sick mortals and to a divided society. Just as Curcio remains by his own choice beyond the pale of divine mercy and love, so too in *Prometeo* Discordia stands as a reminder of the instability that characterizes human life. Apolo has saved most of the participants in this averted tragedy, but the goddess Discordia symbolizes a negative force never totally defeated that may return at any time to sow "ojerizas, disensiones, / odios y aborrecimientos" (2083a) among us.[12]

Notes

1 The text of *La estatua de Prometeo* cited is the Valbuena Briones edition, pp. 2065-97. See also the edition of *Prometeo* prepared by Margaret Rich Greer, with a study of the music by Louise K. Stein, (Kassel; Edition Reichenberger, 1986).

2 "Las comedias mitológicas de Calderón," *Revista de literatura*, 5 (1954), 64. For dissenting views, see Hildner, pp. 68 and 72-3, and Cascardi, p.151.

3 "Una tragicocomedia pura: *La estatua de Prometeo*. Estructuración, funciones gramaticales y juicio de valor," in *Hacia Calderón. Sexto coloquio anglogermano. Würburg 1981*, ed. Hans Flasche (Wiesbaden: Franz Steiner Verlag GMBH, 1983), p. 121.

4 See my article "Calderón and Reason's Impasse: The Case of *La estatua de Prometeo*" in *La Chipsa '81: Selected Proceedings* (New Orleans: The Second Louisiana Conference on Hispanic Languages and Literatures), 1981, pp. 229-37.

5 Cascardi exaggerates this dimension when he states that Prometeo is not a character, but a self-aware symbol (p.143).

6 For an overly enthusiastic association of the myth play with the *auto*, see Morón Arroyo, p. 20, and Hildner, p. 67.

7 See *La estatua de Prometeo*, ed. Charles V. Aubrun (Paris: Centre de Recherches de l'Institut d'Etudes Hispaniques, 1965), p. XVI.

8 It is important to note that Epimeteo's attempt to steal the statue of Minerva comes immediately after his brother's theft of fire. Whereas Prometeo was urged on by high ideals, but betrayed them by the evil means he employed, Epimeteo, urged on by love and reverence, employs the same means, theft, to avoid fulfilling Palas's command to destroy the offensive statue. The world of innocence has been invaded by guilt, and both brothers demonstrate their participation in this guilt through their betrayal of their society's most basic law: thou shalt not steal.

9 This love-hate antagonism calls to mind the tragic love of Eco and Narciso. Whereas in *Prometeo* there will be Apolo's divine intervention to preclude a tragic issue, in *Eco y Narciso* the characters were left totally alone in their hostile and tragic world.

10 See Jack Sage, "Texto y realización de *La estatua de Prometeo* y otros dramas musicales de Calderón," in *Hacia Calderón: Coloquio Anglogermano. Exeter 1969* (Berlin: Walter de Gruyter, 1970), pp. 37-52.

11 Aubrun refers to the chasm between men's idealization of woman and her reality. See "Abstractions morales et reférénces au réel dans la tragédie lyrique, notamment dans *La Estatua de Prometeo* de Calderón," in *Réalisme et poesie au théâtre* (Paris, 1960), p.56.

12 Robert ter Horst's *Calderón: The Secular Plays* is in many ways an extended commentary on *Prometeo*, one distinct from my own, but not necessarily antagonistic. I would agree that the play stands as one of Calderón's finest myth plays "and ranks with his best dramas of any category" (p. 60).

Conclusion

Calderón's use of mythological tales indicates, on the surface, a return to traditional plots and the abandonment of the will to be faithful to experience. But in fact his myth plays attempt to transcend individual experience by configuring a plot with a more universal claim, and thus such a plot, while less verisimilar, becomes nonetheless more liberational in the sense of freeing the spectator or reader from the limitations of time and space.[1] After exploring nineteen of his works, we may legitimately ask ourselves: In the myth plays does Calderón create a dramatic reality of radical novelty? Radical beauty and exquisite experience indeed, but these works are ultimately referential to our world, to our concerns, and to our lives. Though known for his conceptual acuity and artistic conciseness, we oftentimes ignore or overlook the powerful exercise of imagination found in his myth plays. They are in reality what James Hillman has labelled "an exploration and discipline of the imaginal" (p. 194).[2] While the *autos* stand as majestic tribute to theological thinking and the comedies and tragedies to comprehensive exploration and expression of human life, the myth plays reveal an imaginative appreciation of our humanity caught in a conflictive and contradictory world.

A major contribution of this study results from the examination of the structures of time in these plays. The sense of time I have labelled *KAIROS* supports those plays we may broadly call comedic and romantic, and even serious works such as *La devoción de la Cruz* may be substantially affected by the providential structure of time in its plot. Tragic plays, be they mythic or works like *El médico de su honra*, contain a sense of time I have labelled *CHRONOS* in which only the absence or ineffectualness of providence permits us to define what could be called a uniquely Calderonian notion of fate. These critical first steps in an attempt to develop a taxonomy of Calderonian genres demand broader explorations that space does not justify here.

On examining the role of the gods in these myth plays, we have often discovered a dualistic vision of life ultimately defined by the interaction of the divine with the human plane. While this dualistic vision corresponds to the mythological tradition that sanctions such interaction and records it for posterity, underlying this repeatedly antagonistic relation there is a semi-Manichaean appreciation of both spheres of operation. The gods may be benign towards and supportive of human creatures, such as Palas and Mercurio of *Fortunas de Andrómeda y Perseo*, or they may be vengeful, spiteful, egotistical, and cruel like Apolo of *El laurel de Apolo* or Marte of *La púrpura de la rosa*. Humans, too, reveal this Manichaean split, and Fitón of *Apolo y Climene* immediately comes to mind. Calderón's dualistic dramaturgy, while not technically Manichaean, reveals strong tendencies in this direction.[3]

The area where the Manichaean possibility breaks down is Calderonian tragedy. Rather than an evil presence or fate that guides the action to horror and death, Calderonian tragedy normally depicts the absence or ineffectualness of provident intervention in the characters' lives. Comedy celebrates deliverance from evil and harm; tragedy chronicles how humans, left to their own devices, tumble willy-nilly toward destruction. *Médico* is a pristine example of it. But the myth plays display an unusual frankness and challenge commonly held beliefs by positing the possibility of evil forces governing the world. Júpiter is often an ambiguous god more frequently ruled by lust and timidity than by justice and duty. Calderonian myth plays are not reassuring tales, but challenging works that raise more questions than they provide answers.

The most eloquent and thorough depiction of the valences of love and lust are found in Calderón's myth plays. In them we confront the stylization of passion. Plays like *Los tres mayores prodigios* and *El mayor encanto, amor* are negative in their appreciation of passion and love, whereas the later plays, especially *Ni Amor se libra de amor* and *La estatua de Prometeo*, are positive endorsements of the redemptive nature of human and sexual love. The most stylized narrations of affection occur in the plays of court intrigue, *La fiera, el rayo y la piedra* and *Fineza contra fineza*. The latter drama summarizes the positive power of *finezas*, honor's obligations, to energize and give direction to human life. To understand Calderón's depiction of how life should be lived and regarded, we must capture the dynamic power and directional thrust of *finezas* in his dramaturgy. The diametrically opposing force to *fineza* is egotism, and its most negative manifestation is rape. Rape is so negative that it is frequently the initiator of tragic action, as seen in *Eco y Narciso*. Only when providential forces are operative and powerful, as in *Fortunas*, can rape's deadly inheritance be avoided. What stirs passion and lust in males, be they gods or humans, is feminine beauty, the hallmark of misfortune and tragedy for those cursed by its gift. There are many heroines tainted by its touch: Andrómeda, Liríope, Eco, Dafne, Deyanira, to mention but a few.

The issue of fate versus freedom appears in terms of supernatural prophecy and astrological prediction. While these foreshadowings inevitably carry through to completion, Calderón emphasizes how the partial and incomplete interpretation and understanding of these events form the counterpart to that prophecy or prediction. *Eco y Narciso* and *La fiera, el rayo y la piedra* are good examples of how human action, decision, and will are the source of the tragedy that follows, not its result.

There are many metamorphoses that conclude myth plays, but they are not examples of a cosmic rhythm leading to serene resignation. Transformation of substance most often represents a loss, a loss of humanity, a phenomenon that forms part of Calderón's larger tragic vision. Just as rape transforms a woman from person into object, metamorphosis signals a loss of being whose sign is vegetative life, as in Dafne's laurel tree, or mineral existence, like Anajarte's stone. In these plays metamorphosis is not a tribute to love, as some have interpreted Ovid's great poem, but a statement about loss and absence. Only where metamorphosis leads to apotheosis, as in *Ni Amor se libra de amor* and in the case of the stone Statue in *La fiera, el rayo y la piedra*, do we find a positive depiction of transformation.[4]

I would like to end this study by reminding the reader of the innovative and experimental nature of many of these plays. Experiments in staging, as found in *Los tres mayores prodigios*, problematizing of existing genres, such as the *comedia palaciega* of intrigue, in *Fieras afemina Amor*, the creation of new genres like the *zarzuela* (*El laurel de Apolo* and *El golfo de las Sirenas*) and the renovation of the opera, once tried by Lope but subsequently abandoned (*Celos, aun del aire, matan* and *La púrpura de la rosa*) characterize these mythological productions. But along with innovation and experimentation we have discovered what I call a Calderonian mythology, the larger connecting whole that unites the individual narrations of myth. While this mythology exhibits continuity, for example, regarding rape and *finezas*, it also manifests growth of understanding, especially regarding the role of human love in achieving terrestrial happiness. My study of Calderón's myth plays attempts to appreciate each one as a unique dramatization of human experience, albeit from a richly imaginary perspective, that nonetheless respects its human dimension while it at the same time encompasses a broad context. As readers of these plays we become ambushed first by their narrative brilliance and second by their mythic resonances. If you the reader feel more strongly their artistic allure and appreciate better their dramatic richness, then my purpose will have been realized.

Notes

1 It is curious that the more distant from reality and from life the mythological plot becomes the more refined its composition. See Paul Ricoeur, *Time and Narrative*, II, p. 12.

2 Hillman contrasts the "development of the imaginative mind and its power of imaginative understanding, in contradistinction to both the theological mind of Church philosophy and the feeling heart of mendicant and monastic Church orders" (p. 195).

3 For ter Horst's observations on Calderón as a "Manichean fusionist," see *Calderón*, p. 36.

4 For a detailed account of this phenomenon see my "Metamorphosis as Challenge in the Theater of Calderón," a paper presented 18 October 1987 at the University of Calgary's "Parallel Lives, Spanish and English National Drama, 1580-1680" and to be published in the Proceedings.

Bibliography of Works Cited

Aguilar Mora, Jorge. "Notas sobre la loa a *Fieras afemina amor.*" *Nueva revista de filología hispánica* 23 (1974): 111-15.

Alonso, Dámaso and Carlos Bousoño. *Seis calas en la expresión literaria española.* 2nd ed. Madrid: Gredos, 1956.

Aristotle. *The Nicomachean Ethics.* Tr. H. Rackham. Cambridge, MA and London: Harvard UP and W. Heinemann, 1975.

Aubrun, Charles V. "Abstractions morales et référénces au réel dans la tragédie lyrique, notamment dans *La Estatua de Prometeo* de Calderón." *Réalisme et poesie au théâtre.* Paris, 1960, pp. 53-59.

—. "Les Débuts du drame lyrique en Espagne." *Le Lieu Théâtral à la Renaissance.* Paris, 1964, pp. 423-44.

—. "*Eco y Narciso*: 'Opéra fabuleux' de Calderón et son épure dramatique." *Homenaje a William L. Fichter.* Eds. A. David Kossoff and José Amor y Vázquez. Madrid: Castalia, 1971, pp. 47-58.

—. "Una tragicocomedia pura: *La estatua de Prometeo.* Estructuración, funciones gramaticales y juicio de valor." *Hacia Calderón. Sexto coloquio anglogermano. Würburg 1981.* Ed. Hans Flasche. Wiesbaden: Franz Steiner Verlag GMBH, 1983, pp. 114-22.

Augustine, St. *Basic Writings of Saint Augustine.* Vol. 1. Ed. Whitney J. Oates. New York: Random House, 1948.

Avellaneda, Francisco de. *El templo de Palas.* Nápoles: Gerónimo Fasvlo, 1675.

Barthes, Roland. *Critical Essays.* Tr. Richard Howard. Evanston: Northwestern UP, 1972.

—. *Mythologies.* Tr. Annette Lavers. New York: Hill and Wang, 1972.

Bidney, David. "Myth, Symbolism, and Truth." *Myth: A Symposium*, pp. 3-24.

Blue, William R. *The Development of Imagery in Calderón's "Comedias."* York, South Carolina: Spanish Literature Publications, 1983.

—. "Dualities in Calderón's *Eco y Narciso.*" *Revista Hispánica Moderna* 39 (1976-77): 109-18.

Booth, Wayne C. *Critical Understanding: The Powers and Limits of Pluralism.* Chicago: U of Chicago P, 1979.

—. *A Rhetoric of Irony.* Chicago: U of Chicago P, 1974.

Brown, Jonathan and J. H. Elliot. *A Palace for a King: The Buen Retiro and the Court of Philip IV.* New Haven: Yale UP, 1980.

Calderón: Actas del "Congreso Internacional sobre Calderón y el Teatro Español del Siglo de Oro." 3 vols. Ed. Luciano García Lorenzo. Madrid: C.S.I.C., 1983.

Calderón de la Barca, Pedro. *Las armas de la hermosura.* Num. 38. Salamanca: Imprenta de la Santa Cruz, n.d.

—. *Autos sacramentales, alegoricos, y historiales.* Madrid, 1677.

—. *Celos aun del aire matan.* Ed. and tr. Matthew D. Stroud. San Antonio: Trinity UP, 1981.

—. *Comedias.* 19 vols. Ed. facs. D. W. Cruickshank and J. E. Varey. Westmead, Farnborough, Hants, England: Gregg International, 1973.

—. *Comedias religiosas: La devoción de la Cruz y El mágico prodigioso.* Ed. Angel Valbuena. 3rd ed. Madrid: Espasa-Calpe, 1963.

—. *Dramas de honor: El médico de su honra y El pintor de su deshonra.* Vol. 2. Ed. Angel Valbuena Briones. Madrid: Espasa-Calpe, 1965.

—. *Eco y Narciso.* Ed. Charles V. Aubrun. Paris, 1961 and 1963. Reviewed by Pierre Groult in *Lettres Romanes*, 16 (1962): 103-13.

—. *En la vida todo es verdad y todo mentira*. Ed. Don W. Cruickshank. London: Tamesis, 1971.

—. *La estatua de Prometeo*. Ed. Charles V. Aubrun. Paris: Centre de Recherches de l'Institut d'Etudes Hispaniques, 1965).

—. *La estatua de Prometeo*. Ed. Margaret Rich Greer. With a study of the music by Louise K. Stein. Kassel: Edition Reichenberger, 1986.

—. *Fieras afemina Amor*. Ed. Edward M. Wilson. Kassel: Edition Reichenberger, 1984.

—. *Obras completas: dramas*. 5th ed. Vol. 1. Ed. A. Valbuena Briones. Madrid: Aguilar, 1969.

—. *Tan largo me lo fiáis* [by Tirso]. Ed. Xavier A. Fernández. Madrid: Revista "Estudios," 1967.

Cameron, Alister. "The Myth and the Maker." *The Identity of Oedipus the King: Five Essays on the Oedipus Tyrannus*. New York: New York UP, 1968.

Cardona Castro, Angeles. "Función de la música, la voz humana y el baile a través de los textos de *El laurel de Apolo* (*Loa para la zarzuela* y *Zarzuela*), y a través de la loa *La púrpura de la rosa*." *Calderón: Actas*, II, 1077-89.

Cascardi, Anthony J. *The Limits of Illusion: A Critical Study of Calderón*. Cambridge: Cambridge UP, 1984.

A Catholic Dictionary. Ed. Donald Attwater. 3rd ed. New York: Macmillan, 1958.

Chapman, W. G. "Las comedias mitológicas de Calderón." *Revista de literatura* 5 (1954): 34-67.

Colahan, Clark and Alfred Rodríquez. "El Hércules de López de Zárate: Una posible fuente de *Los tres mayores prodigios* de Calderón." *Calderón: Actas*, III, 1271-76.

Crane, R. S. *The Language of Criticism and the Structure of Poetry*. Toronto: U of Toronto P, 1953.

Cros, Edmond. "Paganisme et Christianisme dans *Eco y Narciso* de Calderón." *Revue des Langes Romanes* 75 (1962): 39-74.

Cruickshank, D. W. "Don Juan de Vera Tassis y Villarroel." *Aureum Saeculum Hispanum. Festschrift für Hans Flasche*. Eds. Karl-Hermann Körner and Dietrich Briesemeister. Wiesbaden: Franz Steiner, 1983, pp. 43-57.

de Armas, Frederick A. "The Betrayal of a Mystery: Botticelli and Calderón's *Apolo y Climene*." *Romanische Forschungen*, forthcoming.

—. "Metamorphosis in Calderón's *El mayor encanto, amor*." *Romance Notes* 22 (1981): 1-5.

—. *The Return of Astraea: An Astral-Imperial Myth in Calderón*. Lexington: UP of Kentucky, 1986.

Diccionario de autoridades. 3 vols. Real Academia Española. 1726-39; facs. Madrid: Gredos, 1969.

Dictionary of Theology. Ed. Louis Bouyer. Tr. Charles Quinn. New York: Desclee, 1965.

DiSalvo, Marilyn. "The Myth of Narcissus." *Semiotica* 30-1/2 (1980): 15-25.

Domínguez Ortiz, Antonio. *El estamento eclesiástico*. Vol. 2 of *La sociedad española en el siglo XVII*. Madrid, 1970.

Dunn, Peter N. "Garcilaso's *A la flor de Gnido*." *Zeitschrift für Romanische Philologie* 81 (1965): 288-309.

—. "Honour and the Christian Background in Calderón." *Critical Essays on the Theater of Calderón*. Ed. B. W. Wardropper. New York: New York UP, 1965, pp. 24-60.

Edwards, Gwyne. "Calderón's *Los tres mayores prodigios* and *El pintor de su deshonra*: The Modernization of Ancient Myth." *Bulletin of Hispanic Studies* 61 (1984): 326-34.

Eliade, Mircea. *Myths, Dreams and Mysteries: The Encounter between Contemporary Faiths and Archaic Realities*. Tr. Philip Mairet. London: Harvill P, 1960.

Elizalde, Ignacio. "El papel de Dios verdadero en los autos y comedias mitológicos de Calderón." *Calderón: Actas*, II, 999-1012.

Ellis, John M. *The Theory of Literary Criticism: A Logical Analysis*. Berkeley: U of California P, 1974.

Faulkner, William. *As I Lay Dying. William Faulkner, Eugene O'Neill, John Steinbeck*. New York and Del Mar, CA: Alexis Gregory and CRM Publishing, 1971.

—. "The Bear." *Go Down, Moses*. New York: The Modern Library, 1955.

Fischer, Susan L. "Calderón's *El mayor encanto, amor* and the Mode of Romance." *Studies in Honor of Everett W. Hesse*. Lincoln: Society of Spanish and Spanish-American Studies, 1981, pp. 99-112.

Fox, Dian. *Kings in Calderón: A Study in Characterization and Political Theory*. London: Tamesis, 1986.

Frye, Northrop. *Anatomy of Criticism*. Princeton: Princeton UP, 1957.

Gadamer, Hans-Georg. "Religious and Poetical Speaking." *Myth, Symbol, and Reality*, pp. 86-98.

Girard, René. *Violence and the Sacred*. Tr. Patrick Gregory. Baltimore and London: Johns Hopkins UP, 1977.

Gómez Mingorance, Margarita. "*Apolo y Climene. El hijo del Sol, Faetón* (análisis de dos comedias calderonianas)." *Calderón: Actas*, I, 161-76.

Graff, Gerald. *Literature Against Itself: Literary Ideas in Modern Society*. Chicago: U of Chicago P, 1979.

Green, Otis H. *The Literary Mind of Medieval and Renaissance Spain: Essays by Otis H. Green*. Lexington: UP of Kentucky, 1970.

Habermas, Jürgen. *Toward a Rational Society: Student Protest, Science, and Politics*. Tr. Jeremy J. Shapiro. Boston: Beacon P, 1970.

Hamilton, Edith. *Mythology*. New York: Mentor Books, 1942.

Häring, Bernard. *This Time of Salvation*. Tr. Arlene Swidler. New York: Herder and Herder, 1966.

Hathorn, Richmond Y. *Greek Mythology*. Beirut: The American UP, 1977.

Haverbeck Ojeda, N. Erwin. "La comedia mitológica calderoniana: soberbia y castigo." *Revista de filología española* 56 (1973): 67-93.

Hawthorne, Nathaniel. *The Scarlet Letter*. Boston: Houghton, Mifflin, 1889.

—. *Tanglewood Tales*. New York: J. H. Sears, n.d.

Hernández-Araico, Susana. *Ironía y tragedia en Calderón*. Potomac, MD. Scripta Humanistica, 1986.

—. "Mitos, simbolismo y estructura en *Apolo y Climene* y *El hijo del sol, Faetón*." *Bulletin of Hispanic Studies* 64(1987): 77-85.

Hesse, Everett W. "Calderón's *El monstruo de los jardines*: Sex, Sexuality, and Sexual Fulfillment." *Revista Canadiense de Estudios Hispánicos* 5 (1981): 311-19.

—. "Estructura e interpretación de una comedia de Calderón: *Eco y Narciso*." *Boletín de la Biblioteca de Menéndez Pelayo* 39 (1963): 61-76.

—. "Sexual Problems in the Achilles Plays of Tirso and Calderón." *Kentucky Romance Quarterly* 28 (1981): 177-87.

—. "The 'Terrible Mother' Image in Calderón's *Eco y Narciso*." *Romance Notes* 1 (1960): 1-4.

—. "The Two Versions of Calderón's *El laurel de Apolo*." *Hispanic Review* 14 (1946): 213-34.

Hildner, David Jonathan. *Reason and the Passions in the "Comedias" of Calderón*. Amsterdam/Philadelphia: John Benjamins, 1982.

Hillman, James. *Re-Visioning Psychology*. New York: Harper and Row, 1975.

Hirsch, Eric D., Jr., *The Aims of Interpretation*. Chicago: U of Chicago P, 1976.

Hyman, Stanley Edgar. "The Ritual View of Myth and the Mythic." *Myth: A Symposium*, pp. 136-53.

"'I Love You': Charity in the Home." *Christopher News Notes* 282 (1985).

Jaspers, Karl. "Basic Characteristics of the Tragic." *Tragedy: Vision and Form*, pp. 43-52.

—. *Man in the Modern Age*. Tr. Eden and Cedar Paul. New York: Anchor Books, 1957.

The Jerusalem Bible. Garden City, NY: Doubleday, 1966.

Jung, Carl G. *Symbols of Transformation: An Analysis of the Prelude to a Case of Schizophrenia*. Bollingen Series XX. Tr. R. F. C. Hull. New York: Pantheon Books, 1956.

Jung, C. G. and C. Kerényi. *Essays on a Science of Mythology: The Myth of the Divine Child and the Mysteries of Eleusis*. Tr. R. F. C. Hull. Bollingen Series XXII. Princeton: Princeton UP, 1969.

Kerényi, C. *Prometheus: Archetypal Image of Human Experience*. Tr. Ralph Manheim. New York: Pantheon Books, 1963.

Kitto, H. D. F. *Greek Tragedy: A Literary Study*. 3rd ed. New York: Barnes & Noble, 1961.

Kohut, Heinz. *The Restoration of the Self*. New York: International Universities P, 1977.

Laing, Ronald D. *The Divided Self*. New York: Pantheon Books, 1969.

Lara, Gaspar Agustín de. *Obelisco funebre, pyramide funesto que construia, a la inmortal memoria de D. Pedro Calderón de la Barca. . . .* Madrid, 1684.

Levin, Richard. *New Readings vs. Old Plays: Recent Trends in the Reinterpretation of English Renaissance Drama*. Chicago: U of Chicago P, 1979.

Lévi-Strauss, Claude. *Myth and Meaning*. New York: Schocken Books, 1976.

—. *Structural Anthropology*. Harmondsworth: Penguin, 1968.

—. "The Structural Study of Myth." *Myth: A Symposium*, pp. 81-106.

Lewis, C. S. *A Grief Observed*. New York: The Seabury P, 1961.

—. *Surprised by Joy*. New York: Harcourt, Brace, 1955.

"Life: There's Nothing Like It." *Christopher News Notes* 283 (1985).

Lipmann, Stephen H. "Sobre las interpolaciones en el *Eco y Narciso* de 1674." *Segismundo* 27-30 (1978-80): 181-93.

Man, Paul de. "Shelley Disfigured." *Deconstruction and Criticism*. New York: The Seabury P, 1979, pp. 39-73.

Maraniss, James. *On Calderón*. Columbia: U of Missouri P, 1978.

Martin, Henry M. "The Apollo and Daphne Myth as Treated by Lope de Vega and Calderón." *Hispanic Review* 1 (1933): 149-60.

—. "The Perseus Myth in Lope and Calderón with Some Reference to Their Sources." *Publications of the Modern Language Association* 46 (1931): 450-60.

Mason, Herbert. "Myth as an Ambush of Reality." *Myth, Symbol, and Reality*, pp. 15-19.

Massar, Phyllis Dearborn. "Scenes for a Calderón Play by Baccio del Bianco." *Master Drawings* 15 (1977): 367-75 and plates 21-31.

McCarthy, Thomas. *The Critical Theory of Jürgen Habermas*. Cambridge: The MIT P, 1978.

Mendelson, Jack. "The Habermas-Gadamer Debate." *New German Critique* 18 (Fall 1979): 44-73.

Merrick, C. A. "Neoplatonic Allegory in Calderón's 'Las fortunas de Andrómeda y Perseo.'" *Modern Language Review* 67 (1972): 319-27.

Merton, Thomas. *The Seven Storey Mountain*. New York: Harcourt Brace, 1948.

Moll, Jaime. "Sobre las ediciones del siglo XVIII de las Partes de comedias de Calderón." *Calderón: Actas*, I, 221-34.

Morón Arroyo, Ciriaco. *Calderón: pensamiento y teatro*. Santander: Sociedad Menéndez y Pelayo, 1982.

Myth, Symbol, and Reality. Ed. Alan M. Olson. Notre Dame and London: U of Notre Dame P, 1980. "Introduction," pp. 1-12.

Myth: A Symposium. Ed. Thomas A. Sebeok. Bloomington: Indiana UP, 1955.

Neumeister, Sebastian. "Calderón y el mito clásico (*Andrómeda y Perseo*, auto sacramental y fiesta de corte)." *Calderón: Actas*, II, 713-21.

—. "La fiesta mitológica de Calderón en su contexto histórico (*Fieras afemina amor*)." *Hacia Calderón: Tercer Coloquio Anglogermano: Londres 1973*. Berlin: Walter de Gruyter, 1976, pp. 156-70.

—. *Mythos und Repräsentation*. München: Wilhelm Fink, 1978.

The New Testament. New York: Catholic Book Pub., 1957.

O'Connor, Thomas A. "Calderón and Reason's Impasse: The Case of *La estatua de Prometeo*." *La Chispa '81: Selected Proceedings*. New Orleans: The Second Louisiana Conference on Hispanic Languages and Literatures, 1981, pp. 229-37.

—. "The Father Figure in *Fortunas de Andrómeda y Perseo*: A Comment on the Father-Son Motif in Calderonian Drama." *Proceedings of the Fifth Annual Golden Age Spanish Drama Symposium*. El Paso, TX: The U of Texas at El Paso, [1986], pp. 29-35.

—. "Formula Thinking/Formula Writing in Calderón's *El golfo de las sirenas*." *Bulletin of the Comediantes* 38 (1986): 25-38.

—. "Hércules y el mito masculino: La posición 'feminista' de *Fieras afemina Amor*." *Estudios sobre el Siglo de Oro: en homenaje a Raymond R. MacCurdy*. Ed. Angel González, Tamara Holzapfel y Alfred Rodríguez. Madrid: Cátedra y U de New Mexico at Albuquerque, 1983, pp. 171-80.

—. "Metamorphosis as Challenge in the Theater of Calderón." A paper presented 18 October 1987 at the University of Calgary's "Parallel Lives, Spanish and English National Drama, 1580-1680." To be published in the Proceedings.

—. "On Love and the Human Condition: A Prolegomenon to Calderón's Mythological Plays." *Calderón de la Barca at the Tercentenary: Comparative Views*. Ed. Wendell M. Aycock and Sydney P. Cravens. Lubbock: Texas Tech P, 1982, pp. 119-34.

—. "El 'optimismo' de *Ni Amor se libra de amor*." *Calderón: Actas*, I, 533-40.

—. Rev. of *La gran comedia Gvárdate de la agva mansa. Beware of Still Waters*. Tr. David M. Gitlitz. *Bulletin of the Comediantes* 38 (1986): 151-53.

—. "Violación, amor y entereza en *Fortunas de Andrómeda y Perseo* de Calderón de la Barca." *Homenaje a Gonzalo Torrente Ballester*. Salamanca: Biblioteca de la Caja de Ahorros y M. de P. de Salamanca, 1981, pp. 573-82.

Ovid. *Metamorphoses*. Tr. Rolfe Humphries. Bloomington: Indiana UP, 1955.

Palmer, Richard E. *Hermeneutics: Interpretation Theory in Schleiermacher, Dilthey, Heidegger, and Gadamer*. Evanston: Northwestern UP, 1969.

Panofsky, Erwin. "*Et in Arcadia ego*: On the Conception of Transience in Poussin and Watteau." *Philosophy and History: Essays Presented to Ernst Cassirer*. Oxford: Clarendon P, 1936, pp. 223-54.

Paris, Pierre. "La Mythologie de Calderón: *Apolo y Climene—El hijo del Sol, Faetón*." *Homenaje ofrecido a Menéndez Pidal*. Madrid, 1925, I, 557-70.

Parker, Alexander. "Metáfora y símbolo en la interpretación de Calderón." *Actas del Primer Congreso Internacional de Hispanistas*. Oxford, 1964, pp. 141-60.

—. "*El monstruo de los jardines* y el concepto calderoniano del destino." *Hacia Calderón: Cuarto coloquio anglogermano. Wolfenbüttel 1975*. Berlin and New York:

Walter de Gruyter, 1979), pp. 92-101.

—. "Towards a Definition of Calderonian Tragedy." *Bulletin of Hispanic Studies* 39 (1962): 227-37.

Peñuelas, Marcelino. *Mito, literatura y realidad*. Madrid: Gredos, 1965.

Pérez de Moya, Juan. *Philosophia secreta*. 2 vols. Ed. Eduardo Gómez de Baquero. Madrid, 1928. Original edition, 1585.

Raglan, Lord. "Myth and Ritual." *Myth: A Symposium*, pp. 122-35.

Reichenberger, Kurt and Roswitha. *Bibliographisches Handbuch der Calderón-Forschung*. Vols. I and III. Kassel: Thiele & Schwartz, 1979-81.

Ricoeur, Paul. *Hermeneutics and the Human Sciences: Essays on Language, Action and Interpretation*. Ed. and tr. John B. Thompson. Cambridge and Paris: Cambridge UP and Editions de la Maison des Sciences de l'Homme, 1981.

—. *Time and Narrative*. Tr. Kathleen McLaughlin and David Pellauer. Vol. 1. Chicago: U of Chicago P, 1984. Vol. 2, 1985.

Righter, William. *Myth and Literature*. London: Routledge and Kegan Paul, 1975.

Ruiz Ramón, Francisco. *Calderón y la tragedia*. Madrid: Alhambra, 1984.

Ruthven, K. K. *Myth*. London: Methuen, 1976.

Sage, Jack. "Texto y realización de *La estatua de Prometeo* y otros dramas musicales de Calderón." *Hacia Calderón: Coloquio Anglogermano: Exeter 1969*. Berlin: Walter de Gruyter, 1970, pp. 37-52.

Scheler, Max. "On the Tragic." *Tragedy: Vision and Form*, pp. 3-18.

Seznec, Jean. *The Survival of the Pagan Gods: The Mythological Tradition and Its Place in Renaissance Humanism and Art*. Tr. Barbara F. Sessions. Bollingen Series XXXVIII. New York: Pantheon Books, 1953.

Sharpe, Eric J. S. *Fifty Key Words: Comparative Religion*. London: Lutterworth P, 1971.

Shergold, N. D. "The First Performance of Calderón's *El mayor encanto amor*." *Bulletin of Hispanic Studies* 35 (1958): 24-27.

—. *A History of the Spanish Stage from Medieval Times until the End of the Seventeenth Century*. Oxford: Clarendon P, 1967.

Shergold, N. D. and J. E. Varey. *Representaciones palaciegas: 1603-1699. Estudio y documentos*. London: Tamesis, 1982.

—. *Teatros y comedias en Madrid: 1666-1687. Estudio y documentos*. London: Tamesis, 1974.

Steinbeck, John. *The Winter of Our Discontent*. New York: Viking P, 1961.

Stevenson, Robert. "The First New-World Opera." *Américas* 16 (1964): 33-35.

Stroud, Matthew D. "Stylistic Considerations of Calderón's Opera Librettos." *Crítica Hispanica* 4 (1982): 75-82.

Subirá, José. "Calderón de la Barca, libretista de ópera: consideraciones literario-musicales." *Anuario Musical* 20 (1965): 59-73.

Sugerman, Shirley. *Sin and Madness: Studies in Narcissism*. Philadelphia: Westminster P, 1976.

ter Horst, Robert. *Calderón: The Secular Plays*. Lexington: UP of Kentucky, 1982.

—. "From Comedy to Tragedy: Calderón and the New Tragedy." *Modern Language Notes* 92 (1977): 181-201.

Thomas, David M. *Christian Marriage: A Journey Together*. Willmington, Del.: Michael Glazier, 1983.

Thompson, Stith. "Myth and Folktales." *Myth: A Symposium*, pp. 169-80.

Tillich, Paul. *The Courage To Be*. New Haven: Yale UP, 1968.

Torrence, Robert M. *The Comic Hero*. Cambridge: Harvard UP, 1978.

Tragedy: Vision and Form. Ed. Robert W. Corrigan. Scranton, PA: Chandler, 1965.

Twain, Mark. *The Adventures of Tom Sawyer*. New York: Harper, 1922.

Valbuena Briones, Angel. "La construcción artística de *Fortunas de Andrómeda y Perseo.*" *Homenaje a José María Solá-Solé*. Barcelona: U of Texas at Austin and Puvill, 1984, pp. 91-102.

—. "El simbolismo en el teatro de Calderón: La caída del caballo." *Romanische Forschungen* 74 (1962): 60-76.

Valbuena Prat, Angel. "La escenografía de una comedia de Calderón." *Archivo español de arte y arqueología* 16 (1930): 1-16.

Vellacott, Philip. *Ironic Drama: A Study of Euripides' Method and Meaning*. Cambridge: Cambridge UP, 1975.

Vickery, John B. "Literature and Myth." *Interrelations of Literature*. Ed. Jean-Paul Barricelli and Joseph Gibaldi. New York: MLA, 1982, pp. 67-89.

Waardenburg, Jacques. "Symbolic Aspects of Myth." *Myth, Symbol, and Reality*, pp. 41-68.

Wardropper, Bruce W. "Poetry and Drama in Calderón's *El médico de su honra.*" *Romanic Review* 49 (1958): 3-11.

Wardropper, Bruce W. and Elder Olson. *Teoría de la comedia; La comedia española*. Barcelona: Ariel, 1978.

Watson, A. I. "Hercules and the Tunic of Shame: Calderón's *Los tres mayores prodigios.*" *Homenaje a William L. Fichter*. Madrid: Castalia, 1971, pp. 773-83.

Watts, Alan W. *Myth and Ritual in Christianity*. London, 1953.

Wheelwright, Philip. "The Semantic Approach to Myth." *Myth: A Symposium*, pp. 154-68.

Williams, Jay. *Medusa's Head*. New York: Random House, 1960.

Wilson, Edward M. "The First Edition of Calderón's *Fieras afemina amor.*" *The Textual Criticism of Calderón's 'Comedias'*. Ed. Don W. Cruickshank. London: Gregg and Tamesis, 1973, pp. 183-200.

—. "The Text of Calderón's 'La púrpura de la rosa.'" *Modern Language Review* 54 (1959): 29-44.

Index

About the Author:

Professor Thomas A. O'Connor is currently chair of Romance Languages at the State University of New York at Binghamton. Most recently he served for eight years as chair of the Department of Modern Languages at Kansas State University and prior to that as professor of Spanish at Texas A & M University. Professor O'Connor received his B.A. degree from Iona College and his M.A. and Ph.D. degrees from State University of New York at Albany.

Widely known as an eminent Golden Age scholar, he has published numerous articles, completed two editions of works by Agustín de Salazar y Torres, served as a reviewer for books and manuscripts, and presented papers and led panels at various scholarly meetings. In addition he has received several fellowships and grants and has contributed to both university and professional activities and committees.

Trinity University Press acknowledges with appreciation that Professor O'Connor submitted the manuscript to the publisher on disks. Through a cooperative effort among author, publisher, and printer, the project was edited and processed onto the printer's system, using those disks.

The printer is Best Printing Company, Inc., Austin, Texas
The typeface is Century Oldstyle
The book design is in collaboration with Jerry Tokola
The binding is by Custom Bookbinders, Austin, Texas